ANOTHER 100 NEW ZEALAND ARTISTS

ANOTHER 100 NEW ZEALAND ARTISTS

WARWICK BROWN

GODWIT

Dedicated to the memory of Rodney Kirk Smith, 1938–1996

Author's acknowledgements

I would like to thank my wife, Kitty, and business partners, Peter and Adrienne Jarvis, for their support during the writing of this book. I made extensive use of the Auckland Art Gallery Library's excellent slide and artists' file resources, and I thank the staff for their patience and assistance. Many of the artists profiled in the book and their dealers were generous with their time in getting together essential resource material, and I thank them for all that. Nicola Hill of Godwit Publishing took on much of the sometimes frustrating task of assembling the illustrations—my gratitude to her. Finally, my thanks to Jane Connor of Godwit for her support throughout and for allowing me to twist her original concept into a two-volume contemporary survey.

Illustration credits

The author and publisher gratefully acknowledge the co-operation of all living artists and the estates of deceased artists, and the galleries named in the captions, in granting permission to reproduce works and providing material for reproduction. Photographers are as follows: Helen Mitchell, 20, 87; Lloyd Park, 14, 17, 44; Haru Sameshima and Mark Adams at Studio La Gonda, 1, 9, 13, 18, 19, 22, 27, 29, 34, 36, 39, 43, 45, 50, 52, 59, 60, 62, 67, 69, 76, 77, 78, 81, 84, 90, 94, 95, 99, 100; Grant Sheehan, 6, 10, 15, 40, 66, 86. In addition, the following are acknowledged: 5, photograph Richard Wootton, Sarjeant Gallery, Wanganui; 8, Jacqueline Bullmore and Donné Daubert, photograph Chris Parker; 20, Weaver Sue Batten, Victoria Tapestry Workshop, Melbourne, purchased with the assistance of the Friends of the Dowse and the Queen Elizabeth II Arts Council of New Zealand; 53, Evan Webb, Len Lye Foundation; Len Lye Foundation supported by Technics Group Ltd; 54, photograph Les Maiden; 73, photograph Murray Hedwig; 83 Museum of New Zealand Te Papa Tongarewa, negative number B.041677. All other photographs were supplied by the artists.

First published 1996 by
Godwit Publishing Ltd
15 Rawene Road,
P.O. Box 34-683
Birkenhead, Auckland, New Zealand

ISBN 0 908877 74 9 (paperback)
0 908877 98 6 (hardback)

Text and cover design: Christine Hansen
Front cover illustration: Chris Booth, *Pumice from the Mountains*, 1993-4, pumice and flexible stainless steel cable, 6 x ca. 4 m dia., collection of the Sarjeant Gallery, Wanganui.
Back cover illustration: Vivian Ward, *People and Pigeons*, 1966, mezzotint, 235 x 135 mm, courtesy Portfolio Art Gallery.
Typesetting and production: Kate Greenaway
Printed in Hong Kong

CONTENTS

PREFACE

This is a companion to *100 New Zealand Paintings*, published in 1995, which introduced 100 painters working in the period 1950–95. It covers another 100 contemporary artists working in the same period whose major focus is in an area other than painting. Included in this group are sculptors, printmakers, photographers, and assemblage and graphic artists. As with the painters, many of these artists work in more than one medium, and where applicable this is mentioned in the text. And again, as with the painters, the artists included in the various categories in this book are only a subjective sampling. Many others could not be included because of space limitations. The wide scope of this volume has aggravated that problem.

To a greater extent than in *100 New Zealand Paintings* I have given preference to senior artists. I have also included three artists in whom we can take great pride but who work or worked mainly overseas. Edward Bullmore brought most of his work back to New Zealand and worked here for nine years before he died. Much of Len Lye's work, and his archives, came back to New Zealand after his death in New York. Bill Culbert lives in France and England but has returned to New Zealand from time to time and has had a number of exhibitions here.

Perhaps most crucially, I have preferred to write about artists whose work I enjoy and whom I feel have something to say to every New Zealander. I believe that no matter how erudite or fashionable the theory behind an artwork, and no matter how popular it may be at foreign invitational shows, the work will not stand the test of time unless it becomes accessible after reasonable contemplation and continues to engage the mind after repeated viewings. In the course of writing this book I found myself saying the same thing about the work of a number of artists whose styles, media and ages differ widely. Each has made art that is complex and enigmatic without being abstract or wilfully obscure. The work presents quickly assimilable information, then leaves the viewer in thoughtful mode for a long time. I wrote about the value of this in my first article for the *Dominion Sunday Times* in 1983: 'The true art lover will find in a work of art that connects up readily to his or her input terminals a source of power, like a battery that energises the mind. The artist has put in a great deal of thought, effort, emotion and commitment, and this feeds out to the viewer through the art work, although not necessarily in the same way that it went in.'

There is a further area of definition that calls for comment. There are many creative people in New Zealand working with materials such as fibre, paper, glass, stone, ceramics and wood, and making pieces of such a high standard that categorising them as artists or craftspersons may not seem to be important. I believe, however, that there is a line between art and craft, although many would not agree with me as to where it should be drawn. All of the subjects of this book are generally defined as artists by themselves and by art writers.

As I stated in the Preface to *100 New Zealand Paintings*, a book such as this has certain advantages and disadvantages. The alphabetical presentation enables the reader immediately to look up a particular artist of interest and find out something about his or her work without having to tease the facts out of a general text which groups artists together. Readers must work out connections for themselves, although there are cross-references to other artists in this book, and in *100 New Zealand Paintings*. One full-page illustration can serve an artist better than a number of small ones, but that one illustration cannot be representative of an artist's work, and will tend to emphasise the importance of its particular period, area of interest or the series of which it is a part. No such emphasis is intended, and readers are encouraged to seek out other examples of the artists' works. This is particularly important in the case of those who work in several different media, such as Vivian Lynn and Carole Shepheard. Again, one page of text can do no more than briefly traverse an artist's activities, and the older the artist the more summary will be the coverage. In many cases a full page of text could have been devoted to discussing just one work. Where appropriate, I have summed up groups of works with a general description, rather than giving an analysis of separate works.

Some brief notes are included on pp.10–12 about aspects of different media, and a glossary of relevant art terms is included on pp.13–15. However, a general comment should be made here about works of art on paper. Because they generally need to be glazed, there is a size limitation, and the glass to some extent interferes with viewers' direct experience of the works' qualities. Consequently, artists who work on paper usually do not get as high a profile as painters on canvas or board. This is entirely unjustified. Indeed, because of the portability of prints, printmakers have been the leading group of artists representing New Zealand in overseas exhibitions over the last 30 years.

The notes in *100 New Zealand Paintings* about the development of contemporary New Zealand art are relevant to the present volume and are re-presented in the introduction, with appropriate amendments. Space permits only the briefest of biographical notes on the artists. A list of the abbreviations used in those notes appears on p. 15.

Notes on the illustrations are at the back of the book, along with a list of foreign artists mentioned in the text. As a first step to further reading, I commend a perusal of *Art New Zealand* magazine, back issues of which have now been indexed up to Volume 70. If your local library does not have a set, complain! The libraries of the major public galleries and art schools throughout the country have a wealth of additional material which is often available by arrangement to genuinely interested members of the public.

Writing this book and its predecessor has been a humbling experience. Before I began, I thought I knew a lot about New Zealand art, but I now know that in many cases my appreciation of artists' work was superficial. Both the range of invention and the quantity of excellent works — some unseen, some sadly lost — have astounded me. More than before, I marvel at the talent this country has produced. The funds available to our public galleries for the acquisition of works of art are grossly inadequate. I exhort my readers to buy New Zealand art — not just to support the artists, but (especially in the case of sculpture) to preserve the art.

Warwick Brown
Auckland
June 1996

INTRODUCTION

Two of the forms of artmaking covered in this book, sculpture and printmaking, have long histories. The others are developments of the modern movement, which dates back to shortly after the invention of the camera. That invention rendered obsolete one of the traditional roles of art, the recording of how a scene or person looked. At the same time it put a new means of making art into artists' hands. Photography took on traditional as well as completely new tasks. Not all artists were prepared to abandon depiction to photography, and so there has been a continuance worldwide of landscape, still life and portrait painting, printmaking and portrait sculpture. That area of art we will call traditional art, even though it has changed its look from that of past centuries by adopting some of the techniques of modernism.

The artists now broadly categorised in the modern school have followed another path, one that winds back into history as well as forward. That path is one of creative communication of ideas and of new ways of seeing the world — art to make you think. It tracks through from past masters such as Bosch and El Greco to Goya and Turner, artists who used ideas such as surrealism and expressionism in their work before the terms were invented. At the moment, art history recognises two phases of development: modernism and postmodernism. The first phase covers the development of modern art ideas from impressionism around 1850 to photorealism, a period bracketed by photographic influences. Around 1979 artists and critics in some of the world art centres came to the reasonable conclusion that nothing completely basic could be discovered about defining and making non-traditional art. They proclaimed the closure of the modern period and the opening of the postmodern period. This freed artists from the impossible demand of constantly making breakthroughs, and enabled them to range over the styles, images and ideas of the past, mixing and re-presenting them. It also allowed them to embrace obscure, untested or esoteric theories of art, language and philosophy. With no dominant '-ism', one could write one's own agenda. Evaluating new art thus became harder than it used to be. There was plenty of room for con artists, but also a wide blue yonder of potential. In this new climate, sculpture and photography have thrived. Formerly painting always led the way, working its way through the stack of ideas that had bubbled up before the First World War and then been cut off in their prime, along with many young artists. Now painting can be seen as having limitations.

Contemporary art (as it is now called) has well and truly come of age in New Zealand. Things here got off to a late start but from each generation since 1960 there has emerged an increasing number of talented artists. *100 New Zealand Paintings* gave an overview of the period. Although painters were more numerous and received most of the publicity, New Zealand has had talented sculptors from the start, among them Greer Twiss and the late John Panting and Carl Sydow. Printmaking too has always been strong, with work of the 1950s being more modern than most painting of the period. In assemblage the work of Don Driver, one of the young turks of the 1960s, has always been of world class. Leaving aside documentary photographers such as the brilliant Gary Baigent, art photography has attained a high profile only in the last 20 years with the emergence of such artists as Megan Jenkinson and Christine Webster. Computer art may become important in the future, if its potential for image overload can be controlled, and in this New Zealand can for the first time toe the starting line with the rest of the world.

NOTES ON ART MEDIA

EDITIONED PRINTS

Printmaking is a time-honoured craft, but techniques have now become so diverse and sophisticated that it is difficult to determine how some art prints are made. Four hundred and fifty years ago, engraving, etching and woodcut were the only media, followed by mezzotints in the seventeeth century and lithography in 1798. Prints can now be made by one or more of those processes, plus screenprinting, xerography, laser copying and computer generation. Many of these traditional and modern systems can include photography by using light-sensitive emulsions or scanning devices. Apart from all this, high-speed photo-lithography allows the mass production of coloured images, such as the reproductions in this book. By use of embossing, these reproductions can now even include the texture of the paint on the original work. Such reproductions are sometimes sold misleadingly as 'limited edition prints'. However, whatever else it may be, a fine art print is *not* a reproduction of anything else. An art print may exist in more than one copy, but it is not a copy of anything. Its genesis is not in another art work, such as a painting, but in plates, blocks or screens — the paraphernalia of its making. For printmakers the magic of the process is often the reason for working in the medium.

Finding out how a print is made can add to one's enjoyment of it. Brief descriptions of the main printmaking methods are set out in the glossary.

Printmaking in New Zealand has grown from small beginnings to some 120 practitioners, making it the second-biggest area of artmaking after painting. It was given a boost in the 1980s by the establishment of professional printmaking studios, where expert printers helped artists to make prints. Some of these have now gone, but the Muka Lithography studio in Auckland (est. 1986) remains a strong force, particularly with its annual release of prints exclusively for young people.

GRAPHIC ART

This category includes most forms of printmaking, such as engraving, woodcuts and lithography, and other directly drawn forms of art in pencil, chalk and charcoal. Artists working in these media have reduced their means of expression to the minimum; nothing obscures the direct mark-making of the artist. This is an unforgiving arena — a minor error can, and usually does, ruin a work. On the other hand, great aesthetic pleasure can be derived from an artist's virtuoso performance.

PHOTOGRAPHY

Art has always been seen as something special and valuable. As countless millions of photographs have been taken by non-artists since the medium was invented, artists using photography have some special problems of acceptance. They must go further than other artists in defining themselves as such, and in demonstrating their commitment and sincerity. One major problem is convincing people to study a photograph in the same way that they instinctively study paintings. A photograph can be art if it meets the basic requirements of originality, technical skill, thoughtfulness and communication. By one extended definition, it must successfully express or record an idea or feeling of the photographer/artist, or be the outcome of a project specifically embarked upon to capture images with an artistic purpose. This last category includes documentary photographers who set out to take a series of pictures with a common theme. Confusingly, the whole definition also covers most commercial photographers who, whenever the job allows, will try to get the most creative result possible. Many books have been written attempting to sort out these dilemmas of definition, and perhaps in the case of photography, art really is in the eye of the beholder. For this book I have selected some photographers who are widely accepted as artists, have developed a recognisable style and consistently produced memorable images. I have omitted a large, diverse and active group of documentary photographers, and to them I apologise. Given the camera's unique ability to capture the way things are at a moment of time, it may well be that in the long run their work will be seen as having the greatest value. Fortunately, the excellent selections of work in the Photoforum publications and other special photography books provide a showcase for serious non-commercial New Zealand photography of all kinds.

It is not widely understood that there is a lot more to photography than just selecting a viewfinder picture and pressing a button. The seeming ease and instant printing of amateur snaps is quite misleading. Before pressing the button there are many decisions for the artist to make about camera, lens and film type, framing, lighting, tone, focus, depth of field and camera stability. In both black and white and colour photography the positive/negative is only the next step. Control of colour and tone during the printing process, deciding on how big a print should be, and how the image should be cropped and framed are just some of the downstream artistic decisions to be taken. Finally, there is the element of chance — something that comes into play in photography just as much as it does in gestural painting or bronze sand-casting.

SCULPTURE

Unlike painting, which has had practitioners and an audience in New Zealand from the earliest days, there is not a tradition here of bringing sculpture into the home as there is in Europe. Until the 1950s, sculpture was largely restricted to decoration on buildings and memorial statues in parks and cemeteries. Even today it is hard for sculptors to sell their work, and many pieces are dismantled or lost after being exhibited. Sculpture is very space-hungry: to be seen at best advantage, one medium-sized piece can require a whole empty room. Notwithstanding these disincentives, New Zealand sculpture is alive and well, covering the full range of possibilities: expressive, minimal, pop, conceptual, environmental, monumental, domestic scale, civic and personal. Many of our sculptors have won accolades overseas. Since the 1960s there has been a move away from sculpture as object-making toward installations and environments. As in other areas of art, the range of materials used in sculpture has expanded greatly from the original stone, wood and metal. Almost anything can be used — fat, felt, wool, wire, cardboard, found objects — but the old imperatives of originality and meaningfulness remain.

ASSEMBLAGE

This form of art stands between sculpture and collage. It owes its genesis to that multi-talented genius Picasso who, in 1912, made a cubist guitar out of snipped sheet tin. He went on to make many welded metal works using scrap and found objects. Marcel Duchamp went one step further by exhibiting as sculpture unaltered objects selected from flea markets, his 'readymades'. These ideas have been hugely influential upon modern art, appearing in work by the Dadaists, the surrealists, pop art and Flux art, and in postmodern deconstructivist art. One of the fascinations of assemblage is the magical transformation of trash into art. In some ways this is even more compelling than the obvious worth emerging from the fashioning of gold and jewels to make a crown or reliquary. We are forced to evaluate the beauty in simple things, to use our imagination, to try to see what the artist sees. Gold, once melted and reformed, loses its past history. A found object has a history which is partly apparent, partly unknowable. By choosing to elevate the object, the artist make its history part of the work. By buying the work, the collector accepts the transformation in the same way that canvas and paint are purchased, not for their intrinsic value, but for what they have become at the hands of the artist. Assemblage, like collage, is simple to do but hard to do well.

MULTI-MEDIA

The development of modern art over the last 150 years has opened up so many avenues of expression that some artists have opted for a flexible stance, so that they can take advantage of whatever seems to meet their needs at any particular time. Such artists may do work in any of the disciplines discussed above, as well as performance, sound, video, installation and other conceptual presentations. As with assemblage, this type of approach can easily result in muddled or superficial work. The challenge is to manage the diversity and to orchestrate it into something of lasting value.

GLOSSARY

Anthropomorphic: suggesting the human figure.
Aquatint: an etching process that creates a range of tones from light to dark. A metal plate is dusted evenly with an acid-resistant powder, heated so that the grains melt, and then etched. The acid eats the plate around each tiny powder grain, pitting the plate. The plate is inked, wiped and printed (see **Etching**).
Assemblage: attaching three-dimensional materials together or to a backing to produce a relief or free-standing sculpture. Usually the materials are found objects.
Cibachrome: a photographic colour printing system which produces an iridescent, glossy, archival print on stiff paper.
Collage: attaching or glueing flat materials such as paper or fabric onto a backing.
Collagraph: relief print made from a plate that has been built up by the use of resins or the addition of collaged material such as cardboard.
Conceptual art: since the early 1960s the originality and relevance of ideas lying behind an artwork, rather than aesthetics, have become paramount for some artists. For a conceptualist, art does not have to be about drawing, colour, shape or texture; other artists have been working out the permutations of those for 140 years. Rather, art can be about anything that the artist finds interesting enough to put thought into. This may seem like a soft option, but as with other forms of art only good ideas will prove to be of lasting value.
Constructivism: a descriptive term to cover sculpture which is geometric and open, and in which the form of its making is clearly revealed. Because of its stripped-down approach, it can be linked to minimalism. It was originally a Russian movement founded in 1917–20 by Gabo, Pevsner and Tatlin, who wanted to make non-representational art forms for a new industrialised age.
Dada: an anti-art, anti-establishment movement of the period 1914–20 which set out to shock the public by making art out of rubbish and staging unintelligible performances. Largely ignored at the time, it became hugely influential from 1955 on (see **Flux art**).
Deconstruction: as a result of various philosophers putting forward the idea that popular images, the structures of language and the signs that we live by are, variously, corruptly manipulated, subjective, untrustworthy and sexually biased, many artists have set about taking such accepted structures apart. On one approach, this may reveal unsupportable precepts; on another, it is akin to the anarchists' approach to society: it is rotten — let's blow it up and see what can be made of the remnants.
Diptych: an artwork made in two halves and displayed either joined or side by side with a small gap. A triptych has three sections.
Drypoint: the simplest method of intaglio — the plate is scratched with a sharp burin. This produces a feathery rather than sharp line.
Engraving: as for drypoint, but the metal is gouged out in grooves of varying widths.
Etching: a metal plate is coated by material which resists acid, called the ground. The artist then draws a design with a sharp needle which removes the ground and, when the plate is put in an acid bath, the exposed metal is eaten away. This produces a sunken line which can receive ink. Areas which are to remain white are not etched. The plate is rolled with ink and wiped, the ink remaining in the pits and grooves. The plate, in contact with damp paper, is passed through a roller press, forcing the paper into the

sunken areas of the plate and producing a reversed image. In photo-etching, a photo negative is projected onto a prepared plate, the acid-resisting emulsion becoming hard or soluble in water depending on whether it has been exposed to light.

Flux art: a movement that began in the mid-1960s, described by one of its founders as non-art that 'forgoes artists' indispensability, exclusiveness, individuality, ambition; foregoes all pretension towards a significance, variety, inspiration, skill, complexity, profundity, greatness, institutional and commodity value'. It was inspired partly by the example of Duchamp and the Dada movement. Ironically but not unexpectedly, this type of non-art soon became high art and one of its practitioners, Joseph Beuys (1921–86), became one of the most influential artists of the late 20th century.

Found material: material of any description which was not originally intended to be used in making art.

Generic: a generalised form, recognisable as typical of the subject but lacking any detail and possibly greatly simplified.

Installation: an art project in which the artist takes over a given space and fills it up — with light, colour or sound, with a number of related sculptural elements or anything else which realises the artist's overall concept for the space.

Intaglio: any form of printing in which the ink lies below the surface of the worked plate, e.g. etching, engraving, drypoint.

Kitsch: work that purports to be art but fails because it panders to the lowest common denominators of popular taste: sentiment, piety, prettiness, cloying colour, illustrative drawing, or the debasement of art masterpieces by reproducing them as decoration.

Lithography: this printing process depends on the fact that grease repels water. The artist draws or paints directly onto a flat slab of limestone with a greasy medium. The stone is processed, wetted, then inked. Ink clings only to the greasy marks, and when stone and paper are passed through a press an absolutely faithful (but reversed) copy of the original marks is printed. A separate stone and printing is needed for each colour used.

Lost wax process: a method of casting bronze by making the form to be cast in wax, sealing the wax inside a matrix of heatproof material, and pouring in molten metal to replace the wax.

Maquette: a scale model, usually in an easily worked material such as clay, wood or cardboard, of a proposed sculpture.

Mezzotints: these are prints which have soft tonalities ranging all the way from pure white to jet black. This quality is achieved by preparing the printing plate with a hard, serrated tool. This is systematically rocked back and forth across the plate, pitting it with thousands of minute indentations with raised burrs. A prepared plate, when inked, would print totally black. Light is brought out of darkness by smoothing the rough surface with a burnisher. The image is reversed on printing.

Minimalist: any art activity which uses reduced means to force the observer to concentrate on such basic matters as shape, colour, texture or materials.

Montage: printing two or more overlaid negatives to produce a double-exposure effect.

***Oeuvre*:** the whole body of work of an artist.

Patina: coloration of the surface of metal as the result of controlled oxidising processes, sometimes enhanced by waxing.

Performance: art in which the concept of the artist is acted out in front of viewers (or sometimes alone). It springs from a rejection of the long-accepted view that art should be static, portable and collectable — and therefore able to be turned into a commodity. What happens may or may not be recorded for posterity by photography or video. The artist's mind and body are the media. Nothing may be left but props or traces of the activity.

Postmodern: art made after about 1980 which treats the many '-isms' of the modern movement, developed since 1860, and the work of individual modern artists, as tools which can be used to make new art, without any guilt about copying or lack of originality (see also **Deconstruction)**.

Relief: sculpture where the form is produced on or against an essentially flat surface, rather than in the round. The effect of side-lighting is usually important to bring out the shapes fully. A common form of relief is the modelling on a coin.

Screenprint: the artist prepares a tightly stretched screen of tough, extremely fine nylon mesh and then blocks out areas not to be printed by coating the mesh with a sealer. Paper is placed under the screen and ink is forced through the still open parts of the mesh with a squeegee. A separate screen is needed for each colour. The image is not reversed.

Suprematism: abstract art of pure geometric form and primary colours.

Tusche: a liquid medium used to paint on a lithographic stone.

Woodcut: a method of relief printing (i.e. the ink lies on the surface of the plate). Usually, the artist draws or paints on plywood the image to be printed and then cuts away everything else, i.e. the 'white' part of the image.

ABBREVIATIONS

ACE: Auckland College of Education
ARCA: Associate of the Royal College of Art, London
ATI: Auckland Technical Institute
BA: Bachelor of Arts
BArch: Bachelor of Architecture
BFA: Bachelor of Fine Arts
BSc: Bachelor of Science
CUCSA: Canterbury University College School of Art
DFA: Diploma of Fine Art
DT: Diploma of Teaching
MFA: Master of Fine Arts
UA: University of Auckland
UC: University of Canterbury
WP: Wellington Polytechnic
100NZP: 100 New Zealand Paintings

Note: all measurements are height x width x depth

1

MARTIN BALL

Born Auckland 1952.
DFA, UA 1973;
DT, Auckland Teachers College 1973.
Lives in Auckland.

Ball draws. He is one of the few New Zealand artists who has largely restricted himself to this graphic medium in order to master it fully (cf. Siddell, 80). He has worked in colour and in black and white, and his subject matter has ranged from the intensely detailed to the minimal, but he has always been a realist. His work of the 1970s was his own version of photorealism — attempts not to copy a photograph but rather to make drawings which resembled *reproduced* photographs, with all the graininess and washed-out tone typical of black and white illustrations in cheap magazines. Later he abandoned camera-based imagery in favour of drawing directly from the subject.

At art school Ball majored in painting, and his graduation works were detailed realist paintings of rubbish dumps. He also did a sensitively realised series of classic drawings of clowns, of which the inflexions in the backgrounds were an important part. Between 1974 and 1984 Ball did a substantial body of work which established his reputation as a major graphic artist. The images were based on magazine photographs, plus a few taken by the artist. Found images were cropped and rearranged. The subjects were bikies in leather jackets, motorbikes, rock stars and random snapshots. In contention for the masterpiece of this period is *Man in Leather Jacket*, 1975 (see *Art New Zealand* 58.50). This image of a contemptuous, self-assured young bikie, along with others of members and artefacts of subcultures which could be seen as threatening to middle-class gallery-goers, gave this group of drawings considerable impact. Close study reveals the full range of possibilities for manipulating graphite — intense blacks, fine, barely perceptible lines, hatching, smudging and rubbing out. This work can be compared to that of American photorealist artists such as Tom Blackwell, although Ball was unaware of the whole American movement until 1975.

Between 1984 and 1988 Ball's subjects were old paintbrushes, each one of which he imbued with character in an ironic confrontation of painting by drawing. Between 1988 and 1991 he was working with leaves and flowers, mainly proteas. Many of these works were in colour pencil, and the best of them were studies of the lush foliage found in hothouses. Done on the spot, they captured as much detail as a camera but were obviously drawings, demonstrating a wide range of shading effects, the peculiar colour blends which only colour pencil imparts, and celebrating the tooth of the paper. Ball did some paintings at this time which closely followed the effects of drawing. In 1994, Ball's exhibition *Drawing Paper* was just that. Many of the works in the show were drawings of scraps of blank, slightly rumpled paper taped to a wall. In the most reductive of these there were only three elements — paper, wall and sellotape. Ball made the most of each. The wall was grainy and inspecific, the tape uncannily real and glossy, and the papers became little cloud- or sea-scapes. Other drawings were of crumpled toy parachutes, excuses for virtuoso drawing but also metaphors for the brevity of youth's playtime.

In 1995–96 Ball has returned to studies of the human head based on his own sketches and photography. One developing series features a female impersonator who changes mesmerically and hauntingly from male to female. The work of the last two years shows a greater involvement by the artist with emotive and symbolic content.

Paper Landscape VIII, 1996
Pencil on paper
600 x 460 mm
Courtesy of the artist

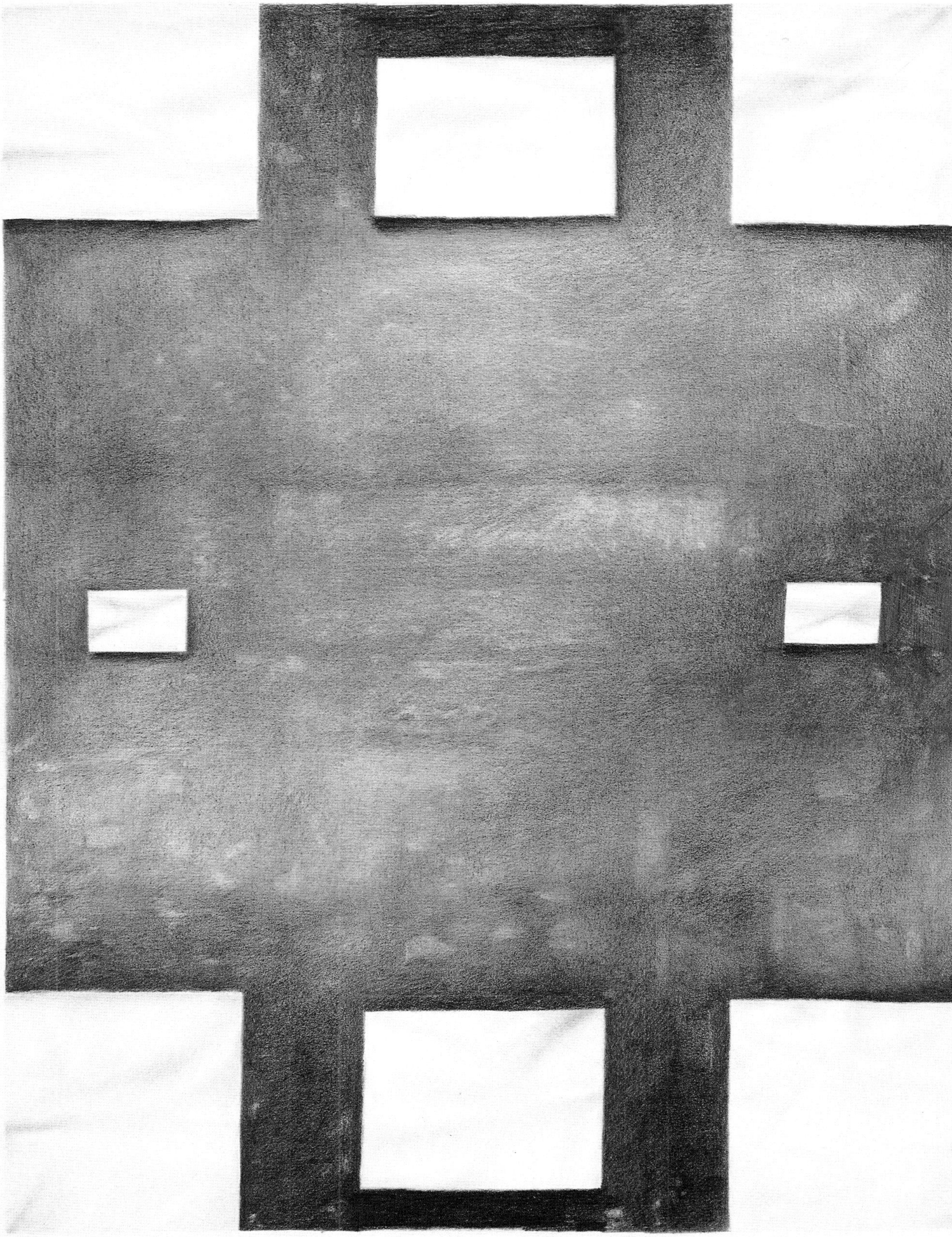

2

WAYNE BARRAR

Born Christchurch 1957.
BSc, UC 1978.
Lives in Auckland.

Barrar describes his photography over the past 10 years as 'filling in the spokes of a wheel'. Having defined as a goal the examination of modified landscapes, he set out on territorial explorations, each one having a specific agenda. At the moment he sees this as an ongoing process, and some 'spokes' are still being worked on. He has worked in colour at the Lake Grassmere saltworks (1987–89), producing stunning images which exploit the horizontally layered landscape and the fact that salt water reflects light differently from fresh water; and in a remote dune landscape on Stewart Island (1988) where dunes look like mangy dogs, trees are buried and stones fall out of moving sandhills. His investigations of new forests show the paradoxes of nature made artificial, while his studies of booms on lakes show how objects made for one purpose completely alter natural phenomena, such as the ruffling effect of wind on water. His work on Nauru Island (1991–95), taken in colour but printed using an old-fashioned black and white process, shows a country with a past but no future.

Barrar's photographs fall into groups (each either black and white or colour), but they go far beyond documentation. Barrar's best images trade on our habit of reading a photograph quickly and making a knee-jerk assessment of what it is about. That habit is formed by the myriad of photographs that we all encounter daily, plus the belief that the camera does not lie. In the hands of an artist like Barrar, the camera can present us with double, treble, even sextuple takes. One suspects that Barrar's agendas are just excuses to go hunting for what Derek Schultz has called 'beguiling ironies'. Because of the specificity of a photograph, a few particular images must be discussed to give some idea of those ironies.

Whanganui River Retention Wall, 1986
147 x 175 mm
Toned gelatin silver print
Courtesy of the artist

The *Landscape of Change* series, 1984– , was Barrar's starting point. He was interested in artificial lakes and the strange things which appear on their surfaces and at their margins. *New lake/new ramp, Marlborough*, 1985 (see *Art New Zealand* 53.67), looks like one of those arty diptyches photographers use to make an image look interesting (take 1). It can't be, though, because the hills at the back are continuous (take 2). It is a submerged boat ramp, the right-hand side exactly dividing the picture vertically at the bottom and fading off at the top (take 3). The illusion is compounded because on the left all is minimal, but on the right there are rocks and weeds (take 4) . . . except that the rocks are artificially placed and the growth is not water weeds, it is drowned paddock (take 5). This work is a masterpiece of New Zealand photography. As a bonus, the artist points out that no one uses this ramp high in the hills — why should they, with the magnificent Sounds to go boating in?

Ngauruhoe and Rock, 1986, shows just that (see *ANZ* 53.67). The rock looks like a mountain, but a protective fence behind it gives its scale away. It looks like those fake *papier mâché* rocks you see in cheap movies. Could this be a set-up shot? No, it isn't. The rock looks fake because it is so young, made of dollops of lava barely weathered. Its shape matches that of Mt Ngauruhoe in the middle distance. Then another cone appears between the first two, part of Mt Tongariro. This study in geometry is a strange landscape intruded upon and divided by humans, and modified both by humans and nature.

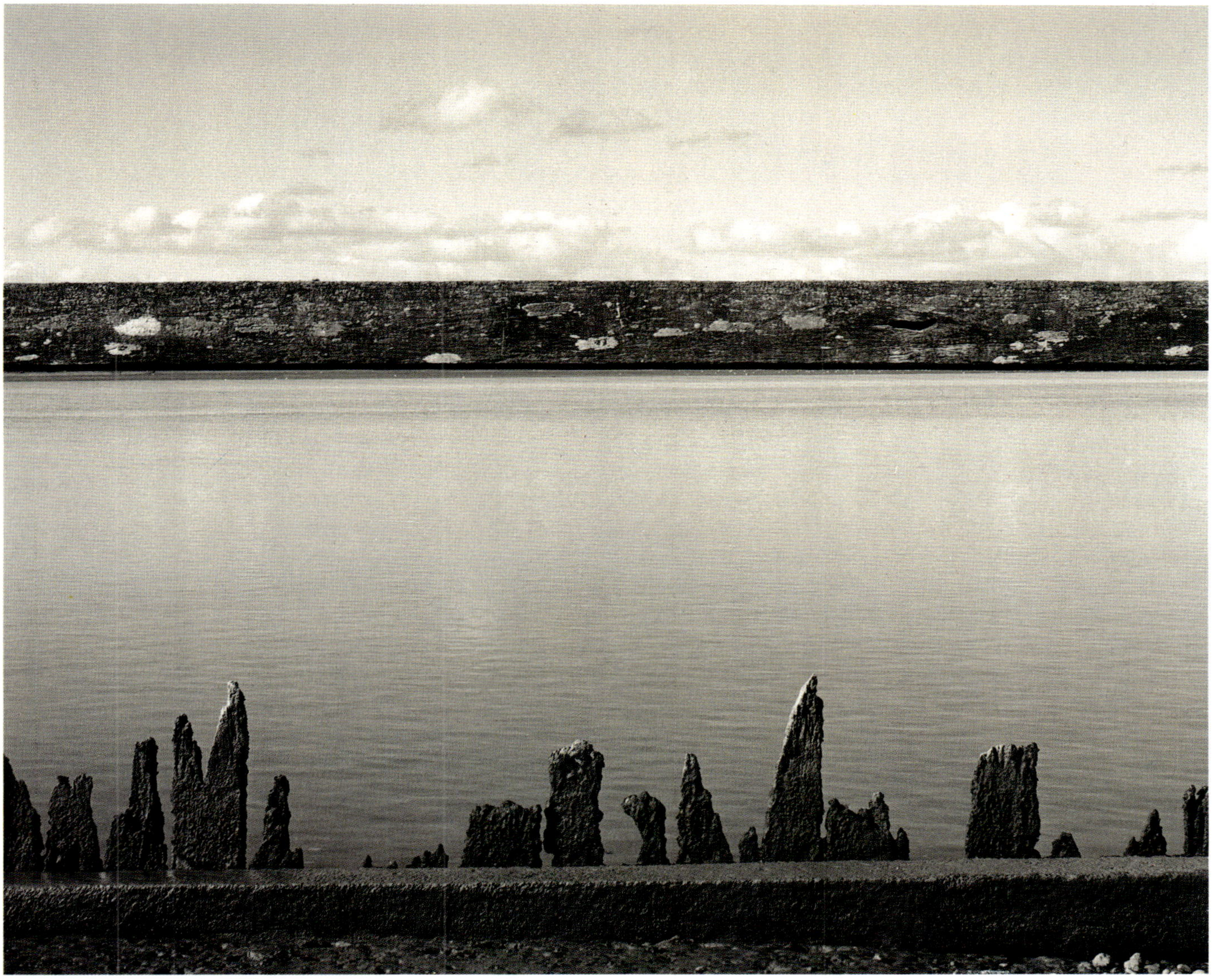

3

PAUL BEADLE

Born England 1917.
Graduated from Central School of Art and Design, London 1939.
Came to New Zealand 1961.
Died Auckland 1993.

Professor Beadle was a versatile artist, skilled at calligraphy, heraldic and coin design, drawing and sculpture. An extensive body of sculptural work done before he came to New Zealand was mostly executed in stone and wood, in realist and deco styles. In New Zealand he did much to revive and popularise the art of working in bronze in the 1960s and 1970s. In 1967 his designs for the new decimal coinage were rejected, but many people still consider them greatly superior to those selected.

Beadle's small, witty, intricate bronze sculptures were immediately popular and became, and still are, keenly sought-after. He used the ancient, lost wax process, whereby the sculpture is modelled in wax, then encased in a heat-resistant plaster and brick mix which is baked hard, evaporating the wax. Molten bronze is then poured into the strengthened mould. Skill and experience are needed to prepare the mould to ensure that air can escape, allowing the bronze to fill every nook and cranny completely. Beadle seemed to ignore such problems when conceiving his works. They often comprised many tiny figures and objects contained within a spindly structure, yet they were always perfectly cast.

Most of Beadle's sculptures are tableaux involving two or more people. Some are scenes from everyday life; others draw on history, religion and mythology. This scholarly background and the often elegant structural presentation contrasts with the jokey figures. With their football heads, goggle eyes, clown mouths, spaghetti hair and wobbly limbs, they could have become merely quaint ornaments in lesser hands. Beadle had a Dickensian ability to observe and describe. A posture, a turn of the head, an expression, an awkward situation — by convincingly working these into his vignettes, Beadle made them touchingly human. Some works are hilarious, such as those depicting folk waiting at bus and taxi stands; in others the absurdity of life often turns to pathos. Beadle also celebrated the joys of life in many Rabelaisian sculptures depicting feasts and orgies, and in the *Loves of Zeus, Nymphs and Shepherds* and *Toys for Young Eros* series.

In many of Beadle's major works, the figures are placed in a cylindrical, spherical or conical matrix. This approach assisted in the casting process by promoting an even flow of metal. Beadle capitalised on this and, drawing on his knowledge of architectural forms, created miniature towers, minarets, cupolas, spiral staircases and archways galore. Candlesticks, chalices and other ornamental forms also fitted the concept.

Beadle was not a 'modern' artist, in that his sculpture cannot be linked to anything similar being done elsewhere this century by non-traditional artists. His approach was closer to that of ancient Egyptians and Greeks, and tribal peoples in Africa and South America, all of whom made small shrine or burial objects from clay or bronze.

In Town Tonite, 1973
Bronze
250 x 160 mm
Collection of the Dunedin Public Art Gallery

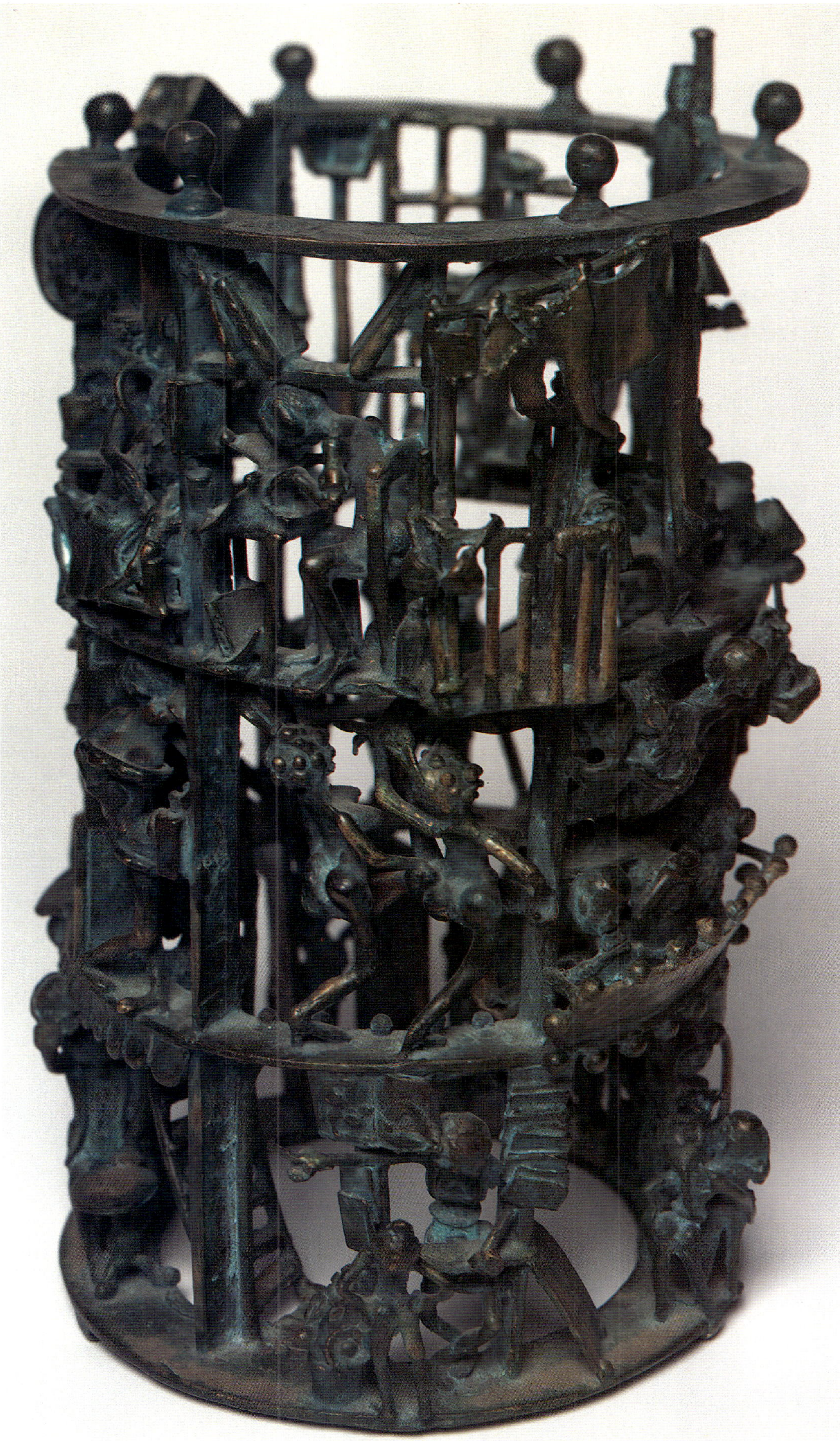

4

GRAHAM BENNETT

Born Nelson 1947.
DFA, UC 1970.
Lives in Christchurch.

For 15 years Bennett has been investigating the dynamics emerging from the blending of two historically opposed art styles — abstract expressionism and geometric abstraction (cf. Mrkusich, 100NZP, 58; Bambury, 100NZP, 5). His *oeuvre* rates with that of Maddox (100NZP, 48) as one of the most consistently focused in New Zealand art. Bennett has done much expressive mark-making, but at other times he has taken a severely constructivist approach. He has worked in the media of painting, drawing, printmaking, assemblage, ceramics, photography, and small and very large sculpture, maintaining throughout a balance of structure and gesture that makes his diverse works immediately recognisable.

Notwithstanding his use of abstraction, Bennett is interested in the way human modifications to the landscape can change our way of looking at it, as well as what we see in it. His works are about views through windows, reflections in glass, shadows in doorways, and about lines — power, fence, railway, pastel and charcoal. He began in the early 1980s with loose drawings which represented three dimensions in two, such as a tent shape on a plain. Gradually the drawings themselves became three-dimensional, with portions lifting off the backing. By 1986 he was using a technique whereby a drawing was laminated between two thin sheets of polyester resin. After such processing, the drawing could be folded and abutted like stiff card to create angled flanges, origami-style. Drawings then became sculptural reliefs in three dimensions (cf. McLeod, 100NZP, 54), the flanges inflected with painted and drawn diagonal and scribbled lines, or sometimes blacked out. The surfaces of the resin sheets could also be roughened or polished. Works changed with the viewpoint and could be made very large without needing frames.

Bennett has made many distinctive drawings and lithographs with a herringbone of V's rising through the centre, and geometric forms and expressive marks clustering around them. Some have co-ordinates of latitude and longitude inscribed in the margins, stressing the link with the real world. Colour is restrained and subtle, restricted to black, white, cream, light brown and blue-green. The stacked V's can call to mind a ribcage, a palm frond or a line of *Coronation Street* gables. One source of the device is the long, natural Boulder Bank which encloses Nelson's harbour, and this is alluded to in the graphics by rectangles resembling navigation markers. Over the years Bennett has moved from a general survey of diagonals, verticals and horizontals to a closer working with permutations of the X shape within a rectangle.

Between 1990 and 1995 Bennett did a number of sculptural installations involving a series of vertically mounted steel and glass frames laid out on the ground. Squares crossed by diagonals, these linear structures provide a multitude of frames of reference by which the surrounding landscape may be viewed. One structure, *Sea/Sky/Stone*, 1991, was erected on the Boulder Bank for two months before moving elsewhere. The diagonals evoke the slope of a hillside and combine to form pyramids (mountains). One may look through to flat land or sea but be reminded of mountains; with the small pieces one may see a stone and think of a mountain. At the same time the hard-edge structures insistently remind us of the works humans have built in and on the land.

Extending the Relationship, 1994
Gramodiorite stone with painted steel and silver-plated copper
150 x 100 x 100 mm
Collection Gallery Miyabi, Fukuoka, Japan

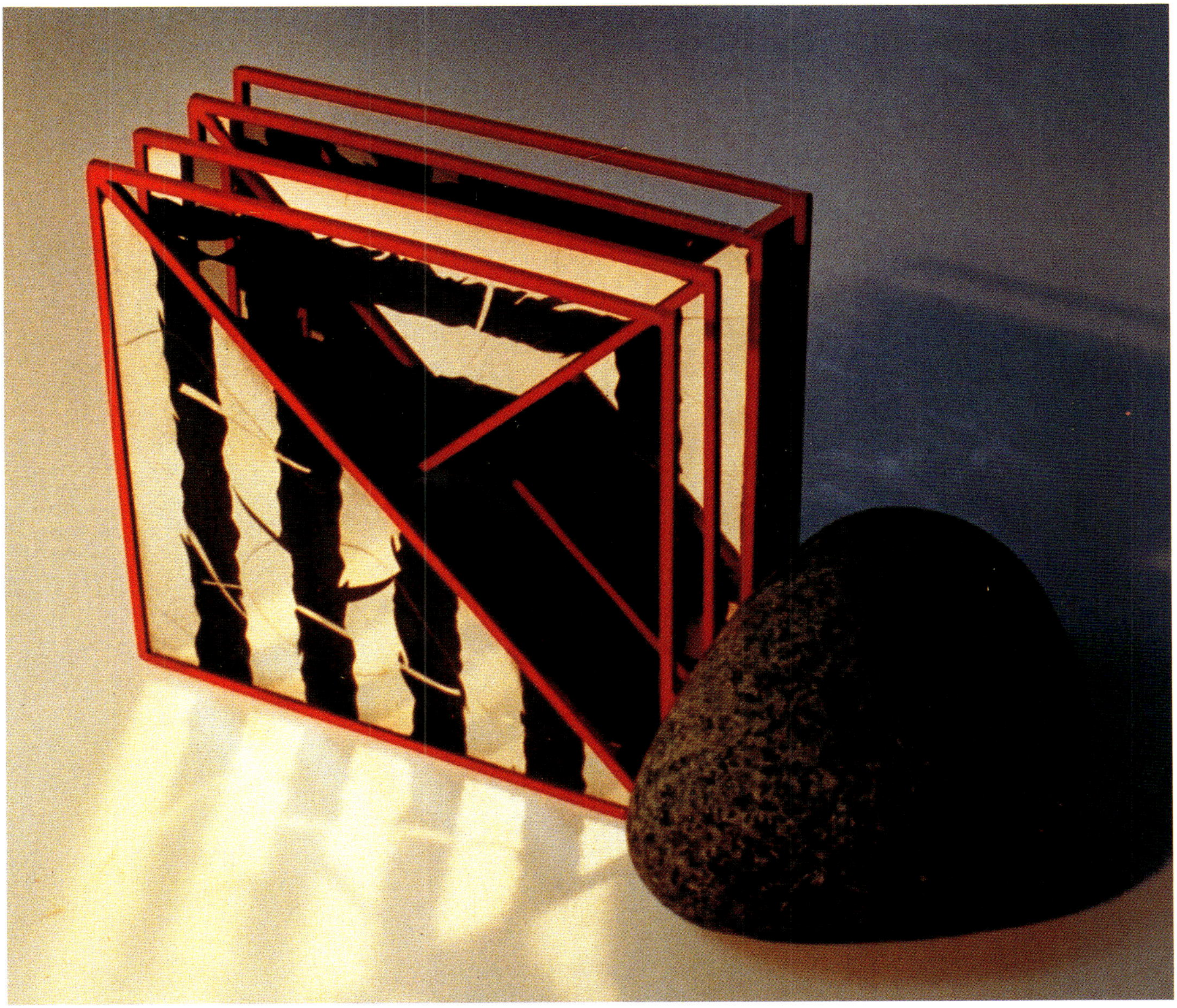
1.

5

CHRIS BOOTH

Born Kawakawa 1948.
Lives in Kerikeri.

Booth studied sculpture at the University of Canterbury before choosing to go overseas to apprentice himself to leading sculptors in England and Italy. He returned in 1971, experienced and determined; set up a workshop and bronze foundry; and has since pursued the challenging career of a sculptor working internationally. The time spent overseas did not convert Booth to an International style. From the beginning he has shown an interest in his environment, its history and sustainability. Although other New Zealand sculptors work with natural materials (cf. Hellyar, 41; King, 48; Shepheard, 79), none does so more directly than Booth. Manuka sticks, huge tree stumps, boulders, slate slabs, basalt columns, lumps of pumice and scoria have been transformed into sculptures of almost classical poise. Sand and cow dung have been used to make impressed moulds for in-ground bronze casting of nikau fronds, sticks and other objects. The bronze works done in 1984–86 have a special quality about them. Supported on stick frames or laid on rock slabs, they are a lacework of castings from organic material, together with the random overflow splatters which fell on the ground during the bronze pour. One moving work included a cast from the corpse of a baby seal. In another, the splattered bronze fan became a storm-tattered sail for an ocean-going raft of manuka poles. One readily viewable work is *Karuhiruhi*, 1986, a bird form hovering over rock-slab hills in Auckland's Finance Centre.

Booth's work has grown in sophistication over the years without sacrificing the use of natural unworked materials. His big bird forms and uprooted stumps of 1983, made from puriri salvaged from Northland scrubland, were sincere but a little simplistic and awkward. His assemblages of lashed manuka sticks of 1972–84 were innovative articulators of space. He now has a sure grasp of the monumental, of materials and of the ability of abstract sculpture to become a powerful, enigmatic presence.

In one important series of sculptures, Booth has been working through variations of an idea which dates back to 1973. Piled-up columns of flaked stone in the form of cairns are a familiar sight to trampers. Stacking up rounded sea or river stones is, however, a near impossibility — but they can be built into high columns, even arches, if drilled through the centre and strung on steel rods like beads. At a variety of scales from small to huge, Booth has made numerous works this way. The toil involved in the hole-drilling is immense, and each stone has to be flattened slightly at the interface to produce a compact look. Two of the most prominent of these works stand at the end of Victoria Street East in Auckland and on a headland at Matauri Bay, Northland. The latter, incorporating the ship's propeller, is a memorial to the *Rainbow Warrior*. These stone towers remind us that there is potential for growth in all things; that humans are just collections of minerals organised in a particular way.

In recent years Booth has travelled abroad, fulfilling residencies, commissions and invitations to exhibit, and his work has become more site-specific and variable in form, with similarities to some of Andy Goldsworthy's work. Booth has developed his own rock-stacking techniques, along with a new method of threading rocks using flexible stainless-steel cable.

Pumice from the Mountains, 1993–4
Pumice and flexible stainless steel cable
6 x ca. 4 m dia.
Collection of the Sarjeant Gallery, Wanganui

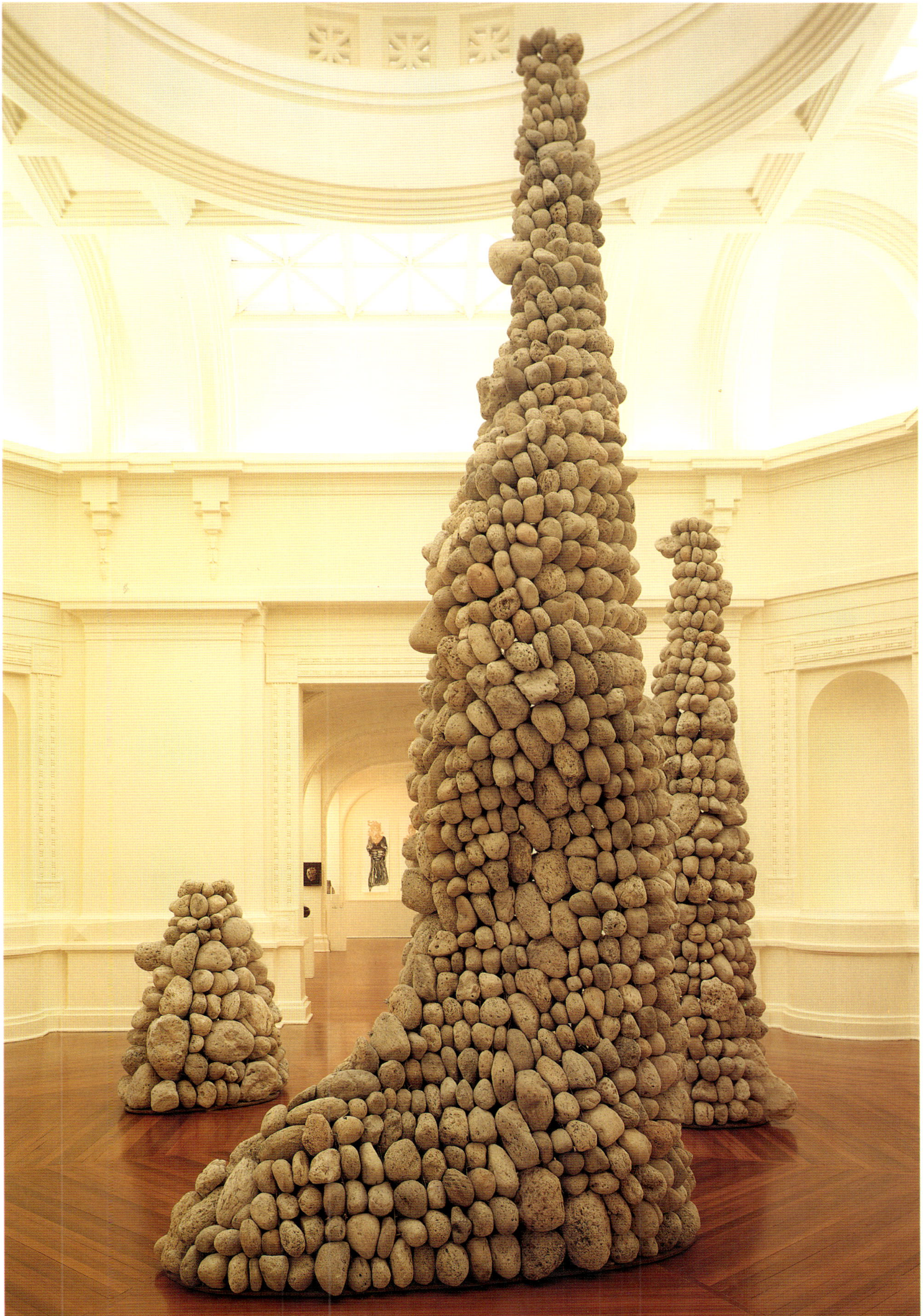

6

JEFF BROWN

Born Nelson 1964.
Lives in Wellington.

Brown is a multi-media artist, although his principal medium is paint. He has moved from completely deconstructing painting without quite turning it into sculpture, to the use of a flat support, albeit the unconventional use of sheet aluminium or galvanised steel, to his recent use of monoprint techniques in his paintings. Two major influences upon this self-taught artist have been Trusttum (100NZP, 91) and Woollaston (100NZP, 99). From the former, Brown absorbed an extremely fine sense of colour and composition, and his work of 1992–94 has stylistic similarities to Trusttum's paintings of the late 1960s. The colour in Brown's work has never failed to satisfy, even if some elements in his earliest works did. Like Trusttum, Brown has based most of his paintings on real-life situations, but abstracted so that the source imagery is barely detectable.

Brown's first show in 1985 was of large portrait heads, vigorously brushed with spatters and drips, surrounded by frames to which painted sticks were attached in random distributions. The heads were perhaps too crudely expressive, and there was a conflict between image and frame that was not fully resolved. In Brown's 1986 work the frames remained but were described by Ian Wedde as 'empty tombs from which the contents have resurrected themselves'. Cruciform shapes, again assemblages of sticks, hung or stood in front of the frames, the whole inflected with streaks of bright but balanced colour. This was a period when neo-expressionism was at its height as an international movement, and these bold and inventive works were right up with the play. Not content to rest there, in 1987 Brown completely shattered and dematerialised his 'paintings'. They became mere shards of painted bark affixed to the wall in a cross-shape. The idea behind these remarkable works was simple, but the results were most original. In effect, each expressive brushstroke was a separate strip of bark, making 3-D wall drawings of quivering apparitions. In 1988 Brown took this idea further, placing collections of painted sticks on the floor. This permitted a greater bunching-up of the elements and a degree of 'cross-hatching', with parallel groups of sticks laid on or tucked under the main form. It was all rough yet balanced, artificial yet natural. The effect was something like coloured phoenix palm fronds, and the critics raved — while noting that any purchaser would have a maintenance problem.

In 1990 Brown began working on paper and on large sheets of hardboard. In works of the early 1990s he built a rich personal style, combing, scraping and dotting paint; juxtaposing broad, flat areas with thin lines and illusory depth; balancing purples and blues with browns and greens. Apart from his development of colour relationships, he did some monochrome works with large areas of the support left bare. In 1993 he exhibited painterly works articulated by angles and planes, distilled from city images such as buildings and trucks. These works were notable for their deep, subtle colours, tight composition and surface incident.

By 1995 Brown was painting on sheet metal, developing allusive works containing stencilled imagery based on truck parts such as hoses and gaskets. In 1996 this imagery was based on builders' tools and working drawings, again using stencils to print with paint. Colours were based on blue, calling to mind the now outmoded blueprint. These works are notable for their use of perspective in strongly three-dimensional imagery of beams, rafters and workbenches.

Untitled, 1986
Oil on galvanised iron
2.4 x 2.4 m
Collection of the artist

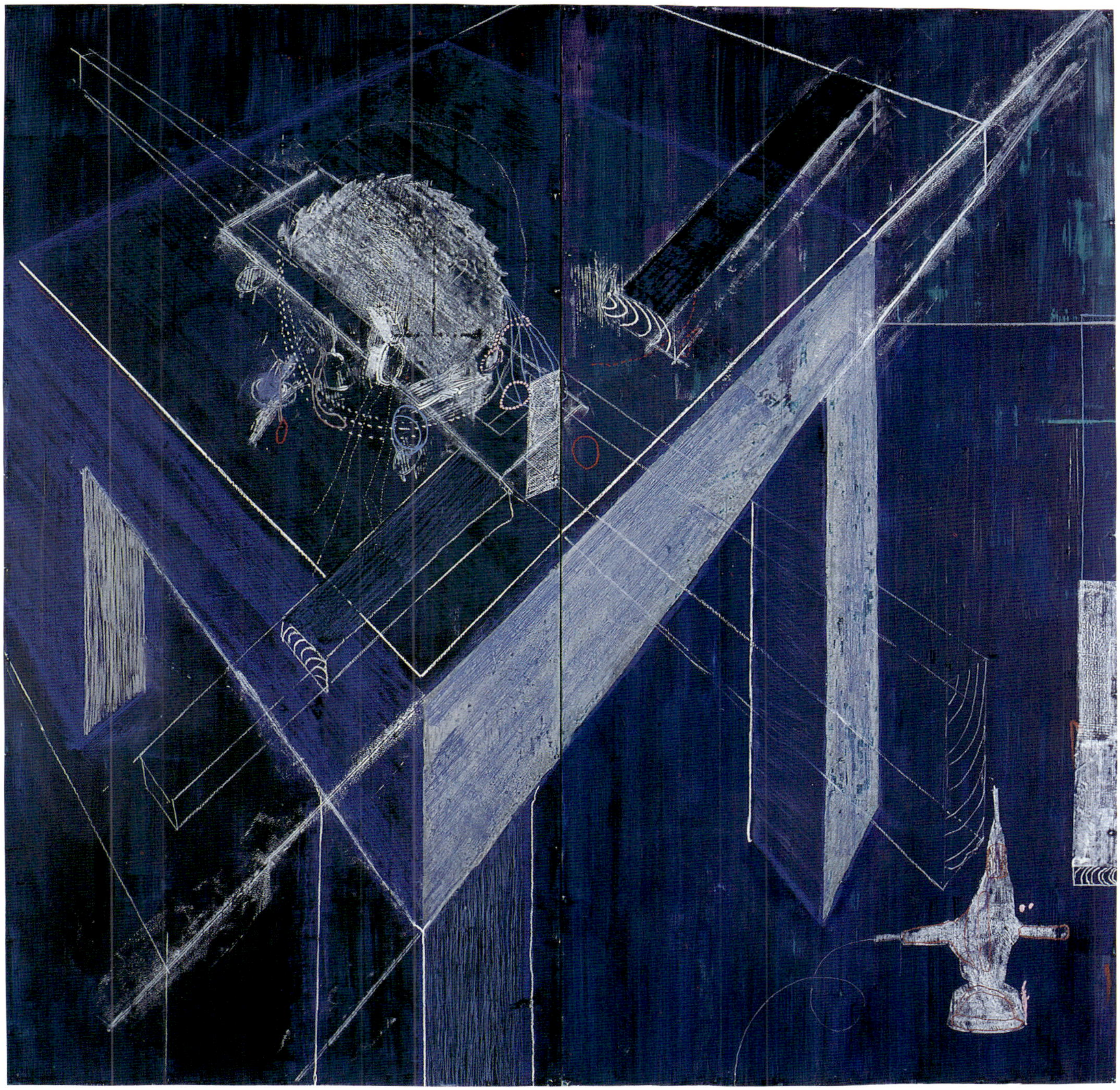

7

L. BUDD

Persona developed 1991–92.

Merylyn Tweedie (born Christchurch 1953) has developed a number of personae since she graduated MFA from Auckland University in 1975. Her avant-garde films and videos have been produced as 'Popular Productions' and other personae have been created for art theory, atelier and readymade art activity. Duchamp and Beuys, two anti-art predecessors, developed personae for themselves as part of their activities, but Tweedie has gone several steps further. The reason for this elusiveness lies in her dissatisfaction with the way in which art curators regard artists as 'names' and use this as the basis for their inclusion in exhibitions (cf. Ffrench, 33). The art of L. Budd, a member of Tweedie's group persona, is aligned with the anti-art-establishment movements of the 1960s such as Fluxus. The original Flux art rejected any pretension towards significance. In the 1970s and 1980s this type of art became ever more intellectualised. Budd's works are set up in what has become a traditional manner for this type of art, and look like they call for a lengthy curatorial essay. In fact they are intuitive, ironic substitutes for those other pretentious set-ups. They thus become anti-art about art that grew out of anti-art. This is about as postmodern as you can get. (This assessment does not apply to an intensely moving work executed by Budd in Poland in 1993 dealing with the Holocaust.)

Budd's work has mainly been concerned with text (cf. Pardington, 67; Carew, 100NZP, 12; Haffern, 100NZP, 30). It has moved cyclically from found to hand-written text and back again. The work grew out of artists' books, which then became large single sheets with smaller pages attached to them and finally works in which the text was incorporated into the work in a wide variety of ways. Even when hand-written, the text is almost always authored by someone else. Another feature of this artist's work is a disinterest in using traditional fine art materials. By using material ready to hand such as wallpaper, secondhand books and furniture, she can make art whenever she wants to and wherever she is. So far, so good — but does Budd's work have any aesthetic merit, however that may be defined these days? Unlike Duchamp's found objects, which were simply declared to be art, Budd's material is usually altered by her in some way. Between 1986 and 1990 Budd's predecessor Tweedie produced a series of works made from xeroxed images collaged onto wallpaper and solidified with coats of yellow resin. Some of these wafer-like pieces were mounted on 1950s pastel-coloured lino-tiles. The imagery was taken from 1950s books such as Arthur Mee's encyclopaedia and, although scrambled, seemed like an ironic commentary on the expected roles of women in 1950s society. This series was strikingly original, stylish and popular with collectors. Budd's works since 1991 have been more informal, the text being on loose-hanging paper exhibited along with items of cheap 1950s leisure furniture — magazine racks, coffee tables, reading lamps and so on. But the work still has a 'look' about it, sourcing it to the artist. It looks earnest, tentative, improvised, half-finished and somehow rather vulnerable. It tests the codes that define art. So, Budd is an avant-garde artist without a theory, who creates a vacuum for theorists to fill — but how long can it be before 'no theory' becomes theory and a self-effacing persona becomes well known? This book is evidence that this has already happened.

Detail from the temporary installation 'Smith & Gröting', Artspace, Auckland, 1992
Variable dimensions
Chair, panel heaters, plastered floor
Courtesy of the artist

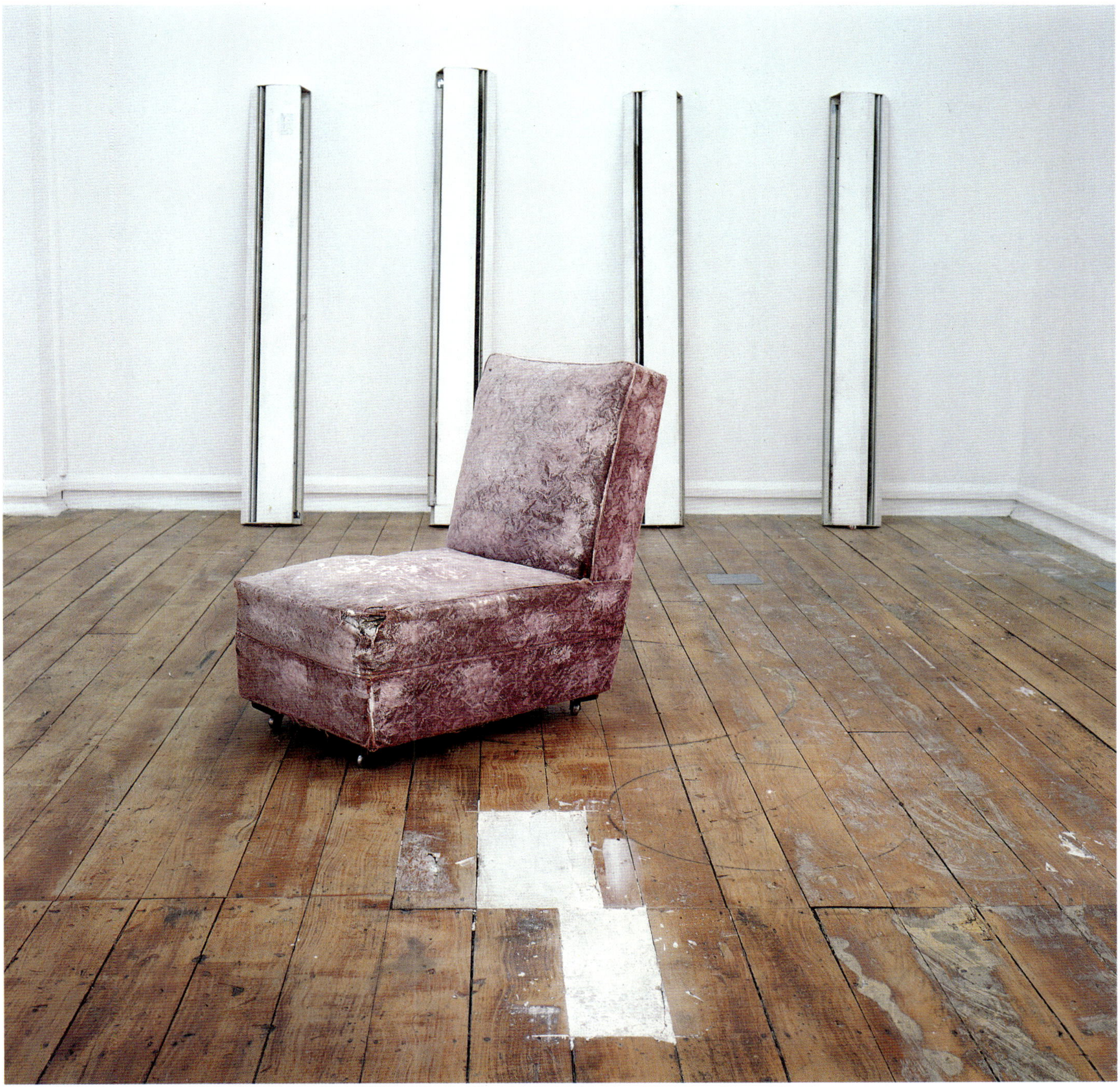

8

EDWARD BULLMORE

Born Balfour, Southland 1933.
DFA (Hons in Painting), CUCSA 1956.
Died Rotorua 1978.

Bullmore's early death cut short the career of an unusually interesting artist. In his youth he played rep. rugby and in appearance he was the archetype of the handsome, burly kiwi bloke. Educated in Christchurch, he produced his mature works in London, and if he had stayed there he would almost certainly have joined Paolozzi, Tilson and Fullard as one of the British pop movement's leading mixed-media artists. His best works can stand alongside anything done contemporaneously anywhere.

Bullmore was an accomplished draftsman from the beginning. Before he went overseas, he drew and painted in the style of the American regionalist T. H. Benton. He also had a taste for surrealist melodrama which carried through to his later work. Throughout his career he drew the human figure with virtuosity in a wide range of styles. During the 1960s he produced a particularly fine series of female nudes in collage and stippled paint whose rounded forms drew on his interest in regionalism and surrealism.

During a brief stay in Florence in 1959 Bullmore honed his drawing skills into an Annigoni-style realism and began experimentations with cubism, naive art and surrealism. In London his art developed rapidly. In 1960–61 he expressed his reaction to cold war tension in the *Transition* series, which depicted ruined cityscapes and despairing people. Other work explored coarse, leering faces in the manner of Breughel and the *Cuba Crisis* series of paintings. Drawings featured anguished heads, severed but living.

With the *Harbinger* paintings of 1963 Bullmore returned to an interest in the female form, moving it towards abstraction. Curved body shapes, with padded and stitched elements, were combined with hovering mechanistic devices. In the following series, these acted to dismember the vulnerable bodies. The *Hikurangi* works were constructed paintings, incorporating 3-D relief elements, rope, wood and canvas. They were big, brutal and exerted a horrid fascination. Some were like the great gangrenous wounds of an interrupted operation. Canvas was slit or torn and the gash either roughly stitched together or pulled apart by cords. Within the frames, what looked like bulging organs were restrained by sheaths of muscle. The colours — browns, khakis and dark reds — seemed to signify death and corruption. The works were intended by the artist to be approached from the viewpoint of landscape. On this reading, this was land twisted by volcanic forces or opened up by humans, ravaged and laid waste. The earthy tones of the earlier works in the series progressed to bright colour, and the look of ripped flesh changed to a more clinical laying-bare. What was previously organic but unspecific became blatantly sexual.

The more abstract and simplified shapes of Bullmore's mid-1960s *Astroform* wall sculptures were a natural progression. These incorporated parts of bentwood chairs and stuffed, stretched canvas to make colourful, vaguely decadent pieces which typify, yet censure, the sixties. Many of these pieces were elaborations on intimate female anatomy. Bullmore also made some very interesting sculptures using old chair parts. He had made a name for himself in London when, in 1969, he returned to New Zealand. Unaccountably, he seemed stifled by the cultural climate here, notwithstanding that at this time the local contemporary art scene was just beginning to take off. He made some more *Astroforms* and *Hikurangi*-style works, but his *Icons* of 1974–76 were like enlarged, suggestive brooches, and his drawings returned to a dated competence.

Astroform no. 9: Conjunction, ca.1966
Mixed media, painted construction
1138 x 1140 x 405 mm
Private Collection, Katikati

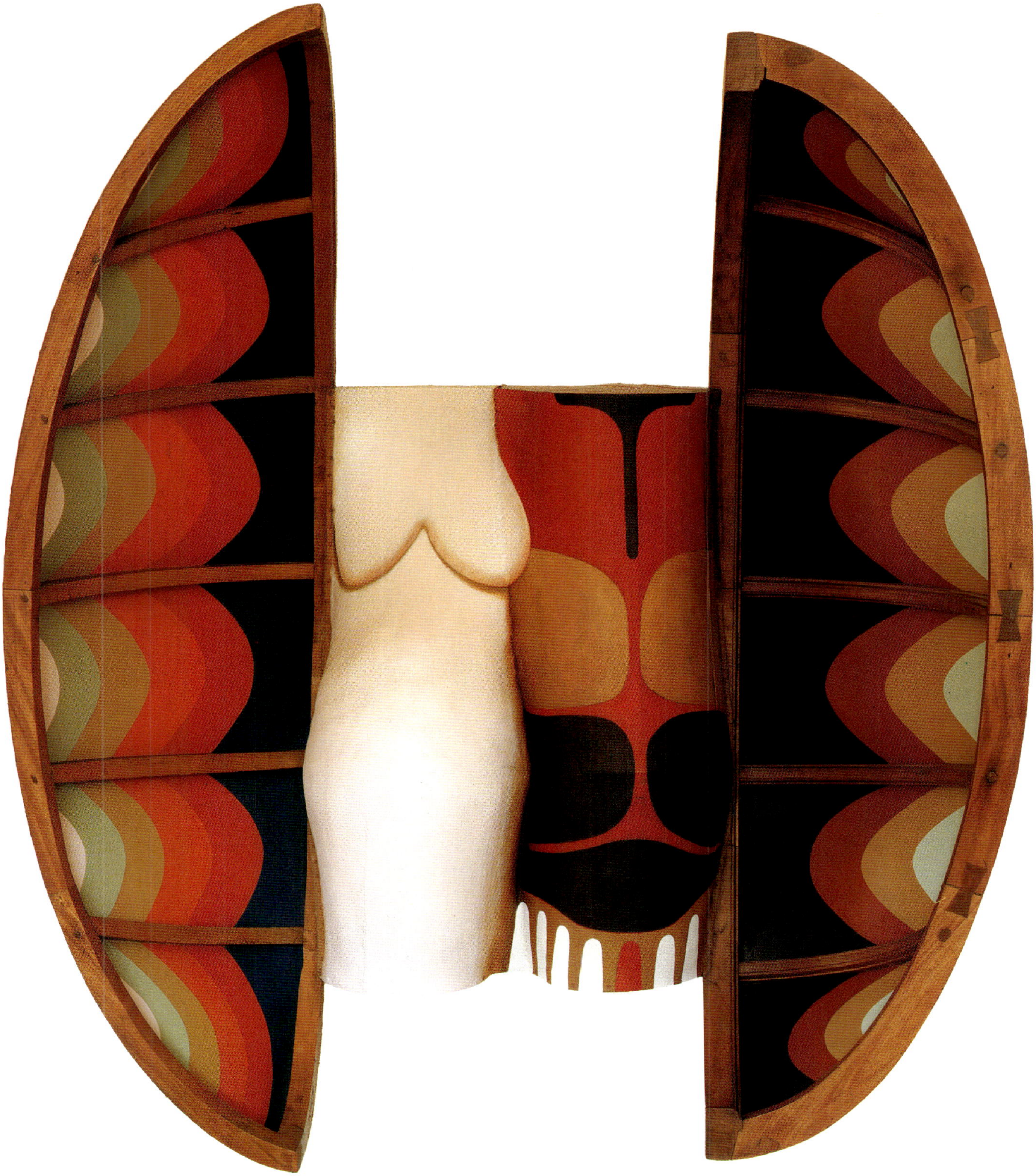

9

BRIAN CAMPBELL

Born Christchurch 1953.
Attended Elam School of Art, UA 1980–81.
Lives in Gisborne.

Campbell is best known for his monochromatic 'corrugated iron' woodcuts, in which the landscape and everything on it seems to be made of the ubiquitous metal. However, these are only the most recent in a series of prints going back to 1985 which have a funky, humorous quality. Campbell makes comments about aspects of society and modes of living, disguised in a surreal, cartoon presentation. His work of the 1980s reflected those years of excess. *Under Pressure*, a screenprint of 1986, shows a large pink city building which appears to be inflated and is constrained from both expansion and levitation by a set of cables. A balloon-like limousine sits athwart a road in the foreground, as if it had just drifted in. The prescient *Downturn*, also 1986, shows a desperate, skull-visaged businessman bending over backwards to touch the ground while office towers wobble and a jet plane is held up by ropes. Other work of the time showed new skyscrapers and the token facades which were all that developers left of heritage buildings. Symbolically, in one print a neon sign is on fire. The colours in these images are quirky pinks, blues, purples and lemons.

Campbell turned to woodcuts in 1986, quickly mastered the medium and produced a major body of work in 1991. In *A World Changed By Science*, a model jet plane on a stand, a diagram of a helix, the frame of a factory under construction, and a rooster are depicted in a bare, hilly landscape. *Living in Interesting Times* shows a shuttered church, a broken-down car and an erupting volcano grouped around a conical, fountain-like form which seems alien. A post-crash, dysfunctional society is clearly indicated in *Neighbourly Relations*, in which two men fight with knives in the suburbs while a third mows his lawn. As line drawings these would be close in style to Chilcott's (100NZP, 13), but the modelling of forms, and harsh light and shade introduced by the flowing woodcut lines make them more portentous. Other woodcuts are strange images of contortionists in orange and green. The background sky in these works assumes the shape of sprays of water arching over the bending figures — a link with the fountains which Campbell is fond of including in his images (for example, *Square Angel and Fountain*, 1988).

The People Who Couldn't Stop Making Things, 1996
Woodcut
540 x 400 mm
Courtesy Portfolio Gallery, Auckland

Apart from the spray device, Campbell used his woodcut lines in the classical manner to give dimension to his forms until he did the 'corrugated' works, when the lines began to simulate the look of iron sheets. Not one to waste a good idea, he hastened to depict everything in the image in this manner, even washing on the line. The result calls to mind the work of Jeff Thomson (87), making these prints a rare example of two-dimensional art following sculpture. Like Thompson's sculptures, Campbell's iron landscapes somehow seem quite convincing. In *Corrugated Kingdom*, 1991, we see a car, caravan, two rowboats and hills made of iron, as well as the more predictable houses and water tank.

Campbell has also been a painter throughout, with similar subjects often being presented in the paint and print media. Technically his painting style is similar to that of Nigel Brown (100NZP, 10), but his imagery is far funkier (cf. Radford, 100NZP, 70). In recent landscapes the surface of the land is shown as gouged all over. This can be read either as shadows or as an expressive link to the woodcut process.

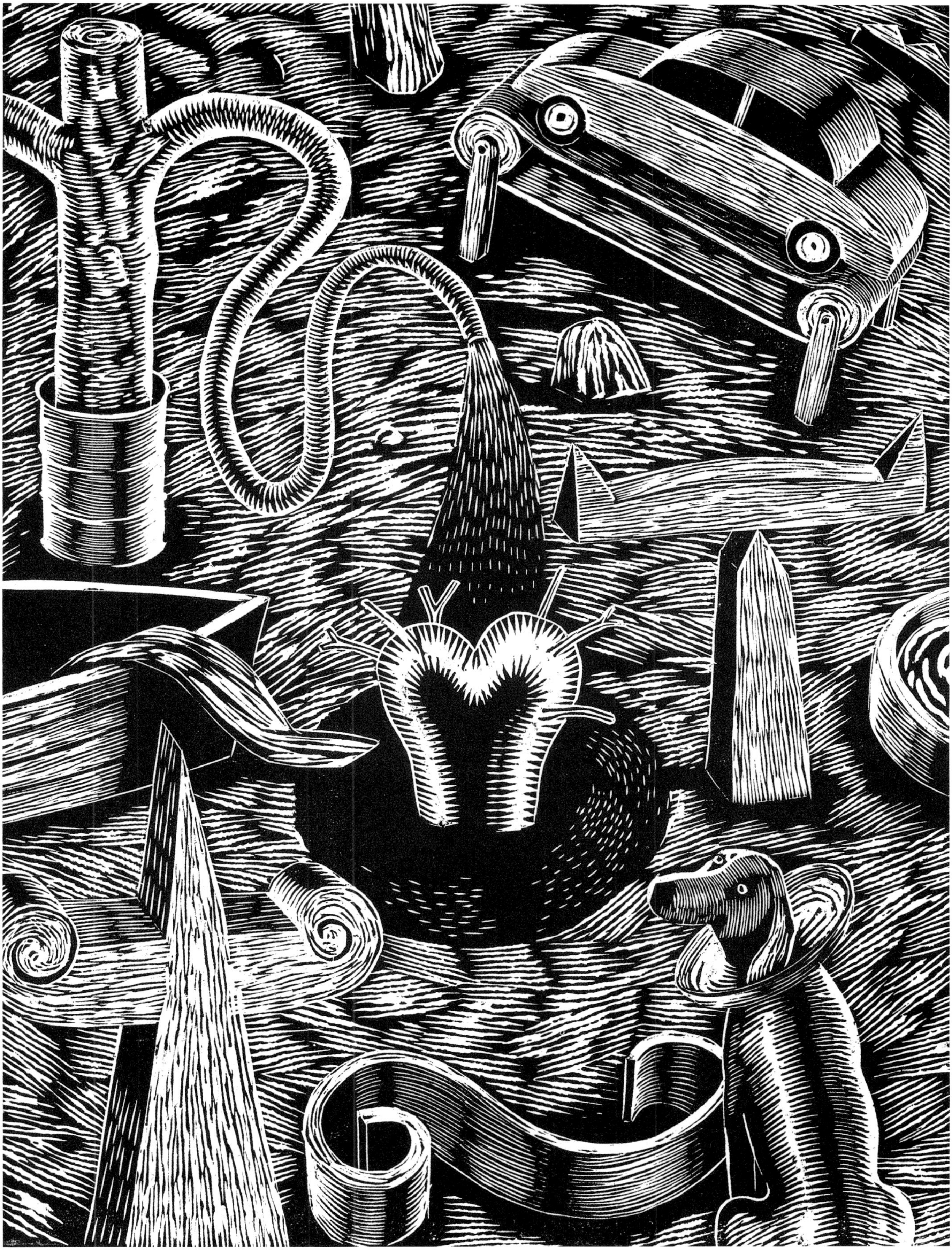

10

CHRIS CANE

Born Kawakawa 1957.
Lives in Wellington.

Cane has developed a consistent, personal style out of a thoughtful amalgam of other artists' styles. There is nothing wrong with this; indeed, it is a source of additional pleasure for those who can read the references. Such reworkings are part of the liberation brought about by postmodernism. Cane's mature work is a blend of the collage techniques of Robert Motherwell, the tentative mark-making of Cy Twombly, the funky drawing of Chilcott (100NZP, 13) and McCahon's wallpaper graphics of 1969.

Cane first came to attention in 1986. At that time he was doing ephemeral installation work using improvised materials. These assemblies deconstructed the safe domestic environment, editing junk material into an array of monotonous greys. As with the work of Beuys, this suggested the grim improvisation of the concentration camp, where things are not made to last because those who use them are soon going to die. In 1987 and 1988 Cane carried this provisionality over into a very fine series of collages. He used humble materials and fragmented signs and messages to create evocative puzzles, poised between absolute balance and absolute arbitrariness. Unframed, tacked together, mainly done on Kraft paper, these works were both elegant and rough, becoming precious ephemera. *Paper Talking* of 1987 was composed of 20 sheets. Stuttering over the surface of the works were blurred lines: fragments of text from media headlines, poetry and mock movie dialogue. In other works a landscape background was a strong feature, with shifting plains near and far — references to McCahon's empty, smudgy Muriwai land/sea interfaces. A low-key harmony was created by the use of ochre pastel marks on the brown paper, which was boldly cut out into irregular rectangles. Some pieces of paper had been prepainted with sweeping brushstrokes to create a grain, and where these were cut and juxtaposed with plain paper a sense of tension was set up. There were specific references to McCahon in the use of his 1974 *Jump* imagery — a dotted line shooting up from the ground across the top edge of a rectangular monolith. There were also loosely drawn boat and tumbler shapes, inferring seasickness or having one drink too many (something McCahon was known to do). The best of these works also incorporated large Rorsharch blots, calling to mind the black shapes in Motherwell's *Elegies*, but also reminding us that, as with the blots, what we see in a Cane collage is always subjective. In 1988 Cane addressed a specific theme, the abuse of dolphins, in his series *Where Dolphins Are.* A typical piece, *Plane*, included photo-based collage elements and a rectangle of blue in the otherwise muted paper colours. These tonalities were a direct reference to Motherwell. In 1989 Cane began working images derived from chaos theory, such as the Menger sponge, into his collage drawings. In 1990 the themes included wheat crop circles and aeroplanes.

Cane has carried his work on into the 1990s with remarkable consistency. As with Killeen (100NZP, 42), Cane's working method allows him to maintain a style while introducing constantly changing 'subject matter'. The fact that the works are not *about* that subject matter, but merely incorporate it into a matrix of readable fragments, is the reason why each work maintains its dynamism.

Geyserland, 1996
Acrylic, charcoal and photocopy on paper
670 x 690 mm
Courtesy of the artist

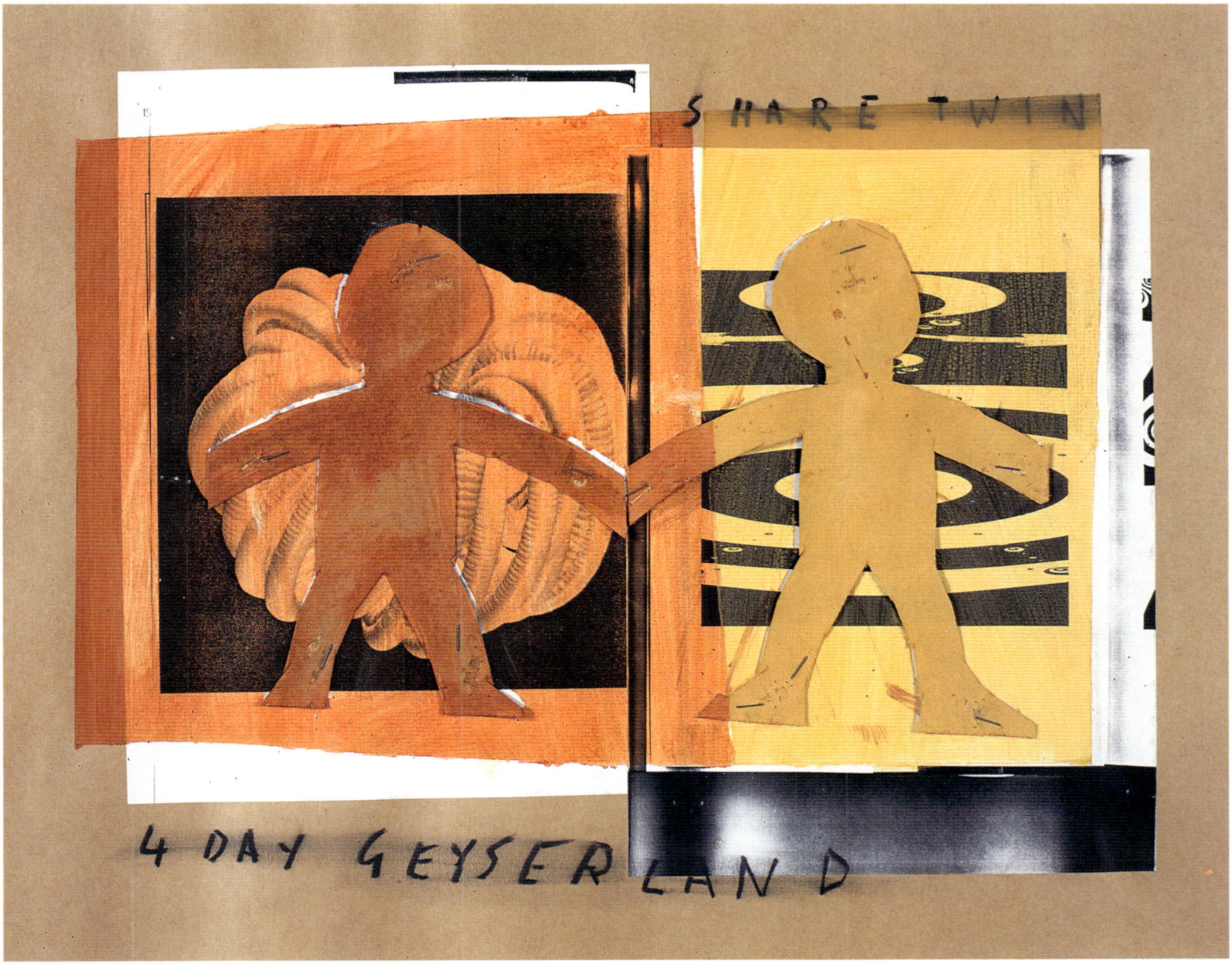
SHARE TWIN
4 DAY GEYSER LAND

11

GILLIAN CHAPLIN

Born Pietermaritzburg, South Africa 1948.
Came to New Zealand 1961.
BA in History, UA 1970; MFA in Photography, UA 1979.
Lives in Auckland and Melbourne.

Chaplin works intuitively; accordingly, her *oeuvre* as a photographic artist covers a wide range. Her early work was landscape-based, including some aerial photography, and from time to time she has returned to landscape. The tactile and volumetric qualities of cloth, and its function as a covering is a theme that has recurred through much of her work (cf. Rae, 100NZP, 71). Self-portraits recur, and there are other linking elements.

In an exercise in nostalgia in 1978, Chaplin reworked and reprinted a series of negatives taken by her father. In 1978–79 she was photographing concrete water tanks, circus tents and light shining through silk fabric. In 1981 Chaplin began using xerox machines to make her images. She was by no means the first to make art on photocopiers, but she brought to the medium a special sensibility, capitalising on things a copier does that a conventional camera does not do. If the item being copied is moved during the copying action, it is smeared and stretched. The images emerge on paper, easily torn and collaged. Pre-existing images can be used and manipulated. Self-portraits can be made by pressing one's face down on the platen. In the 1980s Chaplin made a large number of evocative black and white xerox works using famous images from art history, often distorted as in a fun-house mirror and associated with snatches of the artist's face, as if she were dreaming the images. Rumpled swathes of fabric also appeared in these works.

Supplication, 1996
Cibachrome print
974 x 700 mm
Courtesy of the artist

Chaplin's *Attachment* series of 1982 were night-time images of the bows of boats moored at a marina, the V-shaped tie-lines dominating the foreground while the matching V of the bow faded away into darkness. There were links here to the guy-ropes in the circus tent photos. Also made in 1982 was a series of small, vertical, glass-fronted boxes, all in black and white, which incorporated photographs and found objects. These poised and delicate pieces referred to vulnerability. Backed with photos of eggs, the boxes contained such things as tulle, feathers, dolls' heads, stones, butterflies and snakes. The theme of vulnerability continued in 1983 with xerox collages of a woman asleep, her faced brushed by an owl's wing. These works led to the *Breaking Eggs* series of 1984, which included sculpture of broken bowls, eggshells and hands cast from thin plaster. The associated colour photos were of male and female dancers moving together and apart, symbolising the fragility of human relationships.

In 1985 Chaplin worked on the *Chelsea Project*, the required subject of which was the old sugar works in Auckland. In her photos, taken at night with a flash, golden piles of sugar became dunes, and a plank over an oily puddle became a diving board over a crystal-clear tank of water. Large hanging cloths become the wings of a spirit invoked by a black-coated figure. This figure was seen in some pictures standing before the gothic scene, like one of Friedrich's figures contemplating the sublime. The xerox works were brought to a high point with the magnificent *Mist Areas* of 1990. This was an assembly of identically sized, A3 colour self-portraits, interspersed with black and white images of roses, eggs and bunched cloth. Over the last five years Chaplin has made 20 large assembled works in this manner, some cruciform in layout. At the beginning of 1995 she began the *Mask* series. Much of Chaplin's time in the 1990s has been devoted to audio-visual work for museums.

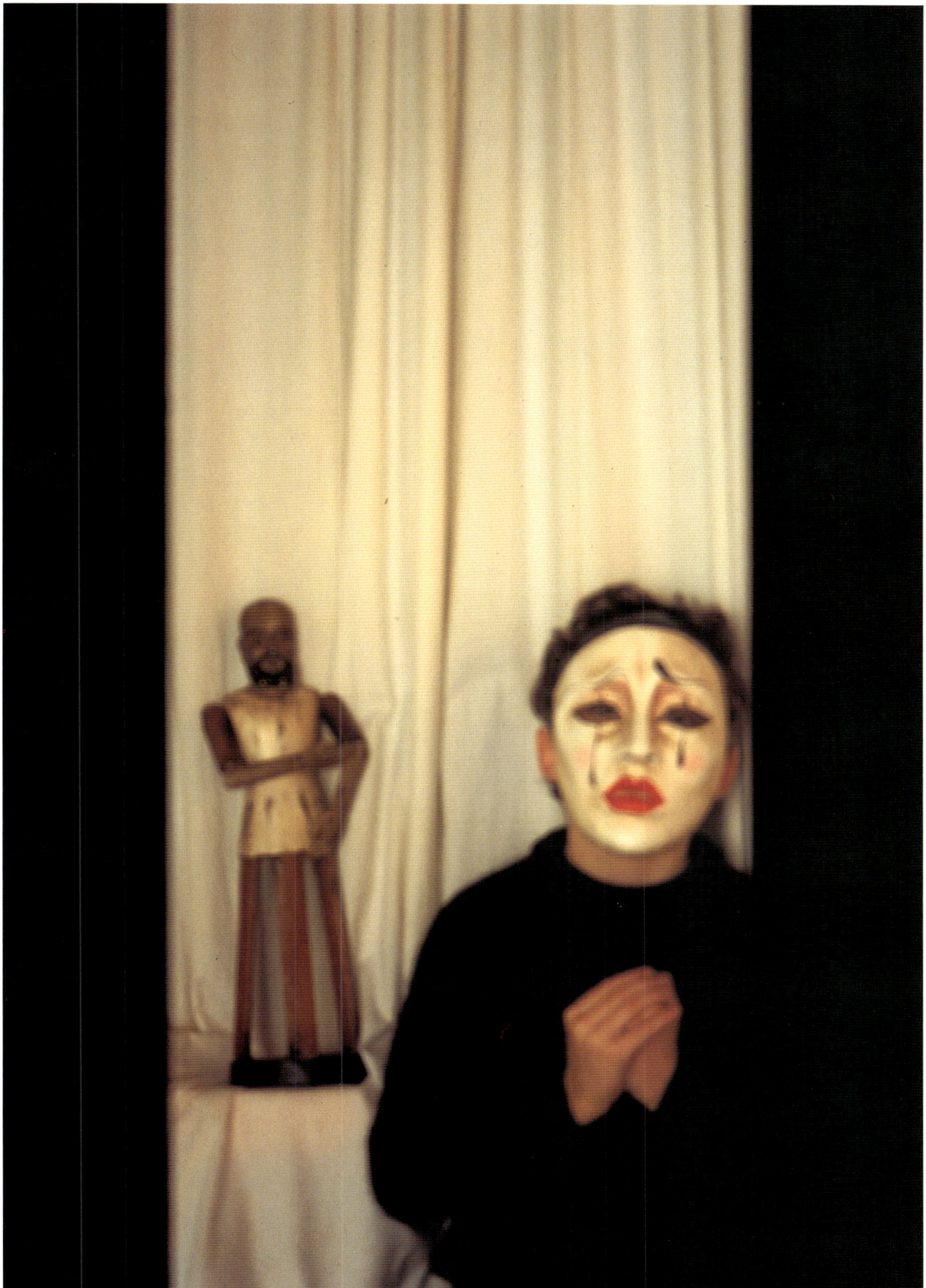

12

DERRICK CHERRIE

Born Auckland 1960.
BFA, UA 1982.
Lives in Auckland.

Cherrie's student sculpture included constructivist frameworks, pillows, and cut-out, quilted figures and beds. These elements pointed the way to his subsequent work, although since 1987 the human figure has been alluded to rather than represented. Cherrie's art arises out of his interest in dysfunctional domestic situations and also seeks to affect the processes by which a viewer of sculpture becomes involved with it. In times past, sculptures were objects that one looked at and walked around. A piece by Cherrie demands more — to be used, or at least to make one imagine using it. This act of imagining enlivens the work and usually disturbs the viewer. Many of Cherrie's works resemble items of furniture modified so that they are fit for some unusual activity: kinky sex maybe, or problems resulting from a physical or mental disability. The sculpture is notable for its immaculate manufacture and ex-factory newness, so that when looking at it one has the sense of being in a showroom. The son of a cabinetmaker, Cherrie knows how to do things right.

In 1985–86 Cherrie's work was divided between black drawings which looked like enormous enlargements of small ink drawings, and white, blocky, horizontal sculptures. Both represented human forms as buildings, or vice versa, and among many other readings they could be seen as commentary on the inhuman, dollar-driven, demolish-and-develop times. In 1987–88 Cherrie's cuboid figures sat or stood upright. One major work, *The Navigator*, was a tall armless figure plodding forward carrying two chairs on his back, and the whole piece was covered with a skin of world maps. Though schematic and featureless, this poignant form seemed doomed to trudge endlessly, weighed down by resting devices he would never use. Other strange works of 1987 looked like block-men metamorphosing into laminated furniture.

Untitled, 1993–4
Plywood, paint, foam rubber and felt
Variable dimensions
Courtesy of the artist

In 1988–89 Cherrie made a series of beds. The *Proluxes* were shiny, moderne horrors and the others were decidedly odd numbers equipped with chromium grip-rails and pool ladders. The most disquieting of these was *Retroflex*, a quilted pink vinyl squab which lay on the floor, tilting slightly up the wall. It was fitted with grip-bars and at its lower end a drain plug was indented, designed to receive whatever fluids might accumulate. This association of bathroom hardware with soft objects continued through 1991 in misleadingly whimsical ring and ball forms. Cherrie returned to beds with the *Supraluxe Suite* of 1992, a set of nine pure white, super-clinical vinyl and formica beds, all subtly different from each other like a set of Robert Ryman paintings. All Cherrie's slick beds seem to repel rather than invite rest. Instead of promoting the freedom of dreaming, they symbolise the slavery of consumerism. In 1993, in *Notes to the House Officer*, a reference to a book instructing doctors how to classify patients being admitted to mental institutions, the bed was stripped to a frame, greatly elongated and fitted out with restraint straps. Parts of this slatted rack were carefully coloured as if to identify them for some special purpose. This important work was the genesis of many ideas developed in 1994 and 1995 in a series of intricate pieces seemingly designed for exercising or restraining the body. Cherrie has always been interested in the invisible structural elements in cabinets. His 1995 works introduced iron screen mesh, bricks, black angle iron and rope, and seemed to be protecting themselves against intrusion. They balanced open and closed spaces, dense and light materials, and lines and curves.

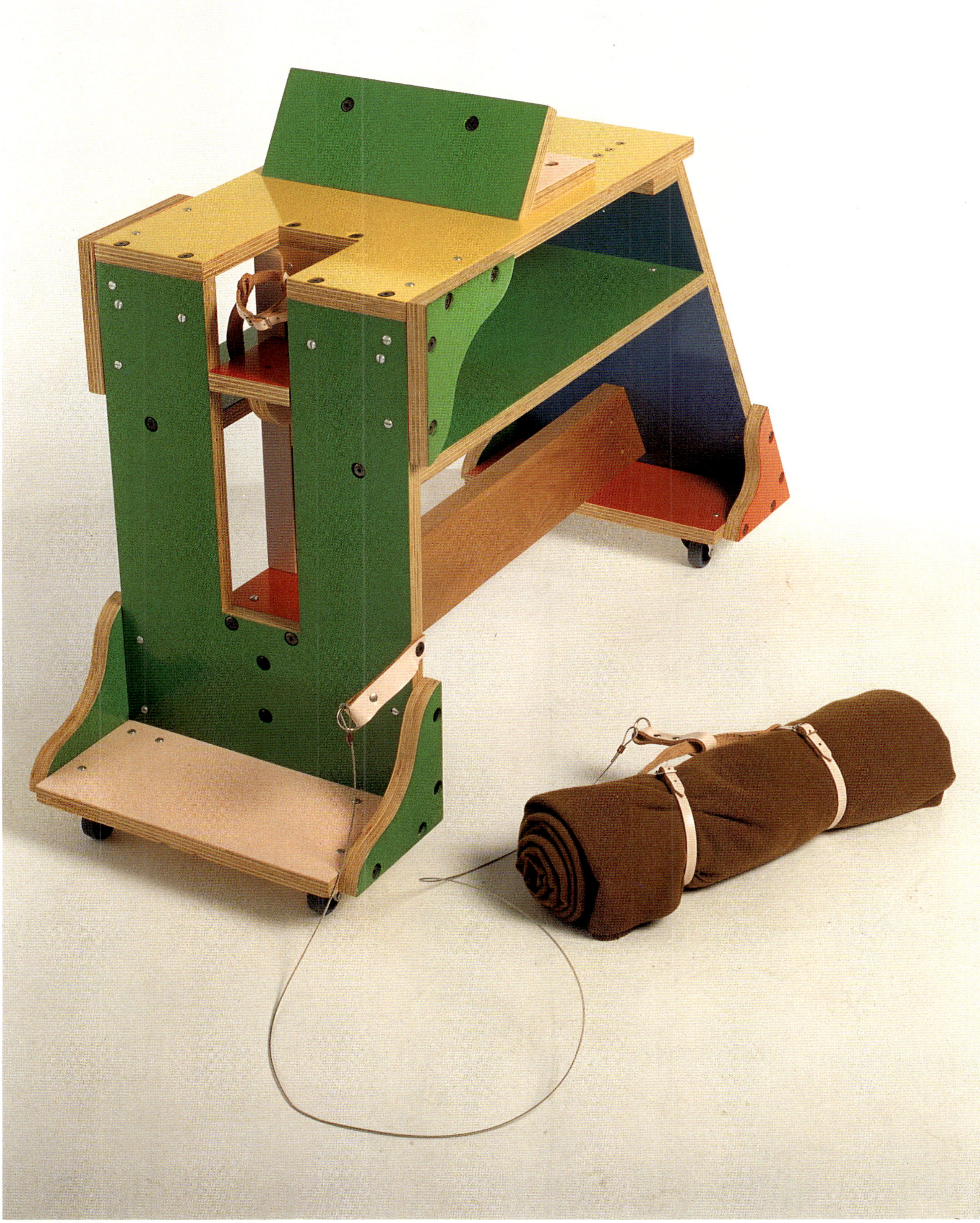

13

LEIGH CHRISTENSEN

Born Auckland 1959.
Lives in Auckland.

Christensen is a non-Maori sculptor with an interest in and respect for the Maori carving tradition. He has studied carving with a Northern Maori master, and his work is a synthesis of European and Maori ideas. This is dangerous territory, and any artist attempting to inhabit it must avoid such pitfalls as trivialisation, pastiche, superficial modernising and kitsch. Many have failed, including artists of Maori descent. Christensen's work succeeds because of his skill, the originality of his ideas and his ability to seek out the areas where the emblems of one culture match another. His work since 1986 has done this with ever-increasing conviction.

Initially Christensen sought to bring out anthropomorphic personifications hiding in particular pieces of wood, but he then moved on to mechanistic metaphors. A fine example of this is *Trouble*, 1992. This is a 1.6-metre-high section of macrocarpa trunk, stripped of bark but otherwise unformed except for the top 50 cm. At the top a natural fork has been carved into the gaping maw of a taniwha, seemingly rearing up from the depths to devour an unwary fisherman. At first glance this terrifying head has a very Polynesian look, but the teeth, eyes and scales soon resolve into cogwheels, nuts and bolts. One then notices that the base of the work is a real gearwheel. This creature does not snap — it minces and grinds. It becomes a symbol for the threat made to a superstitious, pre-European culture by a godless, exploitative, machine-driven one. A related work is *Dyna-saw*, 1991, which has a real sawblade set into it. Christensen has been exploring the theme of human versus machine since 1990 (cf. Roche, 76), all the while looking for resonance between Maori carving conventions and patterns, and the shapes of machine-tooled metal parts. Sawblades, car engine parts, crankshafts and gears have been incorporated into wooden sculptural forms in a seamless way, so that the metal elements seem organically part of the whole (cf. Muru, 61).

Christensen's endeavours have recently reached a high point with a series of works inspired originally by the calculating machines designed and, in part, built by the brilliant mathematician Charles Babbage in the 1830s. Some of his calculations and mechanical innovations have been incorporated into intricately carved totems which magically evoke a whole range of other art without being in the least derivative. Beyond Babbage's Victorian mechanics and the woody complexities of Maori carving there are hints of pre-Columbian American art and Paolozzi's British pop sculptures.

In 1994 Christensen moved on to examining another outmoded calculating machine, the Harvard MKII, a huge computer whose problems with moths in the relays gave rise to the term 'debugging'. A section of this, realised in kauri, proves that the form which follows function can indeed be beautiful to behold. Most recently Christensen has adopted an even more formal approach, using routers to carve layers of complex, repetitive mannikin shapes into a wood slab. From a distance these myriad mini-men resolve into the large figure of a robot, but the figures in meeting-house panels also come to mind. In this work Christensen is drawing closer to Para Matchitt's (57) style.

Transformer, 1992
Carved totara, gear box
2200 x 320 mm
Courtesy Oedipus Rex Gallery, Auckland

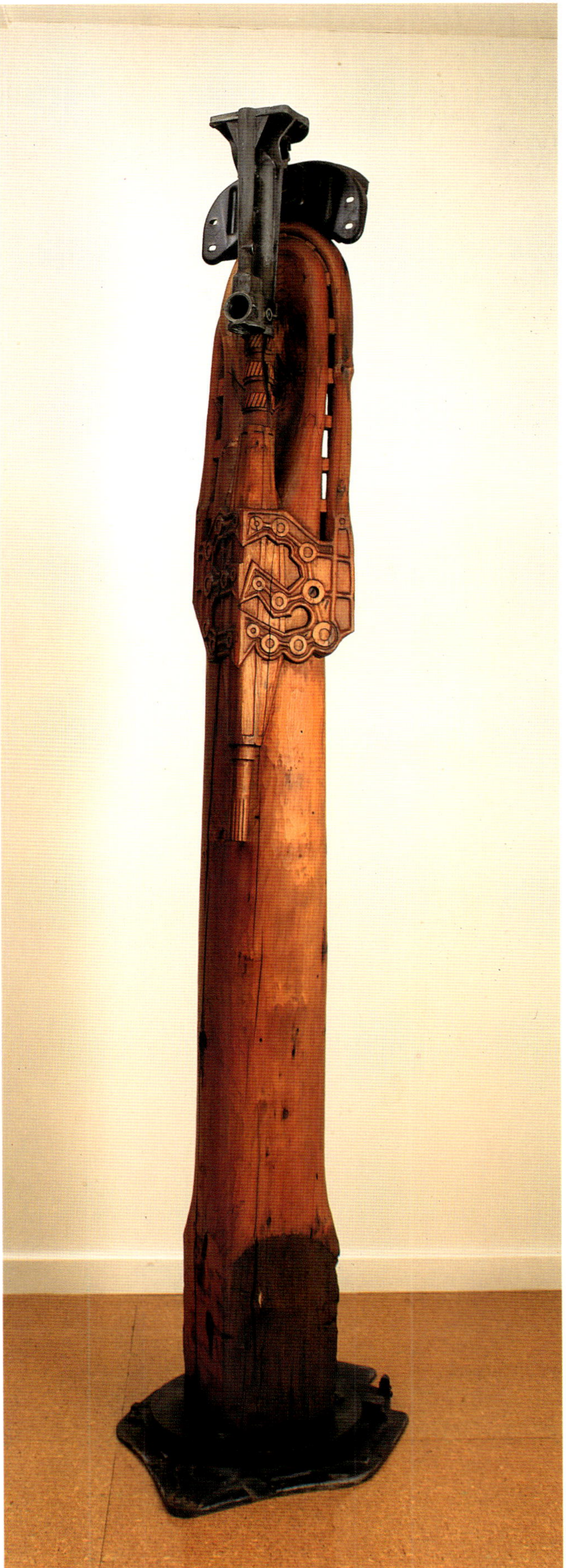
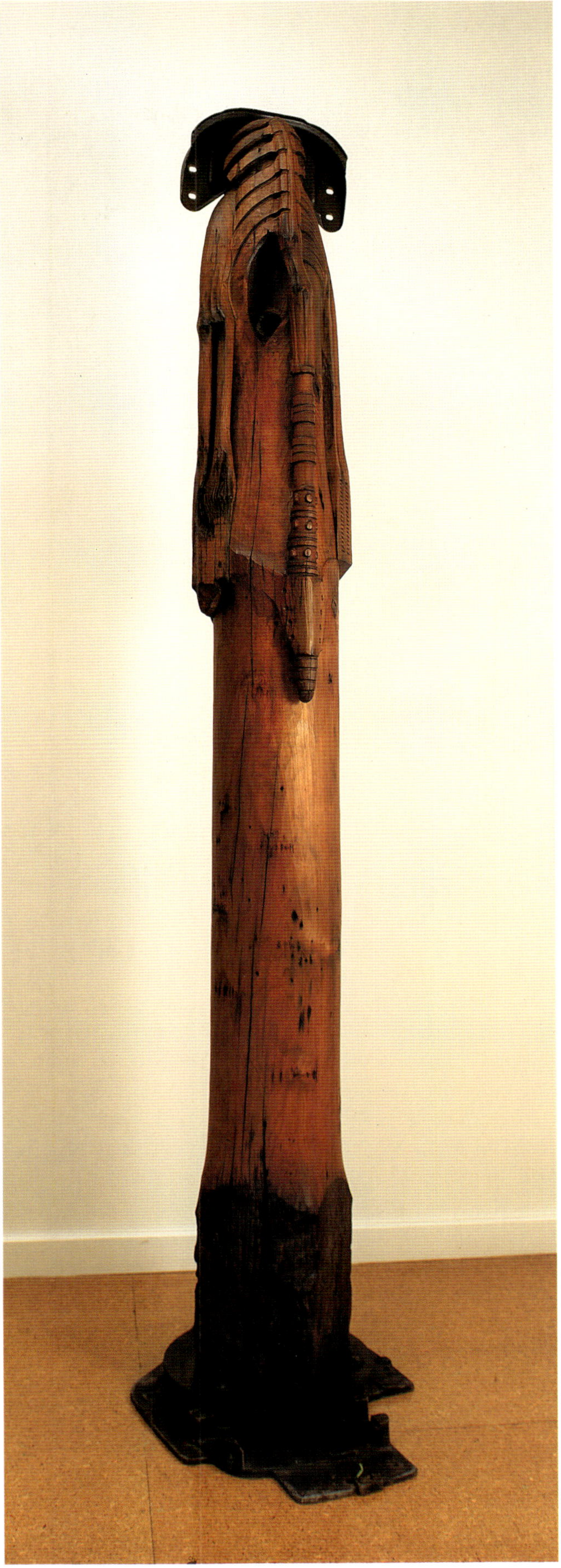

14

BARRY CLEAVIN

Born Dunedin 1939.
DFA, UC 1966.
Lives in Christchurch.

Prints may not often have the impact of a big painting, but they do have the advantage of portability. Consequently, a number of New Zealand artists have built an international reputation through their prints. Cleavin is one of these (cf. Drawbridge, 29; Tricker, 88; Webb, 97). Although he studied to be a painter, Cleavin's drawings attracted attention from the beginning. Cleavin is a consummate draftsman who has the ability to realise in line any thought that takes his fancy. This skill has enabled him to produce an extraordinary body of work in the etching medium: fantastic, surreal, humorous, macabre, frightening, but always convincing. The ill-judged accusations of pornography levelled against some of his work in the early 1970s can now be seen as proof of the power of his images.

Cleavin stands firmly within the centuries-old European tradition of printmaking, a tradition built by such artists as Dürer, Rembrandt, Hogarth, Blake and Daumier. They all produced intense, considered images, graphic in the sense of being vividly descriptive. There is little point in making an image in multiple copies unless it is worthy of wide distribution. So Cleavin takes the time to blend literary, visual and technical elements together. Using little or no colour, and restricted by the medium to line and tone, Cleavin often uses traditional 'vanishing point' perspective to create a 3-D illusion on the flat sheet.

The artist has said, 'Mostly, I reduce the world to absurdity; in that form it is manageable.' Animals and birds feature in many of Cleavin's prints and when the human form is depicted it is often subordinate, distorted or has non-human parts grafted on. One feels that Cleavin has sympathy for his creatures and despairs of his fellow humans. He has a fondness for visual puns, alliteration, anagrams, palindromes and touches of humour (cf. Tricker). An example of this is the *Allegation* series of etchings of 1981. Here, images of alligators hilariously illustrate statements drawn from the language of courtroom reports. *A Number of Allegations Flying About the Room* shows sly-looking, winged alligators doing just that. Cleavin also has a mordant side, using skeletons to make points about the human preoccupation with death and destruction. *Handgun*, 1971, shows a pistol, the butt of which turns into a skeletal hand. *Birds of a Feather*, 1984, shows two warplane pilots with bird skulls for heads, the round craniums matching the helmets held by the flyers. Cleavin's recent *Shadow of Doubt* series shows the skeletons of native birds propped on stands and ticketed, and their shadows cast on a wall. These prints are a fine example of Cleavin's command of the aquatint technique. The wall and the shadow on it are both created on the plate in the same way, the latter image being etched for longer than the former. Beneath all this is a perfect, line-etched grid. These common etching techniques, when used with such mastery by Cleavin, give his prints a satisfying 'rightness' — the sense that the medium is being exploited to the full and that the image could not possibly be improved.

With a Shadow of a Doubt no. 2, 1995
Etching, aquatint, printed on rives velin arches crème 270 gsm, edition 14
300 x 300 mm
Collection of the artist

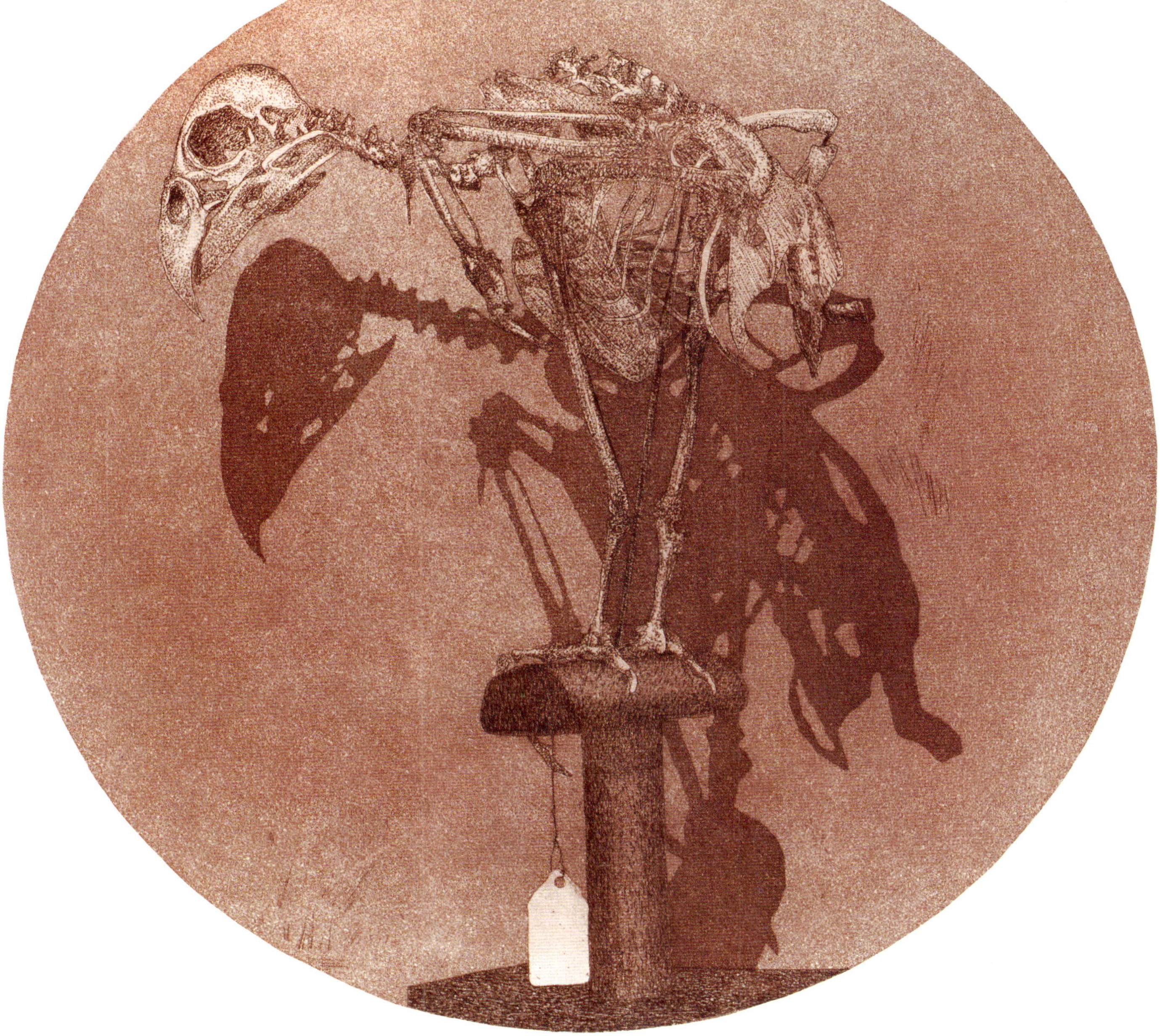

15

KATE COOLAHAN

Born Sydney 1929.
Studied at East Sydney Technical College 1945–50.
Came to New Zealand 1952.
Lives in Wellington.

Coolahan is one of New Zealand's senior printmakers. She has done at least one print a year since the early 1960s, and has exhibited nationally since 1964 and internationally since 1970. Etching has been her main medium, but she has also done some collagraphs and lithographs, combined with other media. She has drawn continuously, and periodically painted, sculpted, made installations and rugs, and made mail art. Her work has always been notable for her willingness to experiment and not to become trapped in any particular style or medium with possibly destructive consequences. She prefers art as 'an opening thing' for both artist and viewer, so some of her work straddles the art/craft boundary.

Coolahan has travelled widely and formed strong views about the state of humanity and of women in particular. Without being too specific or polemic, her work has attempted to set up visual situations which stimulate thought about twentieth-century life. Its diversity makes it difficult to sum up Coolahan's significant and sizeable *oeuvre* over 35 years, but some generalisations can be made. One is her preference for open, loosely composed forms rather than an overall coverage. Even compact works, such as her plastic reliefs or paintings, are made up of fragments. Colour is used sparingly. She may use several intaglio processes in the one plate, and she was one of the first New Zealand printmakers to use multiple plates. In her drawings and prints a variation of line from broad and assertive to very thin and spidery within one work is noticeable, along with a combination of figurative and abstract elements. Coolahan's early training gave her academic drawing skills which come to the fore when required. The curtain, sail or filter has been a recurring device to symbolise the way one perceives 'through filters of knowledge and ignorance'. Stretched and suspended triangles of fabric are often used in her installations, articulating large areas of space and evoking the sails of Pacific canoes. Free-standing forms and kite assemblages in handmade paper and cane also have a Pacific look.

Assimilated Immigrant, 1978
Aquatinted photo-etching and engraving, mounted on machine-stitched hand-cut paper
565 x 758 mm
Collection of the artist

For many years Coolahan has made her own papers to add texture and colour to her artwork (cf. Crook, 20; Lander, 51). The artist has said, 'I have a love for the naturalness of handmade paper. It can be passive and carry images or active and shape forms.' *Lifeguard*, an abstract print of 1987, is an example of this. Two adjoining backing sheets carry expressive black and white intaglio lines, and two other cut and folded papers of different textures make up a relief form in the foreground. In Coolahan's inlaid paper works, colour, form and paper are one, everything being composed at the stage when the paper is still in pulp form. Of necessity imagery is broad in these works, giving them an entirely different look from the etchings and drawings.

Coolahan's earliest works were conventional portraits and landscapes. Her work of the 1950s was expressionistic: both gestural in the manner of Woollaston and textured in the manner of the School of Paris. By the 1960s the landscapes had become stylised, compartmented and semi-abstract, emphasising the ridges and clefts of hills. In the 1960s she began making prints on *papier mâché* and tapa cloth. In the late 1960s and into the 1970s she made some highly original abstract relief prints using moulded plastic. Many of her prints of the 1980s and 1990s have dealt with feminist issues.

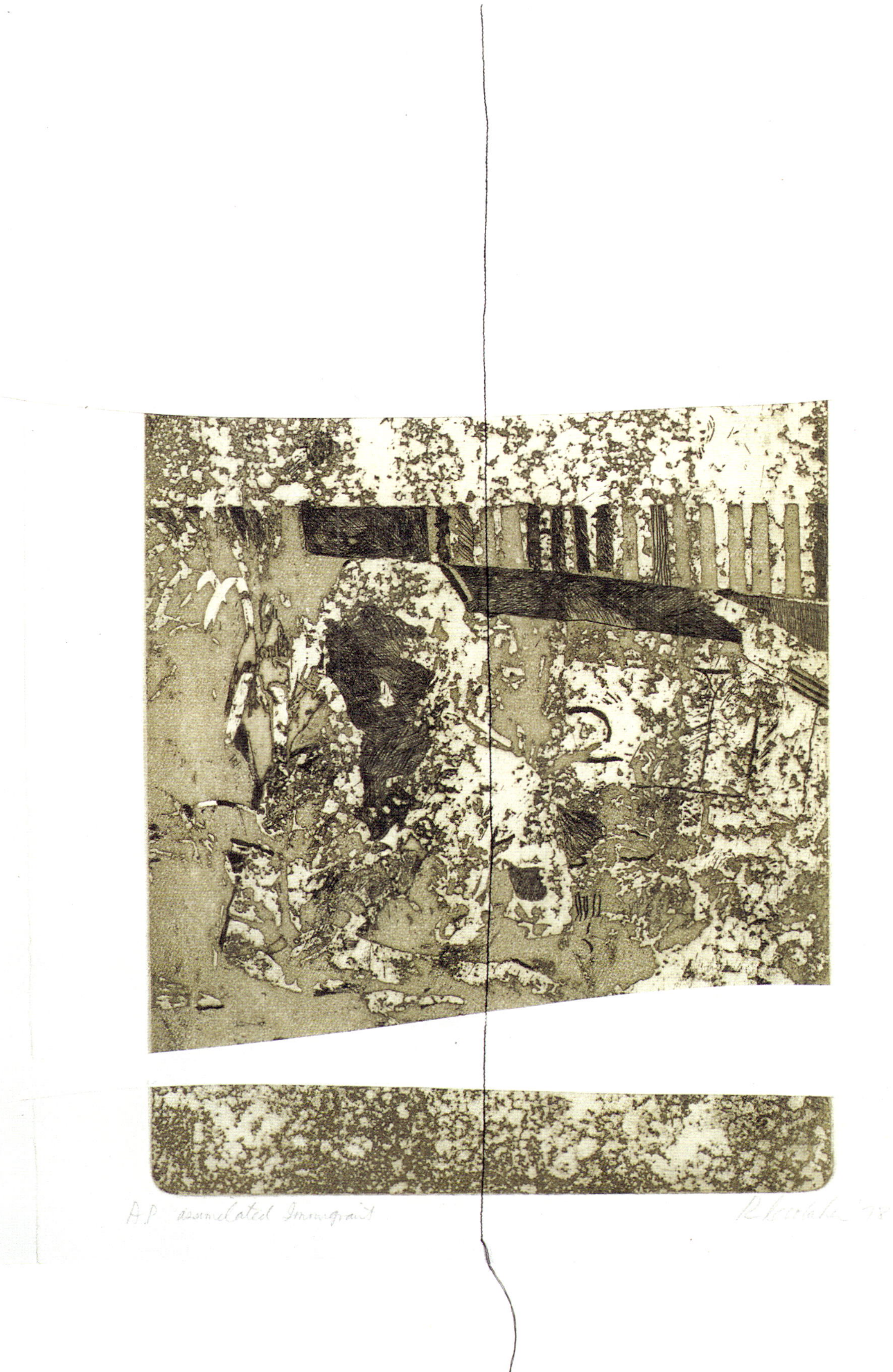
A.P assimilated Immigrant

16

DALE COPELAND

Born Taranaki 1943.
BSc, UA 1965; MA (Hons), Massey University 1992.
Lives in Okato, Taranaki.

At the age of 43 Copeland gave up a career as a maths and physics teacher to become an artist. This late start, and her involvement throughout with an unfashionable branch of art, have resulted in Copeland having a low profile on the dealer gallery circuit. However, her work is in major public and private collections, and as an assemblagist she rates with the best.

A mature and methodical mind informs her work, yet she delights in the very unscientific procedure of bringing together objects with different histories to create a new, artificial repository of meaning. Like a palaeontologist painstakingly boxing and cataloguing fossil bone fragments in the confident hope that one day they will fit together, Copeland has amassed, and constantly replenishes, a storehouse of worthless treasures. Old toys, cheap jewellery, tools, implements, containers, printed matter, and on and on. . . all of them things that once were important and/or useful to someone, and resonant enough to have the potential for another lease of life. Copeland's eccentricity in saving this material has become known to her friends and admirers, who now collect things for her which they think she would like. They rest on her shelves until they are needed as a vital, irreplaceable component of a work of art. One such item, which took 18 years to find its way into a work, was a mummified rat.

Enemies of Reason, 1991
Mixed media
410 x 270 x 80 mm
Collection of Doreen & Noel Bridgeman, New Plymouth

The earliest assemblagists were the Dada artists of the First World War period. Their works were abstract, and designed to shock aesthetes not used to seeing rubbish elevated to art. The father of the genre, however, was Joseph Cornell (1903–72), whose shallow, glass-fronted boxes, full of history and allusion, were like romantic novels. Copeland is a follower, but by no means an imitator, of Cornell. His work tended to stick to the one format, whereas Copeland's is very varied. Pieces may lie flat, or be free-standing, wall-mounted, round or rectangular.

Assemblage is easy to do but hard to do well. It requires an active but reflective mind, patience, inventiveness, and a sure sense of composition and colour. A successful work will touch off in the viewer recollections and feelings which are not necessarily the same as those of the artist. Copeland has written extensively about the genesis of many of her works and hates to part with them, so full of personal meaning are they. Her knowledge of the history of some of the items used adds to her possessiveness. Much of this may be lost on the viewer, who will build a personal set of responses. At times some of the classic images of surrealism (dolls, teeth, staring eyeballs) are used to remind us of dreams, or we may imagine we are inspecting a museum exhibit. Two themes running through much of Copeland's work, evident from some of her titles, are mortality (*The Spice of Life is the Knowledge of Death, Relic*) and facing life in the meantime (*Making the Best of Things, Baggage, Young Girlbox of Dreams*). Some of Copeland's assemblages contain macabre objects, but they are usually tempered by other things which are whimsical or offer hope. Along the way she questions the infallibility of society's edifices and conventions, creating ironic icons which seem both deferential and subversive.

The artist has made a large number of collages and is an expert bookbinder, setting found objects into soft leather covers to make books appear mysterious and precious.

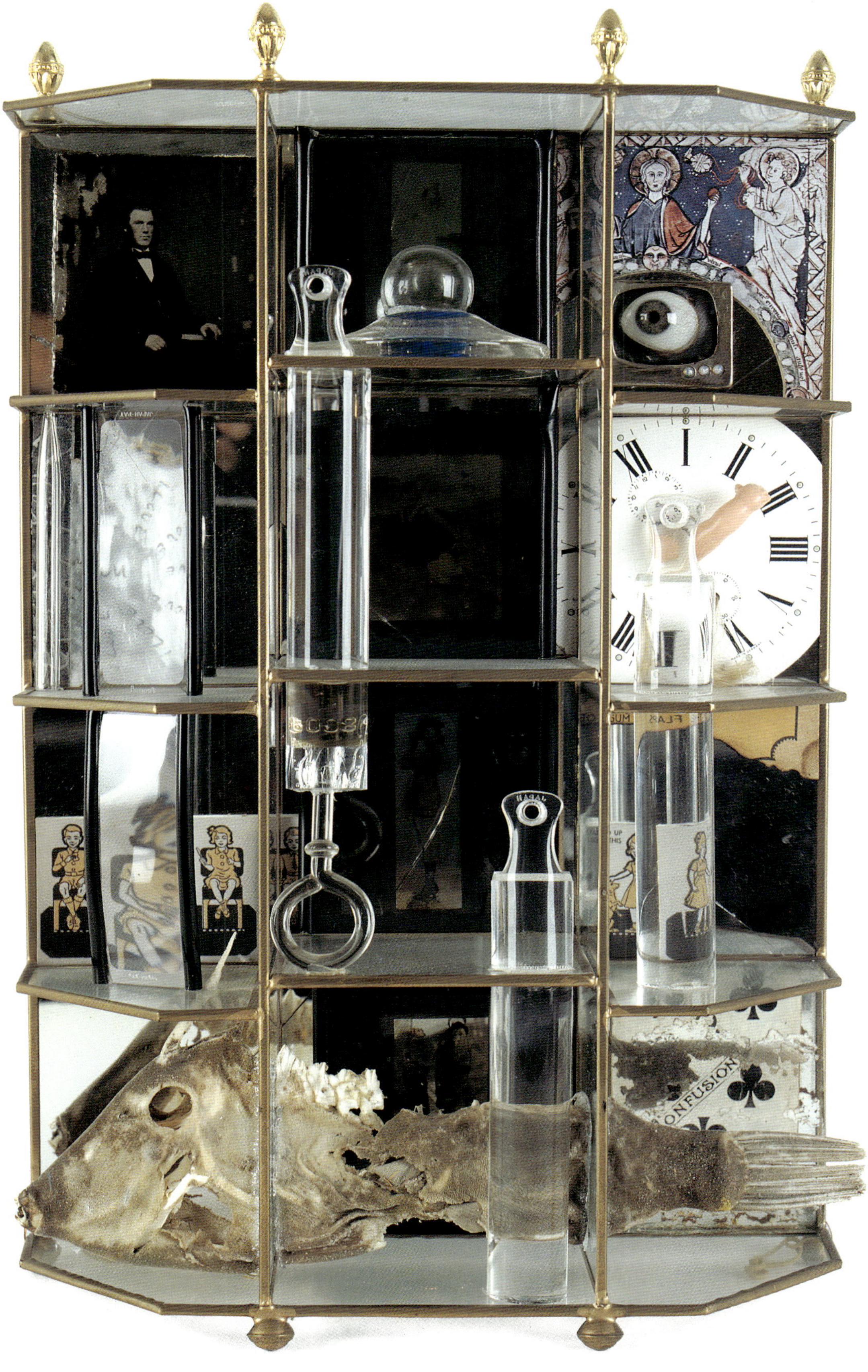
CONFUSION

17

DENISE COPLAND

Born Timaru 1952.
Certificate in Graphic Design, Christchurch Polytechnic 1971;
DFA (Hons in Engraving), UC 1977.
Lives in Christchurch.

Copland's prints are in small editions. She is more interested in the image-making process than in replication. Drawing has always interested her, and the etching medium allows her to do this with added expressiveness and openness to chance and change. Her etchings are notable for their finely drawn lines combined with a wide range of tonal effects and subtle, restrained use of colour.

The works between 1977 and 1979 were a visual diary of the artist's private world of thoughts and experiences. After 1979 she moved away from introspection and began focusing on more universal issues, such as social changes within New Zealand and, in 1982–84, human relationships. At this time some of her prints were from plates deliberately broken in half; paper elements were stitched together; pins were inserted or thread was stitched into the finished print.

Since 1985 Copland's work has been concerned with trees as unique living beings. These arboreal etchings were first inspired by a single elm tree in Dunedin's Logan Park. As well as exploring their forms in different conditions of light, she has looked at contrasts and similarities between trees and people, and the changes, both gradual and sudden, that trees encounter through deliberate intervention by humans or by laws of nature. In her elegant, semi-surreal series *A union between the earth and the sun*, 1988–89, Copland drew analogies between the growth and breathing systems of trees and humans. A feature of works since 1988 has been the view of a tree from its base looking up. This device, used in the past by photographers and painters, produces an odd spatial reversal, because to reproduce the original viewpoint the work should be held overhead, whereas one usually sees these images horizontally or vertically. Copland brought this series to a high point in 1991 with her *Implantations*, four suites of etchings (with aquatint and woodcut) exhibited together. The major *Indigenous* suite explored trees' majestic qualities, as the viewer looked up tall trunks to twisting limbs and branches. At the same time, the sombre, deeply inked presentation of the prints set a gothic tone and some of the trees seemed to be writhing in agony, casting about for a means of escape, presumably from the clearfeller's chainsaw. In contrast, the *Exotic* suite of woodcuts depicted smug, orderly pines set within wide, comfortable borders of printed pine planking. The associated *Avifauna* and *Human Impact* suites showed birds and trees struggling to survive in an uncaring, exploitative environment. *Fragments*, 1993, portrayed fragments of items collected by the artist, such as chips of broken china, cloth scraps, bird skulls and portions of text. Four small plates, their edges eaten away, were randomly positioned for each print, themselves becoming fragments. This series represented a breathing space and stocktaking after the *Implantations*.

Tutoring in printmaking has been a continuing activity for Copland since 1979. In 1985 she produced a limited-edition bound document titled *The Intaglio Print — Chemically assisted processes*. Each book contained 33 original etched test-plate prints with a brief text about how each plate was made. In 1988 she printed plates and blocks by six South Island artists as a boxed sampler set. These have made an important contribution to teaching resources.

And That's Not All, 1995
Etching/aquatint, hand-colouring
6.4 x 3.8 m
Collection of the artist

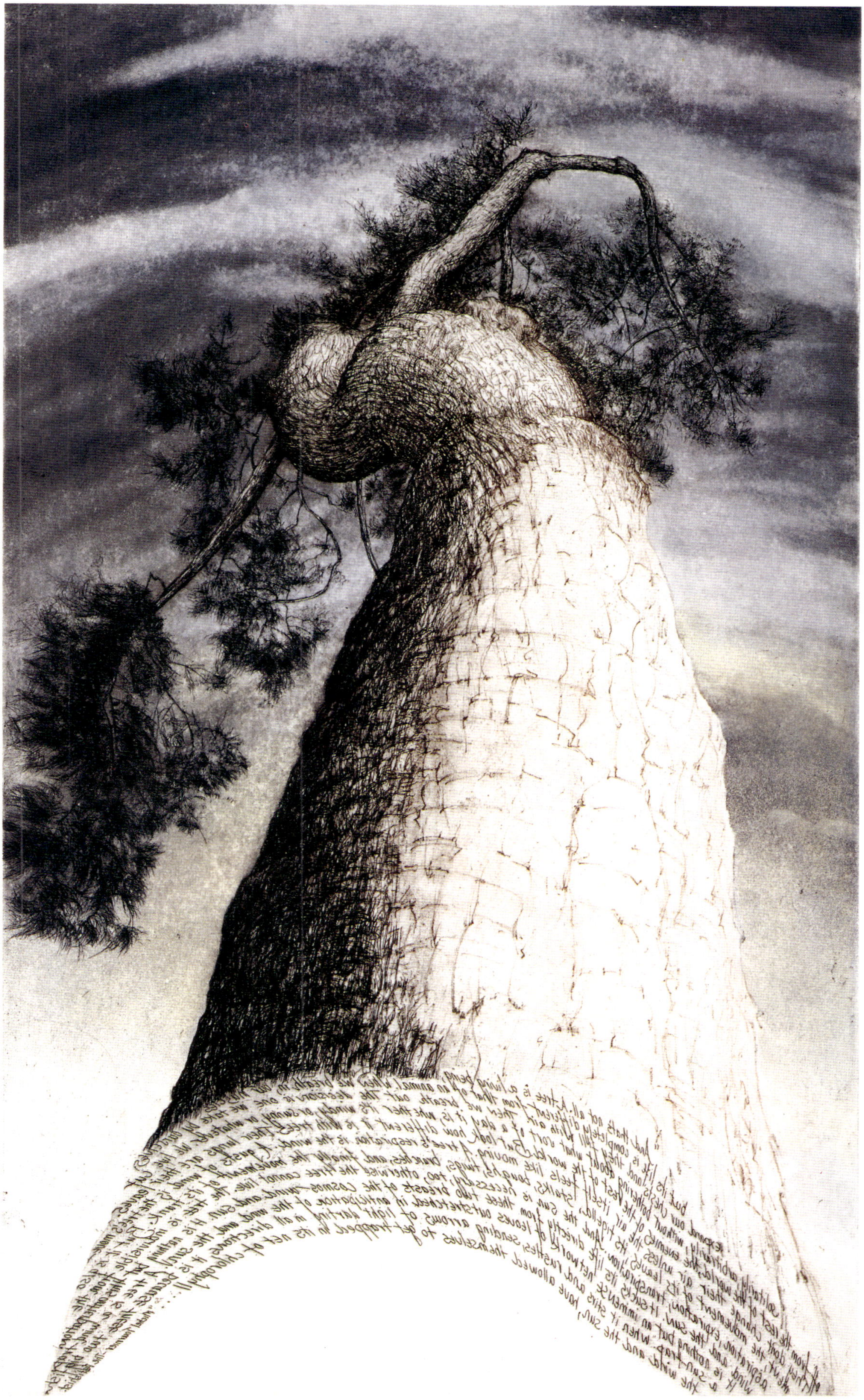

18

CHIARA CORBELLETTO

Born Biella, Italy 1956.
B Arch., Architecture School, University of Milano 1979.
Came to New Zealand 1981.
Lives in Auckland.

By 1987, after working as an art restorer for six years, Corbelletto wanted to start making her own art. Although she had not made sculpture since her art school days, Corbelletto accepted the challenge of tackling a large block of Hinuera stone at the 1988 stone carving symposium at Auckland's Western Springs. Her first effort, a powerful 2-metre-high head in a style which resembled art deco, was one of the best works in the symposium and attracted critical interest. Her works at the 1989 and 1990 symposia were also well received. In 1989 she began working on small stone pieces which were exhibited in that year. Later in the year she began making much larger pieces, using polystyrene coated with a skin of techcrete. This process allowed freedom in the way surfaces were fin shed. In some pieces the effect was of smooth, much-handled stone; other surfaces were like porous sandstone. Since 1992 the artist has worked mainly with creamy, granular Oamaru stone. This will take detail only to a certain degree, and in recent years Corbelletto has pushed it as far as she can.

Corbelletto's work has progressed through three main groups, but all are concerned with stillness, silence and reverence. The earliest pieces, mostly small, had a strong frontal presence and featured smooth, rounded columns and lintels, forming an entrance. In some pieces this entry was open, framed in drawn-back drapery, and one could see inside to another doorway or niche which framed some enigmatic object. In others the opening slanted away, like a fold in the stone. They reminded one of that sense of approach to a spiritual essence that arises when one steps into an old tomb or foreign place of worship. The major work of this series was the large *Know Yourself: Rite of Passage*, 1991. One could walk between what looked like a shiny particle accelerator joined to an anc ent stone dolmen, and there was a palpable sense of energy being transmitted.

Archeologia Del Sentimento, 1995
Oamaru stone
800 x 600 x 500 mm
Collection of the artist

The second category of works had an architectural quality, derived from Corbelletto's studies in that discipline. Mostly tall and thin, they were either talismans or shrines which held bowls or other containers. The firm, boxy structure of the shrines contrasted with the rounded forms of the containers and the loose sand, pebbles or other objects which they held. Humble material so displayed takes on spiritual power. The talismans evoked Egyptian architectural features, Druids' stones, primitive tools — just the sort of things one would expect to find upon entering one of those temple portals. Some had shaped pieces of slate or onyx set into them. Other work in the architectural category included elegant, vertical pieces which look back to the Italian futurist architect Sant Elia. They were made of Oamaru stone, slate and wood surfaced with cement to a seductively silky finish.

The third group of sculptures is the one that has carried over to the present. It includes bowls and pieces with organic shapes, such as corals, shells, gourds and seed pods. Several such pieces make up one work — a 'dialogue between forms'. They invite touching, lifting and careful positioning, and they produce sensuous shadows in oblique light. They are natural forms harbouring spiritual mysteries, infused with a sense of stillness and the aura of ritual.

Corbelletto also makes art furniture which has a close relationship to her sculpture, and is an interior designer.

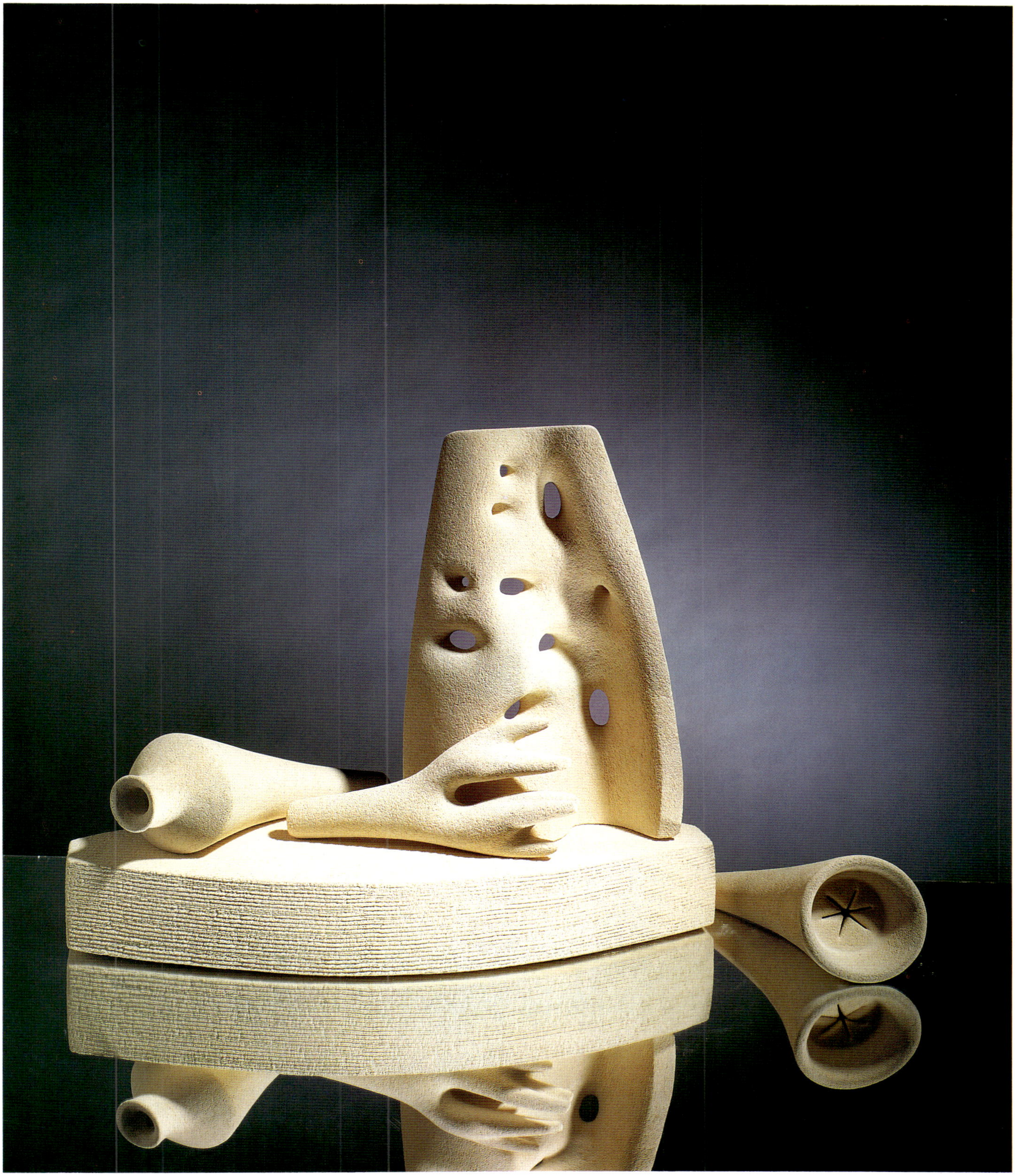

19

BRONWYNNE CORNISH

Born Wellington 1945.
Lives in Auckland.

Cornish describes her activity over the last 25 years as 'pursuing the possibilities of clay'. She is one of only a small number of New Zealand sculptors to work in the medium of ceramics (cf. Hellyar, 41).

Cornish's work serves as a valuable case study for those trying to define the boundaries between craft and art. Seen in isolation, many of the objects she has produced could be defined as ornaments, but Cornish is not interested in decoration, other than as a subject for scrutiny as part of the art process. So when she began modelling domestic objects in porcelain in 1971, they were unpretty things like old boots, kettles, bags and scrubbing brushes, and their facture was disconcertingly wobbly. By 1980 Cornish was making funky, brightly coloured zig-zag objects. Then, late in 1980, she exhibited *Cactus Bay*, her first installation work, intended to be laid out on the floor. The assemblage of objects included a cactus and the accoutrements of a day at the beach — shoes, glasses, bag, and so on. The elements in *Subterranean Desert*, also 1980, and *Floor Piece*, 1982, included cactus plants, a miniature temple and brick structures, animal figures, cast clothespegs and hand-made pebbles.

Since then Cornish, like Hellyar, has made many multi-part pieces. These works are enigmatic, obviously carefully thought out and arranged, but retaining some of their secrets. *Dedicated to the Kindness of Mothers*, 1983, was originally exhibited in a gallery, but ended up as an exterior installation, a large female form lying on its back in the artist's mossy garden. In both locations the work was spiritually moving. The smooth but cracked ceramic face was mask-like but serene, while the rest of the body, made of scoria, seemed to be returning to the soil. This was one of four earth goddesses made over a period of years — one was of unfired clay lumps and two were fired in situ by building a fire over them.

Temple of Hera, 1989
Clay
150 x 140 x 100 mm
Collection of the artist

Working as she does with earthenware, Cornish conveys a sense of the primal relationship that humans and animals have with the earth: it is a source of material to build with, a foundation to build upon, a stage for the action of life, and a place to be buried. The rituals developed to get us through the earthly stage of being are evoked, as is the spiritual world to which, some believe, rituals can connect us. In a 1986 interview with Louise Guerin, Cornish said, 'I try to use really simple objects that everyone can relate to, so I can utilise that primal memory that is in everybody.'

In 1986 Cornish used lopped oak branches with metal appendages to make dancing garden spirits. In installations since 1990 she has been combining ceramic figures with potatoes, piled up or carefully laid out. These works refer to the arrival in New Zealand of Europeans and their cultivars, and their consequent impact on the land. Throughout, Cornish has continued to make miniature Greek temples, sphinxes and animal/human figurines out of porcelain and earthenware. These pieces resemble votive objects from some Mediterranean archaeological dig. The temple as a sanctuary for the spirit, as an oracle's home and as a place in which wonders may be performed has appeared frequently in Cornish's art.

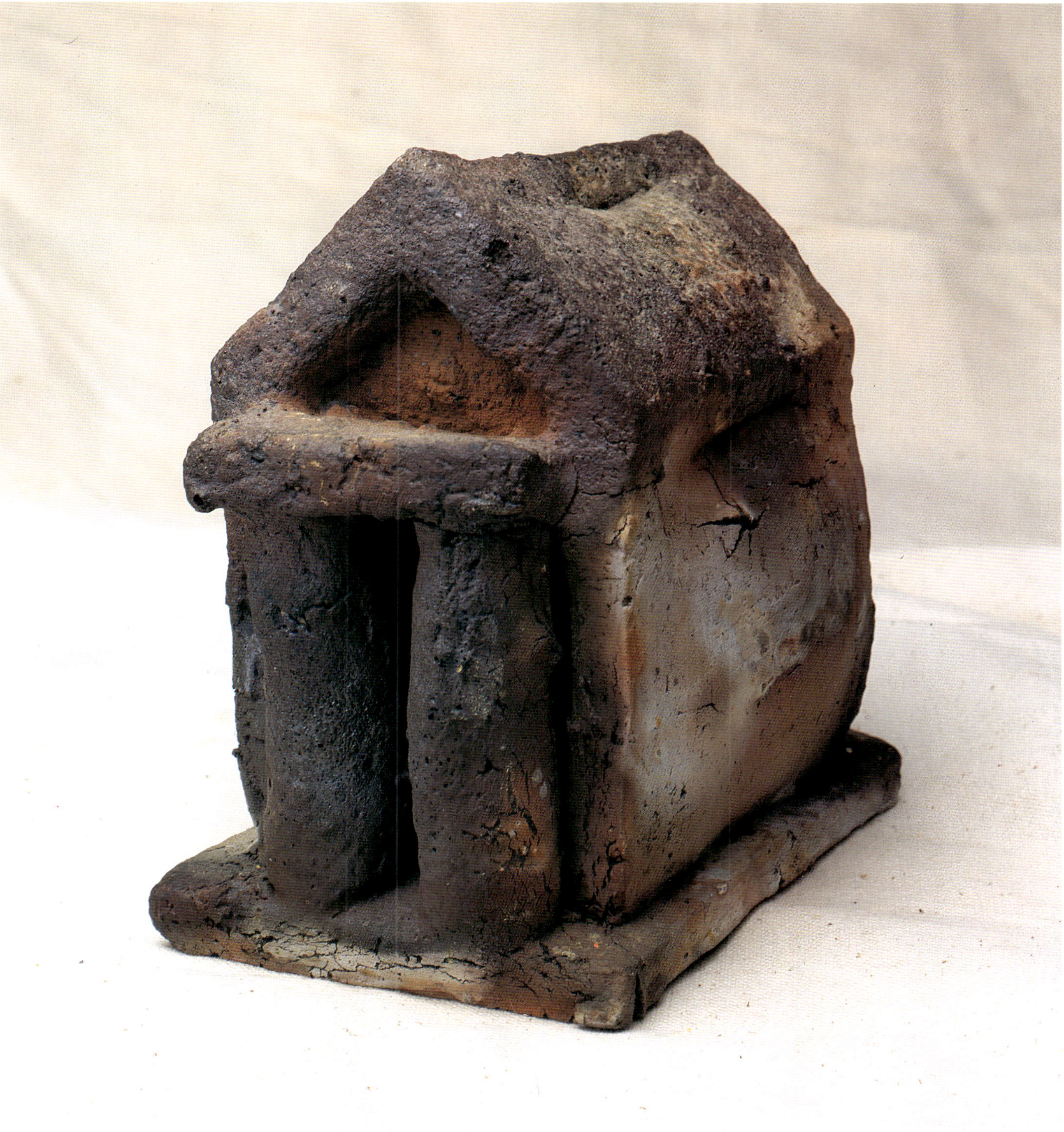

20

GORDON CROOK

Born Richmond, England 1921.
Studied at St Martin's School of Art and Central School of Art, London.
Came to New Zealand 1972.
Lives in Wellington.

In Britain, Crook mixed teaching with freelance design, tapestry making and painting. He came to New Zealand for a change of scene and to work full time as an artist — and stayed. His creativity here as a print and paper maker, collagist, painter, graphic artist, stage designer, weaver, and banner and tapestry designer has been prodigious. The most publicly visible of his works are the large banners he designed for Wellington's Michael Fowler Centre in the 1980s and the New Zealand Chancery in Washington (1979).

European influences are visible in Crook's art. The late work of Matisse (his crisp-cut, floating, gently distorted figures and associated decorative elements), the flying geometric shapes of suprematism, the more formal geometry of Sophie Taeuber-Arp, and the urban pop of Paolozzi are called to mind in many of Crook's screenprints and tapestries. The Matisse influence is particularly noticeable in his 1985 suite of large pastels on the theme of depression and loneliness. His drawings of 1960 are similar to Dubuffet's work, and his collages have something in common with those of Hannah Höch. All this is not surprising, given Crook's educational background. On the other hand, Crook was on the spot during the development of British pop art, and his work from the mid-1950s shows that he was in step with Peter Blake and anticipated the expressive side of Hockney. The infusion into New Zealand art of this sensibility has been a useful antidote to strong American influences.

Crook is both artist and craftsman, but he ignores the art/craft distinction. For him, design equals composition and the medium is whatever best suits the idea. It is ironic that a distinctive feature of Crook's work is that it is anti-design: elements seem to have been thrown together, scattered onto the page, with some bits bunching up and overlapping while elsewhere there are empty spaces. His use of colour combinations is equally reckless. When such an approach is translated into the meticulous, demanding medium of tapestry, Crook's boldness leaves one gasping — yet it all works. The effect is one of vibrancy, vitality, movement and, most important of all, discovery. Crook's work may catch the eye but it does not deliver everything at once.

From over two decades of creativity in New Zealand, some groups of works deserve special mention. Crook taught himself to make paper, and completed many moulded paper-pulp bas-reliefs in the 1970s, well before this activity became popular in the early 1980s. He also used his paper to back his tapestries in his 1978 *Adam and Eve* exhibition. He also taught himself screenprinting, and his trademark cut-out shapes work perfectly in this medium. There was and is nothing like Crook's prints being done in New Zealand — on size alone they lead the field, but their seeming randomness cuts right across the plodding pictorialism dominating this category of printmaking. Technically perfect, they are complex, use many more screens than is usual and sometimes incorporate stitched-on overlays, with the loose ends of the stitching left untrimmed to enliven otherwise flat surfaces. The *Wolf-Man* series of 1991 consisted of 44 prints based on photomontages of faces, cut, mixed and rearranged to create unsettling Freudian images. Crook's most recent collages, coupled in metal frames with photos of themselves, are some of the best work he has done.

A woven tapestry from the 'Maritime' series, 1996
From a suite of 18 miniature tapestries
105 x 125 mm (each)
Collection of the Dowse Art Museum, Lower Hutt

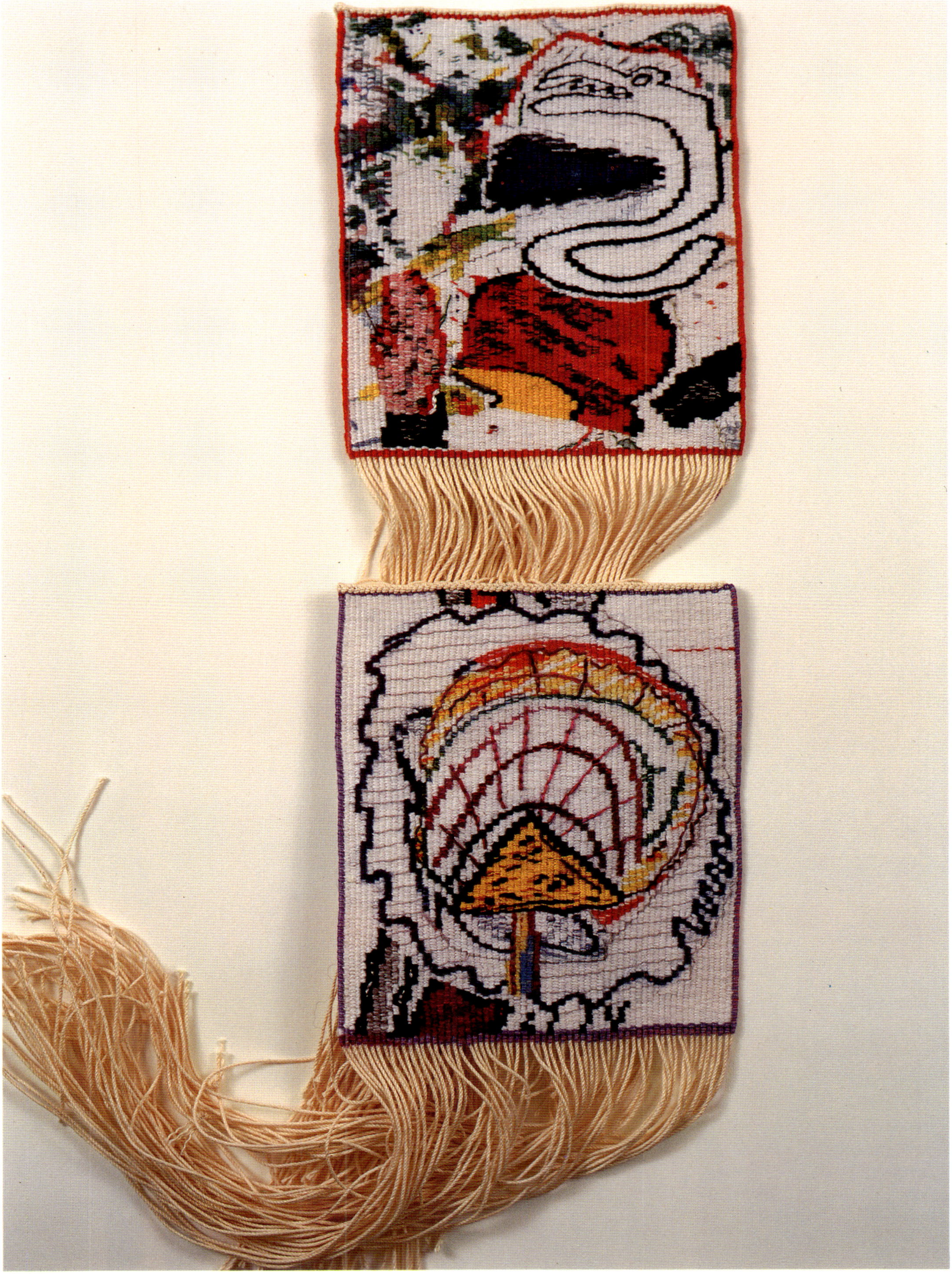

21

BILL CULBERT

Born Port Chalmers 1935.
DFA (Hons), CUCSA 1956; ARCA (1st class Hons and silver medal for painting) 1960.
Lives in France and England.

Culbert is a sculptor and photographer. He has been exhibiting mainly in London and Europe since 1960, but he comes back to New Zealand from time to time to make and exhibit work. A selection of important work made overseas was exhibited here in 1978.

All of Culbert's art is based on an investigation of light. His photographs are not of the conventional arty type, making interesting compositions out of contrasts of light and shade. They are *about* light, recording the way it falls upon objects or the ground and penetrates space. Two examples: a weak, lit bulb in sunlight throwing a shadow of the burning filament; a stubby, partly filled wineglass throwing a shadow in the exact form of a burning bulb. Culbert's sculptures are likewise not about making finely balanced forms, although he often achieves this incidently. Other sculptors have worked with light, but their work differs from Culbert's in that they used light either as one component in a kinetic sculpture (Moholy-Nagy) or as an alternative to paint (Flavin). Culbert's works are demonstrations of things that light does: about the presence or absence of light, its visibility and invisibility, its marking of time. Light can be directed, reflected, cut off, leaked, revealed or boxed in. In conducting demonstrations of these properties, Culbert is content to use whatever comes to hand, and over the years he has made much use of the rubbish tip near his home in a French village. If the improvised look of some of his work should put a viewer off studying what is happening, that viewer will be missing something. For Culbert, the simplest statements are often the most profound.

Flotsam, 1992
Fluorescent tubes, ballasts & plastic bottles
12 x 4 m
Installation, AAA Art Contemporain, France

Culbert began as a painter and worked his way through a range of styles until he became interested in colour theory, then in painting in black and white. At that point he began to consider light as the source of all colour. His first light sculptures were lights contained in perforated boxes or spheres which threw out spatial fields of dots on the surrounding walls (1967–68). The next step was Celeste boxes, translucent cubes upon the interior surfaces of which innumerable bulb images were projected by a *camera obscura* effect (1970).

Through the 1970s Culbert explored all forms of light generation — bulbs, tubes, flames and the sun. He made many ingenious pieces using one-way mirrors to play optical tricks; boxes which completely contained light, discernible only by its heat; boxes with slits along the edges throwing out slices of light; a bent, open tube leaking light from its interfaces with the floor; and many configurations using neon tubing. He also made a series of old farm implements with neon tube handles. He made 10 works in New Zealand in 1978, most notably *Hokitika, Return Journey*, a suitcase with a tube passing through it transversely. He then carried this idea of passing tubes through things much further, piercing buckets, tin boxes and, in the 1980s, a whole range of plastic bottles lined up side by side in rows. One such work made in New Zealand was appropriately titled *Long White Cloud.* It is truly remarkable how in Culbert's hands plastic junk can become luminous, lustrous and lulling. In 1991 Culbert joined forces with his friend Hotere (100NZP, 37) to make two large installation works for New Zealand galleries, *Prop* and *Pathway to the Sea, Aramoana.* The former was a sloping wall of black corrugated iron upon which tubes were laid; the latter was two long parallel lines, one of tubes and the other of paua shells.

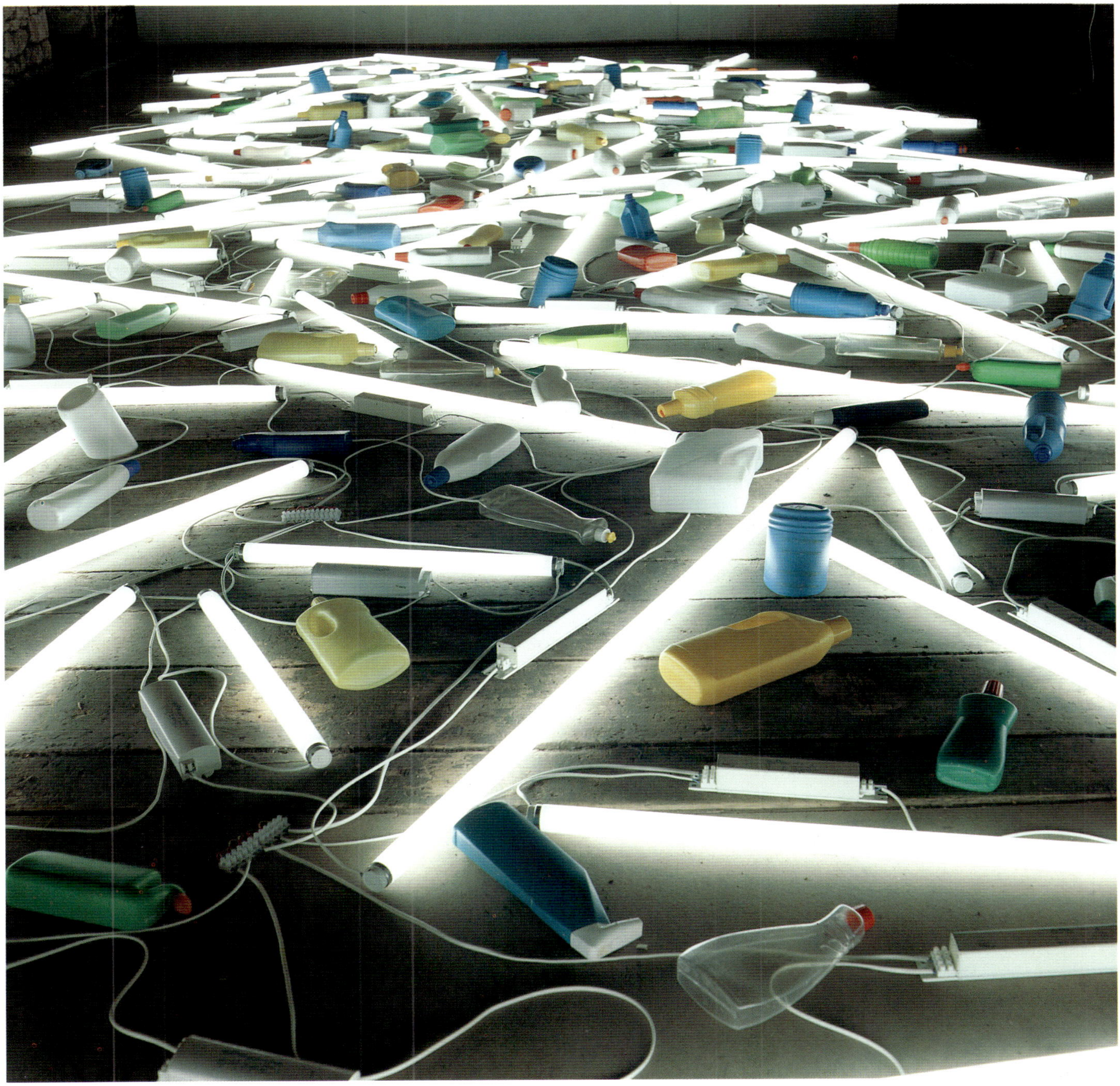

22

PAUL CULLEN

Born Te Awamutu 1949.
BSc, UA 1971; DFA (Hons), UC 1975.
Lives in Auckland.

Cullen is a sculptor whose work exhibits conceptual, minimalist and constructivist tendencies. Trained as a botanist as well as an artist, his work resembles the scientific process of modelling an idea in order to investigate it better. He has had no wish to make impressive objects. A visitor to a group exhibition could miss one of his works, or give it a cursory glance and pass on. That would be a mistake, for Cullen is an artist of finely tuned sensibility. Everything he does is carefully considered and balanced; everything unnecessary to the idea is pared away. Viewers must focus their minds and savour what they see.

Cullen's earliest sculpture (1975) used the most basic materials — string, twigs and stones. The weight of the stones kept a string line taut a few centimetres off the floor; the line kept the twigs balancing on the stones. Roughly tied knots in the string were the punctuation marks in these sparse sentences, which signified the invisible and vulnerable interrelationships of things in nature. By 1977 Cullen was including wooden boxes in the tie-up, signifying human constructions, but the works were still low-lying. In 1978 they rose to vertical orientation, using gravity to provide the tension. In one elegant set-up, two chunks of concrete, string, a piece of glass and a plastic bag with some water in it balanced each other.

By 1979 Cullen had adopted a more formal constructivist style, which he continued with until 1983, using thin, square-sectioned sticks. *Concerning Construction* was made from four sticks and a few cross-struts, but demonstrated how a tower on two legs could be kept upright by an outrigger-type extension. Over this period Cullen made many three-dimensional architectural drawings and small wall-mounted framework pieces using balsa wood. Towards the end of the 1970s Cullen began integrating his models into the surfaces of the chairs and tables they stood on, so that a small sculpture energised a whole table. In 1985 Cullen built miniature gateways, using the minimum number of old bricks required, and these resulted in model Stonehenges. In 1990 Cullen's models became solid and protruded from the wall like shelves. Then they melted into the wall in the form of drawings. His 1991 exhibition was called *The Moon/Navigation*. On the gallery wall he scattered disconnected bits of a landscape seen from above — a model house, a tree, a length of railway track. Pencil drawing on the wall suggested a few more elements — a road edge and a fence line — and a model plane on a stick flew over it all. Shorthand, snatches and sketches, and one's imagination filled in the rest. These works fulfilled in miniature the artist's desire to work at the very large scale of landscape architecture.

At this time the artist began reconstructing furniture, replacing parts with other foreign elements, and this interest has been a subtext in his gallery installations of 1993–96. With links to the early stone and string pieces, these gallery displays have been about tie-ups between spaces, in the form of sound and water piped from one room to another, and between cities by elements shown in one display being reused in another. Full of references to artists such as Beuys, the installations have resembled set-ups for science lectures, without the lecturer or the students. They have also been about the artist coming into a gallery space and asserting his presence merely by altering it, without necessarily filling it with beautiful things (cf. Apple, 100NZP, 3).

Discovery of Oxygen, 1996
Mixed media
Variable dimensions
Courtesy of the artist

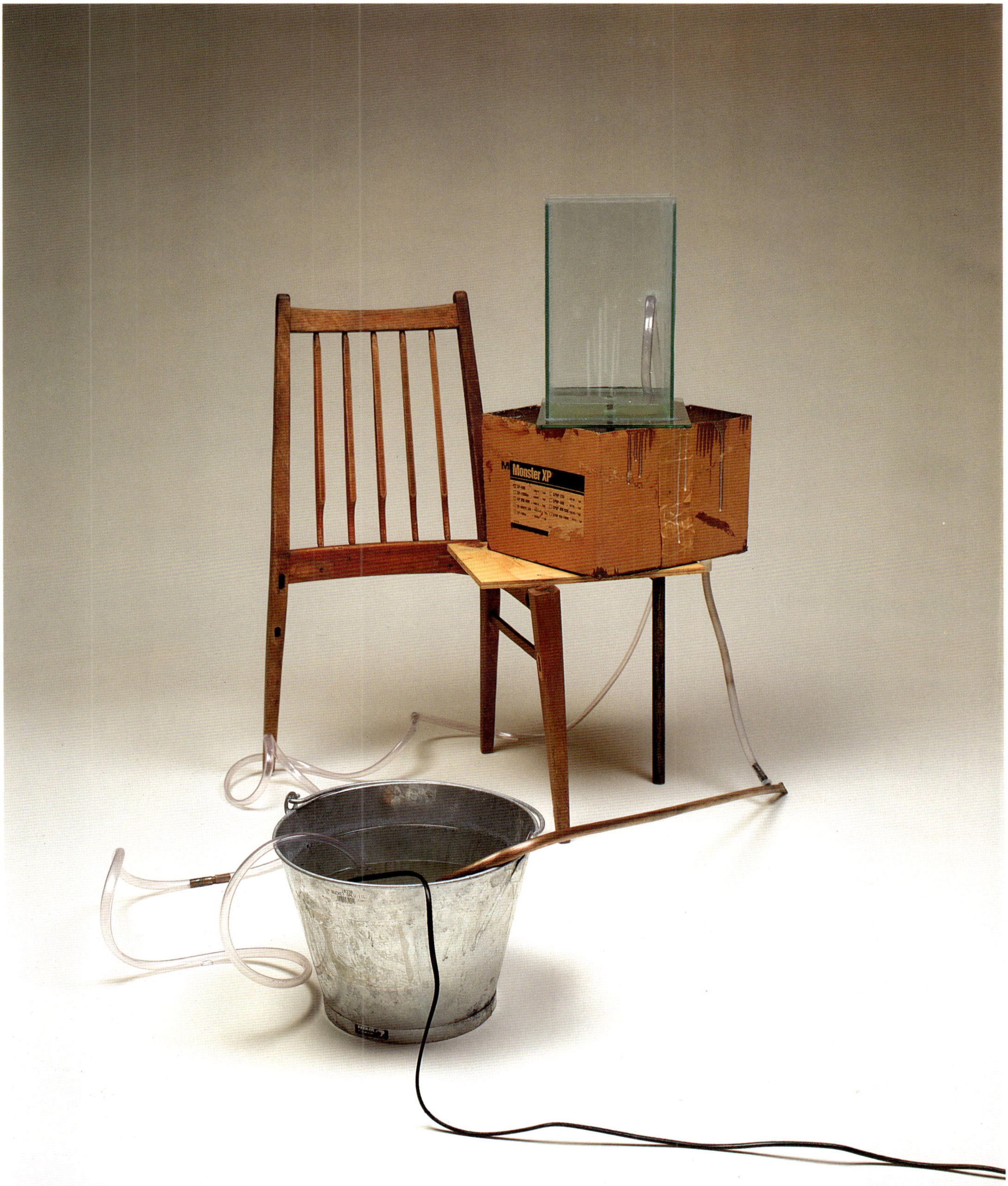
Monster XP

JUDY DARRAGH

Born Christchurch 1957.
Diploma in Visual Communication and Design, WP 1979;
DT, Auckland Teachers College 1980.
Lives in Auckland.

Some people like to make things hard for themselves, like climbing Mount Everest without oxygen or, like Judy Darragh, making art out of kitsch. Kitsch is a generic term covering commercialised sentiment, saccharine romanticism, a surfeit of decoration, the cheapening of tradition, the lowest common denominator of the human response to the beautiful — in short, a lack of taste. And what is taste? It is rational selection of the most valuable qualities in human creativity. It is rejection of the superficial, and respect for original ideas, for the sanctity of original pieces of art. Bad taste is rife in our culture. Greeting cards, tourist souvenirs, religious knick-knacks, teatowels, home and garden ornaments — all are riddled with kitsch. However, Darragh understands that art nowadays can unreservedly embrace everything and anything as its subject matter. She has been working this fertile field now for 12 years.

What she does is take kitsch material wherever she finds it and intensifies its effects to a preposterous degree. Through prodigal accumulation she demonstrates that more really is More. A show of sculpture by Darragh is one of choking, eye-goggling surfeit. She works with tikis, fern leaves, flowers, fruit and figurines, all made of coloured plastic. She combines paua-shell fragments with tulle, cheap mirrors and gold paint. At first glance Darragh's sculptures seem to be appalling examples of kitsch at its worst: a grape and floral clock, a cupid shrine, a leopard lamp, an illuminated Elvis memento with built-in waterfall. Although most of her components are store-bought, the artist carefully alters and adds to them to heighten their kitschiness. Some pieces are hand-worked, such as mats and coffee tables in the shape of the North and South Islands, or a painting of the Southern Alps with an inset real-mirror lake. Darragh's painting standard reaches exactly the right level of formulaic adequacy that one finds on ashtrays and paperweights.

Visible Woman, 1988
Shop display figure, plastic roses, red light interior
600 x 350 mm
Courtesy Gregory Flint Gallery, Auckland

Why does Darragh dignify such anti-art horrors with her polytechnic-polished professionalism? Because she enjoys turning embarrassing dross into gold. Just as the Dada artists used the debris of society to make art during the bloody madness of the First Word War, and the pop artists made us aware of the pervasiveness of advertising, so Darragh challenges us to define for ourselves just what is and is not aesthetically valuable in the image/object overload of the late twentieth century. After all, the components of Darragh's art have been commercially produced by entrepreneurs to meet a market. Could that be the real test of a culture?

Darragh also has an affection for the hobbyists and amateur craftspeople who assemble objects of devotion or pretty things which they hope will bring joy. Pushing that idea a little further, she occasionally includes a plastic phallus amid the bouquets.

Darragh has made some quite big sculptural pieces, such as her memorable *Rock and Rose Bed*, 1989, two beds covered with rocks and roses respectively. Her most recent work is tending to be less overloaded with found objects, more open and restrained in colour. Darragh's *oeuvre* is now large enough for us to see her consistent inventiveness and integrity. Her assemblages are much, much more than the sum of their parts.

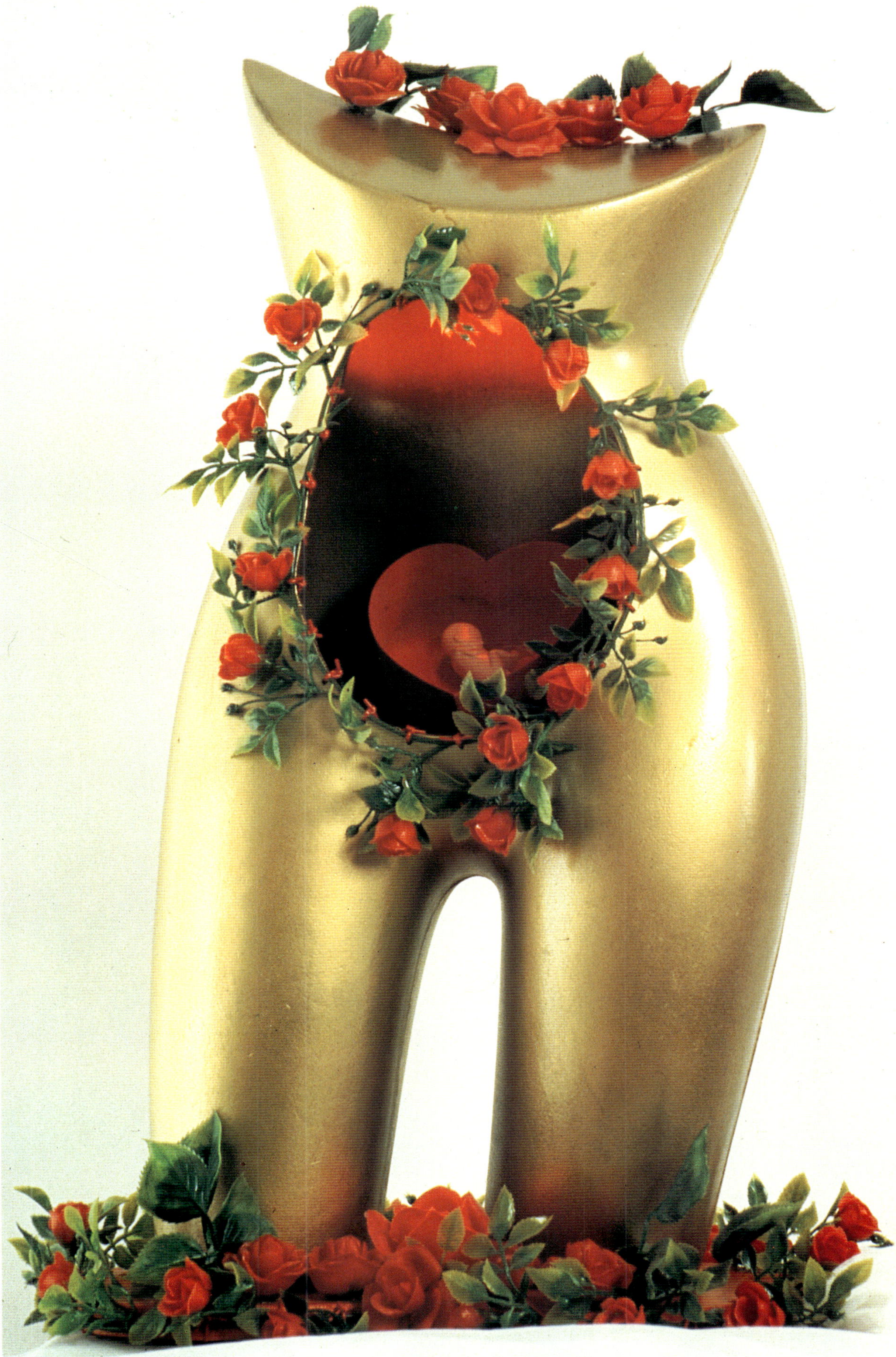

24

BING DAWE

Born Oamaru 1952.
DFA, UC 1976.
Lives in Christchurch.

Dawe is best known for his sculpture, but he is also a printmaker, makes copious drawings and has designed many art rugs. Dawe uses macabre imagery to grab our attention and turn our minds to life-and-death issues. He described himself in 1984 as an environmental protest artist.

In the mid-1970s Dawe's work explored the fusion of engineered and natural structures, looking particularly at joint and tendon mechanisms. He compared the way in which tribal cultures made tools and weapons, using bindings, sticks and drilled stones, with the ways in which tendons attach to bones, and cranes use pulleys and hawsers. The superbly crafted *Tone Arm*, 1978, reproduced the moving parts of a record player while evoking both the grinding of stones in a river and the traditional tools and weapons of the Maori. Dawe also used stretched skin in association with articulated wooden elements and rib-like assemblies to show how a sailing ship can resemble a skinned animal.

Dawe then narrowed his range of subjects to skeletal birds and humans. Between 1981 and 1984 he made a series of large, open works like lines drawn in space — the *Protest Bird* series. A skeletal bird was portrayed trapped in a net, trying to remove a foreign object embedded in its wing, and freed from a cage but also stripped of its bodily covering. Bones were shaped from wood, polished and dark like museum fossils, and some joints were made from aluminium bicycle parts. These works spoke both of humans' cruelty to wild creatures and abuse of the environment, and of the way we are becoming subtly ensnared in technology.

In 1984 Dawe exhibited a major work, *The Cock Fight*. A floor piece, it consisted of a circle of steel signifying both a cockfighting pit and a bomb crater, or the expanding blast of a nuclear explosion. In the ring, and within another smaller vertical ring, a skeletal cock prepared to fight. Entering the ring, released by a skeletal human arm, was another cock, turning from three to two dimensions at the ring interface. Outside the ring a human skeletal form fixed to a grid appeared to be peeling off a block of concrete, leaving an impression behind. The piece was a metaphor for the nuclear arms race and its potential for the flash destruction of the protagonists. The rings inferred the orbits of electrons in the atom, and the impressions on the concrete recalled the famous Hiroshima shadows cast by bodies as they evaporated. This work has had many spin-offs in woodblock prints, circular rug designs and smaller sculptural pieces. Also in 1984 were a series of skeletal *Nuclear Umbrellas*, predominantly made of iron. In 1985 Dawe embarked on a series of very large woodcuts, continuing the theme of how we treat animals and each other. These fine works are full of allusions — to slave-ship plans, printed circuits, arks, umbrellas, killing chains and maypole dances of death.

In 1991 Dawe's work underwent a major change with *Man with face in his chest*, a thin form exquisitely made from laminated kauri sheets. It resembled a peat-bog mummy and related to Dawe's controversial public sculpture made for Christchurch children, a celebration of fabulous and fairytale figures. In the 1990s Dawe's work has remained figurative, naturalistic but grotesque, and in 1994–95 has been associated with empty cupboards or pots, symbolising the fleeting nature of life and possessions.

Still keeping his balance he used the umbrella as a safety net — image of a man with missile, 1985
Wood, steel and stone
2400 x 1300 x 800 mm
Courtesy of the artist

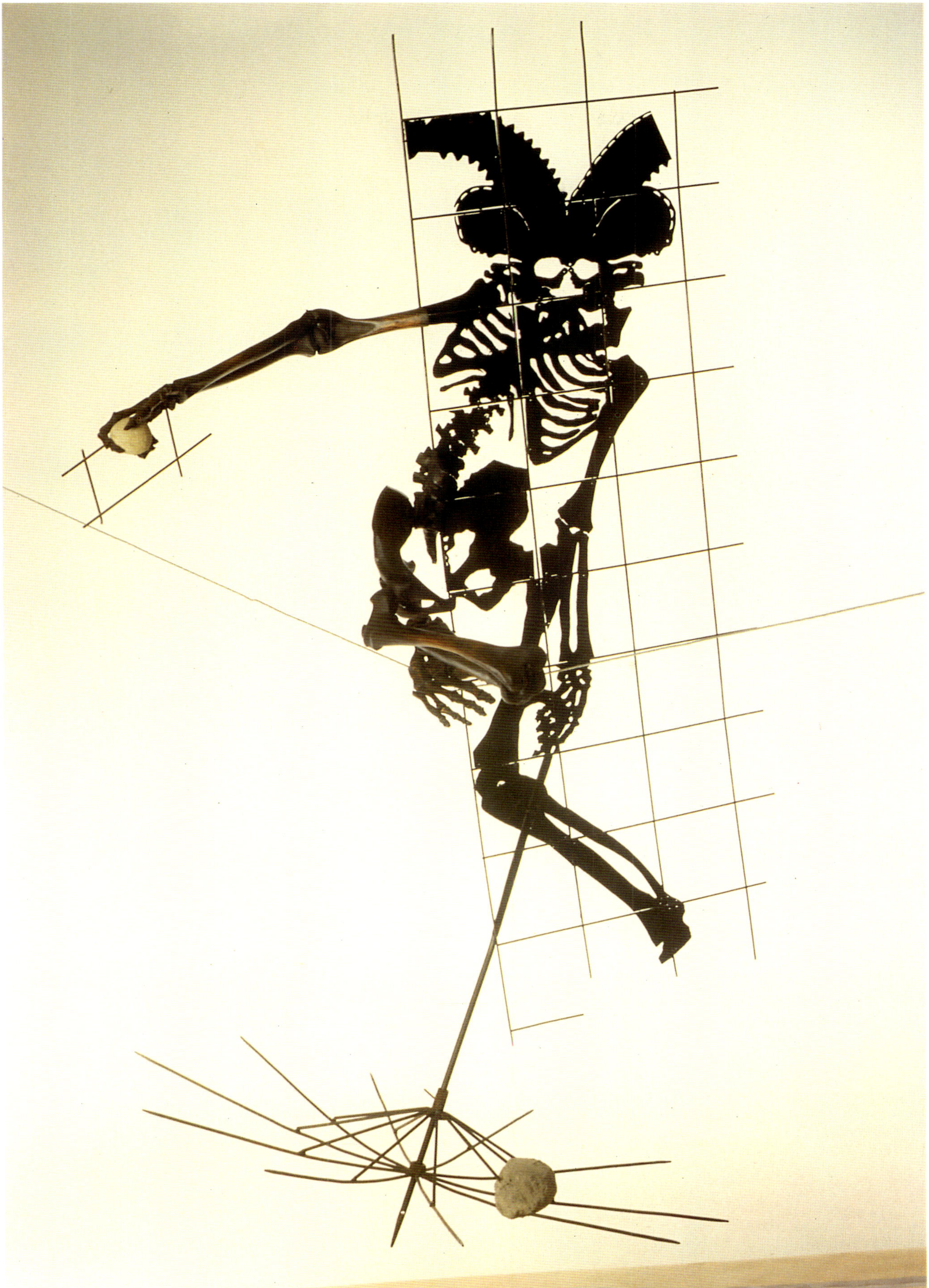

25

MARGARET DAWSON

Born Blenheim 1950.
DFA, UC 1978; DT, Christchurch Teachers College 1981;
MA (1st Class Hons),UC 1995.
Lives in Christchurch.

Between 1978 and 1984 Dawson's photography was of a documentary nature, in black and white. One series of works which pointed the way to future directions was *About Women*, covering a wide range of activities and circumstances. Since 1984 Dawson has been a photographer whose work questions the ingredients of memory and definitions of reality with reference to the lives of women. There is a link to performance art in that she sets up her series of photographs, in some cases assembling extensive props and costumes and using actors (cf. Ffrench, 33; Webster, 88). This part of her work was inspired by Cindy Sherman, who established the idea of the artist assuming various guises in photographs that were self-portraits but also fictions. Dawson has established her own distinctively postmodern, humorous and indigenous variations on this theme. A key work of 1986 was a self-portrait with a stocking on her head. This softened the artist's features, distancing her from the viewer and making her into an abstraction, ready to take on another persona. *Dreams and Illusions*, Dawson's colour photographs of 1984–85, and the *Marginal Persona* series of 1987–88 saw her posed in costume on location in appropriate sites. The works were about women, but with a mixing of roles and time periods, of reality and obvious artifice. Taken as a whole they become an ironic narrative about women in New Zealand — Maori and Pakeha, passive, inhibited or pious, pioneer women, liberated women, women uncertain of their proper roles in the face of feminist agitation. The *Yardbird* and *Canterbury Belles* series of 1989–91 were playful portrayals of women as birds and flowers. During 1990–92 Dawson made a number of large photo tableaux based on famous paintings, using amateur models wholly or partly in costume. She painted the first print of the photograph to create a 'set', then rephotographed it for the finished work. The *Maladies* of 1992 portrayed imaginary domestic disorders, and the *Amusements* of 1993 were humorous translations into 'reality' of Sydney Nolan's stagey, childlike paintings in his *Ned Kelly* series. In 1994 Dawson used photo-collage to produce six works inspired by the drawings of Beardsley (1893–98). She re-created the feeling of evil and decadence which made Beardsley notorious, and this was accentuated by the use of colour and real actors, with a *femme fatale* figure dominant.

One of Dawson's finest bodies of work is the most recent — *The Men From Uncle*. She was caring for an elderly uncle, who had lost his personality and much of his interest in life. He had a handsome, well-proportioned face, a white beard and a fine head of white hair. Dawson realised that he could act as her model in a suite of re-creations of famous photographs. This was a way of giving him an interest while recreating through him personalities and portrayals from the past. She discussed the project with him and obtained his co-operation. Dawson planned the pictures, organised costumes and props, and then worked patiently through the series, doing the long-haired and bearded images first and ending up with short-haired, clean-shaven ones. The resulting series is powerful and moving. For the brief time it took to take each picture, the uncle became a person such as Ingres and Augustus John in the confident maturity of life. In some works he appeared convincingly as a woman, reminding us how old age, like babyhood, gives us sexless, generalised features.

Autographism, 1992
Modified photographic print
1364 x 1037 mm
Courtesy of the artist

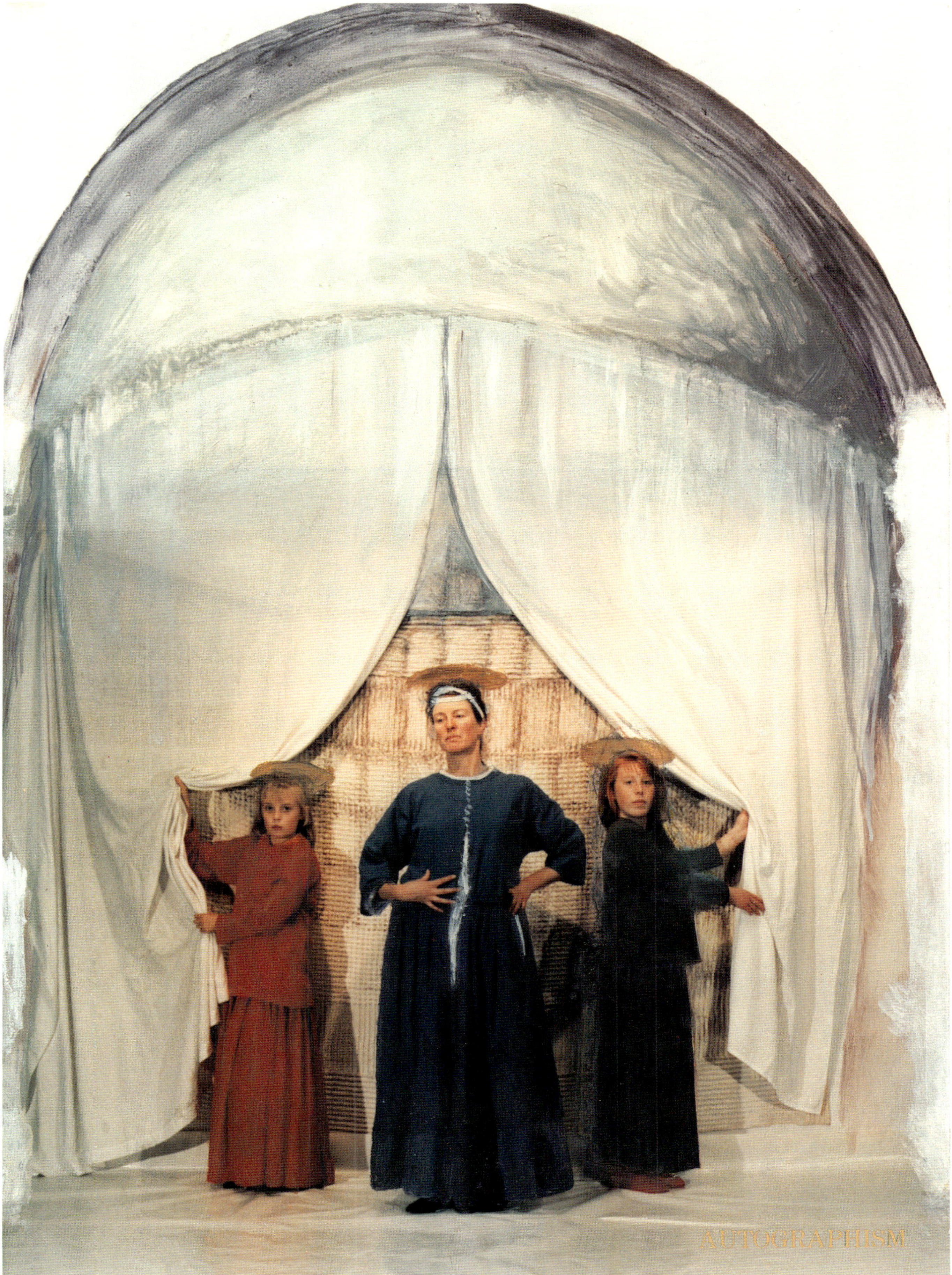
AUTOGRAPHISM

26

NEIL DAWSON

Born Christchurch 1948.
DFA (Hons), UC 1970; Diploma in Sculpture,
National Gallery of Victoria Art School, Melbourne 1973.
Lives in Christchurch.

Dawson made his reputation in the late 1970s with small wall sculptures, most of them no bigger than a shoebox. Since then he has increased the range of his vision to encompass the planet, a 4.5-metre-diameter model of which he suspended outside the Pompidou Centre in Paris in 1989. The creation of spatial illusion is basic to Dawson's art. Using wire and steel mesh, and an unerring command of perspective, he draws in space, making the background wall disappear. His sculptures really do look like big, finely executed ink drawings. He can depict interpenetrating block walls, balls rolling along planks, plumb-bobs swinging in a circle, ripples on water. For the most part his imagery is realistic, and often it is weighty — rocks, blocks, girders, architectural details, even mountains — but they are all magically levitated. Dawson's style has been consistent throughout, and discoveries made in his early work have sustained him over the past decade as a full-time international artist.

In his work prior to 1982 Dawson shrank portions of buildings down to miniature size, sketching their outlines with wires and filling in some wall or ceiling elements with mesh or flat metal. These works, hung on a nail on the wall, were penetrated by light and also threw out shadows. In 1979 Dawson captured miniature yachts in a cone of light, and modelled the light-cones made inside rooms by a single, shaded bulb. In contrast to these tranquil works, pieces based on the Abbotsford landslip showed the violence wreaked upon structures when foundations give way. In 1981 Dawson suspended a wire outline of a doorway and steps, part of the Christchurch Arts Centre, above the Centre's quadrangle. Attention was drawn to the fine old building's architectural details, while also suggesting impermanence. This was the first of many suspended pieces. A series of studies of rocks, begun in the early 1980s, were made of wires which randomly traced the rocks' contours and made one think about the essence of form. The smallest of these works could be held in the hand; the largest is suspended outside a Wellington building; but regardless of size the viewer is inside and outside the rocks at the same time. Other floating rocks were made from crumpled wire netting or foil. The Pompidou planet (now in Australia) was the culmination of this series of works. Dawson has also made images of clouds from time to time. From a triangle of painted corrugated iron with some wires brazed to the bottom side, he created a line of hills against a stormy sky (1981).

Perfection of construction is essential in this art (cf. Snowden, 81), and Dawson has achieved mastery in brazing thin wire and working with metal meshes of various sizes and configurations. He can exploit diamond-shaped mesh to make it look like square mesh seen from an angle, with remarkable results. He can cut bits out of mesh so that the ragged holes look like clouds or rough brush-strokes, and can create emphasis by edging the holes with wire lines. His semi-abstract work of 1985 in this manner, depicting rectangular slabs, was a major achievement (cf. Sydow, 83). From 1991 Dawson has used laser-cutting techniques to reproduce quick crayon sketches out of sheet metal (cf. Wesselman).

Large commissions have been occupying Dawson over the last few years, giving him the opportunity to make monumental pieces, including one based on a sketch 15 years old.

Flying Chairs, 1993
Aluminium mesh
Hung at heights 12–16 m
Temporary installation in Christchurch Botanic Gardens

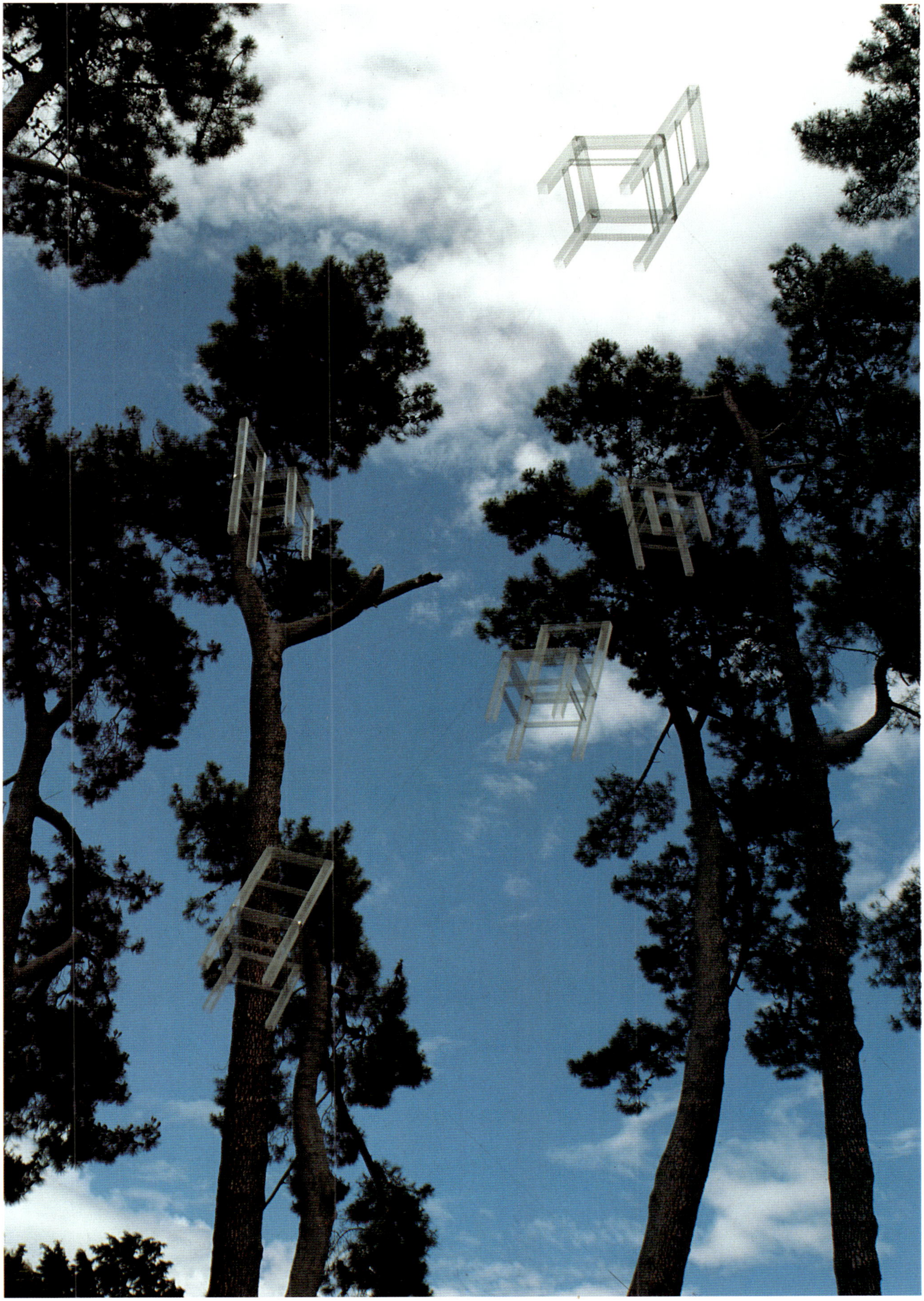

27

ANDREW DE BOER

Born Woodville 1960.
BFA, UA 1986.
Lives in Auckland.

De Boer began carving wood at the age of six, working with his Dutch immigrant father who had developed a consuming interest in traditional Maori carving. He feels that his long exposure to the curved forms in Maori carving subconsciously directs his work. At art school he showed impressive skill at shaping and hollowing out twisting tree branches into complex forms. This set the direction of his future work — the conversion of sinuous lengths of selected natural wood into remarkable anthropomorphic sculptures. His debut show of sculpture in 1987 consisted of a number of tall, thin, knobbly forms reaching upwards, and one pohutukawa root protruding from the wall — a cross between a bladder-seaweed chain and an antelope horn. His 1988 show was even more impressive. He seemed to be able to treat natural unsquared wood like spaghetti, twisting and bending it into zig-zags, arches and continuous wobbly loops. The most impressive among many fine works was *Sleeping Wind*, a life-sized wooden loop resembling an O bent in half and twisted slightly. Made of four tree branches spliced together at the ends, it seemed to change shape rhythmically as one walked around it. Some twisting, swelling pohutukawa forms with carved hands and feet suggested figures. *Trinity* came down from the ceiling like a bizarre clothes-drying rack, and *Rata Arch* was a huge inverted U that one could walk through.

In 1989 De Boer began using metal by heating, bending, winding and welding mild steel around prepared branch forms. The first works of this type were open, like a paper chain, but later he wrapped the branch forms completely to make objects with a segmented, wormlike skin. Some pieces, such as *Stalker*, 1992, combined both open and covered elements, but in all cases the original wood was burnt out in the process. This enabled De Boer to make permanent forms out of untreated wood of all types. By selecting tree branches which, when inverted and trimmed, could become free-standing tripods, he was using nature's engineering. What once reached openly for the sky now straddled the ground as a multi-legged arch.

In his 1990 show *Metal Morphosis/Metal Physics*, De Boer inverted the usual sculptural presentation by hanging the whole show from the ceiling or walls. Some were open zig-zag ziggurats in copper and bronze. The other works were made by the wrap-welding process.

In 1992 De Boer made his first works using the lost wax process to cast forms in bronze, still adhering to the same basic approach to form. He also began using electroplating to give his steel armatures a shiny surface. A fine example is *Reactor*, a twisting arch of 10 worm-like segments which rises from the floor and descends again, the head of each segment biting the tail of the next. The artist's most recent work in polished aluminium has a less organic, more reductive and resolved appearance than formerly. Balance is achieved by splitting the originating branches in half lengthwise, reversing the two pieces and joining them end to end in a twisted loop. Sandcasting has taken the place of the welded strips, allowing a smooth, flat, even surface to be achieved.

Aquaduct, 1995
Bronze and concrete
1560 x 780
x 670 mm
Collection of the artist

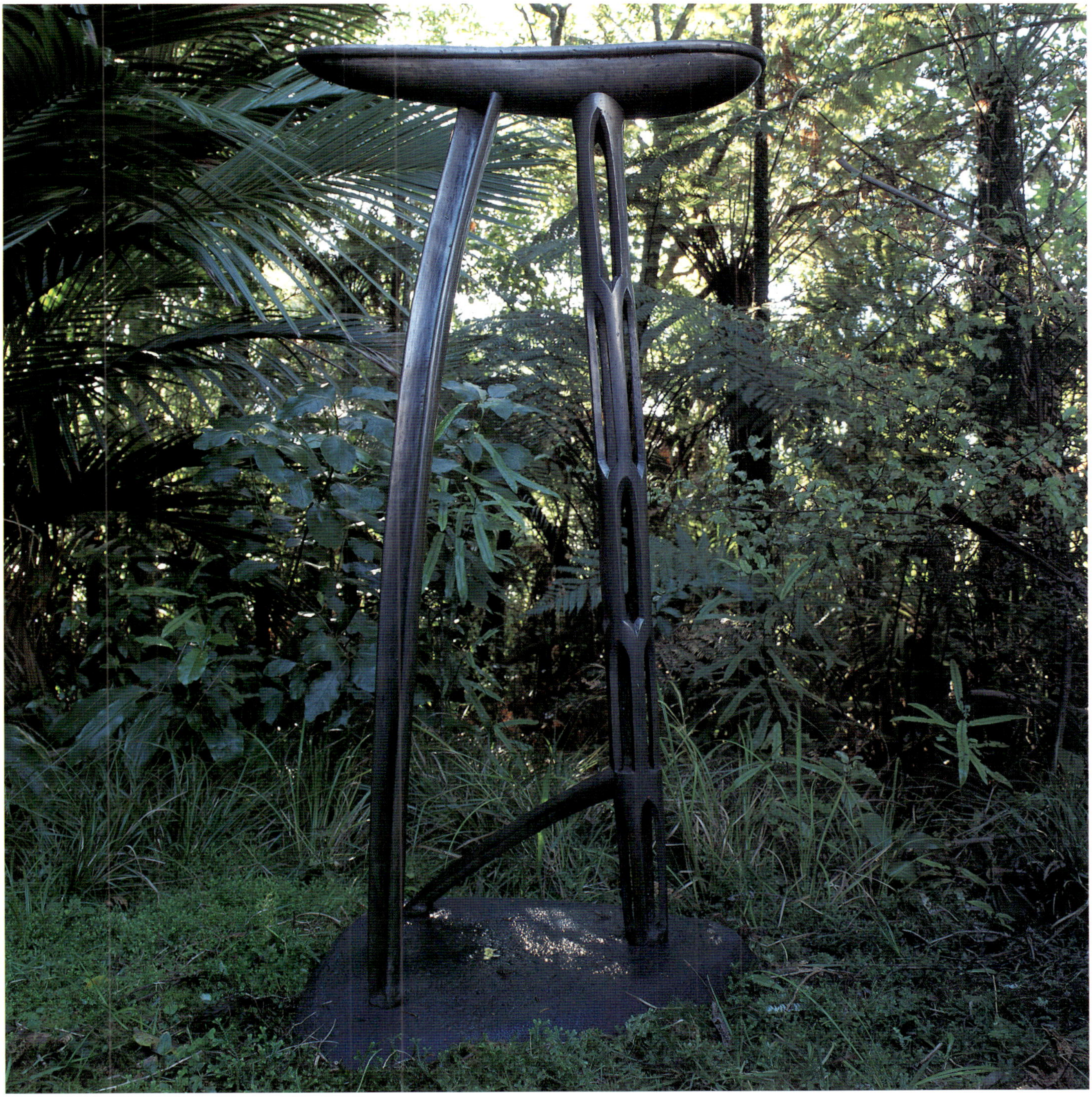

28

PAUL DIBBLE

Born Thames 1944.
DFA (Hons), UA 1968.
Lives in Palmerston North.

Dibble, like O'Connor (65), is a contemporary sculptor with a traditional approach. He works mainly in bronze, and places many of his pieces on hardwood pedestals. They range from table size to 2 metres high, and are notable for their fine, even patina and their sense of calm elegance. This is enhanced in the works which incorporate a plumbline or fishing line held by one of the figures and hanging down below the top of the plinth. In such works an imaginary sea is created in which the viewer is immersed. The sculptures tend to be of a tableau nature, intended to be viewed from the front or back rather than in the round. This is partly a result of Dibble's technique of sewing a shape in canvas and then pouring plaster into it to create a thin, pillow-like form. This enables him to achieve a graceful balance between figures and flat forms such as leaves. The flatness differs from the angular, cubist-based collapse in Stringer's work (82).

Dibble's pieces are fanciful and slightly surreal, showing a delight in flowing curves and precarious balance. Figures with small heads and extremities are distorted in Picasso's 1920 manner. Dibble's style is a sophisticated European one, with similarities to the work of Nadelman and the smooth deco sculpture of the 1930s. This seems exemplified in *Europe Looks Our Way*, 1995, in which one of Dali's burning giraffes looks past two tall ponga trees at a 'down under' figure doing a handstand. Rural New Zealand is, however, Dibble's inspiration. He notes that all cultures are rural before they become urban, and that therefore one must go to the country to find the sources for a nation's cultural identity. Trees, horses, sheep, rabbits, moa and fish feature in many of Dibble's compositions, as do hunters, farmers and fishermen.

Busy Lady, 1995
Cast bronze
ca. 2 m
Collection of Colenso Communications, Auckland

Dibble's early experience in making life-size bronze castings was commercial work commissioned for churches and chapels (1970–77). Over the period 1970–85 he was working on Oceanic themes with mixed-media installations. Boats, swimmers, parrots and cut-out figures on perches and frameworks were depicted in big, loose tableaux, using steel, wax, feathers and whatever came to hand. The artist describes these temporary works as a liberating experience which contributed to the adventurous freedom of his later bronzes.

Dibble returned to bronze casting in 1986 and since then his witty, accessible images have enjoyed wide popularity. As his work is very consistent, it is perhaps best illustrated by looking at a few major works from the period. In 1991 he showed a series featuring mermaids attended by rabbits. The maid, holding a fish, balances gracefully on a spiral conch shell, while the curious rabbit peers into the open end of the conch. *Establishing a New Order*, 1992, portrays a man sawing a kiwi egg in half while a sheep with a sparrow on its head kicks up its heels — an allegory for the replacement of bush by pasture.

Dibble's sculpture has a recognisable style with realistic elements and a clear sense of purpose, but that purpose can be idiosyncratic (cf. O'Connor). The works are joyous and whimsical rather than wilfully obscure, so they are always delightful to have around. As with other art of this type, viewers can make recognitions, connections and assumptions based on their own experience.

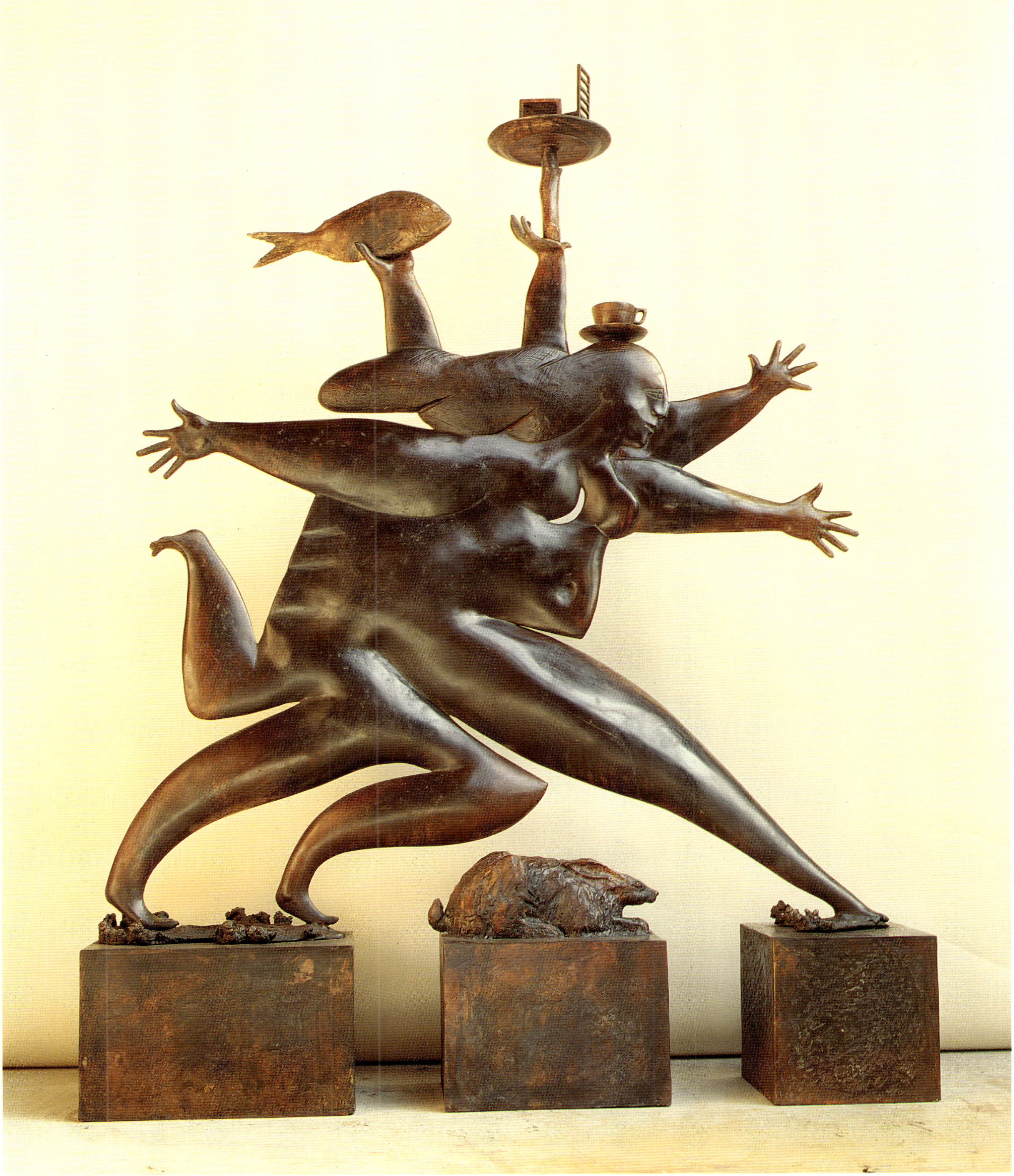

29

JOHN DRAWBRIDGE

Born Wellington 1930.
Art teaching training in Wellington and Dunedin 1949–50.
Diploma Central School of Arts and Crafts, London 1960. MBE 1978.
Lives in Wellington.

Drawbridge is a teacher, printmaker, muralist, sculptor, stained glass and rug designer, watercolourist and painter, and has achieved distinction in all these fields. He has exhibited widely overseas and received many awards. His breadth of interest results from his admiration for old and modern masters who also expressed themselves in many media. These role models include Dürer, Rembrandt, Vermeer, Seurat, Picasso, Malevich and Agam. Drawbridge had ample opportunity to absorb such influences during his 1957–64 study period in London and Paris, where he learned the intaglio printmaking skills that he has developed ever since. Within New Zealand he is perhaps best known for his huge op art murals, such as those in the Beehive and in the National Library in Wellington. His first mural commission was for New Zealand House in London in 1962.

The wider range of Drawbridge's talents is reflected in the scale of his art, for some of his finest works are in the print medium, no bigger than 40 cm square. To produce a desired effect on an intaglio plate is a laborious process, requiring experience and technical skill. Over the years, discerning collectors of prints have noted Drawbridge's particular mastery of this medium. His control at all levels — drawing, design, plate preparation, inking and especially the paper used — is total. The subject matter of his prints is always simple: a bottle on a table, a figure or two, a seascape, an abstract form, a detail from an old master painting. Yet there is a subtlety and complexity in the finished work that can be relished for years. Drawbridge has a fondness for chiaroscuro, settings where there is intense darkness blending through into bright light. The fall of light into darkness and onto figures, objects, walls and floors is the main subject of many of his prints, and mezzotint is particularly suitable for conveying these effects. Drawbridge has developed his own variant of the method whereby he criss-crosses the plate with hundreds of fine parallel lines rather than (or in addition to) all-over graining with a rocker. These slanting lines then work as tone, light rays and abstract elements.

Still Life with Malevich, 1988
Mezzotint
195 x 250 mm
Ellerton Trust Collection, Auckland

In the 1970s Drawbridge's prints were often edged with densely inked vertical oblongs while the central area was expressive and open, and blocks of colour were often included. Some of his mezzotints begun in the early 1980s which incorporate images from Malevich and Matisse are, despite the borrowing, among Drawbridge's finest graphic works. Matisse's curving, dancing forms are echoed by the dimly seen curves of women's bodies, while the angularity of Malevich is used to intensify the geometry of rooms, already multiplied in mirrors. Recent prints have given greater emphasis to realism.

Drawbridge has always painted, and his watercolours in particular are notable for their total command of the medium. He lives with a sweeping view of the sea, and many of his paintings are semi-abstract renderings of rainstorms, the play of light on land and sea, and the glow of sun through hazy sky. In 1969–72 he gave his abstract paintings a unique look by combing the paint into fine ridges. Drawbridge made a series of aluminium sculptures and plexiglass constructions in 1966, and these experiments were drawn on for his 1970 Expo mural which was studded with plexiglass rods illuminated by lights. Works such as this and the 1976 Beehive mural, with their brightly coloured op/pop look, are completely different from most of Drawbridge's graphic work.

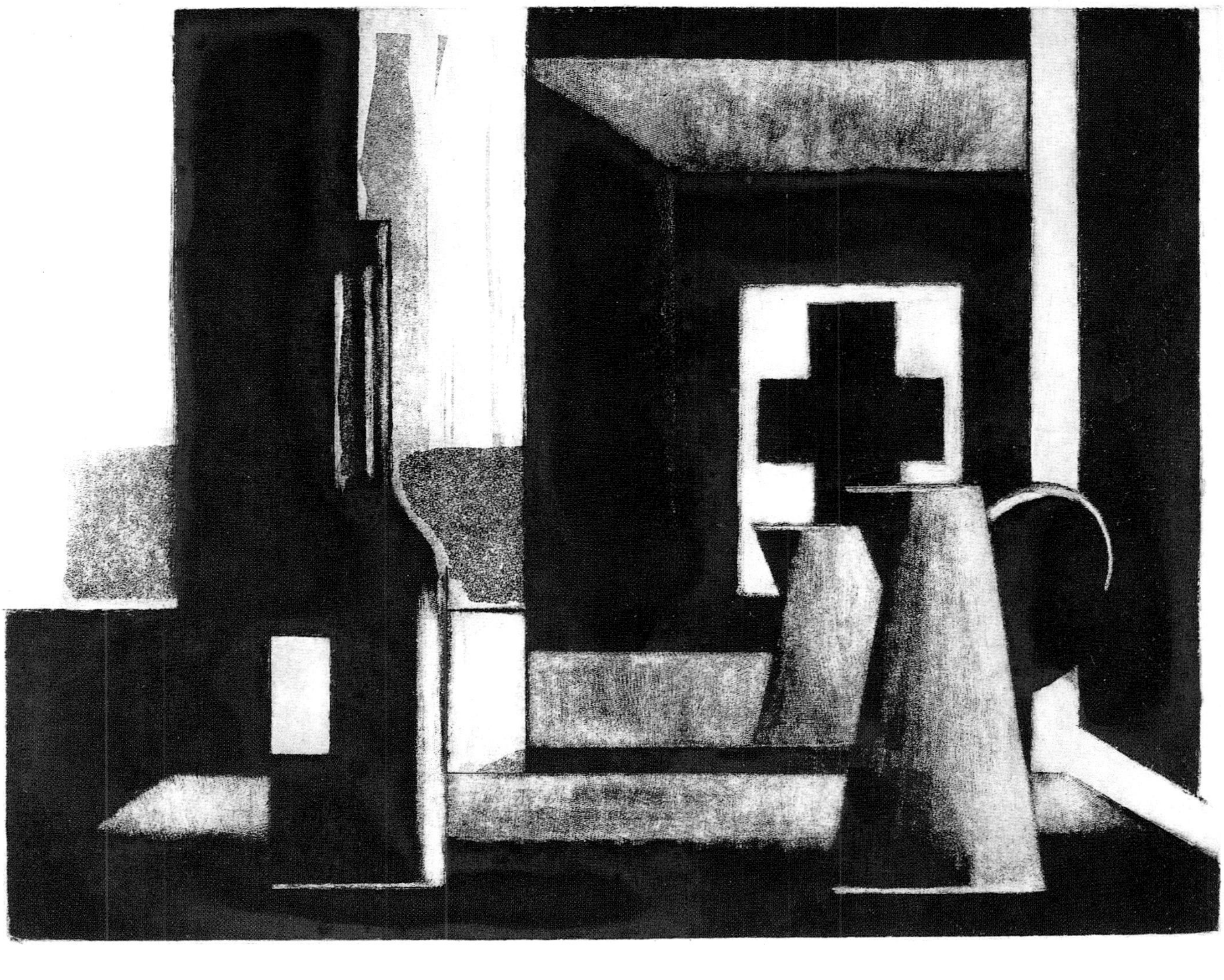

30

DON DRIVER

Born Hastings 1930.
Lives in New Plymouth.

The Dada artists of the period 1915–23 used found objects in their work, mostly cast-off rubbish. This initially anarchic act has been hugely influential in twentieth-century art. However, like any freedom, the wide-open choice of materials must be used in a disciplined way. Anyone can stick bits and pieces onto a board and call it art — indeed, it is a popular kindergarten activity.

Don Driver is a master of assemblage — the art of putting objects together in such a way that an aesthetic resonance is set up. He has ranged in his work from immaculate bands of coloured canvas, plastic or stainless steel layered together like flags (done in the 1960s), through to rough, smelly works made from fertiliser sacks and rusty tools. Driver has made many free-standing junk sculptures, but his creativity is best seen in his wall-based works. There painting and sculpture merge: Driver is painting with the natural colours of objects rescued from the oblivion of the junk heap. Every element is considered, handled and adjusted until the combined elements almost speak to each other and the viewer. Using the techniques of synthetic cubism and his knowledge of how certain colours advance while others recede, Driver overlaps and superimposes his vinyls and fabrics, contrasting shapes and textures, making large-scale collages. The artist is self-taught, but in his youth attended night classes for 10 years studying welding, pottery, painting — anything creative.

Because he uses familiar materials, his works are approachable, if puzzling, to viewers unfamiliar with modern art history. *Soft Hanging*, 1976, consists of a striped blanket with two pastel-coloured, fluffy nylon bathmats attached. At first look one has to smile at the overtones of a suburbia where contemporary art is not high on the agenda. Then one has to smile again at the allusion to the cloudy patches of colour in the paintings of Mark Rothko. Finally one marvels at the precision of the balancing of colours, making the cheap and nasty into the precious and lovely. All of Driver's best works are crammed full of such complexities. There are often allusions to past art, and Driver also uses symbols — dresses and coats are soft, colourful and feminine; tools are hard, muted and masculine. Well-used railway tarps, road signs and stencilled lettering transport us mentally to places elsewhere. Animal skulls on dolls' bodies remind us of our mortality and of the primitive rites of our ancestors. Empty sacks speak of their former contents and also of loss, redundancy and the potential for renewal. Driver's designs of sacks on the floor (poverty) have recently been woven with great success into expensive woollen art rugs.

Driver has made many paper collages over the years, expressing concern about the extinction of species and the brutalising effect of urban living. In his two most recent series of works, empty paint cans jut out as reliefs, and cable-drum ends are used as the bases for stylised aeroplanes.

Bundespost West, 1989
Vinyl, canvas and leather hanging
2095 x 1550 mm
Courtesy Peter Webb Galleries Ltd

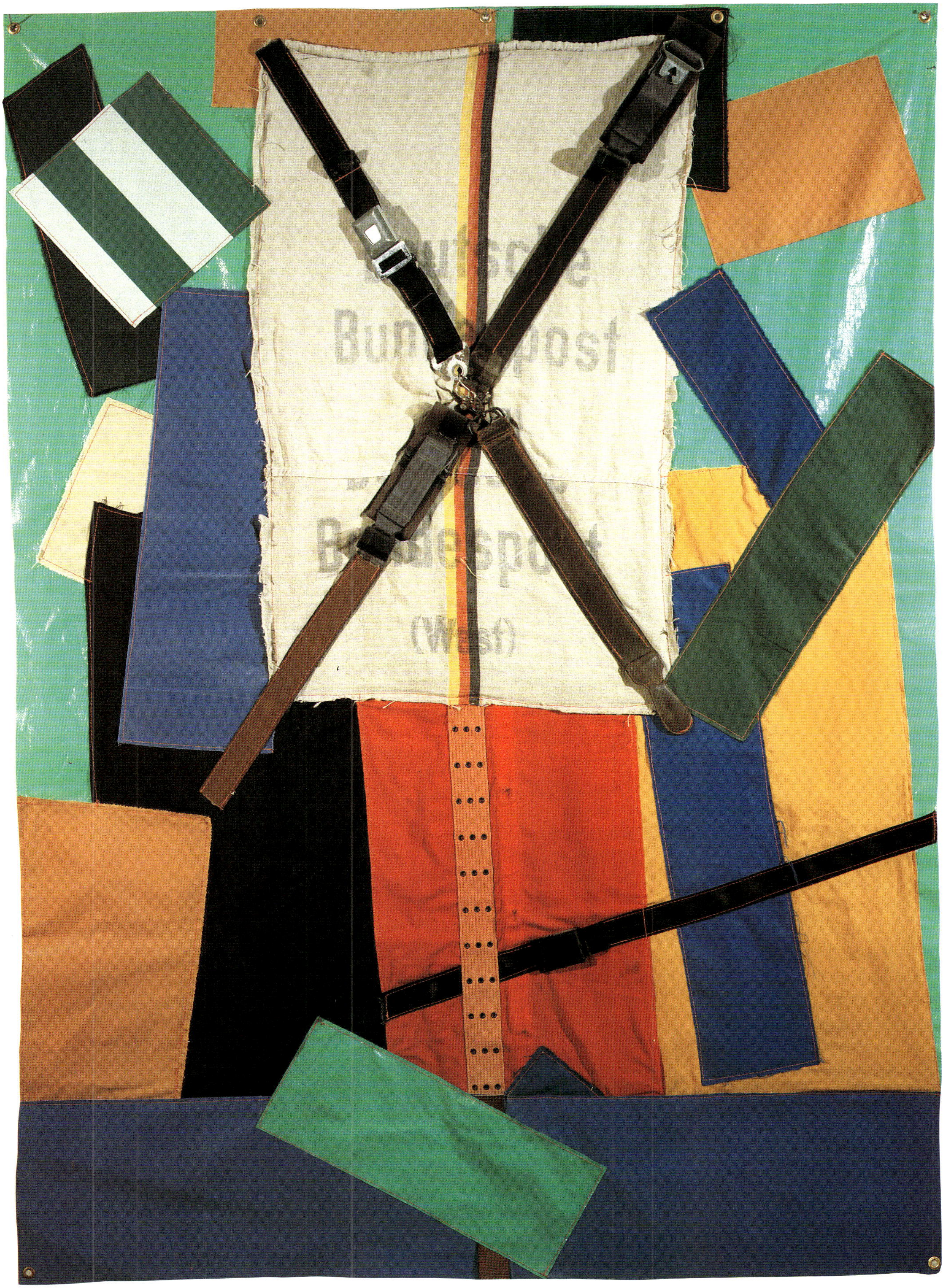
(West)

31

ANDREW DRUMMOND

Born Nelson 1951.
BA (Hons), Waterloo University, Canada;
DT, Palmerston North Teachers College 1970.
Lives in Christchurch.

Drummond is a deeply committed artist who has worked in performance, sculpture and graphics. Following in the footsteps of the late, now almost sanctified Joseph Beuys, Drummond developed a philosophy and a performance style in which to communicate it. Clad in a white boilersuit and a sort of fabric aviators' helmet (or sometimes completely unclad), over the period 1978–84 Drummond mused upon spiritual and environmental matters. He was crucified, covered with latex, and then 'flayed' and suspended in space by ropes attached to his limbs. He conducted purification rituals on the mud flats at Aramoana. In a gallery installation, a white cast of his body sprawled on the floor; projected slides and willow branches spoke of helplessness and uncertainty in the face of onrushing time and relentless natural forces.

Having established his credentials as a modern shaman, after 1984 Drummond turned to sculpture, large-scale drawings and installations. From the beginning he has used carefully chosen materials — slate, lead, copper, willow, wood, beeswax, bones, stone and rusted iron machine parts to make many enigmatic sculptures and installations. There is a strong alchemical tone to his work, emphasised by his early performance activities. The sculptures focus on the life force, based as it is on chemical and electrical actions and interactions which scientists are still trying to unravel. The image of the body has often been present, drawn in graphite, woven out of willow or cast in metal. One is invited to relate the workings of the body to the veins of metallic ores, braided rivers, flowing magma and magnetic fields of the planet. While reminding us of our dependence upon nature, the artist seems to be attempting to make contact with unknown powers or to harness unknown energies. Many of Drummond's works have potential, in the electrical sense, giving the impression that if we touch them we may be affected in some way. His copper-wrapped tree trunks stand like anodes or cathodes waiting for lightning. His graphite-rubbed boxes house slate shards and screwed-up copper balls. His copper-tube coils remind us of high-tension electrical equipment. What they are for how they work, we can only guess at, but they intrigue and disturb us.

Vented Standing Device with Casting, 1994
Glass, spaghnum moss, copper, slate, brass, powdered enamels
600 x 300 x 300 mm
Courtesy Gow Langsford Gallery and Andrew Jensen Gallery

Drummond has departed from this agenda occasionally. In a series of works in 1988, he juxtaposed metal parts with iron body casts mounted on old warehouse timbers, recalling machinery which once whirred and clanked and the body which toiled alongside, both now stilled and frozen in time and memory. Other works have resembled seed pods, cotton bolls and sprouting forms. In a major multi-part work of 1995, *Cob and Pen*, Drummond explored aspects of sexuality and memory using taxidermised swans.

During the 1980s much of Drummond's work had a rough-hewn and totemic look. Recently his style and materials have changed as he has introduced kinetic elements and begun using glass domes and capsules in conjunction with brass. Another major 1995 piece, *For breathing and reaching*, is a large suspended glass tube into which a piston is drawn and expelled, extending and retracting willow rods as it moves. Here the body is referenced by allusions to artificial lungs and to vein-reaming operations, but the form also takes on the appearance of a mechanical squid. The artist intends first to fascinate and then to provoke thought.

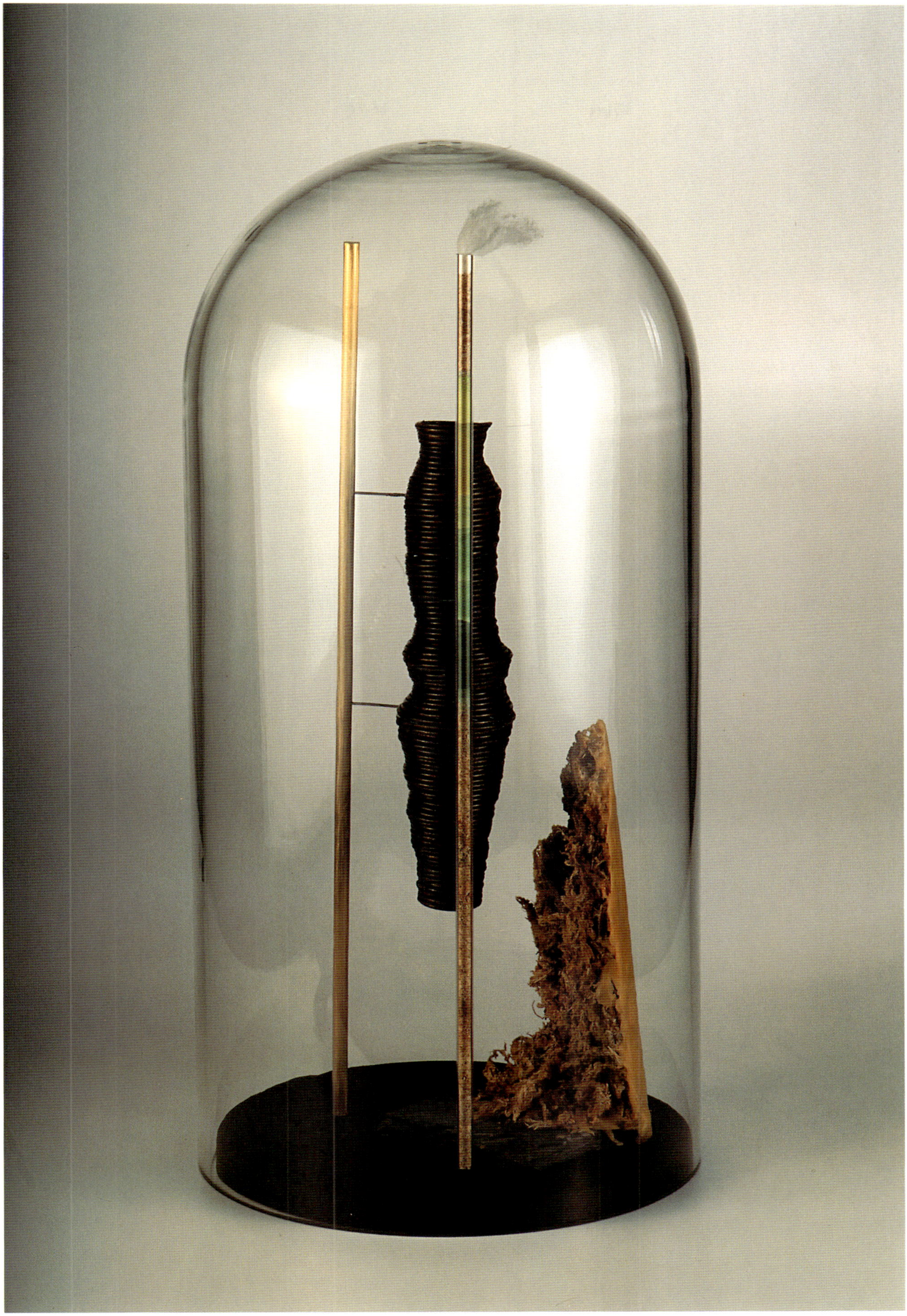

32

SIMON ENDRES

Born Hamilton, 1969.
BFA (Sculpture), UC 1991.
Lives in Wellington.

Endres is an inventive young sculptor who established a reputation in the early 1990s for slick, witty object-making. He is interested in aspects of popular culture and consumption, and the economic pressures that drive and shape them. The title of his first solo show, *(Un)Slick — A Gloss on Life in the Future Perfect*, 1993, summed up the anachronistic irony of the sculptures. Much of the imagery in the show alluded to the 1960s and featured a comicbook futurism that now seems dated.

A feature of Endres' work has been his use of plastic moulding processes to produce unique sculptural pieces that looked as if they were only one of many. He painstakingly carved moulds out of customwood and then had plastic skins vacuum-formed over them. The resulting smooth, glossy shapes were of two types — regular and irregular. The former looked like objects, emblems or badges; the latter like inkblots on glass. Both types could be combined in one work, as in *Light Conversation*, 1994, which was a collection of shapes, or *(dis)Solve (dis)Solve*, 1992, two identical works in which formed frames enclosed photos of a Coca-Cola bottle spilling plastic-formed contents.

The meticulous workmanship put into the plastic moulds was carried over to Endres' other sculptural objects. So, in *The Amazing Escape of Substance X*, 1993, a metal-bound security carrying box (handmade) appears to have dropped from a height and is embedded in the floor, leaking a black viscous fluid (formed plastic). The piece calls to mind 1950s horror films in which lethal things were always escaping from secret labs, and this is confirmed by a miniature 1950s car being carried away on the black ooze. Two other 1993 pieces which involved oily puddles on the floor were colourful plastic containers suspended in space by the stream of liquid pouring from them. One stream turned into pistols, joined butt to barrel, reminding us that lubricant production is often backed by guns.

In 1992 and 1993 Endres reworked Robert Indiana's 1964 EAT/DIE concept. That American pop art emblem, using stencil-type lettering, was an ironic dig at consumer excess. Endres' first version was a stand with a plastic 'Good Housekeeping' emblem on it which lit up to read BUY or DIE. Then, in a 1993 shop window installation, he presented two austere illuminated plastic signs on chrome stands, one embossed with the word WANT, the other with NEED. Each was backed by a panel bearing a W and N logo, making a stylish window display which heightened the pangs of the indigent without even offering them goods to fantasise about. As the shop was vacant and to let, there was irony on both sides of the window. Endres shows how there is something assertive about a word pressed into metal or plastic — it becomes part of the object. He explored this further in 1994 with *Personal Luggage*, three plastic-formed suitcases — one white, one yellow and one transparent. Respectively they were embossed with the words SLEEP, PLAY and WORK.

Endres is now moving away from an overt use of process into work that uses existing objects, and into installations and design commissions which offer the opportunity for spatial and conceptual development. His 1995 show was an enigmatic group of objects including a suitcase, a wire-mesh cage, a padded cocktail cabinet and a photo of a brand mark on a man's neck, and in 1996 he installed an assemblage 35 metres high in a Wellington carparking building.

Transplant (from the 'Concrete Deal' series), 1996
Cardboard, digitally manipulated images, steel, plastic strap
3.5 x 8 m
Wellington installation (dismantled)

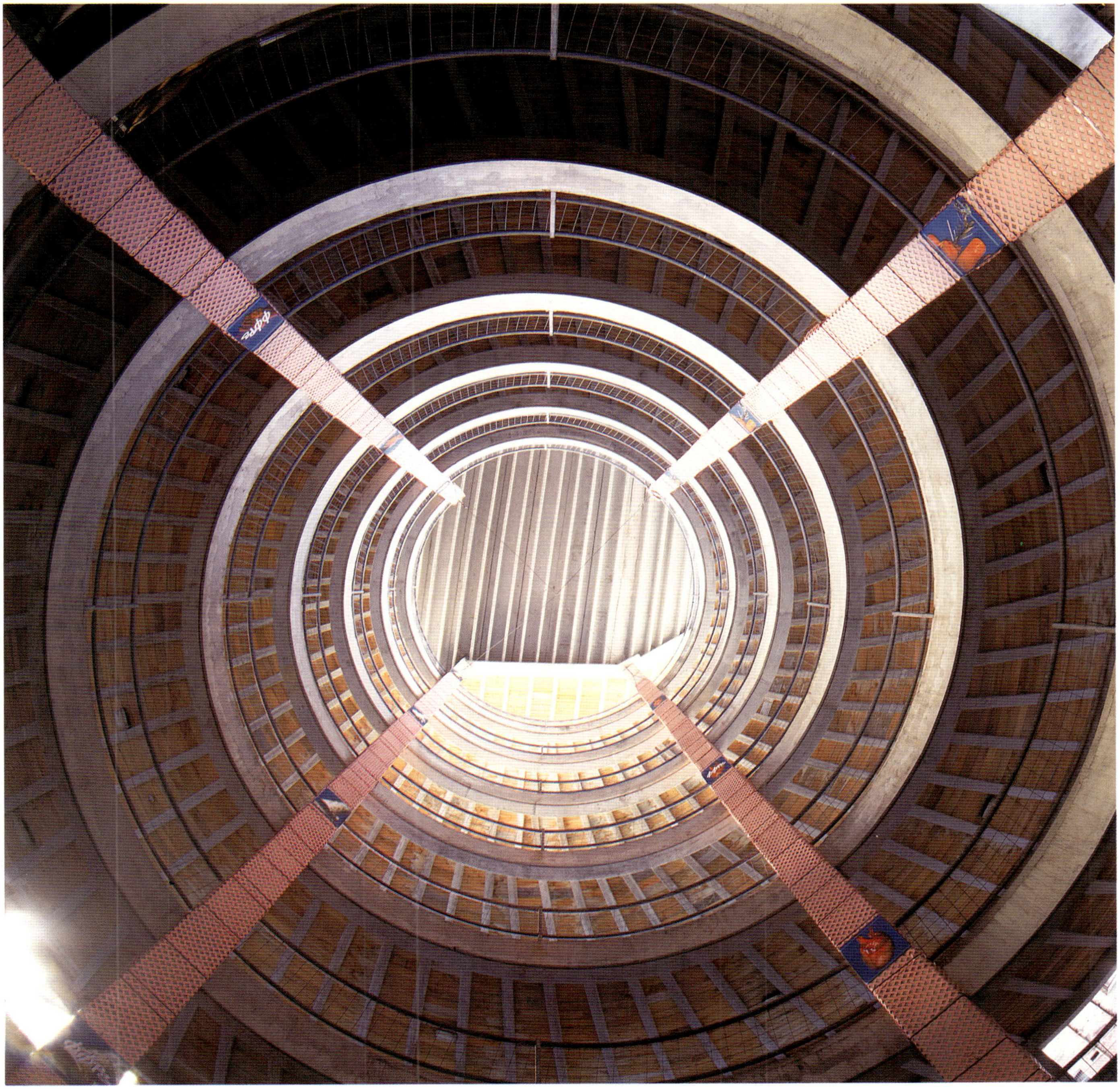

33

DI FFRENCH

Born Melbourne 1946.
Came to New Zealand 1963.
Lives in Silverpeaks, Otago.

Ffrench describes her considerable *oeuvre* in different media as attempts to express poetic ideas visually. Terms applicable to poetry, such as structure, metaphor, symbolism, imagination and passion, apply to her photography in particular. Like those of Webster (98) and Dawson (25), Ffrench's photographs are set up, with carefully posed models and pre-arranged backgrounds. Like Jenkinson (44), Ffrench uses cut-out forms in her work and, as with Webster, nude figures in unnatural lighting are recurrent images, and aspects of gender and social conditioning are themes. Notwithstanding these parallels, Ffrench's photographs are distinctive — showing how creative artists can explore the same territory and make individual discoveries. Ffrench is also a prime example of an artist who uses photography thoughtfully to achieve effects obtainable no other way, while at the same time suppressing the look of a conventional photograph.

Ffrench began as a conceptual sculptor in the 1960s, working both inside and outside. In the 1970s through to 1985 she was a performance artist, working more as a facilitator than as an actor. Her activities included the preparation of sites and the projection of photographic transparencies across them. Additional photography recorded her performances, but was not always done by the artist. The unusual look of these residual photographs, plus some dissatisfaction with the demands and short life of performance work, led Ffrench in 1983 toward her present creative method. Basic ingredients in her complex technique are preparation, photography to make black and white transparencies, further preparation, projection, re-photographing and final printing in cibachrome (only one print is made). This enables the artist to meld two or more images seamlessly together on and/or into a prepared surface (the ground). The ground consists of refractive material such as coke, in consistencies ranging from granules to blocks, sometimes partially overlaid with sheets of plain materials which act as 'screens' for the projections. The shimmer of water or texture of rock can be applied to skin; colour can be introduced to all or part of the image by pigmenting the ground; and extra objects can be introduced through placement on the ground. All of this must be planned and co-ordinated by the artist — action in the studio akin to performance, resulting in a permanent, portable piece of visual poetry. The colour in Ffrench's work is particularly subtle, often giving the effect of an old, hand-coloured black and white photograph.

Over the last 12 years Ffrench has produced numerous series of photographs in which male and female nudes appear. These have been the subject of much theoretical analysis by writers of various persuasions: feminist, gay, sociological, deconstructivist and postmodern among them. Ffrench knows her art theory, but she is also well read in general literature. She does not make her art under the sway of any theory, but only in pursuit of her own ideas. These can emanate from an observation, thought, something read or a desire to explore such things as musculature, sensuality, dreams, passivity/aggression and the role of the nude in historical art. The works are tableaux, confronting the viewer with a dramatic, posed scene which demands an immediate response. The artist readily accepts different readings of her work as part of the art process. Ffrench has made films and videos, and continues to make sculptures, both as ingredients in her photographs and for separate display.

Oscillating for 'Significant Little Opera' series, 1996
Source image; final work presented in form of cibachrome print with viewfinder and powdered steel frame
400 x 400 x 200 mm
Courtesy of the artist

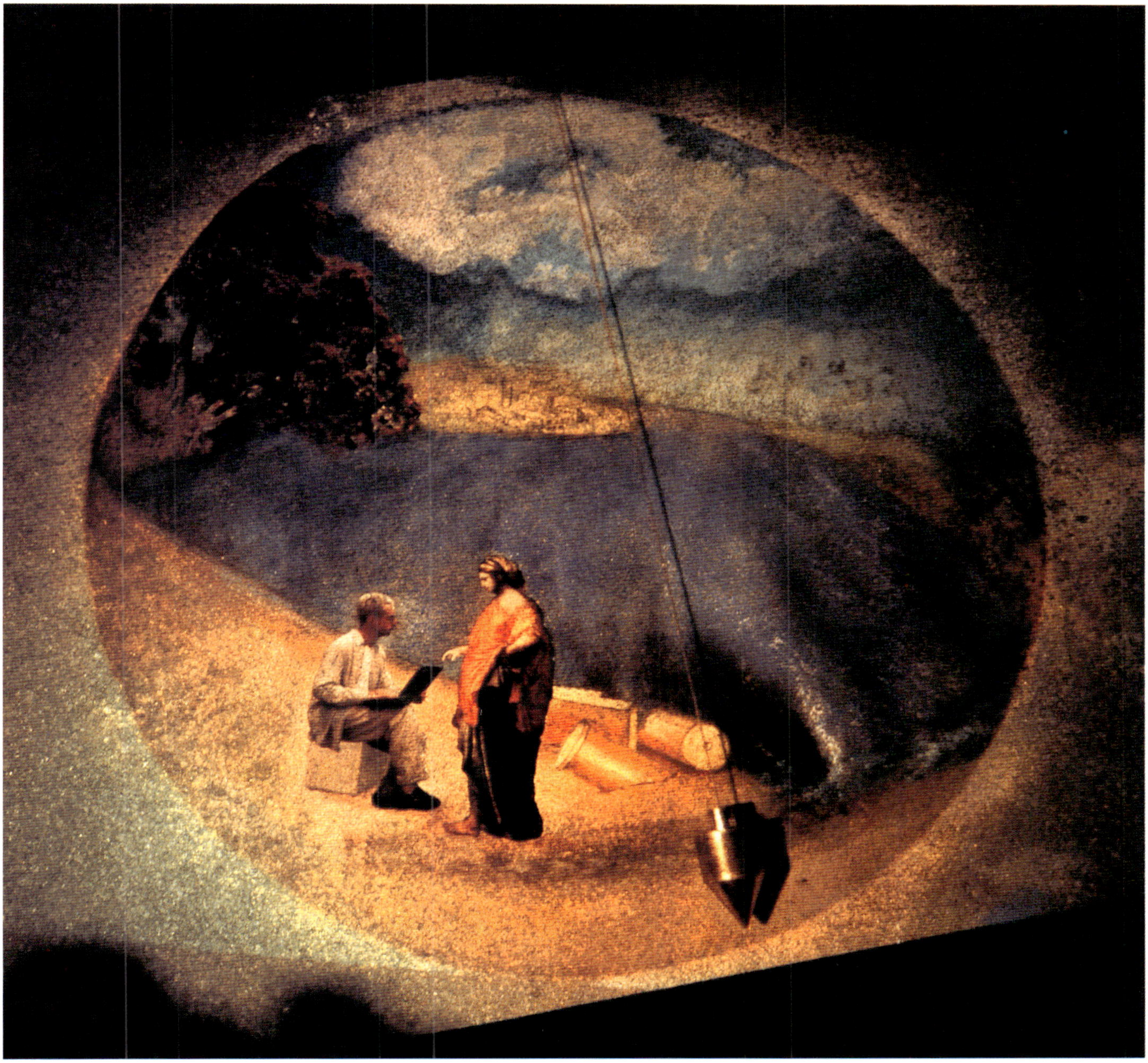

34

CHARLOTTE FISHER

Born Whangarei 1959.
BA (Art History), UA 1981; BFA, UA 1989.
Lives in Auckland.

Fisher has said that her sculpture deals with the organic, the elemental, abstract and associative form. In her 1988 graduation show was a work made of driftwood called *Arch of Ages* which illustrated the artist's statement. It contained many of the forms which, in a more refined manner, she has used since: the column, the round-ended stump, the horn or arc shape and the finger-like protrusion. Made from jetsam and cave-like in form, *Arch* also evoked the sea. A boat shape has been another of Fisher's associative forms, which she sees as a symbol for the bearing and caring role of women. She seeks archetypical forms in her work to link it to an ancient chain of human endeavour whereby signs, symbols and objects meaningful to people long dead can speak to us today She has always held a concern for the environment, and her sculptures can often be seen as reminders of the beauty handed to us by nature in growth forms and water-worn materials.

Fisher was a mature student, and this showed in her debut exhibition in 1989. Her work was confident, original and appeared fully resolved. The balanced, double-ended blunted horn, coracle boat, tall support-post and nailed-on copper skins which made their appearance at this time have been used since in numerous variations. In a 1990 exhibition in Rotorua, Fisher symbolically transported materials found on the coasts east, west and south of that landlocked city in her small carved wooden boats, each sitting on a column. Her persona as a northerner made up the other compass direction. In 1990 and 1991 Fisher made two versions of a form derived from ancient pictograms which could have stood for either a reed boat with standing crew or a comb. One version, *She Stands*, was in wood and the other in Hinuera stone. These pieces, and also *Ancestor* of 1991, relate back to a form made intuitively by Fisher when still a student. The horn/arc was refined further in 1992 in the major piece *Mine Eyes Are Dim With Weeping*, a tribute to the artist's late mother. Concentrating on possibilities in using just a standing column, Fisher made two related works, *McCahon Waterfall*, 1991, and *Pour*, 1993. In each case a streak referring to water ran vertically down a tall, adzed section of tree trunk. In 1993, at an outdoor symposium, Fisher made two blade or leaf-like forms which echoed a cavity in the tree behind. In 1995, these pieces and three others were combined with found curved kauri screens standing behind them to make up the impressive *Still Life* series.

Arc, 1994
Kauri, driftwood, Australian hardwood, copper, graphite
2125 x 1850 mm
Courtesy Gow Langsford Gallery, Auckland

In addition to these eloquent but abstract forms, Fisher occasionally makes pieces with a specific reference. One of her boats, filled with found copper objects, became a peace ark in *Still Life for Bougainville*, 1992. *Endless Columns*, 1994, was a copy of a famous work by Brancusi, papered with impenetrable art-writing texts; while her site work at a 1995 eco-art symposium was a leaf shape (the medieval *vesica piscis*) on a lawn, planted with seedlings of the species that would normally occupy such a space in the bush.

There is no angst, no polemicism, no gimmickry in Fisher's work. Until recently colour was restricted to naturally occurring tones, plus black and white. Her sculptures pursue beauty of form without becoming decorative, and balance primitivism with sophistication. They are calming idols for a stressed-out secular age.

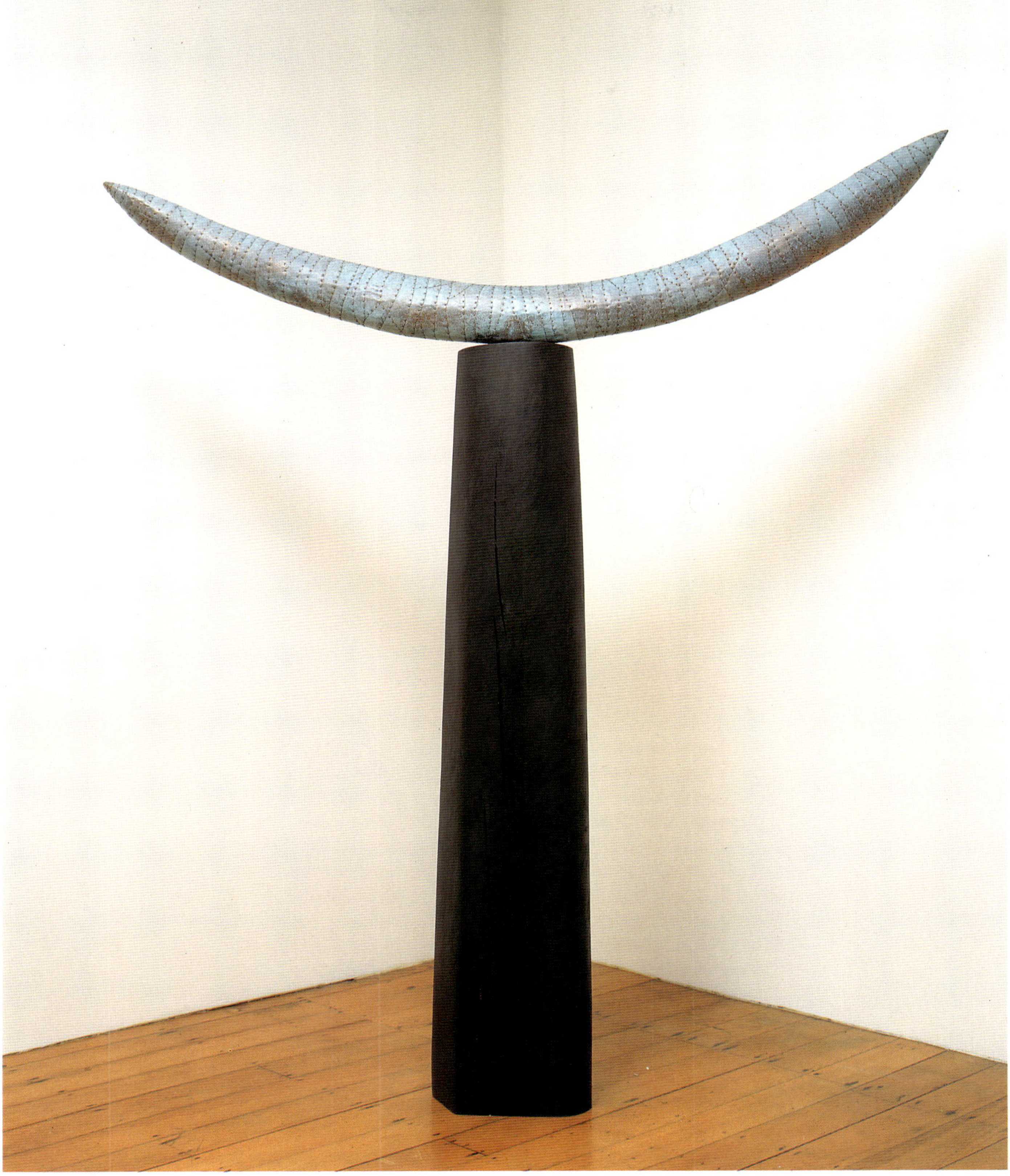

35

RODNEY FUMPSTON

Born Fiji 1947. Came to New Zealand 1956.
MFA (1st Class Hons), UA 1972; graduate in Advanced Studies in Printmaking,
Central School of Art and Design, London 1974.
Lives in Auckland.

Fumpston is a dedicated printmaker and teacher of printmaking. He is a master of intaglio techniques and has also made a number of lithographs and woodcuts. Pastel drawing and collage have provided a break from the rigours of the printing process over the years.

His prints cover a range of styles from meticulous realism to loose, expressive and gestural images. Some of his work approaches abstraction, but it always remains based in the real world. Although noted for his joyous use of colour, Fumpston can surprise us with shadowy, monochromatic mezzotints. His subject matter is equally widely cast, including landscapes, sky and seascapes, garden studies, and objects as diverse as icecream cones, shells and tiki. If there is a unifying element in Fumpston's work it is an unerring sense of mood and place. Whether it be a jet trail in the cold sky above Marble Arch, a sunset at Egypt's pyramids, dusk in the artist's back garden, moonlight on an Indian temple or a gloomy museum cabinet of artefacts, Fumpston can capture the moment. This gives his best prints a special quality of identification with, and communication of, the artist's finely tuned sensibilities.

Fumpston has a warm and generous personality, a self-effacing manner and an unabashed love of beauty. His is a romantic vision and he leaves angst, social and industrial realism and pure abstraction to others. As with John Papas (100NZP, 63) Fumpston has travelled widely, and memories of time spent in London, Europe, Egypt, Japan and India have come together in series of prints. He is also a homebody, finding inspiration in his garden and in such mundane activity as renovations (the *Home Improvement* series).

Part of the enjoyment offered by original prints is an appreciation of the techniques involved, and how different methods alter the look of the finished work. A mezzotint will usually be softer and subtler than an etching; the latter can demonstrate the graphic power of lines and the changing densities of rolled ink. A look through a folio of Fumpston's prints illustrates the diversity of these qualities. The effects seem effortless, but are the result of great labour and meticulous care, both in the preparation of plates and the inking and printing of them. The inking of the 1990 mezzotint series of Indian vignettes can only be described as masterful. Etchings such as the *Egypt* series of 1980–81 contain large areas of pure colour in dark blue and gold. The ink is rolled onto the plate after careful mixing and merging of colours on the roller itself. Under the huge pressure of the etching press, tiny imperfections in the plate, uneven inking or a speck of dust can ruin a print. Fumpston's immaculate technique ensures that this never happens.

By imparting his enthusiasm for the print medium, his organisational skills and his personal discipline to students since 1978, Fumpston's influence has been considerable.

Tropical Garden II, 1980
Etching and aquatint in an edition of 40
500 x 440 mm
Courtesy of the artist

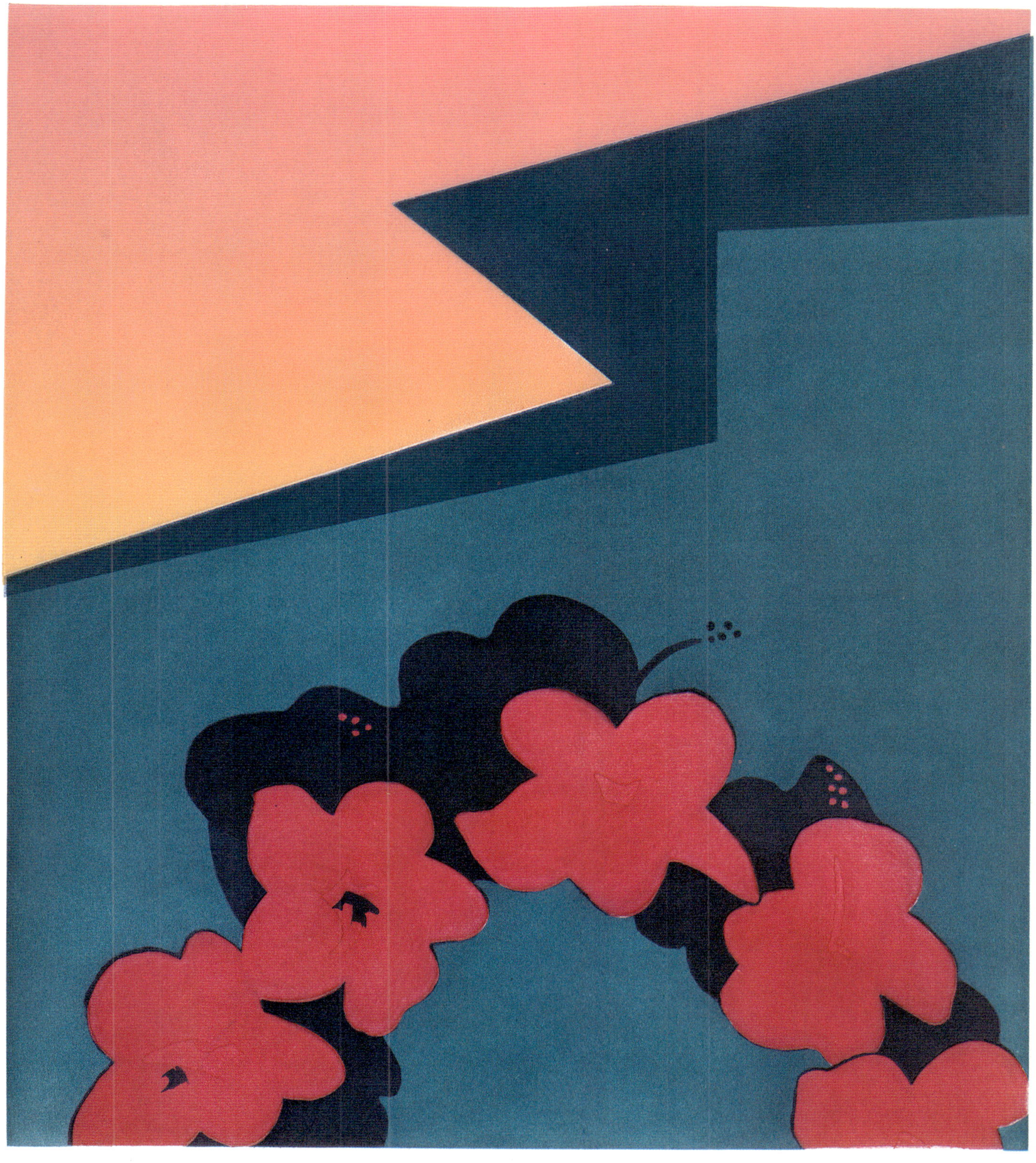

36

RUDOLF GOPAS

Born Lithuania 1917.
Graduated with Honours from Kaunas Art School, Lithuania 1938.
Came to New Zealand 1949.
Died Christchurch 1983.

Gopas ranks with Louise Henderson (100NZP, 35) as one of the most influential art teachers in the period after the Second World War. Without that war he would almost certainly not have come to New Zealand, as a penniless refugee. He brought with him a background of painting and a first-hand knowledge and theoretical understanding of the expressionist movement in Europe. After struggling to establish himself in New Zealand, supporting his family by working as a photo-processor, Gopas was appointed a lecturer at Ilam in 1959. He taught there for nearly 20 years.

Gopas's own expressionist paintings done in New Zealand, judged on an international level, display little originality, but compared with the much more restrained and tentative landscape work being done by his contemporaries here, they must have seemed revolutionary. Although not trained as a teacher, a painter of Gopas's persuasion, and particularly one with his European experiences and exotic foreignness, could hardly fail to influence students eager for a real taste of modernity. Expressionism is more of an attitude of mind and far less confining stylistically than the cubism demonstrated by Henderson. Gopas's enthusiasm for the learning process — the need to explore, experiment and ask questions — communicated itself to his students, particularly as he was involved throughout with the development of his own painting. He was a formative influence upon Trusttum, Clairmont and Fomison (see 100NZP, 91, 14, 23), and yet the art of those three artists is very different from each others' and from Gopas's. They learned from Gopas to hang onto their personal visions, and gained the confidence to draw and handle paint freely. Gopas showed how the weave of the canvas can be an important element in a painting, and that using hessian accentuates this aspect.

Gopas had other enthusiasms to impart. From his early youth he had maintained a keen interest in astronomy and poetry. These two passions came through in his art from 1965 onwards, moving it away from the landscapes, still lifes and portraits that had previously comprised his subject matter. Between 1965 and 1976 Gopas did a series of paintings inspired by his astronomic observances. They showed nebulae, stars and galaxies, but rendered in a gritty and glossy media which militated against any illusion of the velvety vastness of space.

In 1975–76 Gopas completed his series of *Paintings for the Sun*, semi-abstract works incorporating diagram and text. These showed the influences of Klee and McCahon (100NZP, 50), but without the richness of colour of the former or the profundity of the latter. However, the sketches for these paintings were a prelude to Gopas's finest works, his poetic/astronomic/mystic drawings. These works, of extraordinary graphic power, seem to concentrate the artist's whole lifetime of thoughts, dreams and experiences, and offered him the opportunity to blend art and literature. They bear comparison with the sketchbooks of Da Vinci and William Blake. Coincidentally, because much of the text in them is indecipherable, they are also the first examples of decontextual art in New Zealand (cf. Budd, 7; Haffern, 100NZP, 30).

A Spaceship for the Galaxy, 1976
Ink and pastel on paper
280 x 200 mm
Private collection, Auckland

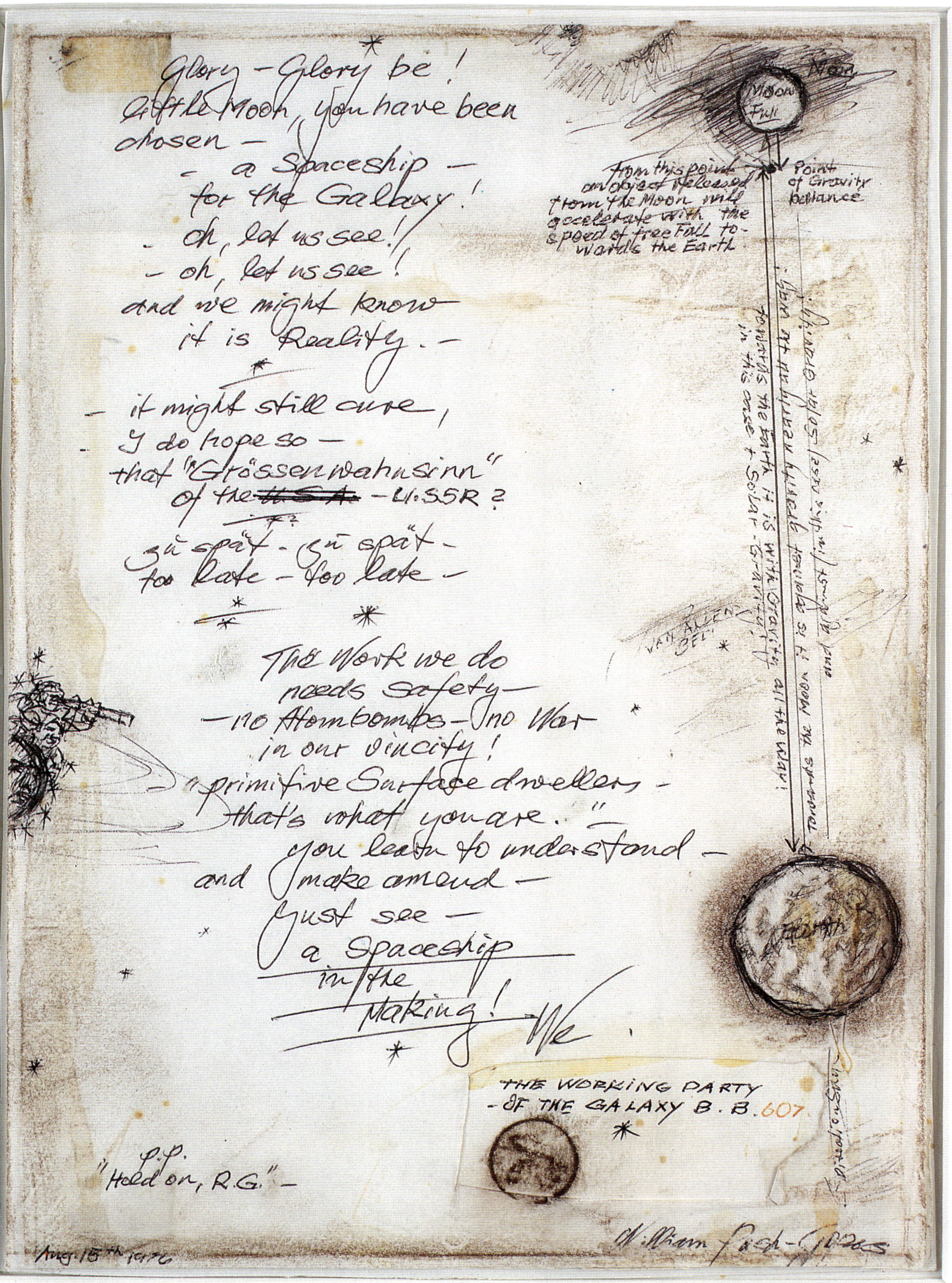
Glory - Glory be!
Little Moon, you have been
chosen -
- a Spaceship -
for the Galaxy!
- oh, let us see!
- oh, let us see!
and we might know
it is Reality. -
- it might still cure,
I do hope so -
that "Grössenwahnsinn"
of the ~~U.S.A.~~ - U.S.S.R.?
zu spät - zu spät -
too late - too late -
The Work we do
needs safety -
- no Atombombs - no War
in our vincity!
primitive Surface dwellers -
that's what you are..." -
you learn to understand -
and make amend -
Just see -
a Spaceship
in the
Making!
We
Moon
Moon Full
From this point an object released from the Moon will accelerate with the speed of free Fall towards the Earth
Point of Gravity ballance
Towards the Earth it is with Gravity all the way!
in this case + Solar-Gravity
Van Allen Belt
Earth
THE WORKING PARTY
- OF THE GALAXY B. B. 607
P.S.
"Hold on, R.G." -
Aug. 15th 1976
William Fish-Jones

37

BARBARA GRAHAM

Born Dunedin 1946.
Studied etching 1980–83.
Lives in Auckland.

Graham has been exhibiting her prints since 1980. She usually works in series, and has produced over 20 of these to date, displaying an inventive mastery of the intaglio medium. Her work prior to 1985, multi-plate etchings freely interpreting trees, skies, seascapes and landforms, showed the influence of her tutor Fumpston (35). Soft, glowing colour was contrasted with graphic gestures. The *Eruptions* of 1984 were the culmination of this period.

The *Space Odyssey* series of 1985 was the first of three inspired by the photographs taken by orbiting weather satellites. These etchings were a remarkable departure from the visual flatness which can plague printmaking. Graham married the distancing effect of the satellite view with that of the etching plate to make compelling images in which the sense of great height was preserved, even enhanced. Careful inking of the plates captured the gradation of blues in the atmosphere from pale to dark, and the rich textures and unusual colours of large land masses.

In 1987 she came right down to earth with the *Structures* series, a set of seven etchings which depicted parts of massive historic or modern buildings. Seen from a low viewpoint, the structures seemed to tower dramatically into the sky. All the prints were made over a uniform background of marks imposed by a separate plate. In the *Inroads* series of 1988 Graham made expressive, uncompromising etchings based on that most unaesthetic of human interferences with the land — the road cutting. The *Apollyon* series of 1989 continued with the satellite images, concentrating on those which depicted areas altered by human activity, such as California's Salton Sea. After a further series of *Space Odyssey* works, Graham used drypoint techniques on acetate film to make the haunting series *Sacred to the Memory*, 1990, in which she first used some collaged photographic prints.

A perfect suite of abstract prints, *After Mondrian*, followed in 1991, then the *20th Century Iconography* series in 1992. This suite juxtaposed images taken from fifteenth-century religious painting with scenes of violence and despair from the twentieth century to question the relevance of the familiar Christian iconography. The related 1994 *Belief Systems* were about the images which represent belief, and suggested that mass-produced religious images have the same aim as advertising and should be treated with equal suspicion. The excellent *Bedrocks* and *Exhibits* series of 1992–93 explored realism and surrealism respectively. Graham's most recent works are the *Dreams v. Reality* series and the *Anthropomorphic* series. The former are surrealistic images concerned with how we can distort reality in our search for the ideal, particularly the ideal human form. In contrast, the *Anthropomorphic* series finds similes for aged and deformed human bodies in the roots of Moreton Bay fig trees.

Over the years Graham has ensured the distinctiveness of her prints by the use of separate plates, the working-over of some prints with pastel or graphite, and the use of collage. This was introduced as part of the *20th Century* series, and the technique also used in the *Belief Systems* and *Dreams v. Reality*. It enables the artist to contrast well-lit, sharply focused, realistic images with gloomy, less distinct, enigmatic backgrounds.

Anthropomorphic Series, 1996
595 x 275 mm
Solarplate etching
Courtesy of the artist

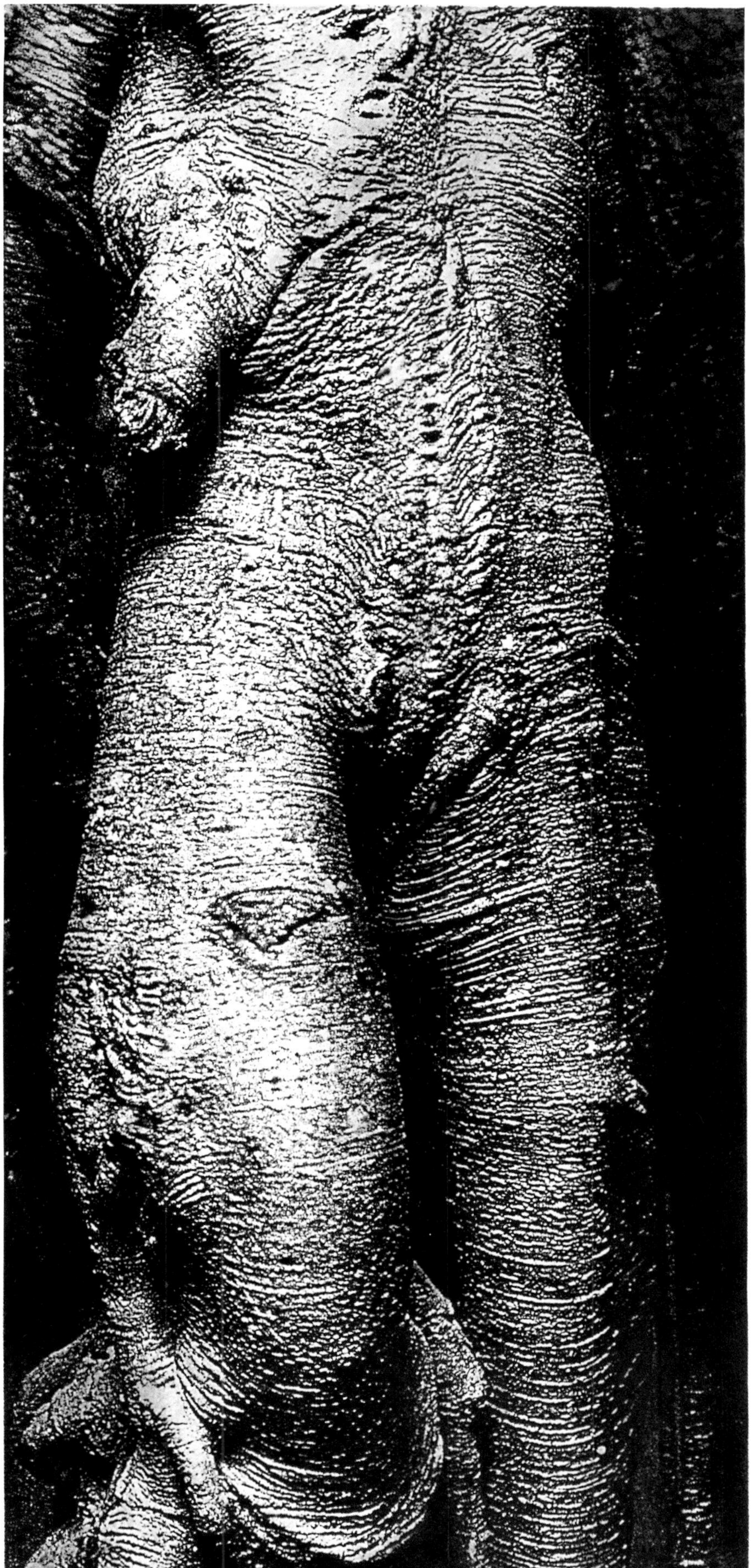

38

BRETT GRAHAM

Born Auckland 1967.
BFA, UA 1988; MFA, University of Hawaii 1991.
Lives in Auckland.

In the 1960s a movement developed against the idea of sculpture being a carved or formed object with so-called aesthetic qualities. The 'post-object' artists used cheap, everyday materials and assembled them rather than formed them (cf. Cullen, 22; Viscoe, 93). Graham is a sculptor whose work represents a return to the evocative form. His sculptures are very much individual objects — adzed, grooved, carved, sometimes rubbed with graphite or stained with colour. Working in stone or wood, he draws on his heritage as a Maori artist as well as the modernist tradition of sculpture epitomised by Brancusi, Moore and Hepworth. Artists of both traditions have sought to make objects with presence and a timeless quality that would retain relevance and meaning down the centuries. Graham's works have this quality. They are generic, based on age-old universal forms of life, growth and containment (cf. King, 48). They do not attempt to incorporate specific Maori forms or motifs — they could have been found in a Pharoah's tomb or an alien spacecraft. There are, however, links to traditional Maori art and life, and titles are always in Maori. Subtle male or female symbolism can be read in some works.

Graham made an impressive start with his graduation show in 1988. He exhibited two tall obelisks and a winged wall relief, both sheathed with thin lead sheets over wooden formwork which had been incised all over with unspecific symbols based on Pacific cultural sources. This was followed in 1989 with a commission for his university's theatre foyer, the *Maidment Muses*. Here nine semi-abstract forms are lined up like ancestor figures in a Maori meeting house. While in Hawaii in 1990–91, Graham carved figures with limbs like seed pods joined end to end and narrow heads sprouting horns. He also went to Japan in 1991 and worked with the sculptor Okamoto, from whom he learned techniques for splitting stone. He used these on his return to make some distinctive forms from Oamaru stone, complete but sliced up into rough cubes and reassembled. There were bowls; a form resembling a font; and another like a tall, lidded wine jar which suggested a sarcophagus or cocoon.

Rangiatea, 1995
Pinus radiata
1900 x 690 x 460 mm
Courtesy Artis Gallery, Auckland

The title of Graham's 1992 show, *1492–1642*, referred to the dates of arrival on the shores of America and New Zealand of Columbus and Tasman respectively. The works told a story of the establishment, growth and flowering of a culture in a new land, followed by its change and possible death when faced with the threat of a new, more technologically advanced culture. Images included a perched bird form, a growing nikau tree, a stylised terraced pa, a dead tree and an ark/coffin.

In 1994 Graham fulfilled a commission at Waikato University with a large, plant-like form opening up to the sky. The inside edges of the 'leaves' are shaped in the traditional Maori poutama (stairway to heaven) steps, and the sculpture is a synthesis of flower, nikau palm and mechanical grab.

Graham returned to the stele in 1995 with fluted forms 2 metres high and similar to cactus stems, both representing a needle, but also reading as a plant shoot or a phallic symbol. Another piece, representing the eye of a needle, evoked a tall ark or canoe with a vaginal-shaped opening at the top; while another resembled a huge saddle, grooved above and smooth below.

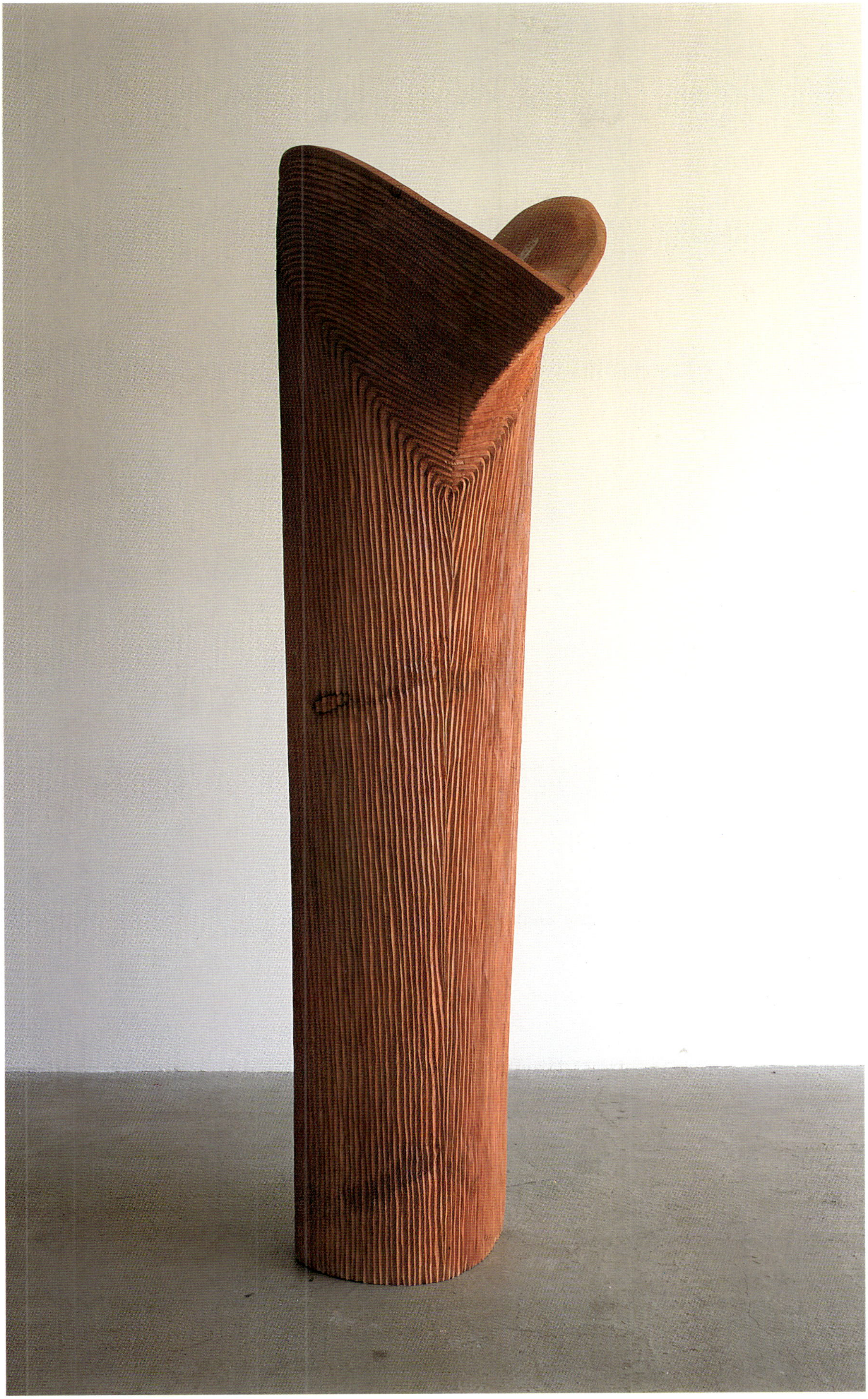

39

DAVID GUERIN

Born Waipukurau 1956.
Studied sculpture and photography at East Sydney Technical College, 1984–85.
Lives in Havelock North.

Guerin works in two modes — stone sculptures, and assemblages of found objects which often incorporate small stone carvings. His stone works range from monumental outdoor pieces to small-scale interior ones. His interest in stone carving from all cultures has resulted in a surprising mix of styles. Some pieces resemble pagan idols with a pre-Columbian or Pacific look; others are like small shrines or fragments from a Roman ruin. He has a fondness for relief carving of the type found on monuments.

Notwithstanding his use of found objects, stone remains Guerin's great love. He sees it as the medium which has defined the growth of human civilisation. His sculptures are muted in colour and gothic in feeling. He regards the medieval period as a time when codes of good and evil were apparent and the images of both were made clear for all to see. Like the carvings in European cathedrals, his works are controlled, tranquil and seem designed to teach us something. He sees signs and symbols combining to isolate cultural beliefs within a manageable, closed unit — and therefore as useful devices for a sculptor to work with. The affinity with the gothic is reinforced by curving arch shapes in some works. These are either cut into or out of wood, or appear in the form of salvaged window frames or fragments of wheels. In a work such as *Justice*, 1988, the curves gather in the elements of the work and also serve as the balancing arms of a scale. This equilibrium is a hallmark of Guerin's work. He seeks balance and order in a world which spins in a cosmos where chaos reigns. Fairness and trust are cornerstones of the artist's moral sensibility. Some of his pieces have words incised into them, such as EQUITY, FATE, JUSTICE, CHANCE, ERROR. These pieces are dogmatic, but they leave room for personal interpretation of the details. Other pieces are less specific. While science has discovered much, Guerin still sees a great deal that is unexplained. Folklore has a purpose in expressing a collective imagination which tries to make sense of the mysterious. In his work, religions, cults, myths, moral tales, folklore and fancy combine into objects which are presented as an act of faith. Guerin often incorporates animals to represent broader themes, as symbols of implied narrative, interpreting tales of character, motivation, inspiration and action.

Work, 1989
Wood, iron and ceramic
1800 x 1000 x 90 mm
Ellerton Trust Collection, Auckland

The challenge of assemblage is to create a unity of forms so that the separate elements become essential parts of a new entity with a life of its own. Guerin achieves this, notwithstanding his use of baulks of old timber, metal parts, tools, ceramic insulators and chunks of stone. He is a magpie who cannot resist the lure of an interesting discarded object. These are often craftsmanlike things — turned wood, decorative cast iron, handmade tools — and have stories to tell of buildings, technologies and activities that are now outmoded. Like other assemblagists, Guerin enjoys these traces of a past life and the interaction between pieces from widely different sources.

Guerin also makes bronze medallions, and casts other small sculptural pieces. He is an active photographer and, like most sculptors, he also draws a lot to work out ideas.

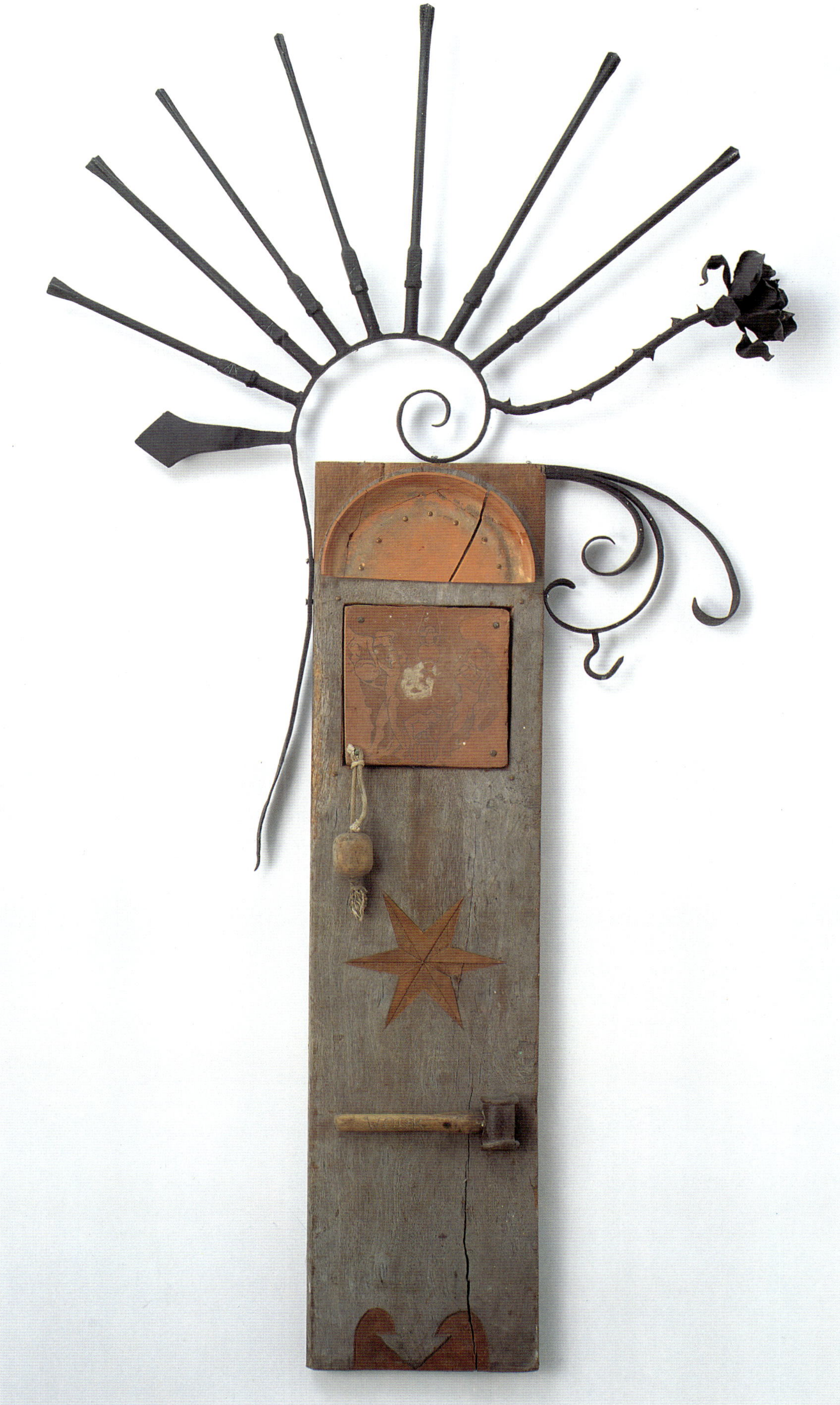

40

TERRENCE HANDSCOMB

Born Wellington 1948.
Attended School of Design, WP 1971.
Lives in Wellington.

Although Handscomb has been making art for 20 years, much of his activity until the mid-1980s was private workings in notebooks and unexhibited drawings. He has shown more often in the last decade, but his work is still not widely appreciated or understood. His art presents us with very specific information — diagrams, words and formulae, precisely rendered and big enough for the short-sighted to read. It seems ordered in accordance with a detailed plan and, to reinforce the feeling that this material is for active use, Handscomb works on big sheets of the translucent polyester film used by architects. You can roll up one of his works and take it to anywhere you may need its guidance — but study it as you may, you cannot make anything of it. This ironical reversal of art's traditional show-and-tell role puts Handscomb in the postmodern group of deconstructivists. One of their somewhat anarchic aims is to break up the connections in what they see as atrophied systems in the hope that new truths may be liberated. Upon these, perhaps, a better world can be built. The description of art galleries as the new churches is now often heard. Symbols, mysticism and philosophy have been ingredients in religions, freemasonry and other movements which call for faith rather than certain knowledge, so why not in art? Confronted with one of Handscomb's large works of the 1980s, the viewer can visualise the artist as priest, initiated into the mysteries and allowing us to view (and worship) symbols which only he can interpret for us. This response was accentuated in Handscomb's 1986 paintings by black cosmic backgrounds and the effect of glowing light from a central device. In more recent works, the difficulty of the interpretation process seems evident in the switches of language from English to Greek to German, and in scribbled notes and amendments built up around larger, more defined elements. A metaphor for enlightenment struggling to escape from the clouds of ignorance and deliberate obfuscation is found in most of Handscomb's works in the form of a dark area of pigment which adjoins or blends into a light area. This device, and the use of text, forms a strong link with McCahon's work (100NZP, 50). Whereas McCahon used allegorical landscapes and readable text to engender spiritual awareness in his viewers (often, at the time, unsuccessfully), so Handscomb gives viewers the option of assigning transcendental meaning to his works. McCahon wanted viewers to find their own inner peace and harmony with nature, but some rejected his work and others just ignored it. The same can happen with Handscomb's works. They are devices for illustrating the intersection of nature and culture (the latter including faith and religion) and the difference between learned codes (language) and intuitive responses. He suggests that grasping the work intuitively is better than a polluted response via language. However, Handscomb's works are not random gibberish. They have very specific meanings for him, but his interest in complex philosophical theories, personal methods of expressing meanings in formulae and his working methods all conspire to render his inscriptions unintelligible to the average viewer. He both accepts and intends this.

In the 1990s Handscomb has become interested in new technologies and is experimenting with video art and image projections. Text is not fragmented in this work and is mixed with figurative imagery.

Model for World Decline, 1989
Oil alkyd on polyester film
2200 x 2970 mm
Fletcher Challenge Collection, Wellington

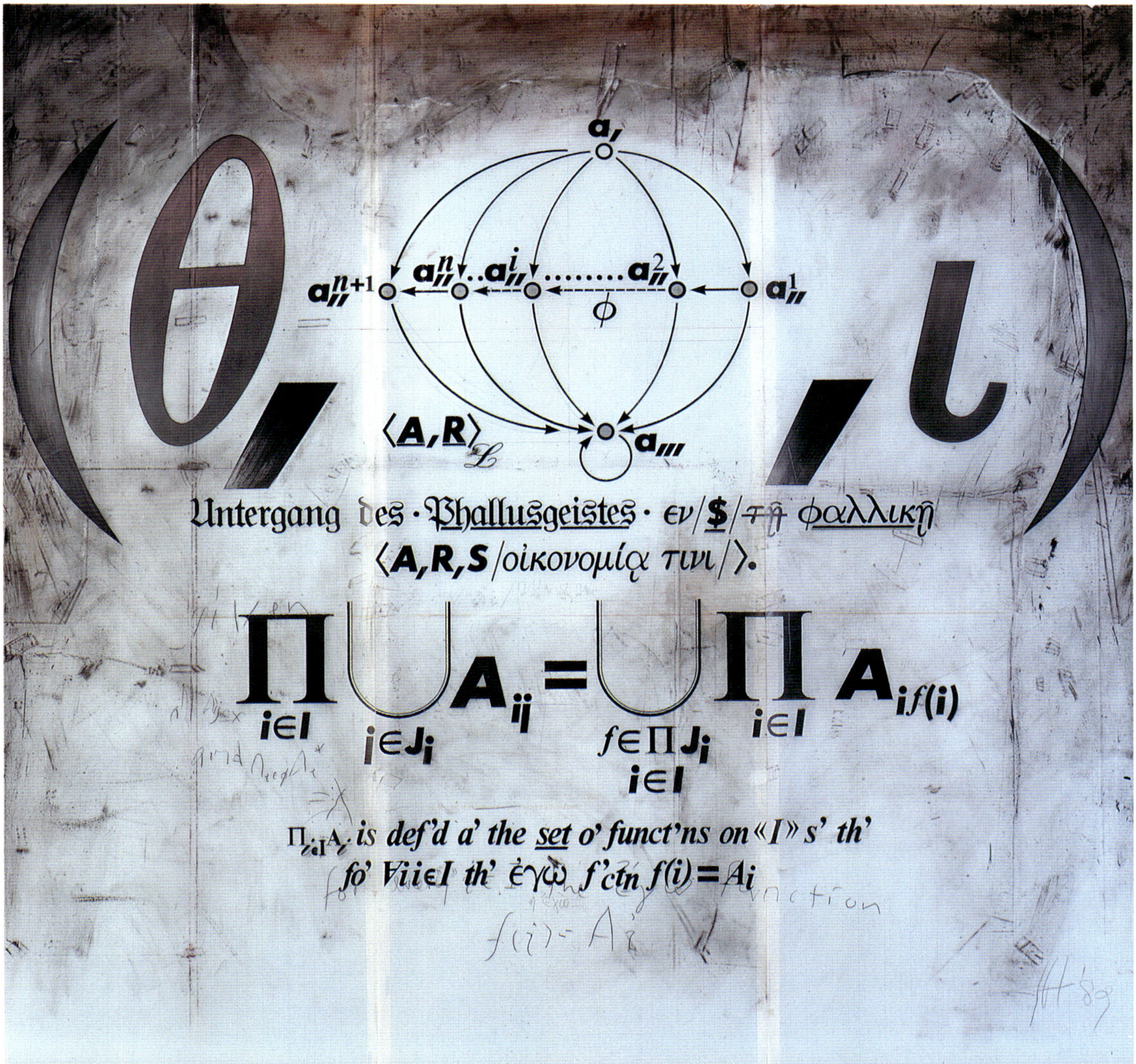
a'
a''n+1
a''n
a''i
a''2
a''1
φ
⟨A,R⟩
a'''
Untergang des · Phallusgeistes · εν/$/τῇ φαλλικῇ
⟨A,R,S/οἰκονομίᾳ τινι/⟩.
Π⋃A = ⋃Π A
Π A is def'd a' the set o' funct'ns on «I» s' th'
fo' ∀i i∈I th' ἐγώ f'ctn f(i)=Ai
f(i)=Ai

41

CHRISTINE HELLYAR

Born New Plymouth 1947.
DFA (Hons), UA 1970.
Lives in Auckland.

Hellyar avoids the human form in her work, feeling that there has been much narrow-minded narcissism in sculpture in the past. Her aim is to turn people's minds to an awareness of their past and its links with the plant, animal and insect world. Early humans had to gather food and make tools, utensils and weapons to survive. Other life forms have to trap prey, grow shells, make lairs or adopt disguises. Hellyar blends these aspects of life with natural forms to produce objects that are redolent of ritual and mysticism. She is a reserved, low-key sculptor and her works seldom look like art to put on a pedestal or coffee table. They are more like the curios that travellers in previous centuries used to bring back from foreign lands. Hellyar often uses a museum display approach to invest her objects with the aura of rare objects from dead cultures.

Hellyar studied biology at school and has an eye for the throwaway details of nature — leaves, twigs, feathers, bones, clay and rocks. She has made sculptures from these overlooked but often eloquent items, working them into baskets and cages made of flax or enclosing them in stitched cocoons. Sometimes she will make homes or nests for them out of baked clay, settle them in jars or trays like museum specimens or tie them to sticks to make strange-looking tools or weapons. Other works are simply laid on the floor in sets. The hand of the artist gently manipulates the handiwork of nature, creating artifacts which are at the same time art.

Meat Cupboard, 1981
Mixed media
1167 x 914 x 279 mm
Courtesy of Govett Brewster Art Gallery, New Plymouth

At art school Hellyar was encouraged to experiment with new materials. By the early 1970s she was working with rubber latex, a medium she has used on and off for 25 years in opaque and translucent states. It has been cast in plaster moulds taken from leaves, the organs of animals, items of clothing or small sections of the forest floor. The rubber leaves have been piled in trays or jars. The clothing, leaving its impression in sheets of rubber hung on lines, has seemed like animal skins or baroque drapes, and the viscera, associated with brass fittings or containers, made totemic objects. In a memorable 1979 exhibition the artist showed 70 small, soft sculptures made of stitched, unbleached calico enclosing various natural materials. Antennae ventured out of folds and pockets; furry, feathery things hid in cocoons or webs. Each small work had its own identity, and the spectator seemed surrounded by sheltering, reclusive life, gathered in a laboratory for study or experiment. In 1982 Hellyar filled a large gallery with flimsy containers of various kinds — huge enclosing webs, nests, baskets and caves inhabited by more of her spindly, seemingly lifelike forms. At the same time the artist made her first *Thought Cupboards*.

More recently Hellyar has been working in bronze, casting fern shoots and spindly stems. She has been using latex to cast multiple leaf forms which are then built up on the gallery floor or wall into large but delicate constructions resembling lichen or dense petals. Taking her view of nature from microcosm to macrocosm, she has been making circular desiccations from coloured, dried clays which read both as laboratory specimens and views of the earth from space. Throughout her career Hellyar has made numerous drawings and some 40 artist's books.

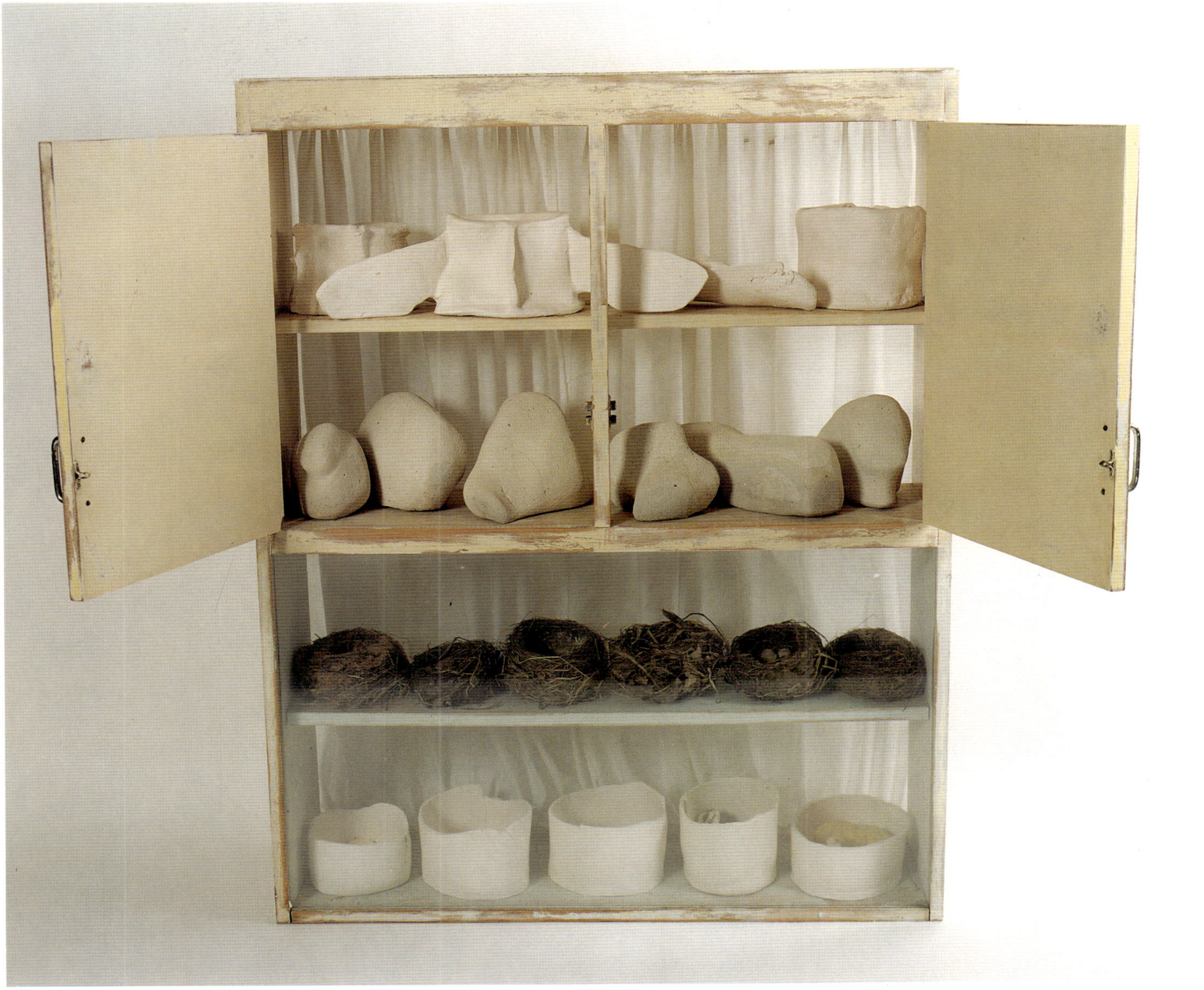

42

JOHN HURRELL

Born England 1950.
Came to New Zealand 1951.
DFA, UC 1974; BA 1975.
Lives in New Plymouth.

Hurrell is one of New Zealand's first conceptual artists (cf. Billy Apple 100NZP, 3). Between 1978 and 1980 Hurrell was an abstract painter, working his own permutations on the geometry of the grid (cf. Scott, 100NZP , 80). Snatches of buried colour appeared as the grid was adjusted slightly — a feature which was to appear in very different work five years later. In 1980–81 Hurrell adopted a procedure used by several other conceptual artists: prescribe a formula for some activity and then follow it. He worked with maps, most of which were whited out in accordance with a principle unique to each work. The map thus ceased to work as a map and became self-referential.

In 1981 Hurrell became one of the first of a new wave of New Zealand artists taking an interest in text, an area pioneered in New Zealand by Colin McCahon (100NZP, 50) but more recently the focus of much philosophical thought overseas. Hurrell's way with words was to assemble them out of pasta alphabet-soup letters. He lined the text up in paragraphs and glued them down onto boards, then coated them with many layers of white acrylic and satin-finish varnish until they became embedded in a translucent skin. The finished works were lovely to look at, with a silky, honey-coloured surface. However, their only content was the blocks of text, readable with difficulty, the words half submerging in the polyurethane. A viewer making the effort found that the texts were quotes from critical writing about art published in the press. It soon became obvious that the artist (himself an art critic) considered the quotes to be trite, glib and unworthy of preservation. Yet he had preserved them — in irreverent but durable material. Like flies in amber the words were trapped; drowned, perhaps, in a soup of superficiality. Hurrell challenged the writers to pit their worth against his in the test of time. If future viewers of his art think that the preserved writings are profound, the laugh will be on the artist.

In another series of map works, begun in the mid-1980s, Hurrell took large-scale maps of the streets of Christchurch and then copied onto them linear images taken from contemporary German and Italian figurative paintings and other sources. Where lines in the overlay touched or crossed streets on the maps, those streets were retained, but all the rest of the sheets were blacked out. The outline of the copied form appeared, but fantastically elaborated by twisting, multicoloured, hairy lines, each one extended to the literal end of the road. The result was a foreign form symbolically imposed on a local landscape In a further reference to cultural dislocation, the artist titled the works with the latitude and longitude map references of European restaurants found in Christchurch. Once one discovers the basis for the works, the blacked-out areas themselves become important. The ink is on top of the maps, but creates a void. Most of the city, though still there, has become a black background to the artist's work. Is this a description of the practising of art in New Zealand? The map works have continued with deceptive 'self-portraits' and works in which the lines delineate boundaries rather than create hairy apparitions.

Self Portrait I, 1993
Rubber latex and India ink on maps
1960 x 1580 mm
Courtesy of the artist

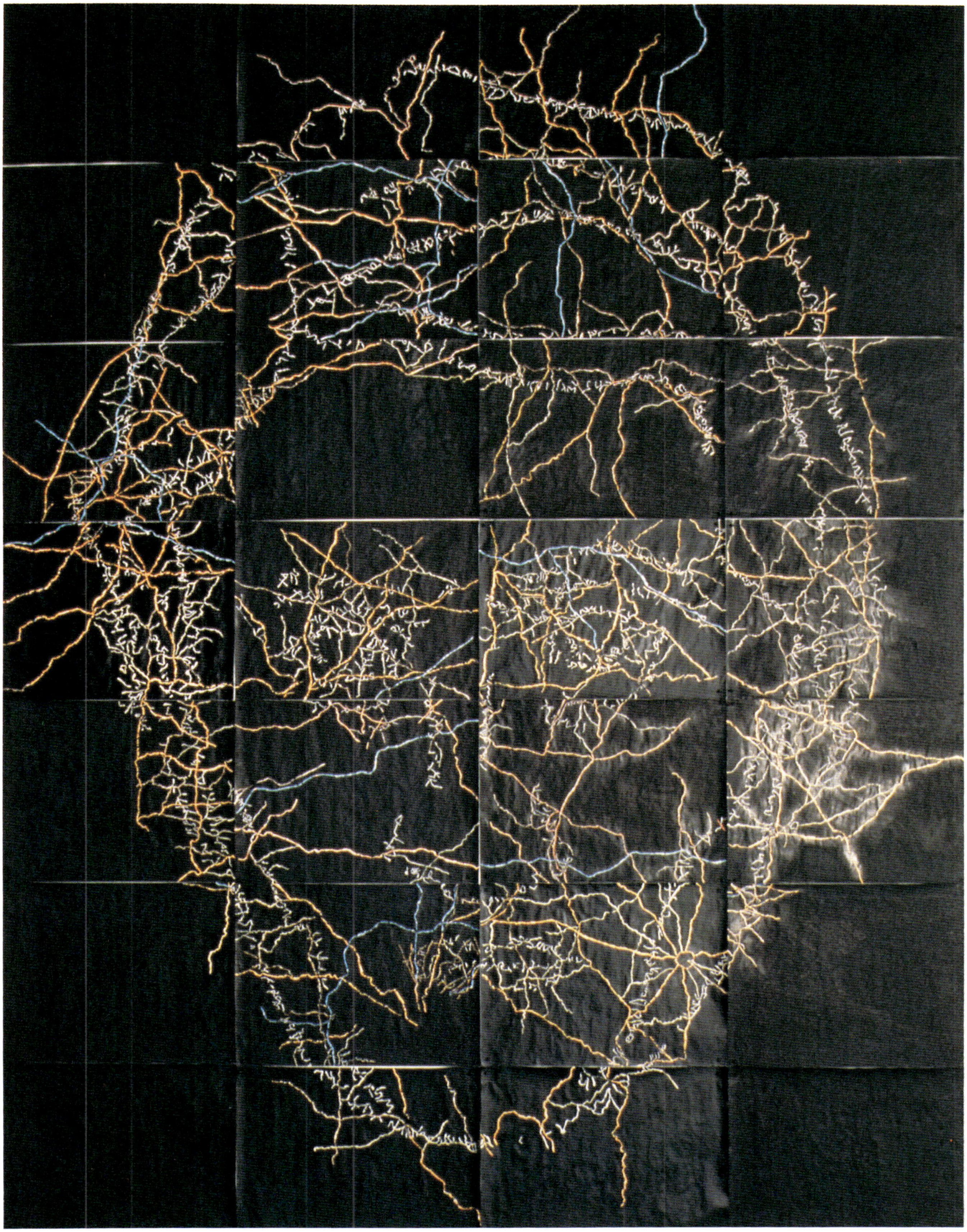

43

ROBERT JAHNKE

Born Waipiro Bay 1951.
MFA, UA 1978; MFA (Film Graphics and Experimental Animation),
California Institute of Arts 1982.
Lives in Palmerston North.

Although his training was in design and film, Jahnke has become an important sculptor. His German/Samoan/Maori/Irish ancestry makes him a personification of the Pacific/European mix that is 1990s New Zealand. He is an advocate of biculturalism, but he is knowledgeable and concerned about past wrongs done to the Maori. His work has moved from an interest in the dynamics which arise from joining design and message elements from two cultures, to a more ironic and critical stance.

As a younger artist in the 1980s he absorbed the culture of his times and created exciting work of his own by advancing the ideas of others. He also led a flowering of creativity based on traditional Maori forms and techniques, but reworked and made relevant to our multicultural society. His early sculpture had some similarities to that of Para Matchitt (57) and Ralph Hotere (100NZP, 37). From Matchitt came constructivism, carving and inlaying; from Hotere burnishing, burning and written elements. These references appeared openly, as quotes or points of departure.

Much of Jahnke's sculpture of the period 1988–92 called to mind eaves, weatherboard walls and church windows as well as storehouse fronts, palisades and spirit figures. Although all Jahnke's pieces at this time had a grandeur of overall design, much enjoyment was in the details. Metalwork; lead inlays; wirework; patina; glass rods; subtle, small-scale, half-erased paint details; and a particular feel for aged, weathered or oiled wood became the focus of attention. Scraping, incising, polishing, sandblasting, torchwork, sawing, hammering, painting, drawing and stencilling were evident. Complex relationships of numbers, symbols and words were built up, while multi-layered concepts underpinned everything. Like Te Kooti's meeting houses, built with a knowledge of European structures and incorporating joinery and tongue-and-groove linings, or Rua's appropriation of European symbols, Jahnke's works were hybrids, suggesting a culture beset by change but preserving its secrets. Some of his pieces were less like building facades and more like totems, tools or stylised weapons. He was making enigmatic, optimistic icons for a new society.

In 1993, with his *Second Reflection* works, Jahnke took the form of the Doric column — an imported symbol of wealth, power and law — and presented it supporting nothing and paired with a negative cut-out twin, its shape defined by a solid surround. Glass was used in some of these extremely elegant works, as well as roman lettering and numerals and Jahnke's other subtle marks and touches. They were metaphors for the shadow and the substance of promises to Maori by colonials and the double standards of their ethical systems, but they also incorporated the reversals found in Maori carving patterns. Similar works in 1992 had a pediment with Roman arch — a link with storehouse facades, but also a symbol for the weight of colonialism settling on the tangata whenua. *Con Version 3.33r*, 1994, was a solemn group of works sheathed in lead and featuring axes joined with symbols of church and state. Axes were used as barter for Maori land, but the unfairness of the deals has created many axes to grind. Remarkable works of 1995, involving aerial photography and using giant rubber stamps and pepper pots as symbols, have moved into neo-pop to make serious statements about integration and the contentious proposal for a 'fiscal envelope' to settle Maori land claims.

Preservation, 1994
Photograph, timber, steel, glass, copper patina, wood shavings
2400 x 800 mm (dimensions vary)
Courtesy Fox Gallery, Auckland

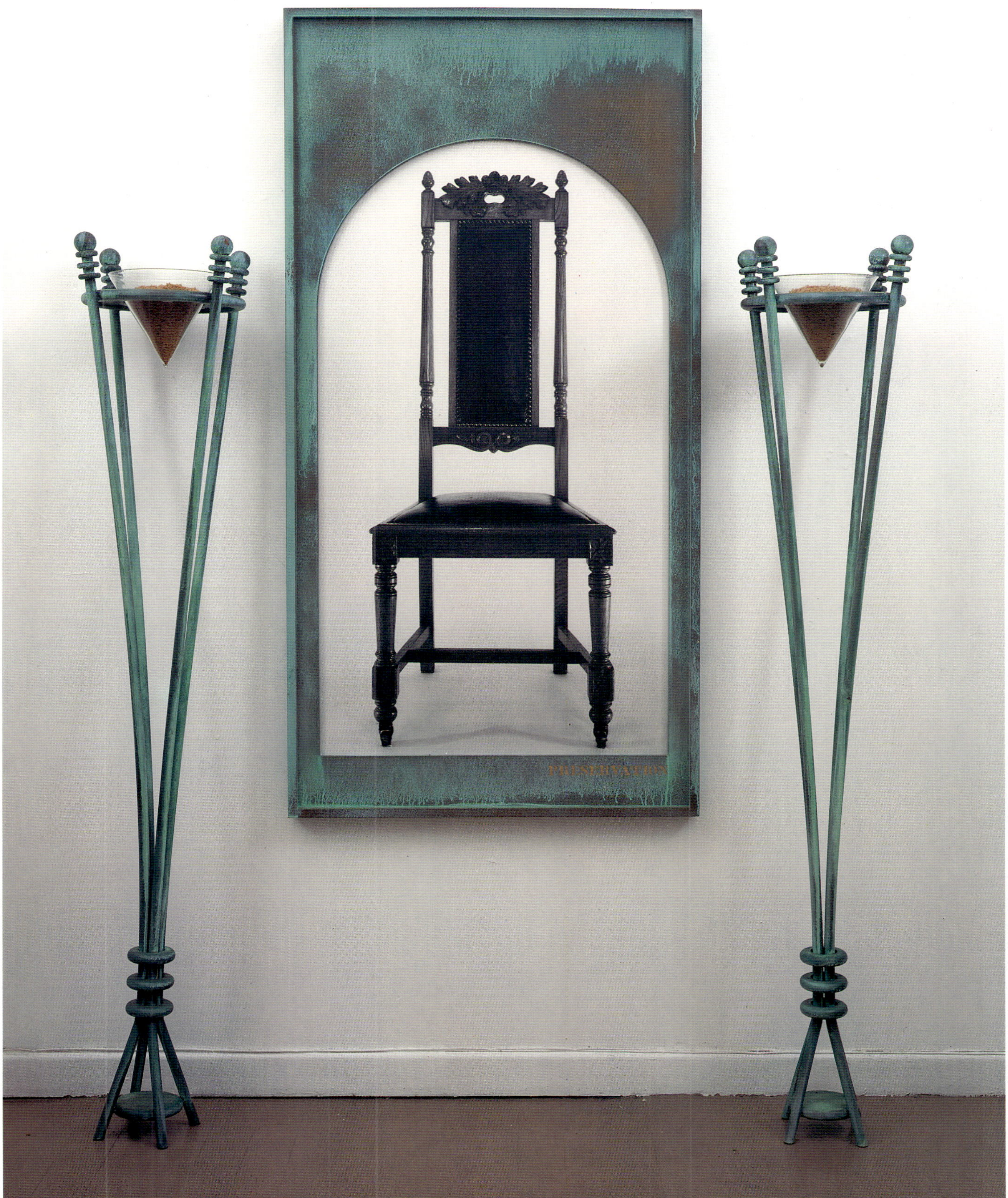
PRESERVATION

44

MEGAN JENKINSON

Born Hamilton, 1958.
BFA, UA 1980.
Lives in Auckland.

Jenkinson is a highly literate artist with an interest in the ancient classics, conservation, the nature of time and the position of modern women. She has always treated her photographs as the start, not the end, of the art-making process. On the other hand, her works contain only photographic material, and often stretch the flexibility of colour printing to the limit. Although the photo is celebrated for its ability to freeze time, precise dating of Jenkinson's work is pointless. Photographs taken over a period of 15 years form an image bank from which she draws when required. Her early work, done in the 1970s, involved hand-colouring, sepia toning and creative cropping. Since 1981 she has been using the cibachrome printing method. Photographs are taken with an eye to a concept worked out in drawings, then carefully cut up and reconstructed into elegant collages, some with three-dimensional elements. Leaves and flowers are frequently used. Offcuts are stored for possible future use. Many of Jenkinson's works have the look of museum displays or pages from a precious book. She works on them slowly, shifting and reworking them until everything is in balance. Her experience gained as a photo technician enables her to control the tonalities of the prints, often to obtain delicate autumnal colour. The immediate effect is always luminous and exquisite, but each work is rich in metaphor, mixing, interlacing and juxtaposing images. The original photographs are thus both refined and rendered more complex.

The contents of museum cases have often been photographed by Jenkinson, and the final form of some of her collages resembles them. She exploited the luminosity of cibachrome in her series *Rediscovering Galapagos*, 1982, with photographs of butterfly and snail specimens cut out and mounted on pins in a box, like the originals. As well as cutting out actual images, Jenkinson will cut out the shape of something from a photograph of something else, creating a new image in which truth and fiction are mixed. In her *Five Waters* series of 1987, images of drinking vessels were made from strips cut from photographs of the sea. The strips alternated normal views with views tilted up vertically, creating a spatial dislocation and a decorative effect such as one finds on cut crystal. Beyond that, the works were about the attributes of natural water and its malign aspects after interference by humans. The image of a vessel or urn has been used at various times since 1986.

In her *Virtus Moralis* series, begun in 1986, Jenkinson used herself as a model, transported into a dreamworld where classic myth mixed with twentieth-century reality, to make statements about the breakdown of traditional moral codes. The elegant, poised figure of the artist seemed like an angel of grace trying to bring order out of chaos. This series has been expanded during the last few years into 40 works in the *Virtues* series, to be issued in book form in 1996. As part of an overall classical referencing, Jenkinson has revived a partheon of goddesses, and uses Latin in her titles and imagery found in Roman decorative reliefs such as urns, ribbons and wreaths. The *Emblemata* series are illustrations of aphorisms in roman script which are inscribed on the works' mounts or embedded in the imagery.

In 1990 Jenkinson exhibited seven works in the series *Per Genus et Differentiam*. Each work showed two different things of the same type — chairs and shoes, for example — and in the nature of the differences lay complexities and subtle allusions.

The Crystallography of Refinement, 1995
Photo collage, ilfochrome
Installation of 7 framed works
ca. 2200 x 1600 mm
Courtesy of Jonathon Smart Gallery, Christchurch

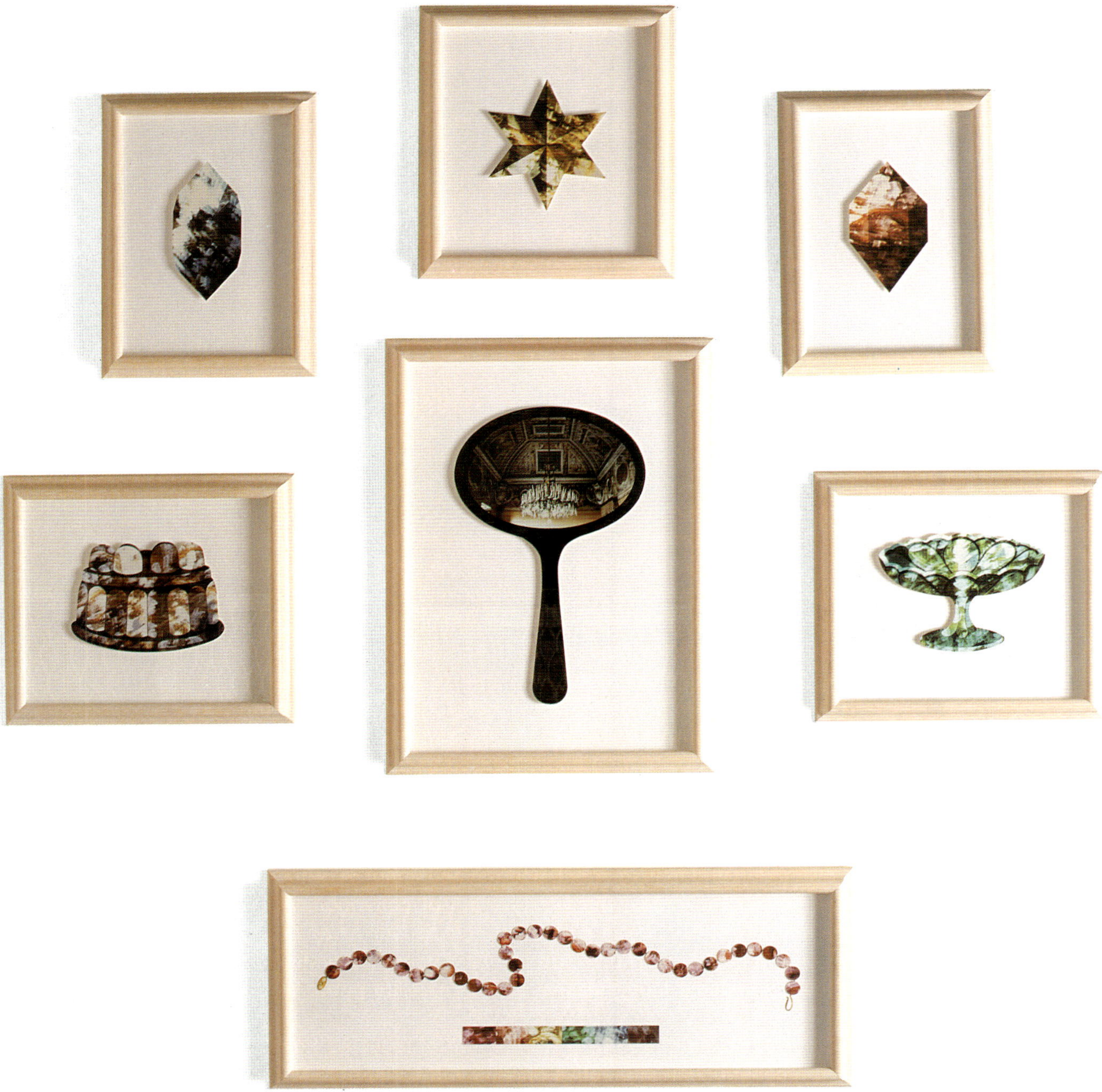

45

PAUL JOHNSON

Born Wanganui 1947.
BFA, UA 1972; BA, Nova Scotia College of Art and Design 1976;
Certificates in Teaching and Museum Studies 1975–82.
Lives in Wanganui.

Johnson is a sculptor, painter, photographer and assemblage artist. Much of his time in the 1980s was occupied with figurative ceramic relief sculptures, to which he returns occasionally, and steel and slate sculpture.

In 1988–89 Johnson was working with the environment in a manner similar to Pauline Rhodes (75). He painted an existing mooring structure in the Wanganui River bright orange, erected a fence made of orange plastic mesh along shallows in the river and unrolled the same material on a nearby beach, in each case documenting the work in photographs. At the same time Johnson made a series of simple but elegant table sculptures for exhibition in Japan, which could be seen as maquettes for large outdoor works. White or black columns supported curving coloured grids, and a graphic component on the base traced parabolas for movement.

In 1990–91 Johnson began making assemblages — elegies to the abstract expressionist painting style using found plywood, hardboard, tin and other sheathing materials. As with the work of Driver (30), Johnson's assemblages are carefully constructed, their regularity and formality of shape contrasting with the actual materials, which often introduce looser, gestural elements.

Harbour Entrance, 1991
Mixed media
800 x 600 mm
Private collection

Black and White, 1994, was an important exhibition with the painter Kura Te Waru-Rewiri: here a Maori female artist and a white male artist were joining forces to explore differences. Johnson's wooden wall reliefs were allegories of tentative cultural and spiritual encounters. Spiral forms found in Maori art were compared with Celtic stone reliefs to form a link between the ancient heritages of European colonists and Maori. The bar codes of modern western technology were compared to the stick charts of Polynesian navigators. Black and white was used in these works symbolically but not superficially. In *Aotearoa*, 1993, two cloud-like shapes, white above and black below, were held apart by manuka sticks. The lower form could be read as the mere shadow of the other, or as the solid earth propping up the lightweight upper form. Again, the sticks could be feelers, probing for common ground. By using plywood backgrounds for unshaped native woods, the artist raised the issues of colonial destruction of forests, exotic farm forestry, land ownership and management, and the economic benefits and detriments flowing from all these. Bar codes, the very symbol of commodification, portrayed by wobbly white manuka sticks, made a metaphorical as well as an actual overlay. The swirling grain on the background plywood signified ocean currents, and black-painted defects in the ply became land masses, as in a satellite photo of the Pacific Ocean.

The uniformly sized *Colonial Boxes* of 1994–95 were made of recycled building materials, which underwent reconstruction into votive objects in the cult of the home handyman. Several of the pieces partly deconstructed the reconstructions. In *Repairs/Maintenance* a 94 x 70 cm box was clad in unpainted, fake timbergrain weatherboards. One board had been damaged and repaired with real timber, the grain patterns matched but the join emphasised with green filler. *Rural Economy* was like a model of a rusty, corrugated-iron shed full of sacks, while *Hospital Cage* was a white box of truck tyre remnants, flapping like skittled magpies. Most recently Johnson has made a number of smaller assemblages on the theme of navigation and migration by sea.

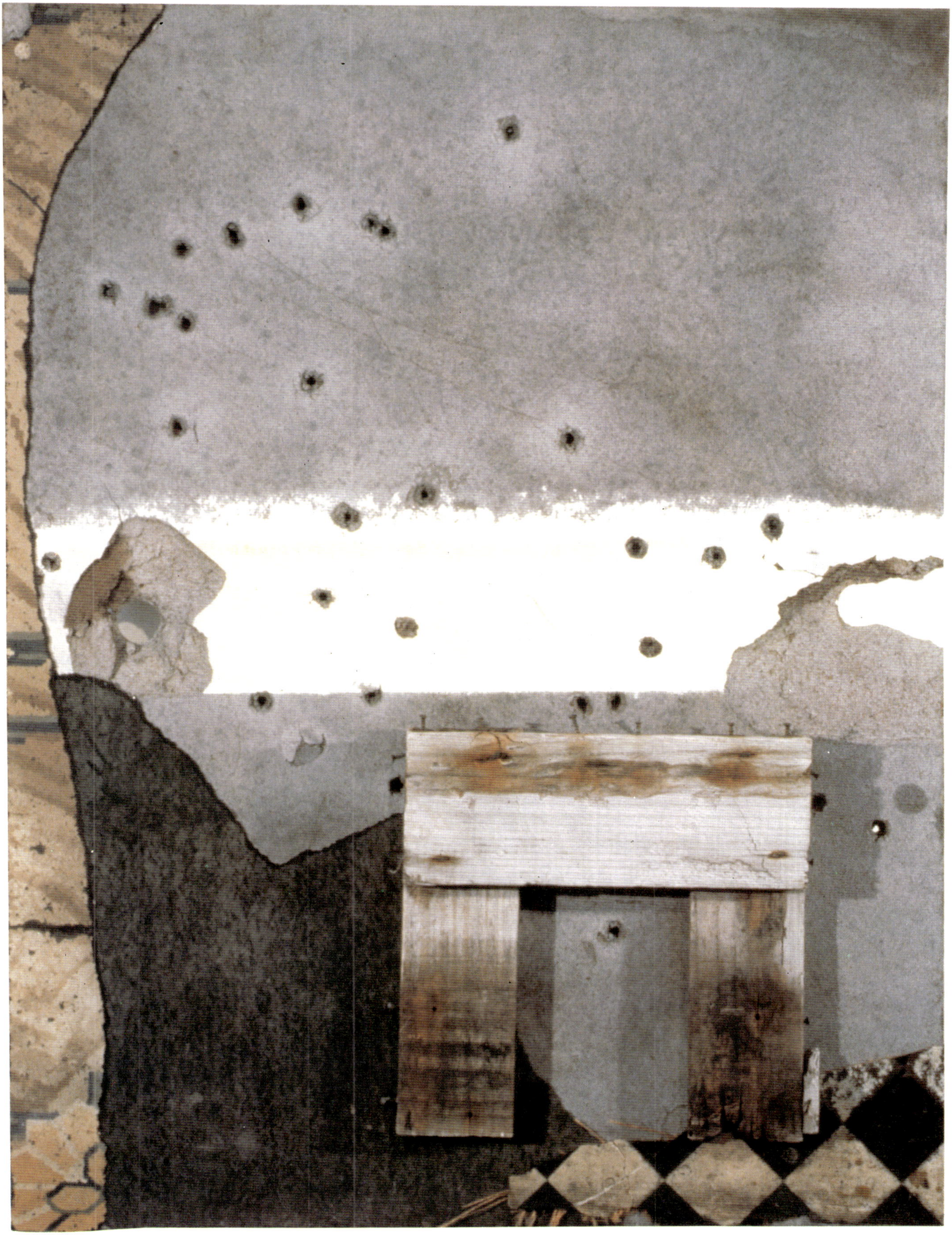

46

PAUL JOHNSTON

Born Christchurch 1949.
BSc, UA 1971; DT, Auckland Teachers College 1971.
Lives in Auckland.

Largely self-taught, Johnston is an artistic generalist, adept at drawing, design, woodworking, sculpture, photography and painting. Most notably, he has been an active printmaker for 15 years. In the *Floating Cubes*, his first series of etchings in 1981–83, he was interested in the depiction of three dimensions in two. The origins of these works were mathematics and Johnston's long-term interest in geometric fabric designs. He took this idea further in etchings and drawings where the cubes were cut out and folded to create shallow reliefs. After a trip to London during which he studied clothing and textiles in museum collections, Johnston produced *Samples, Fragments and Garments*, 1986–88, a suite of semi-abstract collographs and etchings. Garments and designs from Japan (where the artist lived as a child) and Palestine appeared in these works, some of which included cut-out and collaged elements printed from separate plates. Also in this series were a number of prints based on jackets, where aspects of the sea-going environment appeared as fine line drawings in the folds of the garment.

In 1986 Johnston made the first works in his *Arc of Visibility* series, concerned with the coastline of New Zealand and how we relate to it. Matters connected to clothing made their final appearance in a background of dress-pattern lines, which also read as plans for yachts and as navigation plots.

Johnston has developed a photo-transfer process which enables him to make etchings based on collages of his photographs. In some cases the image looks fresh; in others it has an old, faded and yellowed appearance. Since 1990 Johnston has produced a number of etchings depicting the Whatipu area, a wilderness of sand, huge rocks and rugged cliffs at the entrance to the Manukau Harbour. The bar offshore has seen many shipwrecks, and in his prints Johnston offers what seem like snatches of maritime history — corroded bits of metal, jetsam, grainy photos of rocks and sea, and glimpses of charts. Pictures of the curved ribs and planks of smashed longboats are juxtaposed with those of scallop shells which, in close-up, look very similar. Another series, *Negotiating a Difficult Passage*, 1993, used the backs of old floor tiles with their curving glue lines as the starting point for images that looked like greatly enlarged fingerprints. The works also had the linear quality of woodcuts, and evoked the rolling sweep of waves and the agglomerate rock of the pudding-shaped Waitakere hills. The tile impressions were lined up in horizontal sets with small overlaid photo-etchings of Whatipu, the whole becoming a semi-abstract narrative about a specific landscape, navigational sightings and the clash of sea against land.

In 1995 Johnston exhibited his first paintings, a diverse group of constructed, abstract works which introduced many ideas capable of further development. Narrative was eliminated to focus on symbols, but these still related to the markers and geometrical bearing lines used by coastal navigators. Vertical pole forms divided and interrupted the rectangular, horizontal-format paintings. A few of the paintings were just short, square posts hung vertically, the paint covering all visible sides. Wrapped and stuffed canvas, jute bindings and layered, multicoloured paint revealed in a myriad of tiny rectangular glimpses were features of the paintings.

Traces, 1996
Etching
460 x 350 mm
Courtesy Portfolio Gallery, Auckland

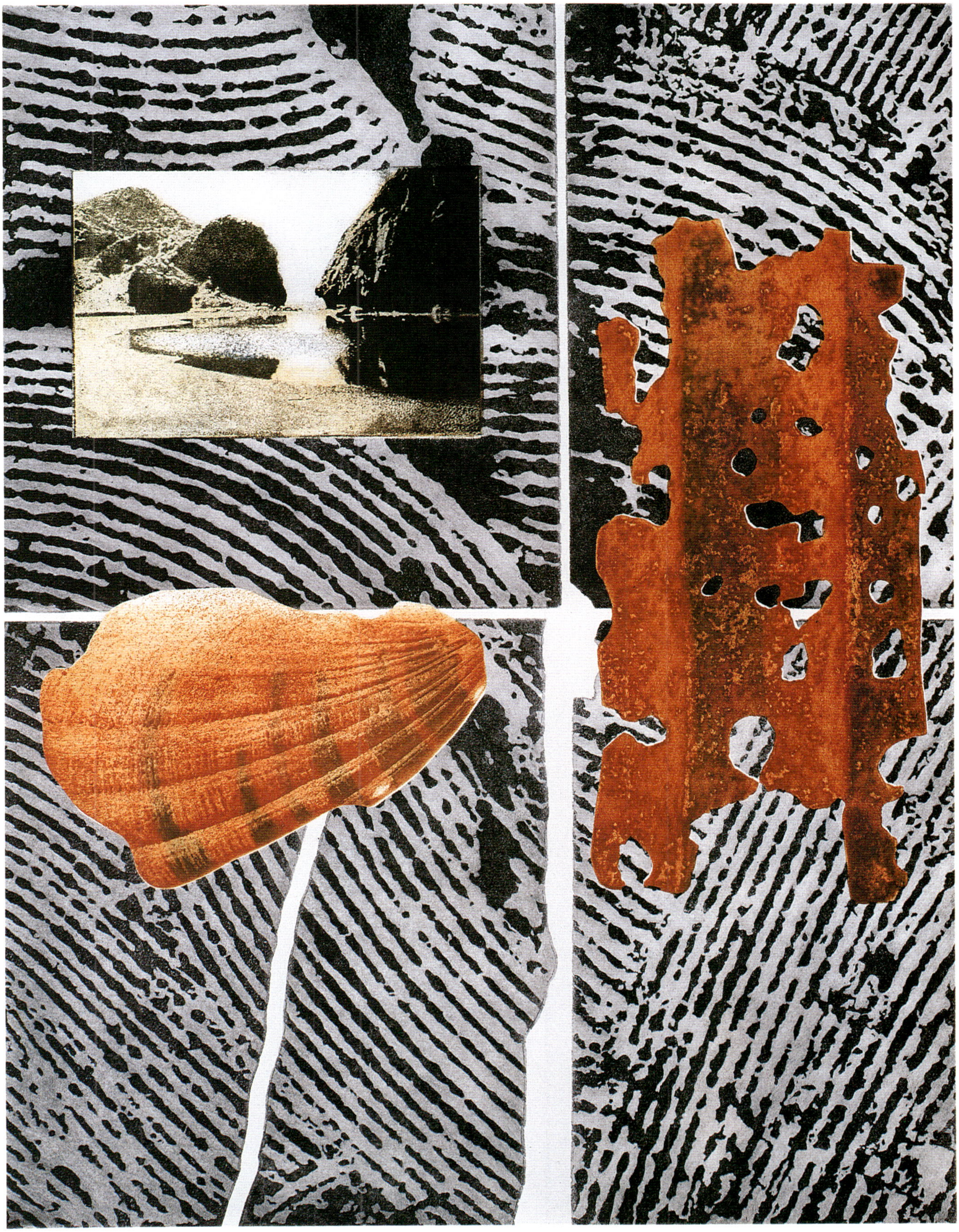

47

MORGAN JONES

Born Surrey, England 1934.
Came to New Zealand 1955.
DT, Christchurch Teachers College 1959.
Lives in Queenstown.

Jones is a dedicated constructivist sculptor (cf. Cullen, 22; Pine, 71). His work over 30 years, notwithstanding his use of basic materials, has been elegant and carefully considered. His sculpture is concerned with freedom and the liberation of the body to move wherever it pleases. Ladders and steps are incorporated into many works, because Jones feels that there is something exciting about ascension. Later works have used aeroplane forms to carry forward the ascension/journeying theme. The opposite of freedom, descent into confinement and oppression, is another of Jones's themes.

Between 1965 and 1975 Jones was carving tall wooden columns into semi-abstract forms with titles such as *Prisoner* and *Judge*. The forms were deeply indented to make small cell-like spaces. Jones notes the influence of Louise Nevelson at this period. In 1975 he took to sculpting in fibreglass and made a series of dynamic, abstract forms enamelled in primary colours. In 1979 Jones made a series of tactile wall reliefs using old harness leather, and this turned his attention to country matters. He switched to working in treated pine and corrugated iron, linking his work to the New Zealand landscape, both literally (several of his pieces are now on farms) and allusively, by mimicking stock pens, sheds and platforms. There was oblique reference to concentration camps, with their cheap construction, guard towers and prisoners herded like cattle (he visited Dachau in 1988). Major works made between 1979 and 1987 in this style include the large *Shelter*, 1981, standing out in the Mackenzie Country; *Natural Selection*, 1985, which referred both to farm races and the aspirations and mixing of races; and *Here and There*, 1986, which encouraged viewers via platforms and steps to an elevated, padlocked outhouse. On peering in a grille in the door one saw one's own reflection in a mirror. *Boom*, 1987 (now sadly destroyed), was a massive painted pine girder, like a section cut out of a railway bridge, supported by struts and crossed ladders on a stepped dais. In England in 1988 Jones made *Axis* in a forest clearing, a work in stone related to *Natural Selection*.

Since 1989 Jones has returned to making interior works and his style has become more diverse, sophisticated and complex, moving closer in feeling to that of British sculptors Caro and Cragg, and making more use of paint. He has abandoned the rural look, except for the use of plywood and finished pine. Curved forms have been introduced and some pieces have been wall-mounted. The *Flights* series of 1989 was modelled on segments of aeroplanes and the theme was uncompleted journeys. In *Escape and Flight*, also 1989, a skeletal wing form hung above works that were meta-phors for the journey through life to death. *Broken Journey*, 1991, showing a resurgence of the Nevelson influence, was a black column and half a pediment emerging from the wall, with small associated fragments. A related work of 1991 was the floor piece *Dreams of a Prisoner*, a black Greek temple surrounded by four ladders and wall reliefs. The stylish, richly allusive 1993 collection *In Search of Go(l)d* involved ramps, steps and yellow ladders. Lumps of stone sought to gain height on forms that suggested bullion vaults, skyscrapers or stepped river valleys. *End of the Line*, also 1993, was a group of buffer-like forms modelled on segments of steam-engine boilers, supporting five simulated railway line lengths: a reminder that a railway once ran through the gallery site.

Pumps, part of 'Escape and Flight' installation, 1989
Aluminium, Plywood, acrylic
1830 x 530 x 203 mm
Collection of the artist

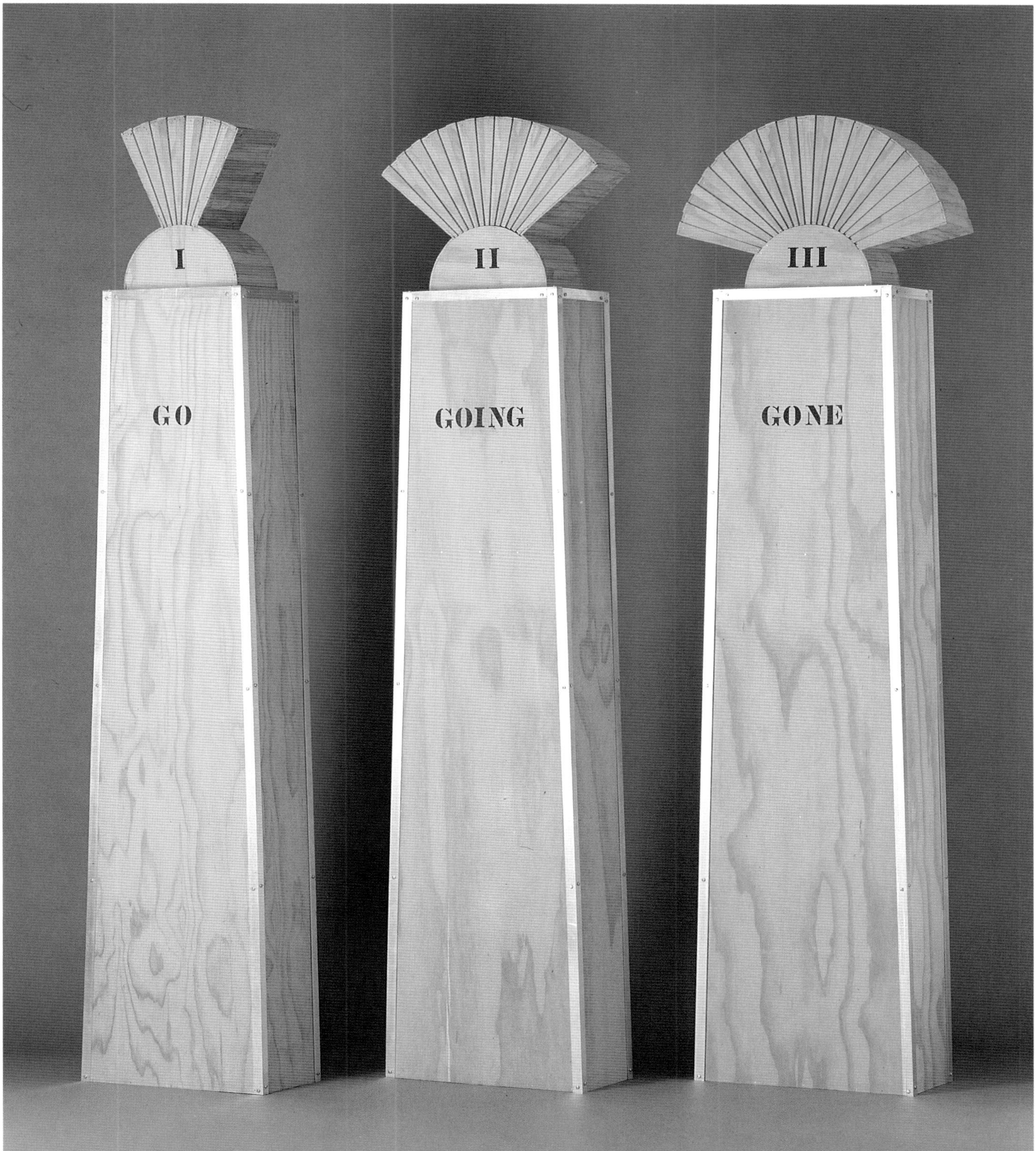
I
II
III
GO
GOING
GONE

48

VIRGINIA KING

Born Ohaeawai 1946.
Attended Elam Art School 1963–64.
Lives in Auckland.

After working in other art media for some years, King began concentrating on sculpture in 1988. Much of her work in stone, bronze and wood has been a response to the organic forms of nature — water, shells, fish, eggs, leaves and trees. Underlying it all has been a concern for the environment and an interest in the history and progress of humanity. King's work also brings to mind the ritualistic and totemic objects found among the cultures of tribal peoples.

From 1987 to 1990 King participated in the Western Springs stone sculpture symposia, hewing monumental columnar forms from Hinuera stone. Used by King in several versions is a free-standing, vertical form about 2 metres high. Tapering down to its base, it resembles a thin leaf or a large flattened urn, but these readings are denied by a hole in what the artist calls a 'tree of life' shape, cut out of the centre. Light falls through the hole, the sides of which are often coloured or gilded. Laid flat, a similar form becomes a paddle or leaf.

King uses demolition kauri in her work, reminding us of the history of this timber. In 1991, under the title *Matter and Spirit*, she exhibited blocks of wood with plaster heads lying beside and on top of them. In 1994 the artist looked back to the felling of the kauri forests of the Auckland district, an act of vandalism which destroyed a unique environment. King made a raft-like form, about one-seventh the scale of the kauri rafts used to float the timber down the coast to the mills. The elements were joined together with hempen cords smelling of Stockholm tar, and each length of timber was engraved with gold-painted words. A smaller version of this using old piano keys was designed to float, as were other works of 1995. King's bronze wall pieces of 1994 were inspired by the structure of leaves and cross-sections of spiral shells. So, in King's work the structures found in nature and the human presence in the landscape are combined in a way that makes us think about forms that are produced in the process of survival.

Table sculptures in the form of wooden-leaved books or altarpieces are another area of interest for King, relating to the books the artist was making back in 1984. Using leather for hinges, and gold leaf, paint, printing and other effects, she creates graceful but mysterious artefacts. In 1995 she explored the potential of the negative and positive spaces resulting from the cutting out of shapes from a slab of wood. The perforated, solid unit could be suspended on wires above water or hung so as to cast shadows on a wall. The cut-out pieces could be laid on the floor or floated on water, or grouped into circles, raft or leaf shapes.

King has always had an interest in poetry, inscribing passages on parts of her sculptures. In 1995 she assembled groups of the wooden letters used in bronze casting to make sand moulds. These were floated on water in a leaf shape, symbolising both the coming together of meaning in the poet's association of ideas and the poem's potential to take on a life of its own.

Phantom Canoe, 1995
Macrocarpa, acrylic paint, beeswax and damar resin
3490 x 580 mm
Collection of the artist

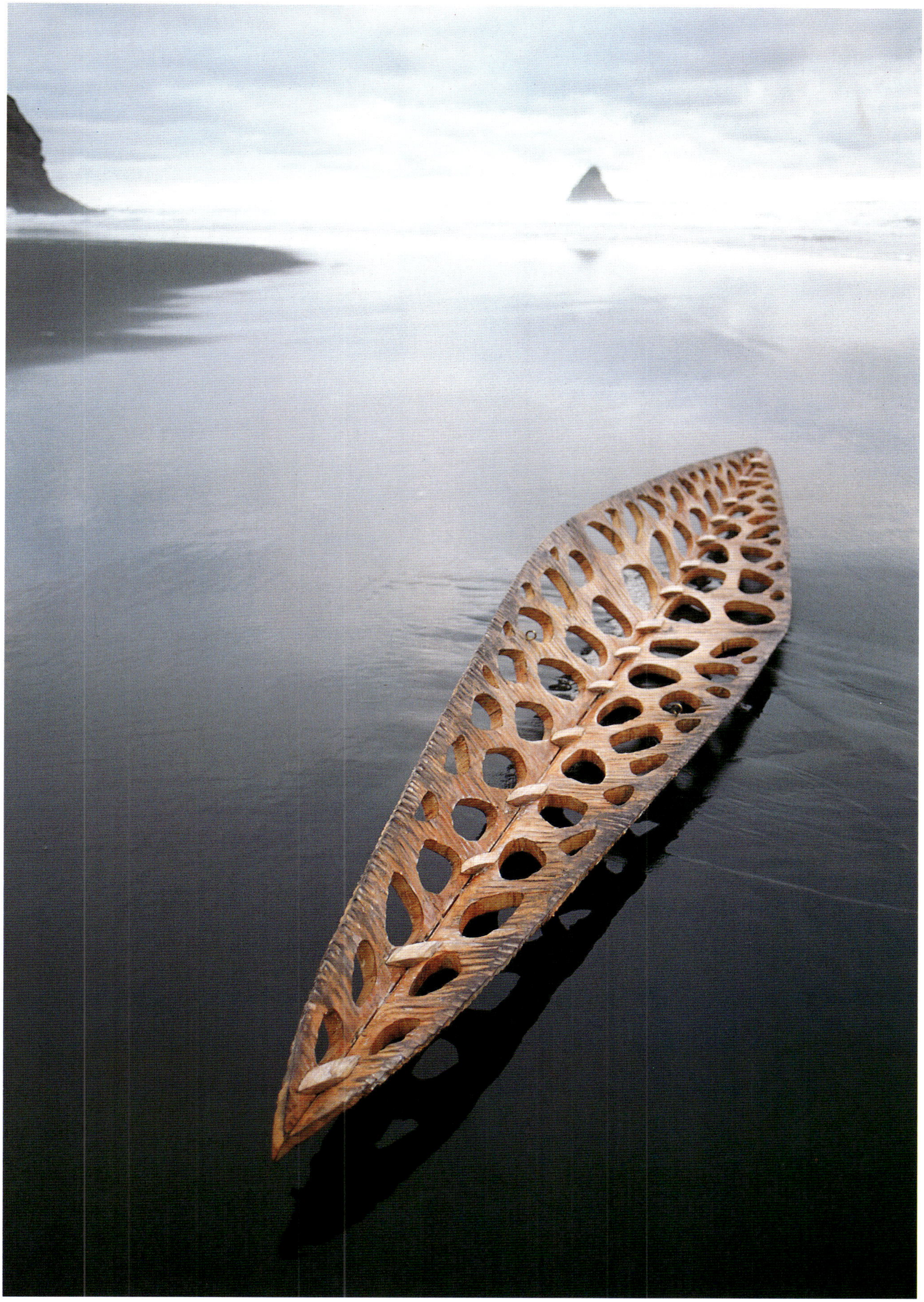

49

SIEGFRIED KÖGLMEIER

Born East Berlin 1953.
Came to New Zealand 1983.
Lives in Dunedin.

Köglmeier's art has mainly been about his involvement with his environment, whether that be a derelict factory, a forest clearing, a beach or an art gallery. By manipulating things found there, making marks, or building an installation by adding handmade objects, he changes the space and the way other people relate to it. Some of the things he has done have been seen by only a few people before being changed or lost in the flow of events, but the sincerity and originality of his ideas remain in photographic documentation of his activities. One example among many, *Build-ups* of 1988, shows clearly that Köglmeier is an artist of uncompromising dedication. It filled the whole of a sizeable Auckland gallery, and yet, from another point of view, it did not exist. Over a period of years the artist had painted an abstract picture; repainted it 500 times; photographed it at each stage; and then cut it up into pieces of the same size as the photographs. Evenly spaced and pinned on the wall, there were enough rectangular bits and photos to fill the gallery.

A sense of order underlies most of Köglmeier's large installation works. Multiple units are arranged on floor or wall in evenly spaced shapes such as circles, rectangles and fans. One series, done in several interior and exterior installations around New Zealand, imitated the effects of magnetism, an invisible natural force. Köglmeier used large numbers of short, pointed, red sticks which, like swarming compass needles, aligned themselves with imaginary 'lines of force' designed by the artist to energise the particular space. These radiated out from a column, entrance or other point. In a 1988 Hamilton arrangement, the flow of the nearby river was echoed as the sticks, like a flotilla of ships, bunched up and swirled around two columns. The use of sticks dates back to one of Köglmeier's first works done in New Zealand in 1983, when he collected and symmetrically laid out driftwood on a Taranaki beach. Other elements used in floor installations include miniature models of the tetrahedons used in breakwaters. In a 1990 piece, Köglmeier reversed the tetrahedrons' role, forming them into a red wave which battered a black wall.

Central, 1988
Painted wood elements
Variable dimensions
Temporary installation, Wellington

Some works have more specific themes than others. In *Exodus*, 1989, Köglmeier built a low wall of red blocks fabricated from scrim. The top few tiers were knocked off in one direction as if by an explosion. Some distance from the wall the scattered blocks began to turn into black eagles, which then flew off into the 'space' of the far wall of the gallery. The work referred to the fall of the East German Wall and the resulting liberation of the people's spirits, but also to the spectre of recurrent Nazism. By limiting his colours to black, white, red and the occasional touch of gold, Köglmeier not only reaffirms his German heritage but also links back to the alchemists who, like him, manipulated basic materials in the hope of achieving magic transformations.

Köglmeier has also done numerous suites of abstract paintings and finely detailed drawings, and has filled notebooks with sketches of remarkable concepts which have regrettably not yet been realised.

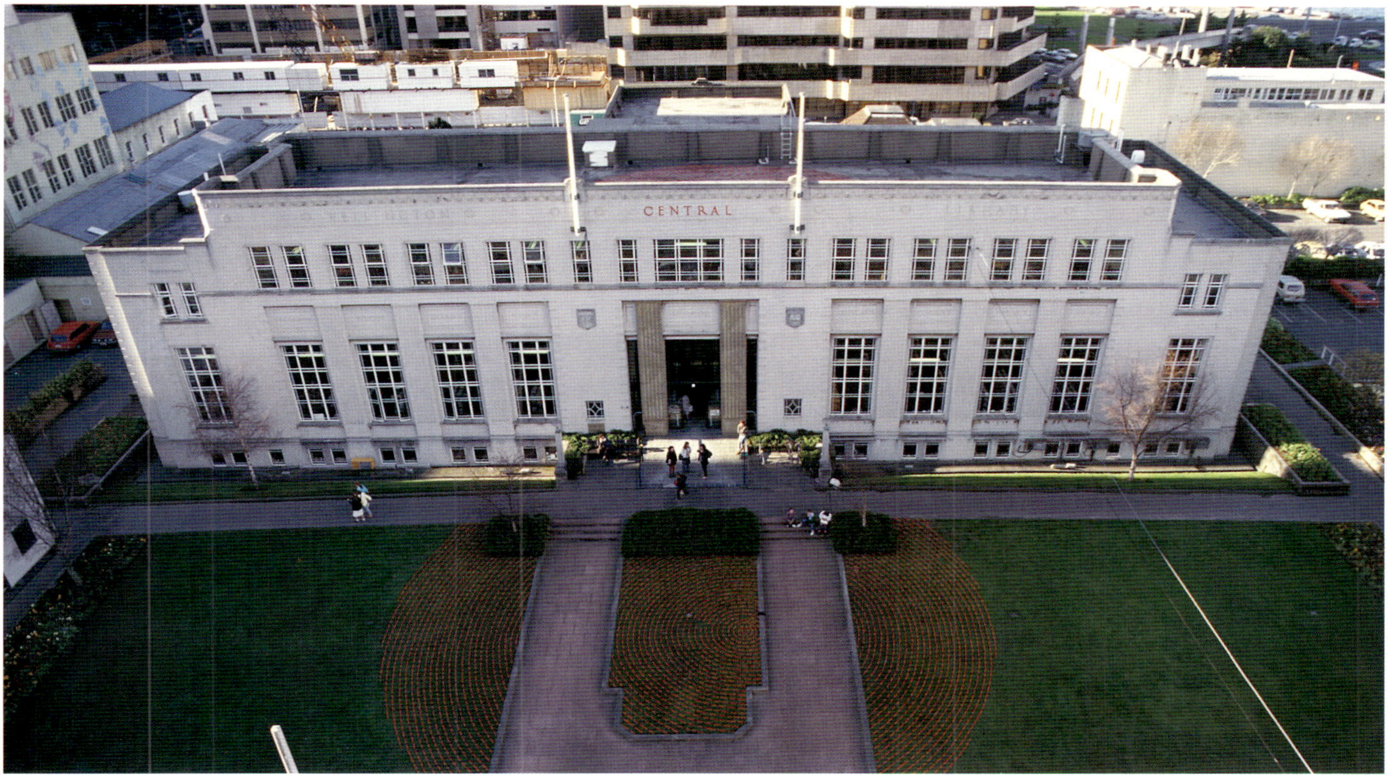
CENTRAL

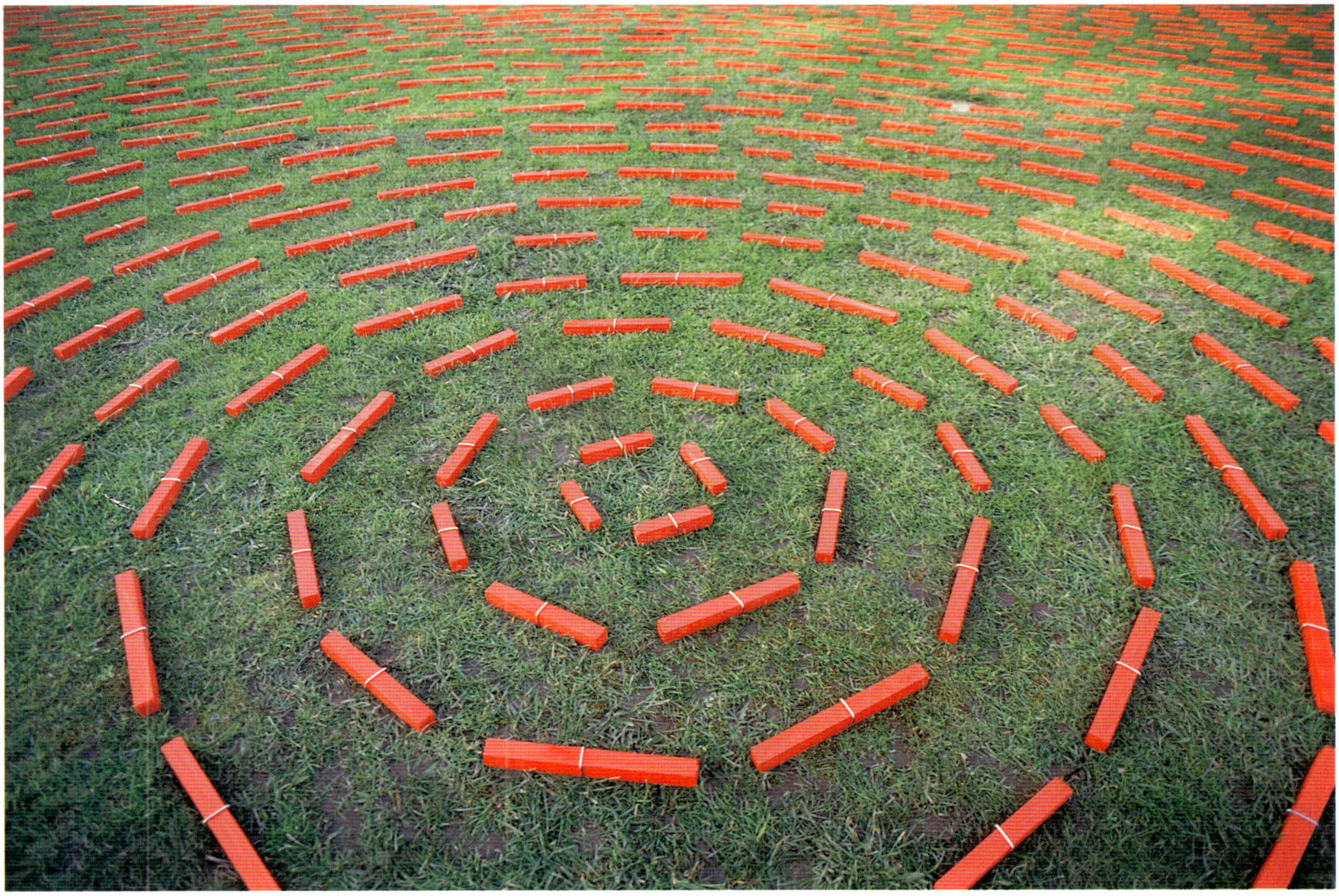

50

DENISE KUM

Born Auckland 1968.
BA and BFA, UA 1992.
Lives in Auckland.

Kum has been accused of putting things in art galleries and, in effect, challenging the public to deny that they are art. It must be admitted that the materials she uses are not conventional. Lists are tedious, but in Kum's case almost a necessity if her art is to be described. She has worked with honey, beeswax, sugar, toffee, rice, water, fungi, dried beancurd, soy sauce, ducks' feet, seaweed, sharks' fins, wire, glass, stainless steel, oils, vaseline, industrial plastics, heat, light and smell. Processes and transformations with and in these materials are part of what her art is about. She has said, 'I prefer working with the essential stuff of sculpture, the qualities inherent in and of the materials. I find out by working on the pieces their potential and possibilities, rather than imposing enforced or preconceived ideas.' Kum is also in the business of generating questions. Many of the materials listed above are consumables, but after passing through Kum's hands they cease to be so, except as art. Consumables become untouchable and the mess they make calls for a clean-up. Who is to do this? Is this a critique of cooking, the burden of women? Is the 'waste' of the consumables really a waste? Are other types of art really just consumables masquerading as collectables? Then there are queries as to the nature of the materials used. New toffee looks like plastic; blown and pulled glass can look like vaseline, as can molten plastic dropped into water. There are art history references: Kum's messy ingredients often separate out in layers like a Rothko or McCahon painting. She often uses multiple units, such as sets of lights or trays of food, calling to mind Bill Culbert (21) and Carl Andre. Finally there is a metaphor for the dangers of science coupled with a dig at B-grade horror films.

Kum's work was distinctive at art school exhibitions, with off-putting jars and tanks of scummy yellow fluids looking like abandoned biology experiments or an old chemistry storeroom. In her work *Suite* of 1992, she cooked/overcooked 36 slabs of toffee to varying degrees. They were then left to deliquesce onto the floor. In 1993 and 1994 she used heat-lamps, normally employed to keep freshly cooked food warm, to keep it warm for days until it rotted and dried out. All of this can be seen as a metaphor for human life (cf. Jones, 47), but equally as a deliberate and experimental pushing of art boundaries.

Kum broke through gallery boundaries in 1994 in Christchurch by mounting a photographic exhibition on the shelves and amongst the stock of a Chinese supermarket. More recently she has been using glass and plastics in association with vaseline to make strange, repetitive shapes. Some of these are blobs tapering off to a wisp at the top; others are twisting, writhing forms like high-speed photos of turbulent water. In any group show Kum's work remains distinctive, and ultimately it is here that her contribution lies. Thanks to Dada, happenings, Flux art and, particularly, the work of Beuys, consistent performance of unusual activity has become acceptable as art. It is outside the norm, it challenges accepted practice, it has a cleansing effect (even if it makes a mess). The one requirement is that it must have style (cf. Budd, 7), and Kum's work has that. In particular, her choice of materials from Chinese supermarkets has been an ironic personal cultural reference.

It is perhaps a little early to evaluate Kum's work fully, but she is building an international reputation. She is also an expert film and TV make-up artist.

Thermo, 1995
Ethylene vinyl acetate, tint, dye, powder, petrolatum, glass, solder, metal trolley
2000 x 800 x 380 mm
Courtesy of the artist

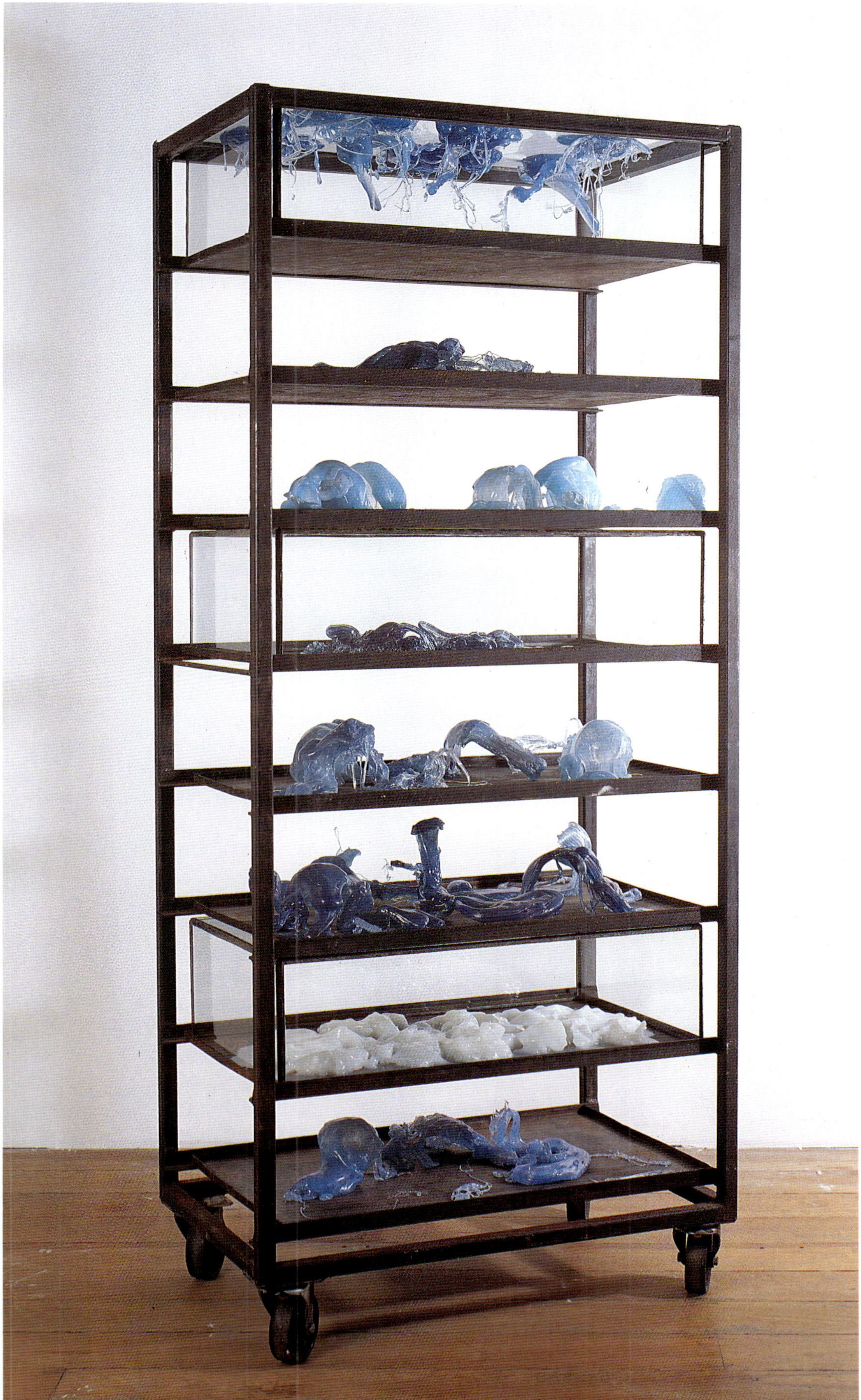

51

MARK LANDER

Born Napier 1955.
DFA, UC 1977.
Lives in Oxford, North Canterbury.

Lander works with handmade pigments and paper, and these give his art a distinctive quality. After experimenting with various modern art styles, by 1984 Lander was working with commercial fluorescent paints, doing large, free-form paintings on hessian and canvas which used a lot of material. He became concerned about both the cost and the toxicity of his paints, and his thoughts turned to the working methods of primitive artists. He began experimenting with natural clay pigments and, later, with handmade flax paper. Working hard over a period of four years, he developed the materials that he has used ever since, although he sees the learning process as ongoing. Coloured clays, found in roadside cuttings and diggings in the Canterbury district, are dried, ground, sifted and mixed with PVA to form archivally sound paints. Much of Lander's imagery is loosely based on the landscape and so imagery and pigment blend in his work. The subdued, subtle range of hues that he obtains is surprisingly large — blues, oranges, mauves, dull greens, umber, red ochre and pinks. Lander scrubs and layers these into his textured papers, creating dynamic and colourful works that are lively without being strident. To replace rag paper and canvas, the artist has found flax paper to be an exciting medium for light and texture. It can be gossamer thin or hard as cardboard, smooth, or crunched and wrinkled. In addition to sheets for domestic-scale art, Lander can make very large pieces of this paper for use in stage settings and gallery installations. The wrinkled paper can be lit to emphasise the texture with dramatic effect, or lit from the front or back to change the look of a drop completely. In installations, the papers are hung freely like long banners to articulate space, and in association with natural materials such as stones, sticks or leaves. So, by ceasing his reliance upon imported art material, Lander has been liberated as to the quantity and size of the pieces he produces. He has also found a comforting sense of place and completeness, and feels self-sufficient and free of overseas influences.

A typical work by Lander will resemble a coloured-in drawing. He delineates forms in bold lines, with occasional dashes and cross-hatching, and then applies colour to the areas enclosed by the lines. Images may include dancing figures, trees, birds, fish, stylised hills, rivers, waves and clouds. Most works have an irregular patterned border, creating an internal frame. His work shows the influence of Klee, with the addition of a little funk and whimsy, and zig-zags drawn from tapa cloth designs. The results resemble some of Chilcott's work of the late 1970s (100NZP, 13), but Lander's colour is more subdued than Chilcott's, and the tapa-like texture of his papers gives his work a distinctive Pacific feel.

Lander has been developing this style for 12 years with freshness and originality. Although his work is decorative and angst-free, it is never formulaic and is always interesting and enjoyable. Lander also makes plates and vases decorated with motifs developed in the paintings.

The Bending Palm, installation view, 1993
flax paper and clay pigments
ca. 6.6 x 7m
Courtesy Robert McDougall Art Gallery, Christchruch

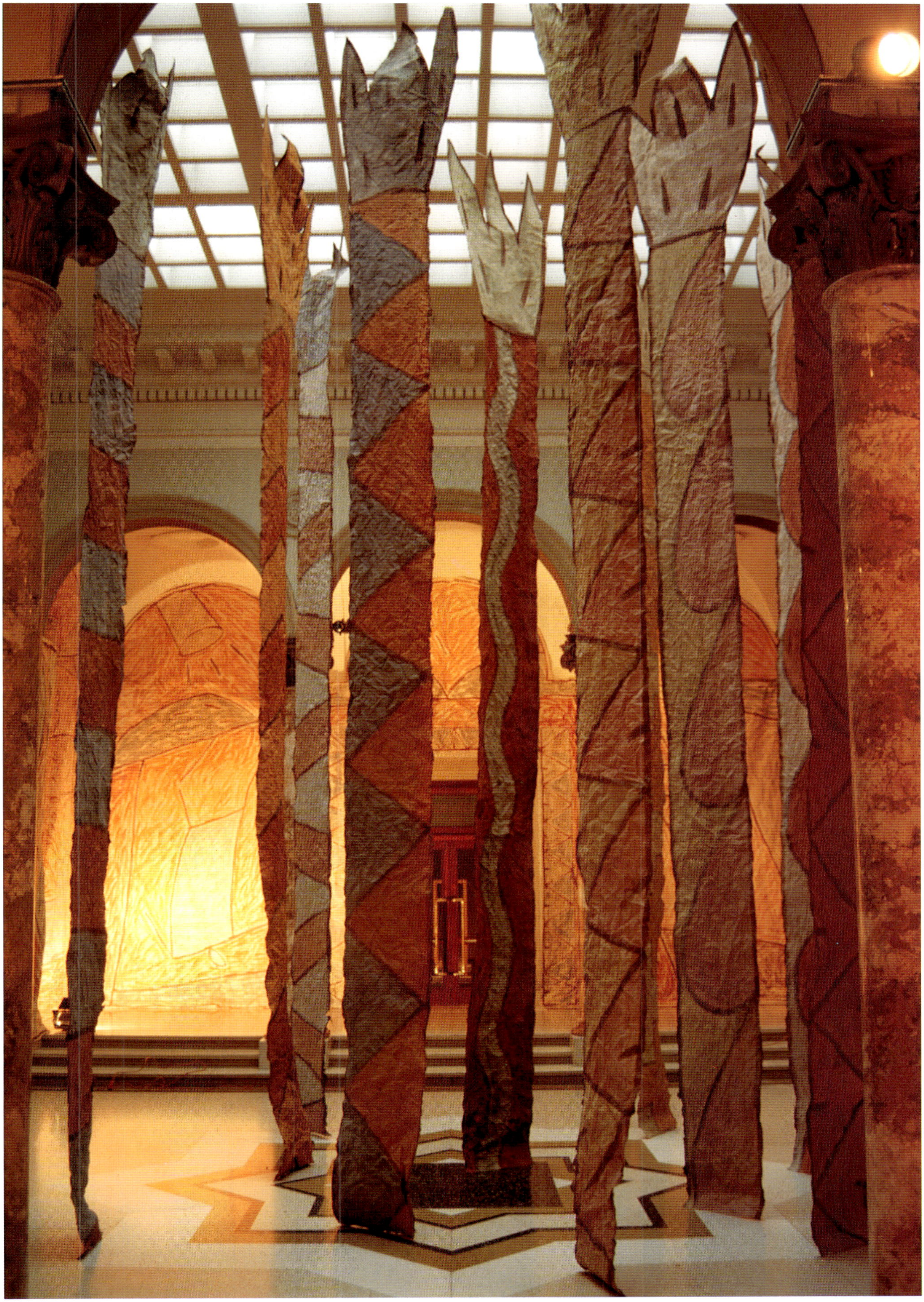

52

BARRY LETT

Born Hastings 1940.
DT, Wellington Teachers College 1960.
Lives in Auckland.

Lett's involvement with art has followed a circular path. He studied art in Wellington and Auckland, and more or less by chance became an art dealer in 1965, his name over the door of one of the country's leading galleries. His urge to be an artist was fuelled by this involvement, and in 1975 he retired from the gallery and began to paint. His first exhibited paintings were portrait heads delineated in bold simplified lines, and he then integrated these into decorative backgrounds. His painting activity culminated in the large mural that he executed at Nga Tupuwae College in Auckland in 1983. This admirably achieves its goal of bright, optimistic, Pacific multiculturalism. Lett encountered Maori carvers at the college and became interested in working with wood. Between 1984 and 1986 he made wooden reliefs, some wall-mounted and others free-standing. They were like huge, child-like drawings turned into wooden cut-outs. First came heads with wooden hair, then figures, then aeroplanes and clouds, then solid, flat wooden dogs. The aeroplanes were particularly effective, hanging in space like mobiles, paradoxically light and clunky at the same time, brightly coloured and joyous.

The dogs led to Lett's first stone sculpture. He covered a wooden dog with cement and embedded rounded river stones in this to produce a pebble-aggregrate pup. This was immediately popular, tying together several aspects of everyday living (toys, pets, ornaments and the fad for bringing the wilderness to town in the form of 'natural stone'). Between 1987 and 1990 Lett made many pieces using this concept, ranging in size from a life-sized four-year-old on a plastic bike to a mother-and-child group towering 3 metres high. The stone dogs appeared in many forms and colours, and there were women protectively holding birds and fish. Overall, this body of work has a surreal air. It is as if the tiny cells of which all living things are made have grown huge; it is a dream world of the artist's creation. One of the finest of the stone works was *Tree Forms* of 1991, two free-standing trees 3 metres high, the trunks stone-covered and the crowns made of jagged slices of granite.

During the period 1993 to the beginning of 1996 Lett was committed to duty as a househusband, caring for two infant children while his wife worked. Sculpture was impracticable and his thoughts returned to painting which retained a dimensional element. Subject matter, unsurprisingly, was domestic. He began with two wall relief works, rough portraits of his two children. These used sawn timber coloured with paint and crayon. The subjects, the naive forms and the media used delightfully evoke childhood. From there Lett went on to a series of assembled relief paintings on customwood. These sum up many of his ideas over the last 20 years, combining and balancing bright and subdued colours and simplified forms with decorative, fragmented backgrounds, and incorporating heads and figures.

Girl with Flowers, 1996
Painted wood and stone
1200 x 420 x 200 mm
Collection of the artist

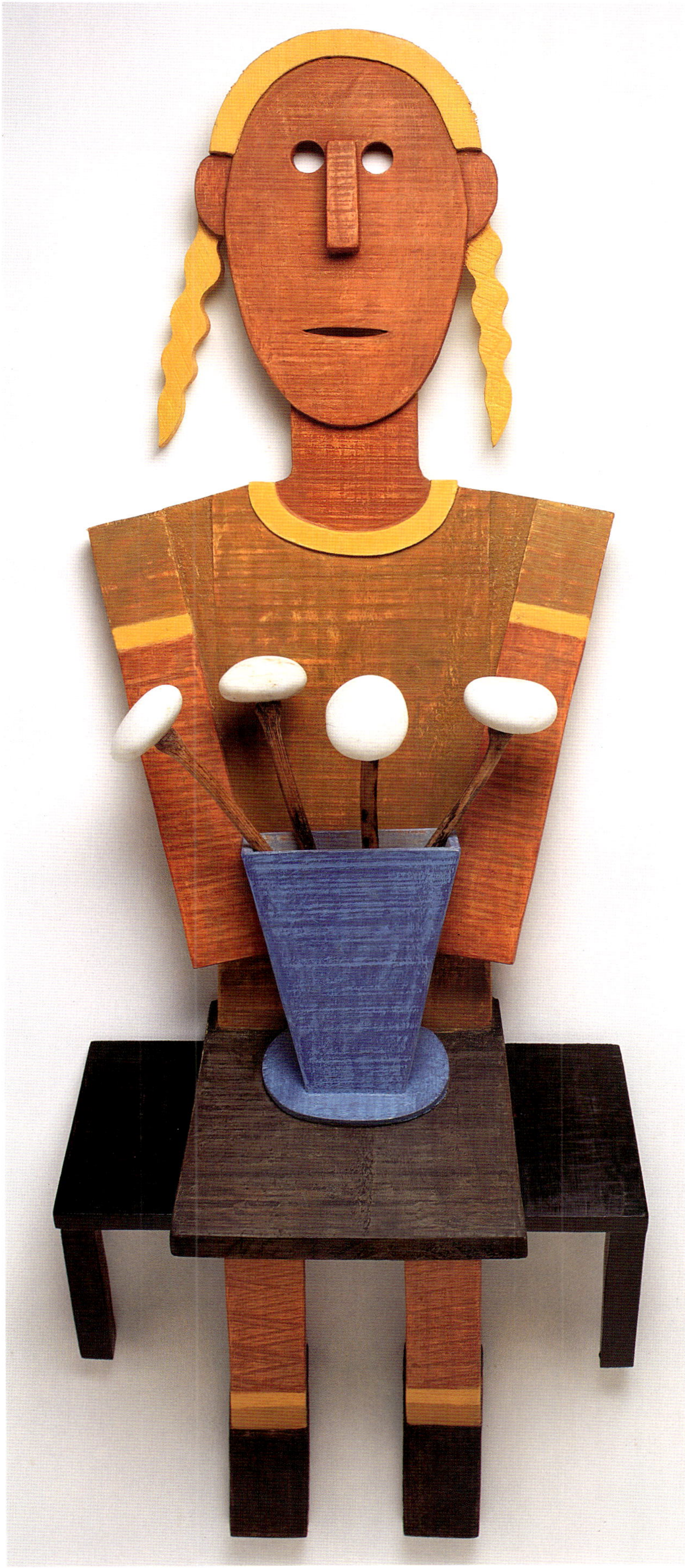

53

LEN LYE

Born Christchurch 1901.
Died New York 1980.

Len Lye did all of his important work outside New Zealand, so it could be seen as inappropriate to include him in a work on New Zealand artists. However, there are special considerations. Two major works were fabricated in New Zealand and acquired in 1977 by the Govett Brewster Art Gallery in New Plymouth. Lye bequeathed many of his sculptures, his archives, films and plans for unmade works to a New Zealand foundation which now acts as trustee for this internationally important material. The foundation has been active in arranging regular shows of Lye's works, and so his life's work has a living presence here. *Wind Wand*, an 80-foot-high fibreglass swaying pole, has been fabricated recently for a New Plymouth collector.

There is no doubt that Lye was one of the most important artists this country has produced. He was multi-talented and innovative. Arriving in London in 1926 after a stint living in Samoa, he was quickly accepted into avant-garde art circles and exhibited textile works and futurist constructions of tin, cardboard and wire, sadly all now lost. He had left New Zealand for Sydney in 1921 to learn about film-making, and in England made thousands of drawings for an animated film, *Tusalava*, which was shown in 1929. In 1935 he produced the first abstract, camera-less films ever made, by scratching into or drawing on the film stock. In the late 1920s he was one of the first western contemporary artists to take an interest in batik. From the 1920s onwards he did innumerable doodles and some drawing, printmaking and painting, working in a rather loose, spiky, Polynesian-influenced version of Mirò's style. He took a great interest in tribal art from his childhood on, and later formed a theory that art can spring from inborn 'memories', like the instinctive behaviour of animals. In another pioneering activity he was involved in experimental writing around the 1930s.

Apart from his films, the most enduring of Lye's works are his kinetic sculptures. Although he was attracted to the possibilities of making art out of motion very early in his life, and knocked together some moveable pieces while still a teenager, it was not until the 1950s that he turned from film-making to kinetic sculpture. What Lye did was to take out the gimmickry typical of such sculpture and replace it with grace and symmetry. Some of his works were restful, others weirdly sporadic, still others explosively noisy, almost terrifying in their power. Lye worked with high-tensile stainless steel, exploiting its light-reflecting qualities and flexibility when in the form of thin rods or strips. He made fountains out of bundles of rods held at the base and mounted vertically so the tops splayed out and swayed. He mounted strips, energised by electric motors and magnets, so that they rolled, shook or twisted, emitting sound either from their own twanging or from colliding with specially placed hammers. He also had truly monumental visions: of wand-like sculptures as high as tall buildings, of temples emitting huge electric sparks, of cities that were sculptures. Most of these remain as dreams only, but the Len Lye Foundation is committed to keeping alive the possibility of making some of the more practical plans.

Fountain, 1976
Stainless steel, motorised, formica base
5 x 5 x 5 m
Collection of the Govett Brewster Gallery, New Plymouth

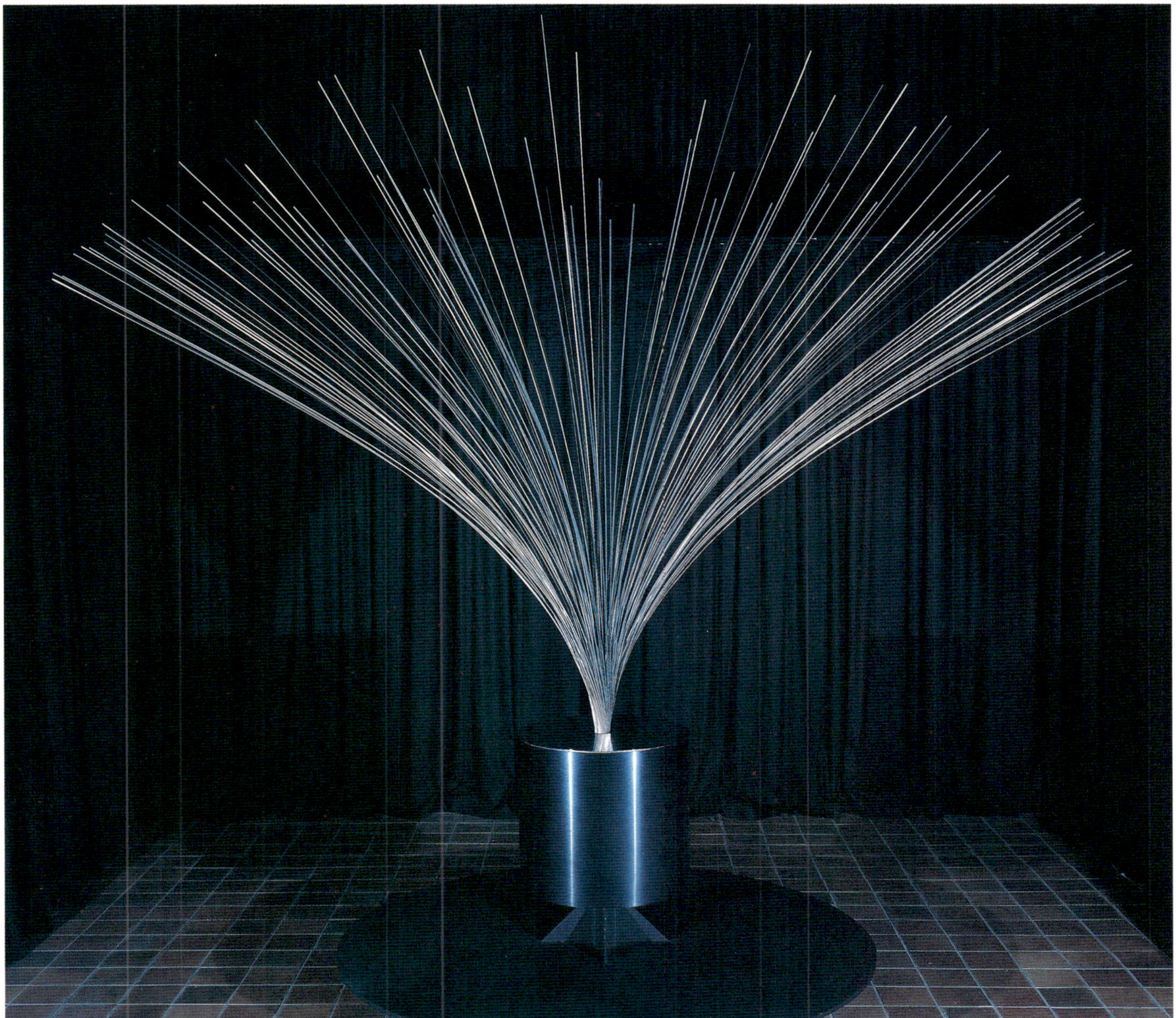

54

VIVIAN LYNN

Born Wellington 1931.
DFA, CUCSA of A 1952; DT, Auckland Teachers College 1954.
Lives in Wellington.

Lynn is a multi-skilled artist who has read and travelled widely. Her work over the years is diverse in several media, but each series of works displays consistency and the marks of craftsmanship and intellectual depth. In some quarters she is acclaimed for her screenprints, in others for her sculpture, and her recent work in collage and assemblage after a period of enforced inactivity has delighted many.

Lynn was one of the first New Zealand artists seriously to address feminist issues in art, and from the early 1970s this interest has continued, but with an awareness of the full social picture. Prior to 1972 Lynn was a painter of landscapes and made relief prints and etchings. Some of these called to mind the work of Klee, but in others, such as *Organo*, 1970 semi-abstract feminine forms dominated. Screenprints in the *Book of Forty Images*, begun in 1972, examined the ways society treated women — the expectations and constraints placed upon them in home, workplace and social institutions. It also touched on environmental issues, something the artist returned to in the mid-1980s and its use of quoted text foreshadowed the wave of text-based art of the 1980s. The six related *Playground* screenprints of 1975 attracted attention for the technical skill exhibited in their making as well as for their oblique statements about the brainwashing and manipulation of humankind by greed, politics and commercialisation. During the 1970s Lynn did a series of drawings critiquing cultural images, particularly the phallus, in order to develop a feminist semiotic. These, together with her more abstract *Asherim* drawings of 1984, represent this aesthetic.

In 1982 Lynn rang the changes again with her *Guarden Gates*, seven constructed sculptures in which human hair was woven into cyclone-mesh steel gates. The artist had complex motivations in making these works, which appeared to speak of the barriers erected to control and deter women's self-expression. In some cases women become trapped and helpless; in others they can use their skills (what men call wiles) to infiltrate the system, to get through. Lynn has used the powerfully evocative materials of hair and skin-like materials in much artwork since. The *Lamellae*, 1983, used paper to simulate both skin and tree bark. The pages of a large artist's book, *Threshold*, also called to mind aged, maculated skin. In 1986 Lynn installed a large *Goddess Gateway* at the Govett Brewster Gallery, using discarded tapa cloth and hair to comment on women's traditional labour. The artist referred to cross-cultural similarities, to trans-historical custom and to work by Mary Daly, *Moving into the wild realm of the prehistoric sacred*, where ritual is explored. A totemic column of hair with a woven face, *Caryatid*, was exhibited in 1986, and the *Intimate Connections* of 1995 were rough, stiff sheets of polyethylene with hair and beeswax. The left and right sides of these emblematic works were balanced, as in a Rorschach blot. A related series, *Your Mental Set*, used a concertina of paper to catch mirror-image blots in its folds.

The elegant *Drawing Connections* of 1986–95 incorporated many diverse materials, including mica, coral and copper, within a lustrous chequerboard — an echo of the grid device used by Lynn in the late 1960s. Her newest works are the *Baroque Drawings* of 1995, where Lynn presents desire masquerading in cultural icons, a continuation of the rigour of Lynn's thought over 25 years.

Baroque Drawing, 1995
Mica, pearls, silver, seeds, jet
590 x 590 mm (each piece)
Collection of the artist

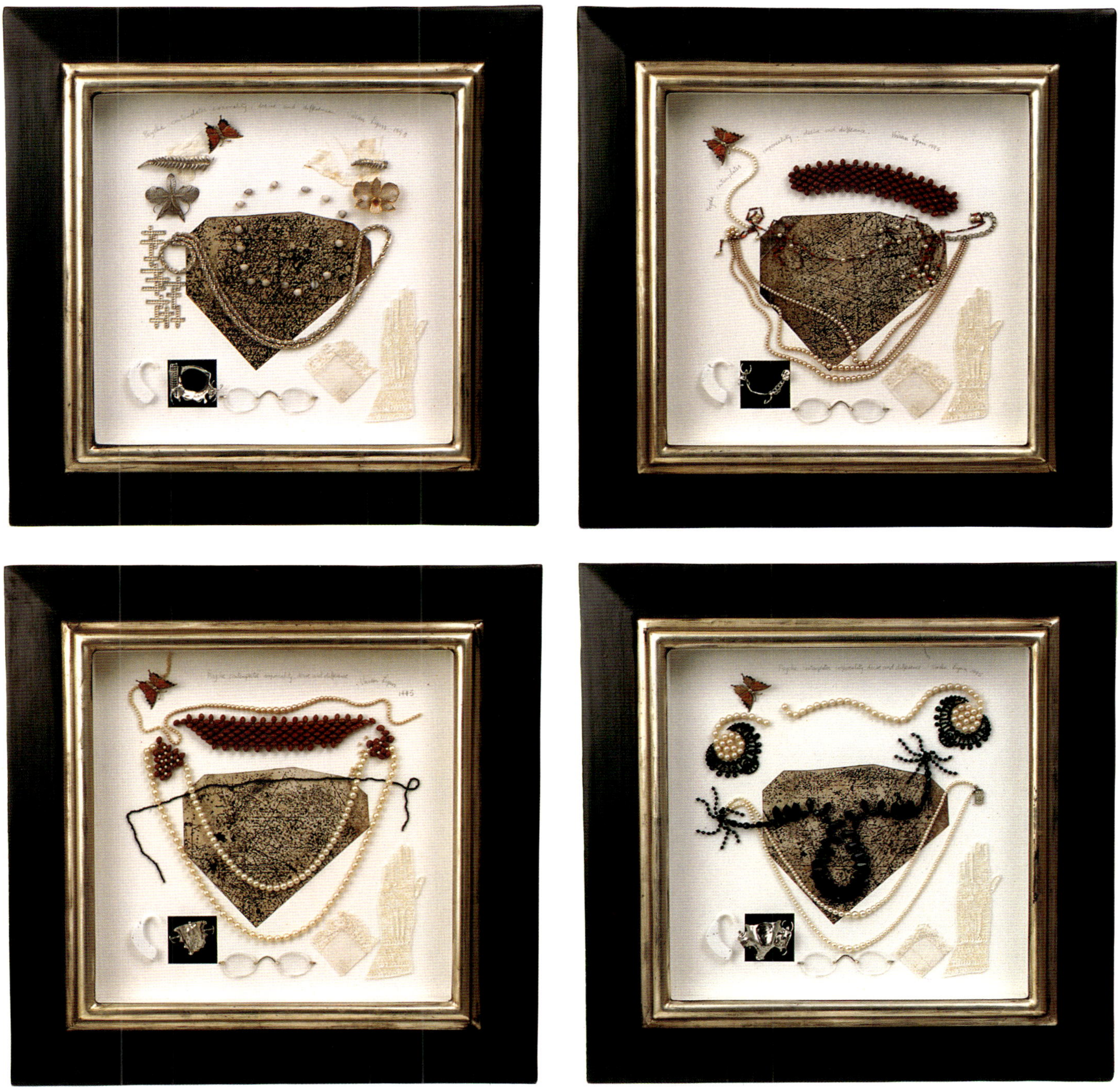

55

EDWARD MACKENZIE

Born California, 1937.
Diploma of Art, Cooper Union Art School, NYC, 1960;
studied graphic design at Royal College of Art, 1966–68.
Came to New Zealand 1982. Lives in Oromahoe, Bay of Islands.

Mackenzie's assemblages are small and usually regular in shape. Rather than the felicitous agglomerations of Darragh (23) or Copeland (16), or the simulated scenery of Simon Shepheard (79), Mackenzie favours repeated forms which resolve into patterns. His exhibitions each follow one theme through many ingenious permutations. Consequently he keeps an eye out for materials which come in sets, or are mass-produced. He develops a language with this material and then adds extraneous items where appropriate. His orderly designer's mind takes more interest in the frame of an artwork than the work inside it. He has long been fascinated by frames, and many of his works consist of rectangular elements which chase each other around a square. This device sets up a visual swirl around the central area. Sometimes the artist will put something there that resonates with the rest of the elements; sometimes, as in the *Frameworks* of 1991–93, the space will be empty. The owner of such a work is invited to put small photos or treasures in the space.

Mackenzie's first New Zealand show, *English Seaside*, 1984, was a report on Englishness by an American 15 years in London. It was built around a set of photographs taken by the late Tony Ray Jones. The next show was literally about NZ, with each work in the show spelling out those letters (Mackenzie is working on a second version of this). *Pyrotechnics* of 1986 was all about matches and matchboxes, beloved of collectors but here rendered collectable because of the artist's invention and intervention. *Les Bateaux*, 1987, were small paintings exhibited with a set of collages, each one made from four identical postcards with a boating theme which were cut and glued to short, square lengths of wood. These were assembled in a square to make a decorated frame surrounding a loosely painted sketch relating to the subject of the card. In 1989 Mackenzie was working with Meccano parts and, in a separate series, bicycle seats. The Meccano pieces clearly demonstrated the artist's remarkable inventiveness, because nearly everyone over 40 has played with Meccano at some time, and the purpose of the toy was to make assembly easy and stimulate creativity. Mackenzie avoided cliché and triggered nostalgia, as well as a 'Why didn't I think of that?' reaction. Such a reaction is a common one when looking at his work.

Piano Works, Frame for a Round Object, 1994
Piano components
160 x 160 x 60 mm
Courtesy of the artist

His 1991 work, the *Oaracles*, was based on the fact that wooden sculling oars are hollow. They were cut on an angle so that the hollow took on a heart shape, or became an open mouth in a Henry Moore-style head. These created elements were then blended with found objects to make table-sized sculptures. His 1994 exhibition, *Piako Piano*, was assembled mainly from old pianos, ideal sources of material for Mackenzie because of their numerous small duplicated components. His 1995 exhibition, *Colour by Numbers*, utilised Cuisenaire rods, an aid used in primary schools to teach arithmetic. When new plastic ones were issued he collected as many old ones as he could, then used both types to make 15 witty pieces.

Mackenzie got into assemblage because shortage of money made the acquisition of expensive art material impracticable. His work, like that of all the assemblagists in this book, proves that the medieval alchemists were right — dross really can be turned into gold.

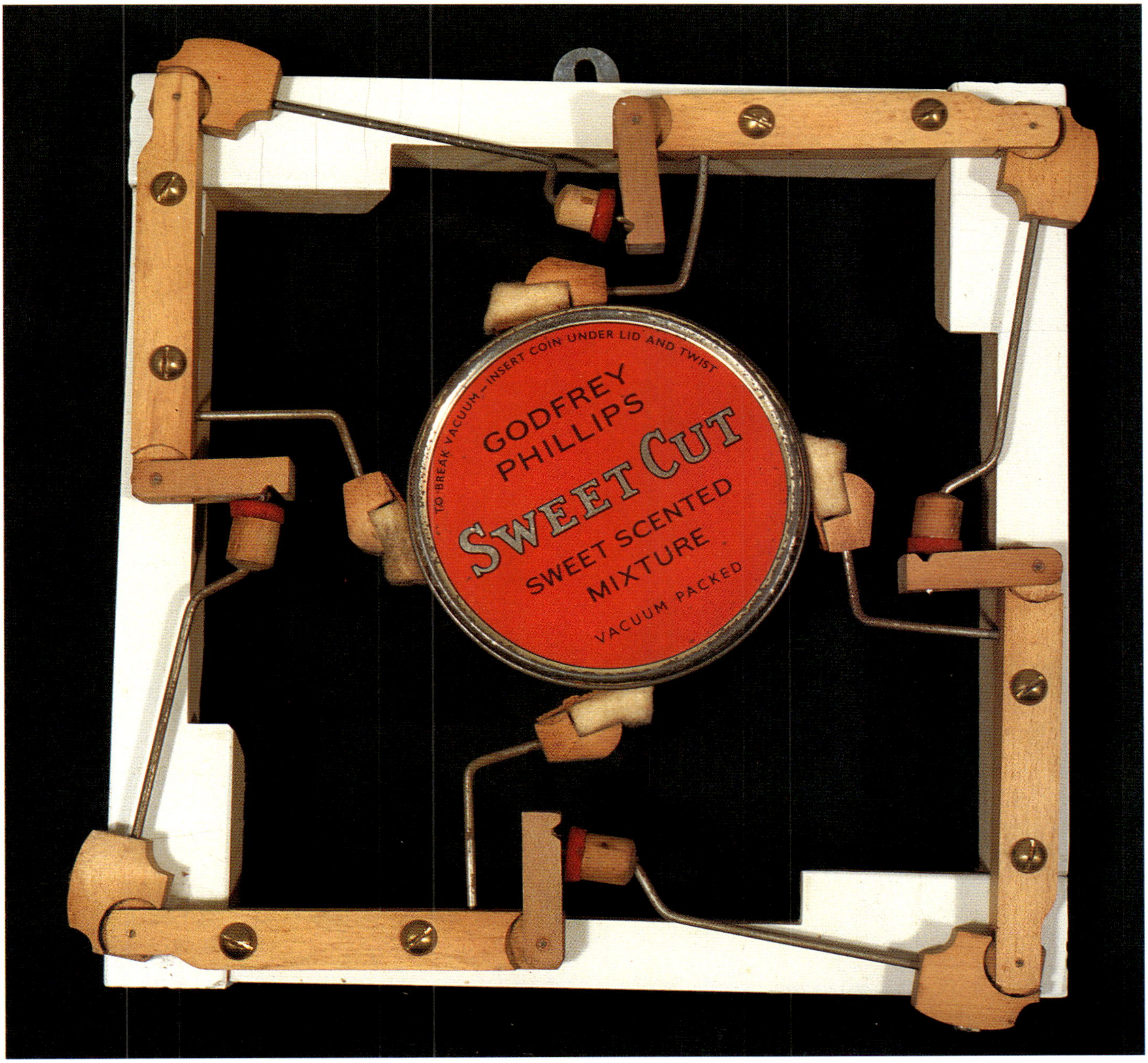
TO BREAK VACUUM–INSERT COIN UNDER LID AND TWIST
GODFREY
PHILLIPS
SWEET CUT
SWEET SCENTED
MIXTURE
VACUUM PACKED

56

KATHRYN MADILL

Born Ruatahuna 1951.
DFA, UC 1971.
Lives in Dunedin.

From 1972 until 1994 Madill concentrated on printmaking, working in drypoint, woodcut, lithography and most especially in mezzotint. Her mastery of the mezzotint process enables her to summon the merest suggestions of light out of the pitch blackness of the prepared plate. She enjoys the fact that in this medium 'the background is done for you before you start'. In 1982–83 Madill did a one-off series of black and white paintings in which white forms seemed to arise from the black and sink back into it.

Some of Madill's images are quite realistic and tell a story, such as a nursery rhyme; others are very loose and surreal, with simplified lines and blocks of primary colour. Often much of a print will remain dark, with emphasis placed on a head, a figure or a few free-floating objects. Levitation is a phenomenon encountered frequently in her work of the 1980s.

Madill's is a fey vision: other-worldly, elfin, whimsical and visionary. She often portrays a female figure as if in a dream — as a fish, a bird, a poet or a circus performer. The idea of the paper or canvas as an arena in which the artist performs has led numerous artists to theatrical themes and modes of presentation (cf. Chilcott, 100NZP, 13; Dolezel, 100NZP, 20; Watkins, 100NZP, 94). Madill has often put her images in a circus ring or on a theatre stage, to emphasise their dreamlike quality. In one of her *Women's Boat* series of lithographs in 1991 curtains are drawn back at either side, and the others have the artificial look of painted sets, simulated sea and stage lighting. The prints depict women in a boat seeking sanctuary, fleeing some unknown threat or looking for a new, better world. This series is notable for the abrupt changes from white to dark, and the sense of drama one experiences at sea on a brilliant moonlit night. The artist's experience with mezzotint was here transferred into lithography.

Dance, 1995
Crayon on paper
300 x 375 mm
Private Collection, Auckland

Since 1994 Madill has been making small, exquisitely refined crayon drawings. She uses a very sharp crayon and, with a myriad of small marks, builds up a dense layer of pigment which is softened hazily here and there with a solvent. These works usually depict a green, open landscape with hills, sea or sky beyond. Often the horizon line is rimmed with light, indicating dawn or dusk. In some works, figures taken from classical religious art appear in their robes, gesturing benignly amid sparse trees. These are nostalgic, dreamy images — a mixture of McCahon (100NZP, 50) and medieval art. They follow on logically from Madill's prints, balancing fine detail with empty expanses, and dull earth colours with jewel-like highlights. Other drawings deal with personalities and themes from Victorian literature, in which the artist has a special interest. She lives and works in a large, isolated, nineteenth-century house with a sweeping view of city and sea — a perfect setting for her nostalgic, poetic art.

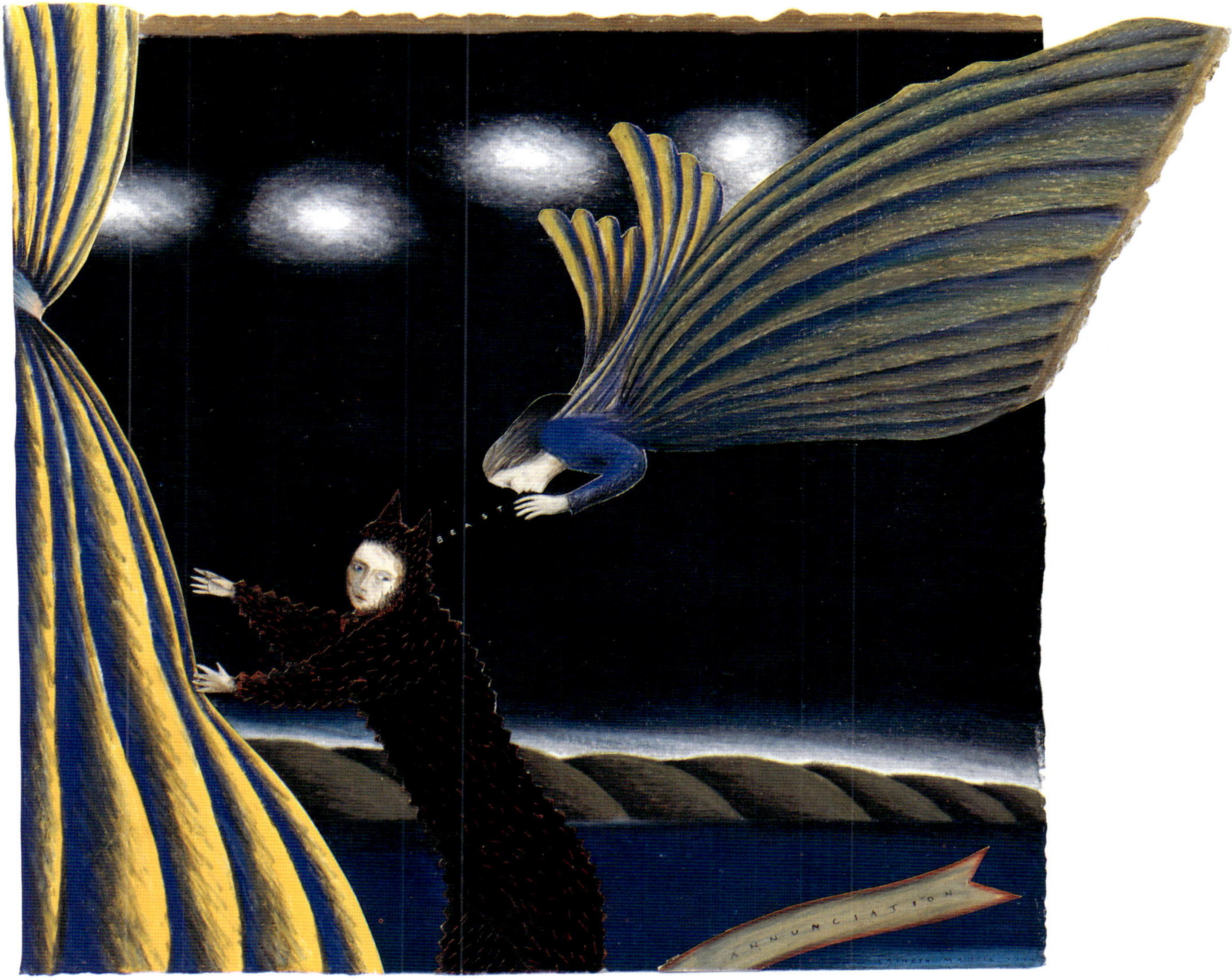
BEAST
ANNUNCIATION

57

PARA MATCHITT

Born Tokomaru Bay, East Cape, 1933.
DT, Auckland and Dunedin 1956–57.
Lives in Napier.

Among contemporary Maori sculptors, Matchitt has been one of the most successful in drawing upon his cultural heritage without 'modernising' traditional forms. Like the greatest Maori carvers of the past he has developed his own style: architectural, constructivist and abstract. Matchitt extracts basic elements found in traditional Maori carving and reuses them, integrating them into his compositions in a simplified, austere way. A few examples: the zig-zag pattern which appears in much carved and woven work; the pitched eave of meeting houses and whare; the palisade post with a round, head-like top; the arched pa gate and symbols used by the Maori prophet Te Kooti. All of these appear in his mighty, 18-metre-long *Huakina Flag,* 1986, in which truss-like diagonals march down the work, pushing it out, contrasted with rounded figurative elements.

Matchitt works in unpainted, rough-sawn native timbers, often skilfully using the subtle changes in colour which have resulted from weathering. He uses power tools to achieve straight lines, sharp edges and exact circles and curves. Wire, nails and the occasional found metal object may be worked into the composition. A fine example of these qualities can be seen in Matchitt's major wall relief outside Auckland's Aotea Centre (1989), which incorporates sections of a steel conveyor track. That element, completely consistent in look with traditional sources, suggests a society coming together and moving on, and the mural wonderfully blends the appearances of tribal gods and the pumping, hammering mechanical gods of industry. Homage is also paid to the gods of art, with sculptural quotes from Brancusi and Picasso. Similar syntheses occur in another major work, *The Gate,* 1989, in which wooden sawtooth shapes are matched by sharp steel teeth in a huge, baroque gateway that would look great in a *Star Wars* movie. In a more austere mode, Matchitt has made a number of large sculptures in the form of A-frame meeting houses, the *Papa Kaainga*. Small, carved openwork sections adorn their apexes. Their resemblance to ski chalets may be coincidental, but they make a point about changing values and lifestyles in both Maori and Pakeha communities. These works can be grouped to create an enclosed, uncovered central area, a reference to marae. To enter these small spaces one must bow low and then crouch down in the gloomy interiors, made aware of the past and present human need for shelter and communion, made conscious that art can indeed affect us. Another major work is the *City to Sea Bridge*, 1993–94, which crosses a busy Wellington street and connects to a park at the water's edge.

Matchitt was known in the 1960s for his expressive paintings, and between 1964 and 1985 he completed a number of sculptural and mural commissions for marae, schools, businesses and public institutions. He has been a full-time artist since 1986. His creativity extends into the areas of drawing, book illustration, printmaking and the design of stained glass windows. Apart from his 30-year career as an art teacher, he has directly influenced younger sculptors such as Christensen (13) and Jahnke (43).

Whakapapa III, 1987
Totara
1965 x 1005 x 88mm
Courtesy Ferner Gallery, Auckland

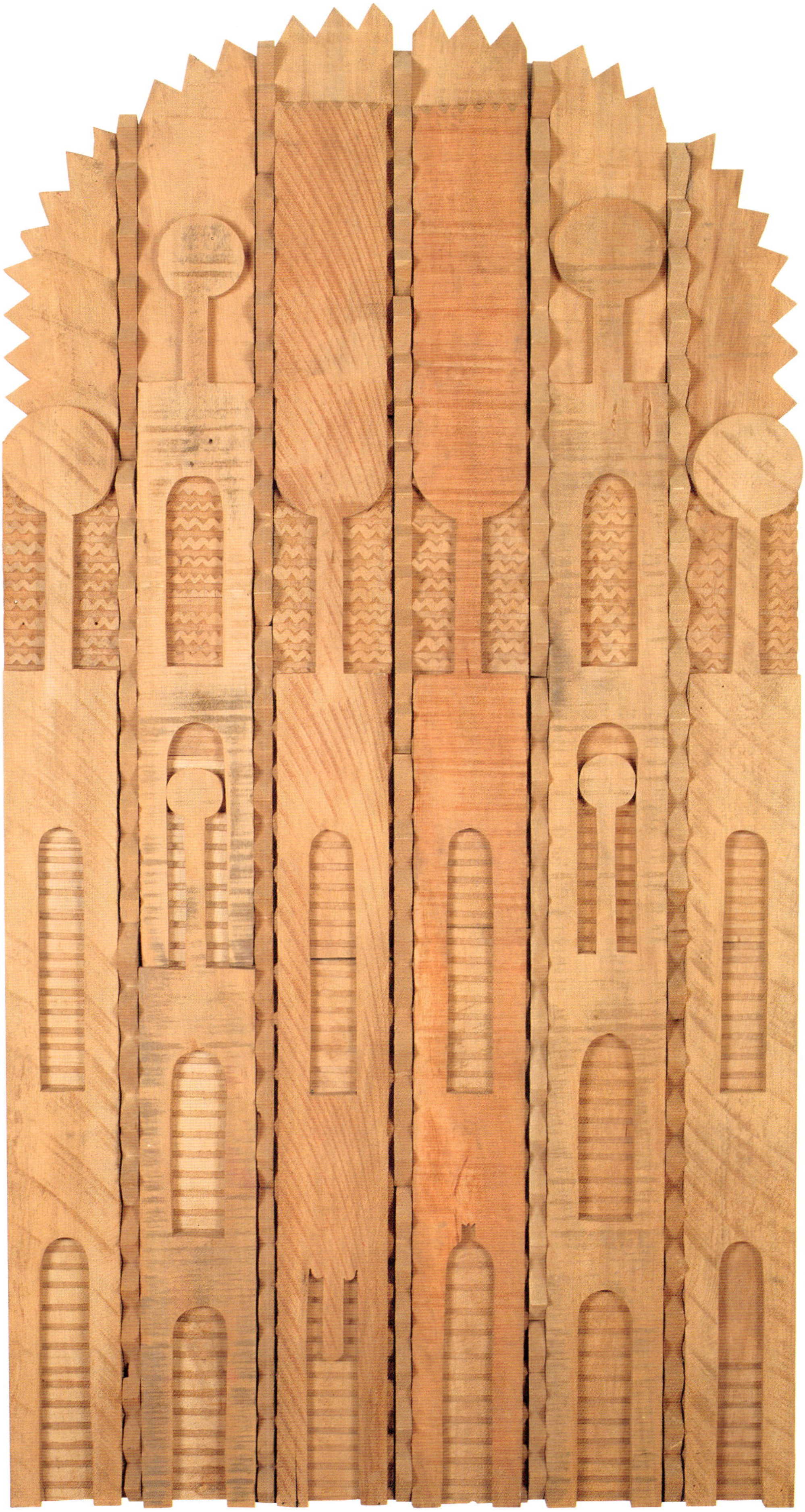

58

BARNARD McINTYRE

Born Wellington 1961.
BFA (Sculpture), UC 1985.
Lives in Melbourne.

McIntyre's sculpture, although it has undergone considerable change over the years, has always consisted of objects, obviously handmade. His works, although by no means confrontational, must be confronted and dealt with by the viewer. They are like things left behind by a previous tenant, made for some use which cannot be discerned. In this they differ from objects by a sculptor such as Cherrie (12), which seem to have specific uses, albeit strange ones.

In 1986–87 McIntyre made a series of small, tar-coated, rusty, folded-metal objects with small V-shaped teeth along the edges. At that time he was using a blocky cruciform shape, albeit in crude form. It appeared then as a cut-out from the side of some works, as a structural member in others and, in the manner of icing forced through a cross-shaped extruder, as a cactus. He was to return to this form later. With the metal pieces he also exhibited a number of white-painted pipes and sticks which leaned against the wall. In 1988 he made a number of elongated, three-dimensional wall-mounted pieces out of variously patterned formicas. Some sides were straight, others curved. Some of these pieces resembled offcuts from a furniture factory while others looked like they were designed to fit into a larger construct. In 1991 McIntyre's forms acquired flanges, so that they resembled assemblies of chunky shelf brackets, but with organic references which conflicted with the factory-made look. The cross shape used earlier reappeared in a more boxy form, like a geometric bud or seed pod. In 1992 these forms became squatter and thicker, and two sets of crosses intersected at right angles to produce a complex object with a three-dimensional cross on each of its four sides. This form could sit square on the floor or lie tilted over on one side. McIntyre also made some vinyl-covered, interlocking cubes at this time. These works of 1989–92 have some similarities to the 1970s work of Richard Artschwager, but McIntyre differed from him in the quality of his finish and the abstract nature of his forms. Artschwager's pieces were immaculately joined, with the formica surfaces chamfered and butted to produce what looked like a factory-made object. McIntyre's joinery was rough; some ends of the forms were left open so that you could see the wooden framework inside; some pieces of customwood sheet were left raw; lino and vinyl laminations did not quite fit, and sometimes overlapped edges. The results looked like an ambitious project made by someone whose skills were not quite up to it. Some critics thought that the roughness just demonstrated lack of skill. Some thought that it was a deliberate attempt, in a 'post-object' sculptural climate, to prevent the objects becoming precious or ornamental. Others discerned a metaphor for the flawed nature of humankind, and still others saw an ironic reference to the kiwi 'do-it-yourself' mentality. The artist did not say who, if any of these, was right. In 1994 McIntyre was working with open, foldable boxes made of vinyl on foam board. In 1995 in Melbourne he began assembling found objects, such as ring-binder files, into complex geometrical clusters.

Throughout his career McIntyre has made drawings. Originally they were in charcoal; they then became collages made from adhesive vinyl with fake woodgrain patterns. Recently he has been drawing using a computer to generate virtual sculpture – forms which can be viewed on the screen from any angle, as if they were being filmed in a gallery setting.

Untitled (from the exhibition 'Surface Tensions'), 1992
Composition board and vinyl
1350 x 1350 x 1350 mm
Collection of the artist

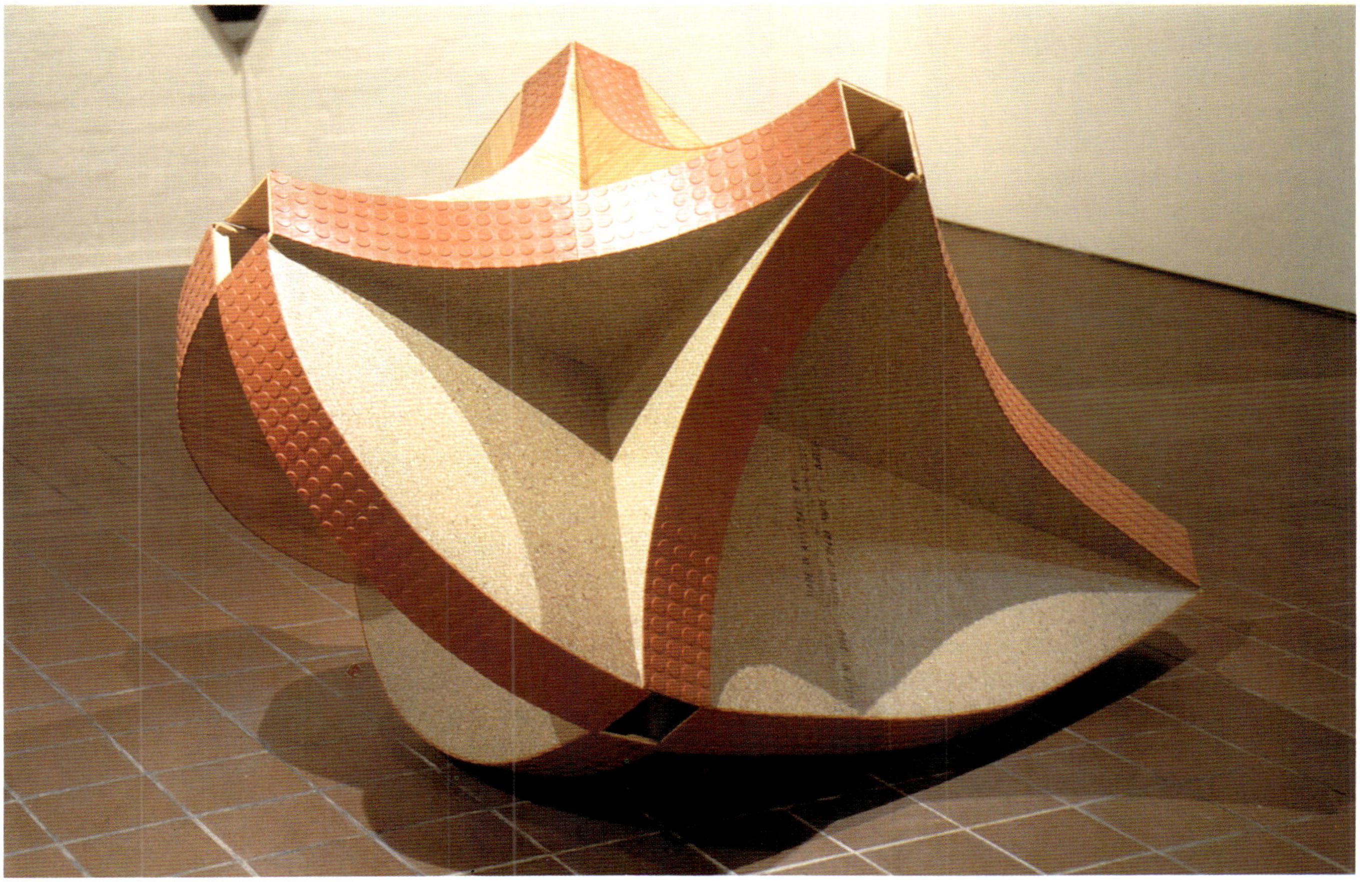

59

NEIL MILLER

Born Sunderland, England 1963.
Came to New Zealand 1975.
BFA, UA 1988.
Lives in Auckland.

Miller defines himself as a painter who works in metals. At art school he enrolled for painting, but it seemed to him that he could learn more in the sculpture department. His working method until 1993 was akin to painting, in that he never sketched or pre-planned; rather he set about using materials at hand, working with them intuitively, a stage at a time from the ground up, until all possibilities were resolved and the work was complete. Accordingly, Miller has avoided the engineering of massive works and most of his work has been at human scale or smaller. He has found metal a balanced, direct and relatively quick medium to work in. Much of his sculpture emulates the forms of nature — the twirling vine, leaf, shell, seed, seed pod, twig and shoot. Unlike art nouveau and subsequent debased decorative metalwork, Miller has avoided florid excess and simplified things down to the bare bones. His style is closer to that of Gonzalez and David Smith, and his organic working method has mimicked the natural growth depicted by his art. Another important element in Miller's work has been the concept of duality (cf. Jahnke, 43). Positive forms have been matched with negative ones; curves with straight lines; weight with lightness; and movement with stasis.

Until 1993, Miller worked with steel rods and plates cut with a torch and welded. His graduation show in 1987 included the prototypes of forms which engaged him for five years thereafter. One was a solid and a hollow cone placed vertically end to end, with a side support of curved steel rod. The other was a more boxy, constructivist form painted in primary colours. In the former manner, *Speaker*, 1988, is a 2-metre-tall seed pod standing vertically and sprouting a loudspeaker horn from its tip. Its roughly cut and welded steel segments recollect cubism, but the form remains graceful, if eccentric. Other pieces from this period resemble groups of leaves standing on their tips, or bundles of thin, straight sticks. Most of Miller's work done in 1991 was in suprematist style: part boxy, part open, with right angles and straight lines, and some elements painted in primary colours. He did a number of drawings at this time, compatible with the sculptures. His 1992 show included a steel split-pod form which could be seen as a chrysalis or even a sarcophagus. It marked the end of the robust, organic works.

In 1993, partly because teaching sculpture, which he had been doing for three years, inhibited his intuitive approach, Miller re-evaluated his aims and began planning his works. They became smaller, mostly two-dimensional, refined, geometric and wall-mounted. Dualities were still explored in the meeting of wedges of different materials, such as gold and silver. Rivets and screws were substituted for welding, and finely scribed lines and impressed letters and numbers appeared. The artist sees these pieces as distillations from, and therefore consistent with, previous work. In *Another Green World*, 1995, two wedges with the tips cut off are joined ambiguously; they could have just edged up to each other or collided violently. One half is inanga greenstone; the other half bronze patinated and waxed to resemble greenstone. This small, abstract piece is a metaphor for the current socio-political climate and may indicate a new line of development for Miller.

Hindsight, 1988
Carbon, cadmium and wax on steel
2.4 m high
Private Collection

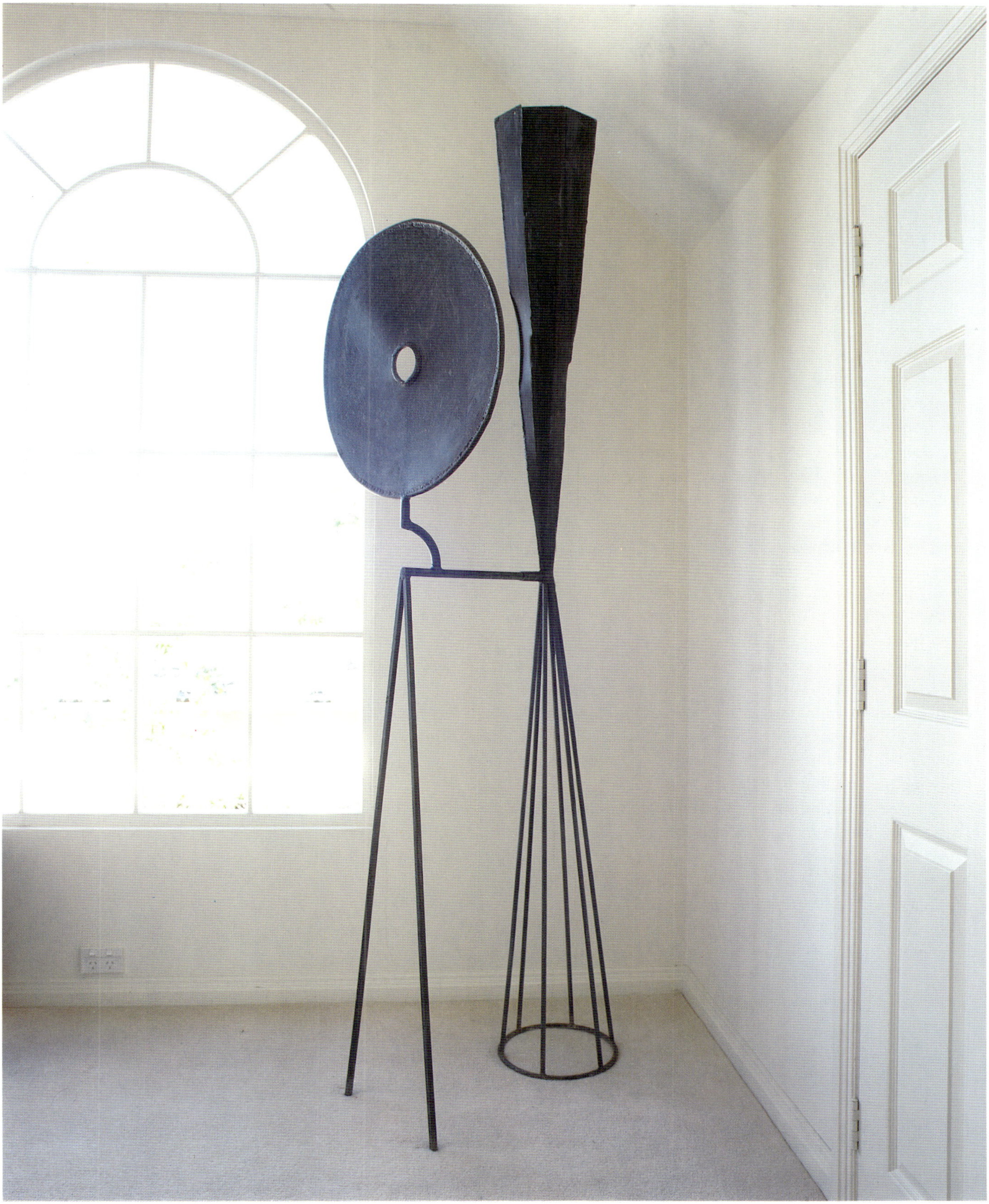

60

CATHRYN MONRO

Born Whangarei 1966.
BFA, UA 1989.
Lives in Auckland.

Monro is a sculptor working in sand-cast bronze. Features of her work are the holes in the castings and the splatter resulting from a deliberately incomplete or over-full pour. This gives the effect of a decayed leaf or seaweed strands, as well as of an ancient and greatly corroded bronze artefact. Monro's pieces are essentially flat, designed initially to lie on the floor but latterly to hang on the wall, and over the last six years they have moved from being very fragmentary to becoming defined shapes.

At the time of her graduation and for two years afterwards, Monro was making multi-part sculptures which presented parts of an animal or human form. Like a reconstruction of a partial dinosaur skeleton, these works left much for the viewer's imagination to fill in. Some parts were castings of actual bones; others were of impressions of body parts such as hands and feet; others were abstract frills and splatters of bronze. Monro was influenced then and subsequently by childhood experiences in the bush and on the seashore with her biologist father, looking at the forms of nature both in life and in death. In her 1991 exhibition *Ekstasis*, the elements became very sparse and dispersed, with a small decorative element in the centre signifying the spirit. These pieces were about the extremes of experience, including out-of-body ones. This show included *Ascension*, an ethereal casting of fragments of a rope ladder, of which the shadows thrown on the wall were an integral part. In 1992, at a time of bereavement in her family, Monro made a series of urn-shaped pieces, ranging in size from small to life-size. These extended the usual understanding of urns as containers for cremated remains. The smallest were for sounds or smells, the medium-sized ones for objects and the large ones for the whole body. They suggested an analogy with the body as a container for memories and the need to respect those memories when disposing of it. Although loss and decay were evident in the eroded look of the pieces, there was also a sense of dignity and tradition.

umilita/umanita (humility/humanity), 1994
Patinated, sandcast bronze
ca. 1710 x 835 mm
Collection of the artist

Monro visited Italy in 1993 and was much moved by her experience of Renaissance art and architecture. As a sixth-generation New Zealander with ancestors in five European countries, she felt the sense of history and returned home with a new sense of being alive. She made a series of amphora-shaped works, exhibited in 1994 under the title *respiro/espiro*. All the works bore one or two Italian words along their centre line — 'compassion', 'peace', 'courage and wisdom', setting out The Virtues. The shape could also be seen as a leaf or a lung, both of which are devices for breathing. The works could be read as a metaphor for the struggle to live and to keep ideals alive (successful survival) or for the corruption and interment of civilised behaviour (failure and spiritual death).

The artist's next series of works involved turning the urn shape on its side and elongating it greatly. Coincidently, the resulting objects, perforated as usual with holes edged by curving ribbons of bronze, resembled at first glance a carved Maori lintel, paddle or taiaha. The thought arises that the designers of Maori carving took their inspiration from the random forms in nature as well as ordered ones, such as the koru. Monro continues to experiment with sand-casting, exploring the possibilities of incorporating glass into the bronze.

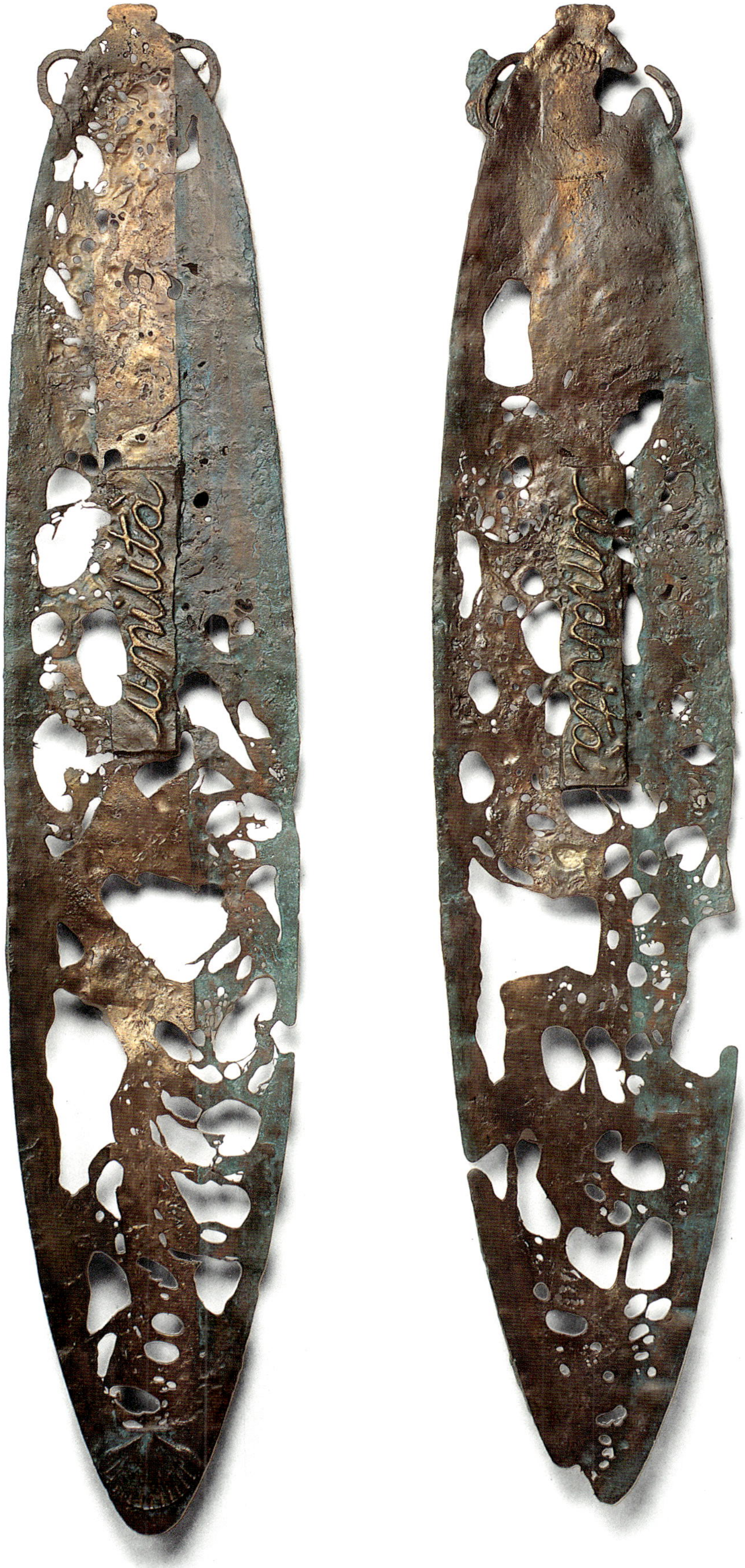
umiltà

SELWYN MURU

Born Te Hapua, Northland 1940.
DT, Ardmore Teachers College 1960.
Lives in Auckland.

Muru began as a self-taught painter, receiving favourable notices while still in his early twenties. His work at that time was landscape-based and heavily textured and expressionistic. In 1968 he began introducing collage elements. In 1973 he painted a series of expressive, sweeping Northland landscapes. In 1975 he began an ambitious project to paint the history of Parihaka (1860–81), a shameful period in the colonisation of New Zealand. He did 45 canvases in a manner that mixed the styles of the Australians Nolan and Boyd. Like Nolan's *Ned Kelly* series, Muru's paintings employed harsh colours and broad brushwork to depict episodes from the Taranaki land-grab. In 1981 Muru contributed a set of anti-apartheid paintings to the wave of anti-Springbok tour protests.

The year 1986 was a very productive one for Muru. He did some richly expressive oil paintings, predominantly dark red in colour, with a moody landscape in the foreground and hills shaped like carved Maori forms in the background. He also took up sculpture. Henry Moore was a strong influence, and Muru's *Te Maaoorii* is a tall figure with its arms folded and a hole where the chest should be. This witty wooden piece incorporates found metal parts for genitals and head-dress (cf. Christensen, 13). Moore died in 1986 and Muru named after him an arch piece he was carving at the time. This impressive work, lopsided, boldly modelled and capped with a flower-like rosette, was a pointer towards *Waharoa* of 1991. *Crucifixus pro Papa*, also 1986, was a more serious, expressionist work in dark-stained wood, made from demolition materials and commenting on the developer mentality of the time.

Waharoa, 1991
Painted wood and sheet copper
ca. 9 x 10 m
Auckland City collection

In 1988 Muru exhibited 14 panels of flattened corrugated iron painted in rich textures with graffiti, poem quotes, Maori proverbs and Ringatu symbols, the whole becoming a visual rhetorical address. Another fine work of 1988 was a wall relief of rich yellow rough-sawn wood and found metal, a palisade of seven figures cleverly blending Picasso and traditional Maori forms. A major work of 1990 was *The Sentinels*, a pre-Columbian style stone panel in Auckland's Regional Authority Building. Tall and white, it sets out in chunky words a Ngati Whatua chant about living with nature.

The following year, 1991, was another important one for Muru. He completed a six-panel mural with a strong anti-nuclear message based on a poem by Hone Tuwhare, and made an impressive installation piece at the National Gallery called *Whatever we do the gods are constant*. It consisted of bird/spirit forms perched on high pedestals above a sea of mechanical debris. In Auckland's Aotea Square he erected a huge macrocarpa gateway, a greeting to visitors, topped with figures of the ocean and forest gods, the god of elements and the heavenly spheres. This work shows Muru's ability to create sculptures which seem essentially Maori but on inspection are seen to be generalised. In 1993 Muru made five immense hangings , described by T.J. McNamara as 'truly an epic painting, a huge, thunderous, aggressive work full of the power of thought and of nature'. Those comments apply to much of Muru's work of the 1990s.

Muru has turned out to be a much more versatile artist than the painter he originally set out to be. He is prepared to work in diverse media, to experiment, reinterpret modernist styles and tackle big projects while remaining true to the spirit, if not the form, of his cultural traditions. He is also a film-maker, playwright and broadcaster.

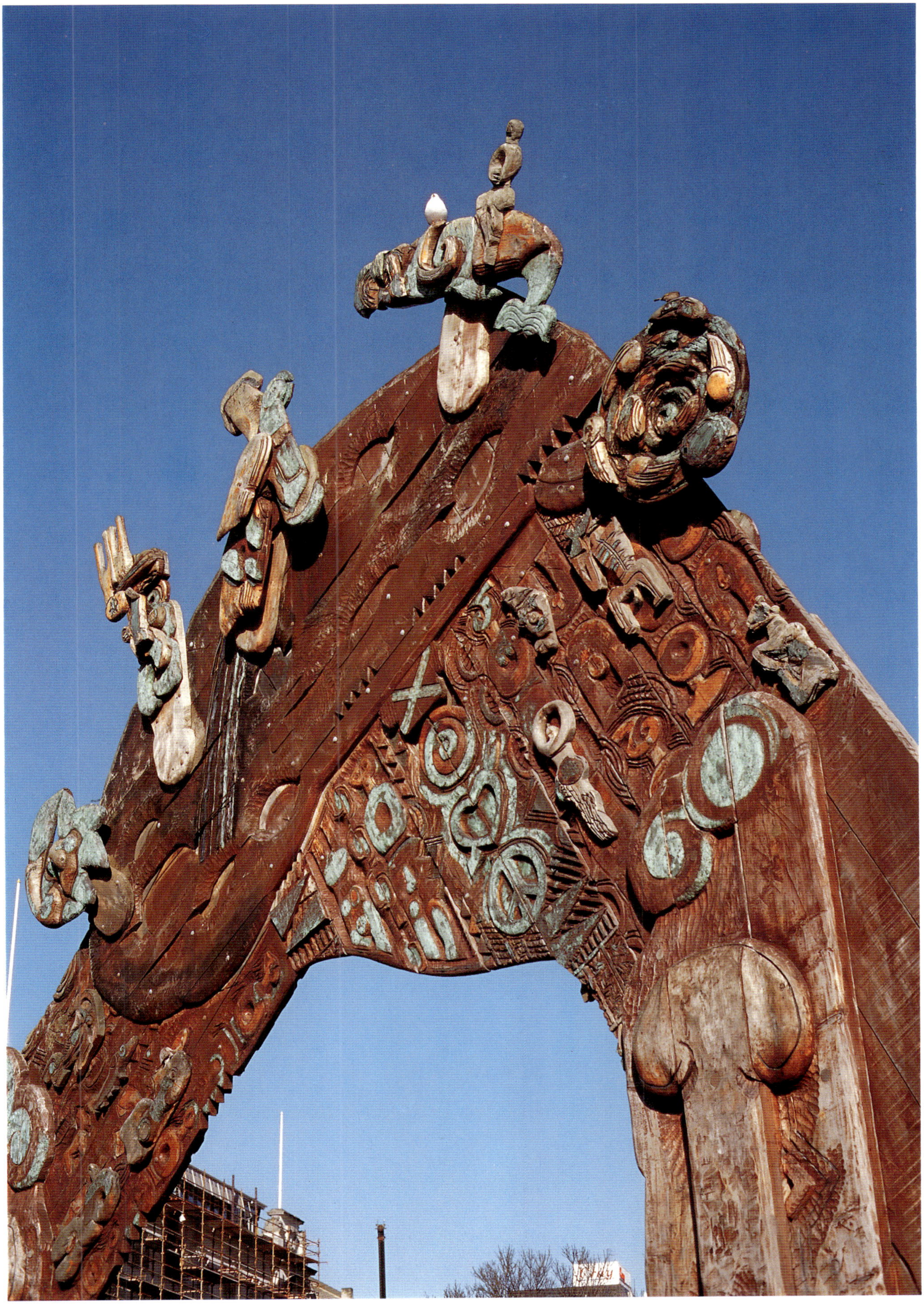

62

KAZU NAKAGAWA

Born Tokyo 1957.
Bachelor of Fisheries (Marine Engineering), Tokyo University of Fisheries 1981;
studied furniture-making, Hatano Polytechnic 1985–86.
Came to New Zealand 1987. Lives on Waiheke Island.

Nakagawa brought with him to New Zealand a set of traditional Japanese cabinetmaker's tools and an extraordinary skill at working in wood. He also bought an attribute rather rare here: patience, a cast of mind willing to spend whatever time it takes to achieve perfection. His early work was boxes and furniture, albeit furniture of such originality, poise and immaculate facture that it seemed too good to use. By 1992 he found this activity an insufficient use of his energies. He moved beyond the utilitarian into the useless, making art which has sometimes incorporated tables and chairs, but only as elements in sculptural assemblies. He began with a set of works which seemed designed to demonstrate his complete mastery of wood. Choosing the old, hard wood of stumps, posts, battens and poles, he fashioned it like cheese, turning rough blocks into miniature architectural follies articulated with archways, steps and passages. In one case five sections of wood were pierced by a gradually widening aperture; other pieces came apart to reveal internal complexities. Grain patterns were in scale with the forms and enhanced by black resin.

Nakagawa's 1993 work was based on the then recently introduced tetrapak milk carton and demonstrated that the artist was not just a woodworker. He used the formal qualities of actual cartons, and their resemblance to tall shrines, to make a series of cast concrete pieces. Some of the forms were distorted and broken; some contained eggs in hollowed-out niches — 'a non-man-made form to contrast with the man-made one'. The human hand was present in one piece, which included the cast of a workman's glove. By filling up empty containers and then taking the old skin away, Nakagawa in effect re-created the forms, making the old inside the new outside. This sort of gentle conceptual game is typical of his art. Another example: in 1994 he exhibited a thin, tall table with three drawers. The table supported a row of wooden blocks, partly planed and partly rough — statements about the transition of wood from the raw to the finished state. On sliding open the perfectly fitted drawers, one found in the first sawdust, in the second a circle made up of long shavings arranged like skins of an onion, and in the third wood offcuts. Here, stored within the work, was the debris of the woodworking process. The artist has stated that his aim is to make the surrounding space — what is 'beyond the edge' — become part of each piece.

Knowing, 1995–6
Wood and cord
3700 mm diameter, average height of balls 1060 mm
Courtesy Aberhart North Gallery, Auckland

In 1996 Nakagawa showed more small monuments to his infinite patience in a sculptural installation which included cradles of sticks holding 108 wooden balls, each requiring 4000 cuts of the bandsaw to produce. Three ellipses in liquidambar wood made a separate work. Their sides and tops were sliced with thousands of fine cuts, so that they looked like piles of paper from the side, but like rolls of paper from above.

The choice of timber to be used is part of the creative act for Nakagawa, as is its finish after the work itself has been made. He uses hard, aged timber, linseed oil, Japanese urushi tree resins and rice-bran polishes to bring every component to just the degree of gloss and tone that is appropriate.

Nakagawa is also a painter of minimal abstractions in the manner of Robert Ryman and Agnes Martin.

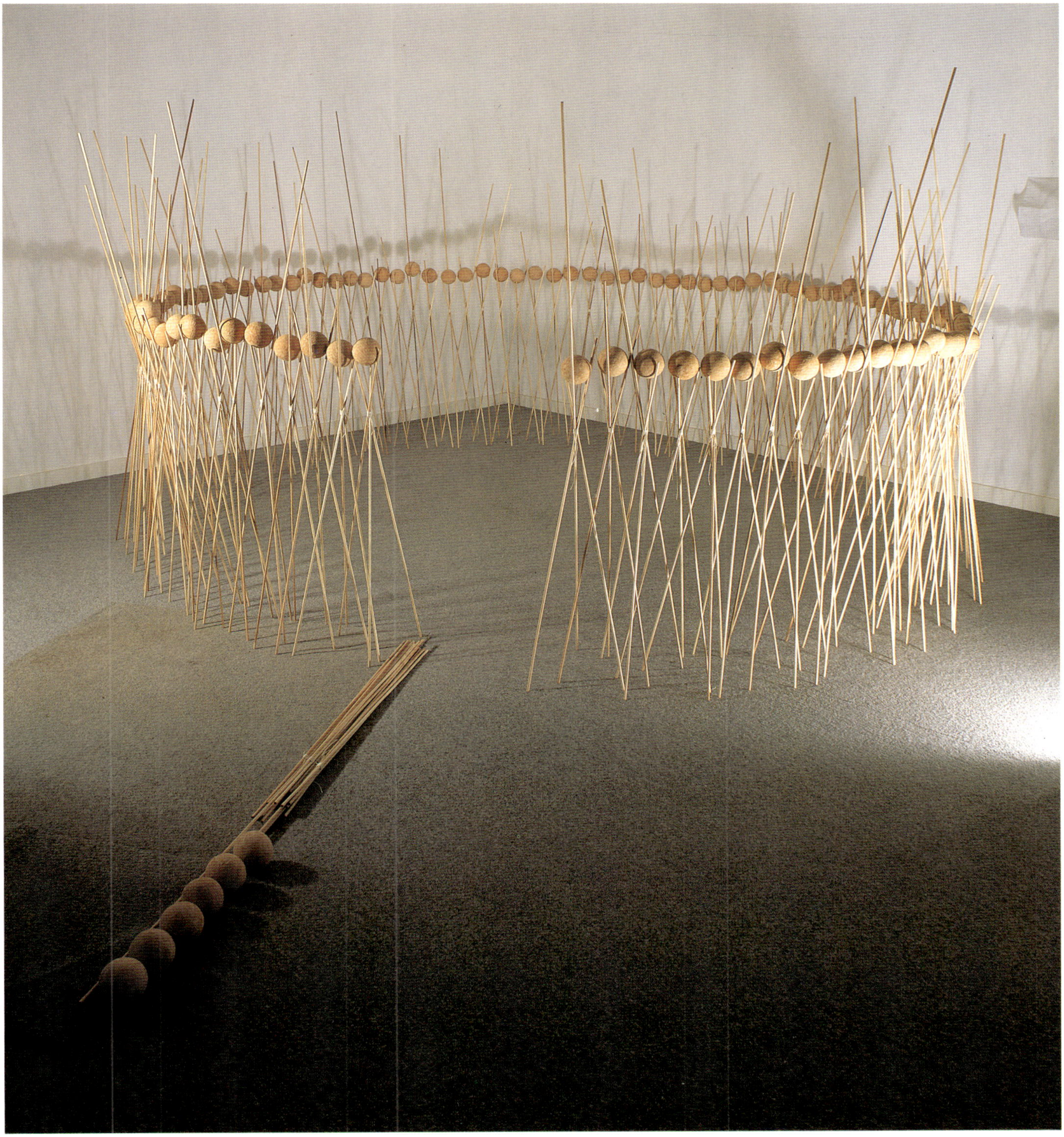

63

PETER NICHOLLS

Born Wanganui 1936.
DT, Auckland Teachers College 1962; DFA (Hons), UA 1963;
MA (Sculpture), University of Wisconsin 1979.
Lives in Dunedin.

Nicholls' work after 1977 has been a robust counter to a trend towards the spindly in New Zealand sculpture. Where others have used sticks he has used massive baulks of timber; where they have used wire and tin he has used heavy chain, hawsers, eye-bolts and sheet steel. Wood is his principal material and he is very much a constructivist: his works are about the relationship of the parts and the way in which they are held together or kept apart. His early work was informal and abstract, similar to work by the Americans di Suvero and Snelson, locked up in a state of tension or stable placement. After 1984 it became quite ordered, arranged like parts of a skeleton, with a sense of potential for movement.

Nicholls' earliest series was the *Probes* of 1970–72, lengths of manuka split lengthwise and joined as mirror images. The *New Land* series of 1975–78 began with angled pieces suspended on taut wires, then developed into more self-supporting pieces, allowing heavy chains to curve under the pull of gravity. These works suggested the bootstrap engineering of pioneer loggers, railwaymen and farmers. The *Wisconsin* series of 1978 used natural or roughly shaped trunks rather than sawn elements, creating a contrast with the nuts and bolts holding parts together and the chains and weights hanging from them. A feature of these works was an apparently precarious balance, and in many subsequent pieces Nicholls has used this device to energise the sculpture by unsettling the viewer. Needless to say his pieces are always completely stable, but he has an ability to levitate heavy blocks of wood so that they seem to be teetering.

Luff, 1988
Bronze, Port Orford cedar and jarrah
6.5 x 5 x 3 m
Private collection, Auckland

The *Constrictions*, 1980, were stubby barrels of ironbark banded with steel and filled with lead, like mallet heads, which stood on the floor. The contrasting *Lissom* works, 1981, based on dance movements and related to the *Probes*, returned to a vertical stance with graceful poise.

Works done in the early 1980s using sheet steel and boulders were diversions from Nicholls' involvement with wood. Wellingtonians will know *Full Stop*, 1982, on the harbour foreshore. This was made by dropping a 3-tonne rock onto a heated sheet of steel which dented gently to enfold the rock like a pebble in a hand. Temporary installation work included *Sprung Arc (Times Three)*, 1984, in which steel sheets were bent into curves and held in place by cables.

In 1985 Nicholls took another side path with a series of small, lively, partly painted forms made of hollowed-out sycamore. They resembled stylised dancers and acrobats in Leger's cubist style. In 1990 Nicholls exhibited a group of works in Wanganui, inspired by the feelings generated on his return to that area after long absence. For the first time he was making specific references to people and places. Aspects of the flow of the river and its historic use as an access route were hinted at in works which lay passively on the floor. The major pieces were made of several driftwood elements joined together to make sinuous river and coastline symbols in which objects relating to journeying, woodworking and river-crossings were embedded. These led to the remarkable 11-metre-long *Cut*, 1993–95, made of shaped walnut slabs, which resembles both a road winding over rolling, faulted hills and a dry, twisted flax leaf.

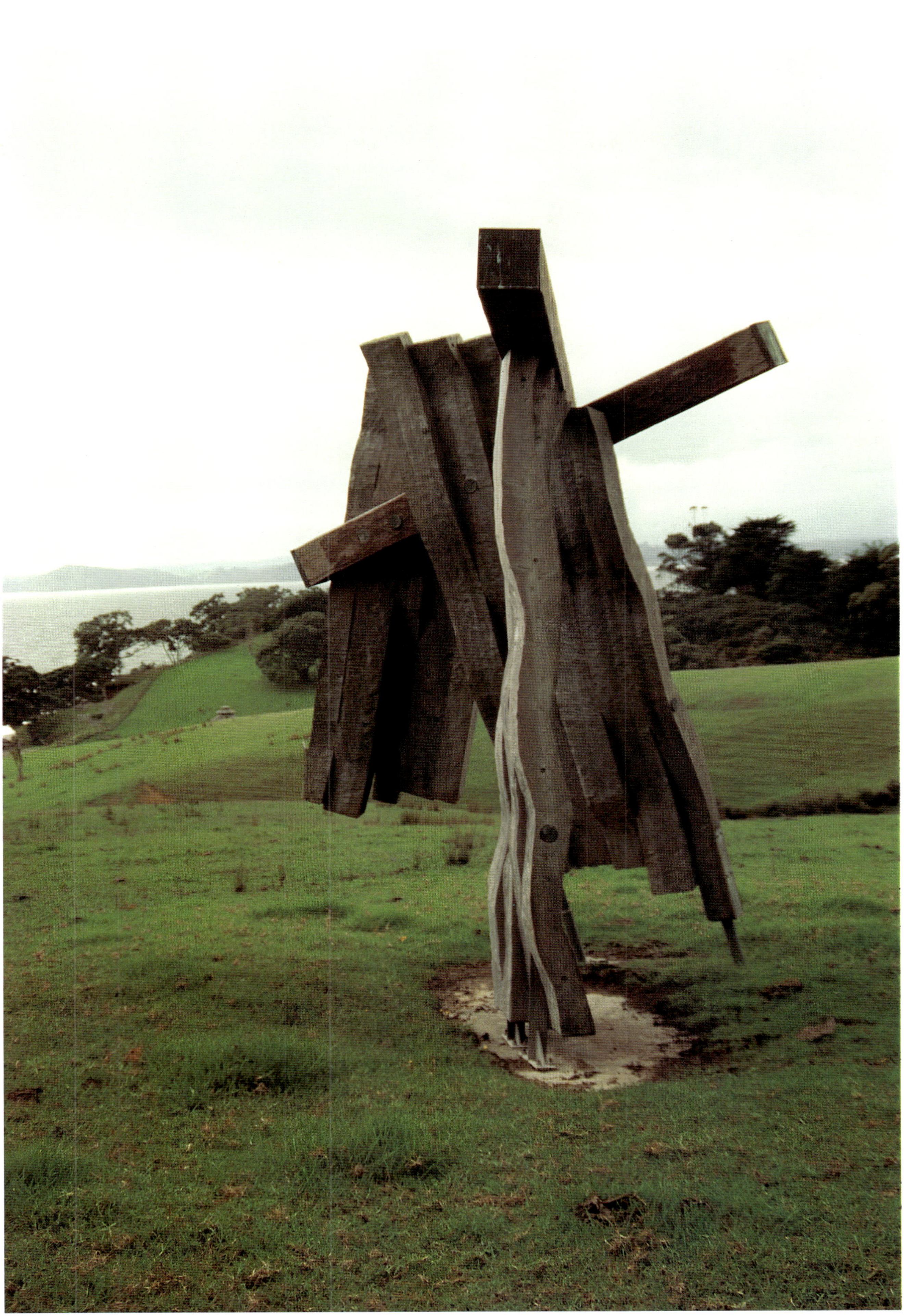

64

ANNE NOBLE

Born Wanganui 1954.
DT, Wellington Teachers College 1974;
MFA (1st Class Hons), UA 1983.
Lives in Wellington.

Noble is a photographer with a finely tuned sense of the evocative and spiritual, and a sure touch when it comes to composition, balancing both the forms and the areas of black and white within each frame. These attributes lift much of her extensive body of documentary photography into the realm of art.

Noble's first exhibition, in 1976, was of white forms fluttering in the darkness, a precursor to her acclaimed 1990 series based on swans. In 1980 she made a series of playfully erotic pictures showing plants, inanimate objects and details of bodies. Two untitled works made at this time demonstrate the power of a good photograph to transcend its subject matter. Seen through Noble's lens, adjoining male and female armpits become curiously surreal. At the top of another photograph there are two head-dented pillows; below, a double mattress is covered with a furrowed sheet. The strongly sidelit ridges sweep away from the pillows, suggesting a landscape of dunes and distant hills. Between 1982 and 1985 Noble spent much time photographing the Wanganui River, resulting in a suite of black and white pictures which captured the river's moody reflections, the scattered communities living along it, the dark bush hemming it in, and its run-out to the sea with its burden of debris from far inland. Many of these works are timeless, with misty skies and a sense of history hanging heavily over all.

Breath, 1995
Iris Jet Print
150 x 100 mm
Courtesy of the artist

Noble's photos for the 1984 *Chelsea Project* were done on polaroid black and white transparency film, transferred to make paper negatives, followed by contact prints. The finished works had a nineteenth-century look, portraying the scarred, gloomy corners of the Victorian sugarworks as gothic and purgatorial. In complete contrast, Noble's documentary series *In The Presence of Angels,* 1987–88, was a study of nuns in a convent in London, showing the daily routine of monastic life. Using black and white, she was able to emphasise the spartan environment, the solitude and silence. The only thing coming into the space was light, and Noble, like Vermeer, treated it as a measure of time and a symbol of timelessness. *Song Without Words* of 1990 was another important black and white series, mainly details of the bodies of swans framed together as one-, two-, three- and four-part works. Because swans can twist themselves into surprising positions, the images were enigmatic and semi-abstract. The white birds' bodies and the black spaces between them and the edges of the paper assumed equal importance. Here was the essence of swans: ruffling, bending, burying heads in wings, the camera finding depths and caverns within the birds.

In 1992–93 Noble did a sensitive documentary series, *Hidden Lives*, about those who care for the disabled. Among these pictures were close-ups of things pinned to walls or held to doors with fridge magnets. These became part of an ongoing series of 'fridge wisdoms' that will eventually resemble a book with many pages, each with a separate, unknown author. *A Beautiful Botany* of 1993 was a series of four-part works of details of plants and flowers. The mesh of forms and out-of-focus elements in the foreground conveyed a sense of being inside a bush. Over the past two years Noble has been working with computers to extend the boundaries of photography as well as making reference to things historical, such as the kinds of colour created by early photographic processes.

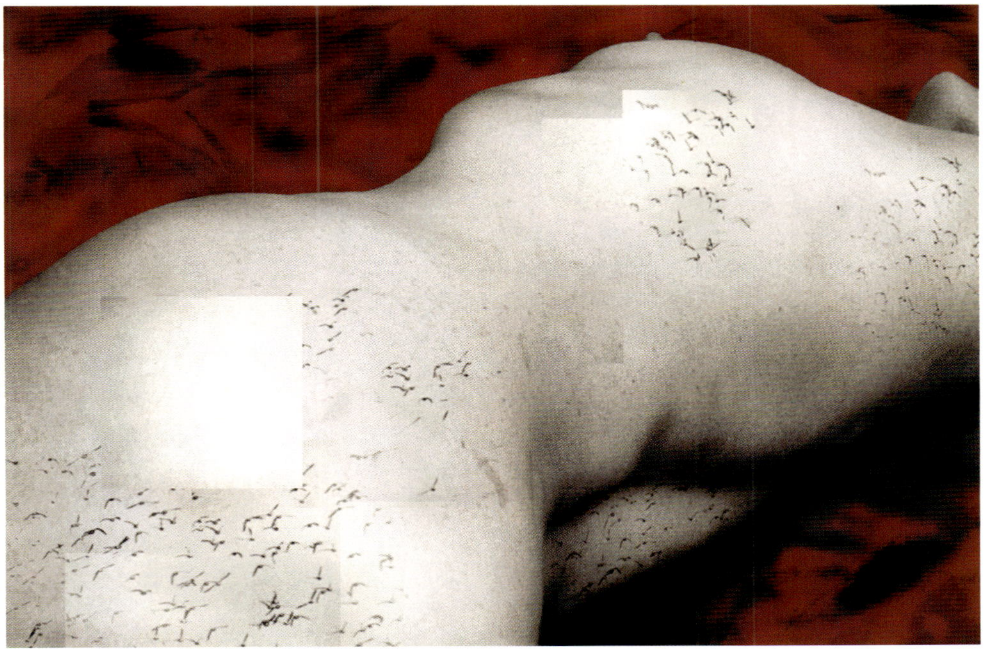

65

DENIS O'CONNOR

Born Auckland 1947.
Studied at School of Industrial Design, Wellington 1966.
Lives on Waiheke Island.

O'Connor is both a thoroughly contemporary artist and a craftsman of the old school. In many of his sculptures he celebrates the achievements of the pioneer masons, builders, sailors and engineers who laboured to found the society we live in. The occasional appearance in his work of finely modelled hands and different kinds of tools reminds us of the disciplines, virtues and pleasures of traditional carved sculpture.

Until 1983 O Connor worked in ceramics. Pieces moulded and fired from Waiheke clay, begun in the mid-1970s, were in earthy colours, and surfaces were glazed or granular. O'Connor explored aspects of the history of the Hauraki Gulf islands, making tablets memorialising the myths and trades of past inhabitants. The intellectual content and size requirements of these pieces grew until clay was no longer a suitable medium. Instead of 'making stones', as the artist decribed it, he began using real stone — at first mainly limestone, then extending into slate in the 1990s. The elements of his sculpture are rendered realistically and with all the care of a monumental mason, but the resulting objects are surreal and enigmatic (cf. Paine, 66). For example, component images in the major multi-part work *The Birdman and the Engineer*, 1987, include the trousered shins, booted feet and lamp of a railwayman; a pile of branches and pinecones; and water-worn stones from which a tyre, a battery, a vice and an architectural fragment emerge. The viewer is obliged to draw conclusions from this collision of the natural and manufactured worlds. O'Connor's sculpture is often fragmentary, having the appearance of something excavated or salvaged from a shattered society. Classic lintel shapes and incised roman lettering are used, adding to the feeling of times and monuments past.

The first stone series was *Songs of the Gulf*, 1982–84, continuing at a more complex level the theme of the earlier clay works. *Branches from The Wishing Tree*, 1985–86, was based on an Irish story about a community which elevates a tree to sacramental status and literally pins its hopes on it. Lopped tree branches lay on the floor with objects attached the branches operating as plinths. After this O'Connor began to think in terms of larger narrative tableaux. *Birdman* had 23 pieces and *The Gorse King* of 1988–90 had 33. The latter work, and his series *Theatre of Dust* of 1991–92 and *13 Stemmata* of 1994, were musings on migration to New Zealand and what happens when one culture is transported into the territory of another. This is something that O'Connor has always been interested in, with particular reference to his Irish heritage. Works such as these have become increasingly poetic, both allusive and elusive, and since the early 1990s have incorporated found objects.

O'Connor's artisanship shows, but doesn't necessarily tell. He spends much time in thought and research before he makes a piece, and he has begun writing associated semi-poetic texts to give some insights into his sources in memory and history. His many public and private commissions and collaborative pieces make more specific statements. A monumental public work of 1989, *Mote Park*, condenses New Zealand history. On one side of what appears to be a massive demolition fragment we see an incised digital display; on the other is a hand holding a leaf; and the whole block is transfixed by a shaft which forms a sledgehammer on one side and an oar on the other.

In his latest work O'Connor is moving from austere stone to luxurious varieties such as onyx.

Tenebrae/Pendulum for an Emigré, 1992
Welsh slate, sandpaper, oils, silver leaf
2658 x 1990 mm
Courtesy of the artist

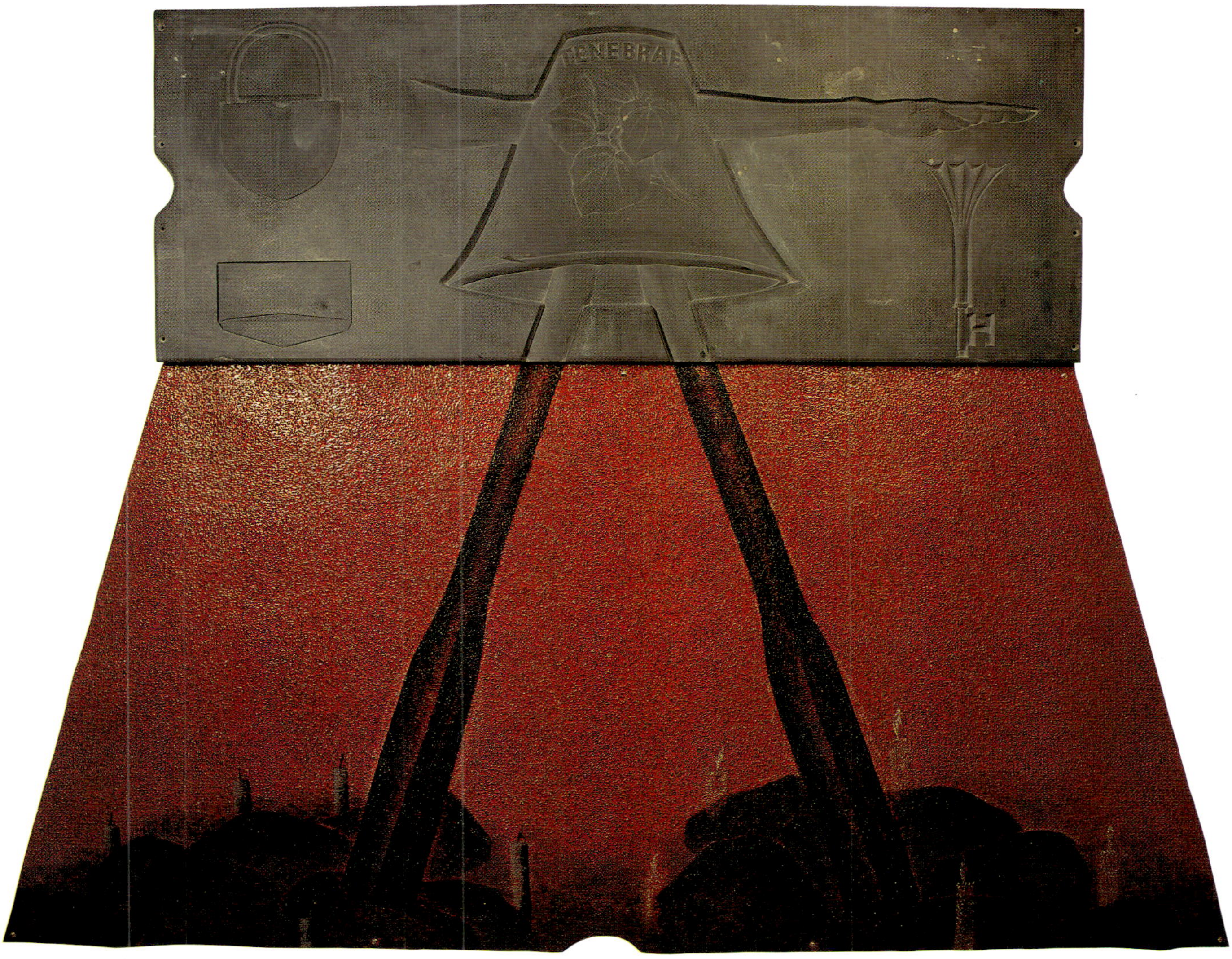
TENEBRAE

66

RALPH PAINE

Born Auckland 1957.
Certificate of Graphic Design, ATI 1976.
Lives in Auckland.

The passage of time sometimes has an odd effect on art — instead of looking out-of-date it can look more and more up-to-date. When Paine began exhibiting in 1977 his work seemed disorganised, loose and eccentric. It now looks like some of the first postmodern work done in New Zealand and a source of ideas for many other artists (see Cotton, 100NZP, 16; Hammond, 100NZP, 31; Budd, 7). Paine was appropriating and deconstructing before the terms were coined. Writing about his work in 1983, Cheryll Sotheran noted that 'it seems that the time has arrived for his blend of whimsy, cynicism and irony with acute political and social perceptions'. After a further decade during which Paine continued to have a low profile, Sotheran's words seem equally applicable to two major pieces Paine produced in 1994 and 1995. The first, *Hegel's Utu*, was shown in the extraordinarily ornate Provincial Council Chambers in Christchurch. The second, *Call Waiting*, was designed for the clinical whiteness of the New Gallery in Auckland. Both consist of long scrolls. The 1994 work, in two scrolls, fell from the lofty ceiling like holy writ, dealing to current holy art cows (McCahon, text, philosophy, deconstruction and the unframed image). The Auckland piece is five scrolls illustrating (very indirectly) aspects of the telephone exchange that used to occupy the building.

With their enjoyably free, graphic feel, Paine's pictures do not seem considered. They are more like inspired doodles. He works on paper and uses watercolour wash, gouache, pencil, ink and collage. Paine's subject matter is always individualistic; his colour either brash or thin and faded; his style a little old-fashioned-looking. Sometimes one is reminded of the rather fanciful creations of the early days of cartography. This is supported by the content of the works, which offer a mix of images and text with maps and diagrams. Guidance is needed and seemingly offered, but often we are left bewildered (cf. Carew, 100NZP, 12; Haffern, 100NZP, 30). Paine's works are like pages from the notebooks that art students are encouraged to keep. In them we find all sorts of references — archaeological, mythological, historical, anatomical, zoological, poetic, philosophical and personal. At times randomly associated images set up arbitrary connections; elsewhere specific points may be made.

Borrowed images redrawn by the artist have featured throughout Paine's work, his sources ranging from comics to classics. His parents were both commercial artists and so he was immersed in dissociated images from an early age. This process continued at design school, where students were 'opened up to everything'. Saul Steinberg was another influence, and when Paine encountered the work of Watkins (100NZP, 94) and Chilcott (100NZP, 13) he was inspired to become a contemporary artist. From the first he reacted against the idea of developing a style. He saw art as a means to make visual poetry and helped this along by developing an individual script, reminiscent of that found on seventeenth-century deeds. McCahon's use of words was a further encouragement.

Since 1990 Paine and Chilcott have collaborated on a number of projects, resulting in artworks started off by one and finished by the other. Because of the artists' similar ways of thinking, these hybrids have been remarkably successful.

Where the garment gapes, 1985
Gouache, India ink and colour pencil on water-colour paper
602 x 469 mm
Collection of Lynn Middleton, Wellington

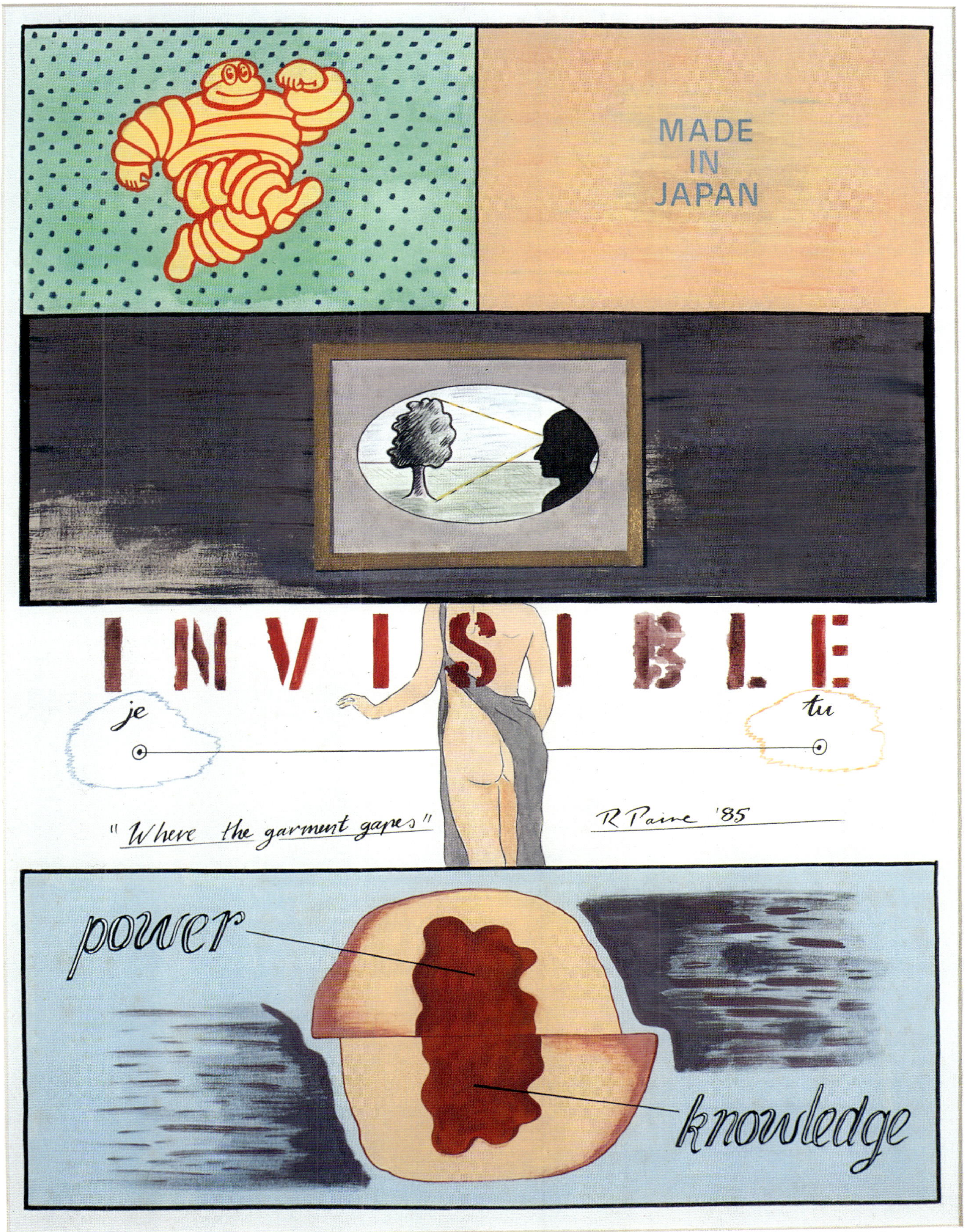
MADE
IN
JAPAN
INVISIBLE
je
tu
"Where the garment gapes"
R Paine '85
power
knowledge

67

FIONA PARDINGTON

Born Auckland 1961.
BFA, UA 1984.
Lives in Dunedin.

The artistic agendas of Pardington and Webster (98) are similar, although their works look very different. The adjective 'decadent' has been applied more than once to Pardington's photographic work, and indeed much of it displays the signs of decadence. Elaborate gold or trinket-encrusted frames enclose imagery which hints at, or overtly presents, themes of sexuality, bondage, fetishism, disease, vivisection and death. To see this as fervid *fin de siècle* excess is a superficial response. Contemplation of Pardington's work brings a realisation that there is much tenderness and compassion mixed in: an understanding of the human condition, that beauty must fade but can give way gracefully to age, that we must live with death, that distasteful bodily functions cannot be avoided and that ecstatic dreams can turn to nightmares. Pardington has also been tagged with feminist and deconstructivist labels, because of her photographs of male nudes and her use of inner frames covered by disjointed snippets of text. These too are simplistic assessments. The artist has professed a fascination with the human body as form: form for its own sake and with the potential for classical and suggestive references. Male and female sexuality are given more or less equal examination in Pardington's photos. Where works incorporate text, the snippets come from one or more sources chosen by the artist for their ability to enhance viewers' responses to the principal imagery. That enhancement must be subjective and can be from short groups of words or an awareness of the general nature of the source books. There is thus much of the surreal in Pardington's work, because Freudian dreams and automatic writing were basic ingredients of surrealism. There are also echoes of the work of Joseph Cornell, who used old maps and fragmentary texts to generate memory and nostalgia.

Heavy Penance, 1993–4
Black and white photographic print
ca. 200 x 240 mm
Private Collection, Auckland

During 1985–87 Pardington was photographing carefully posed male nudes in black and white. Though similar to Mapplethorpe's less explicit work, these photographs had a playful quality. *Saul*, 1987, a very fine image of a well-built man with aquiline features wearing nothing but a beekeeper's mask, expressed disdain and a wish to be left alone but also suggested a hint of fear and a need for protection. In 1987–88 Pardington diversified into gold-toned prints of male arms and legs adorned with jewellery, and into wistful photographs of an elderly woman. The emulsion at the edges of some of the negatives was manipulated. At this time the artist also began making excessive frames encrusted with baubles and fringed with feathers, and, in images like *Descent Into Flesh*, 1987, she hinted at such taboo subjects as ejaculate on pubic hair and the male's wet exit from and re-entry into the female both at birth and later.

In her series *Tainted Love* of 1994, Pardington continued in uncompromising vein, using old medical photographs of communicable skin diseases as well as her own suggestive imagery. Just to list images appearing in photographs by an artist such as Pardington is of limited value, because the context and presentation is so important. Blood-soaked towels, grinning plaster moulds of teeth, roses, model breasts and crusty barnacles could all be the stuff of gothic pornokitsch. Pardington controls them and generates symbols, metaphor, allusion, mystery and disquiet.

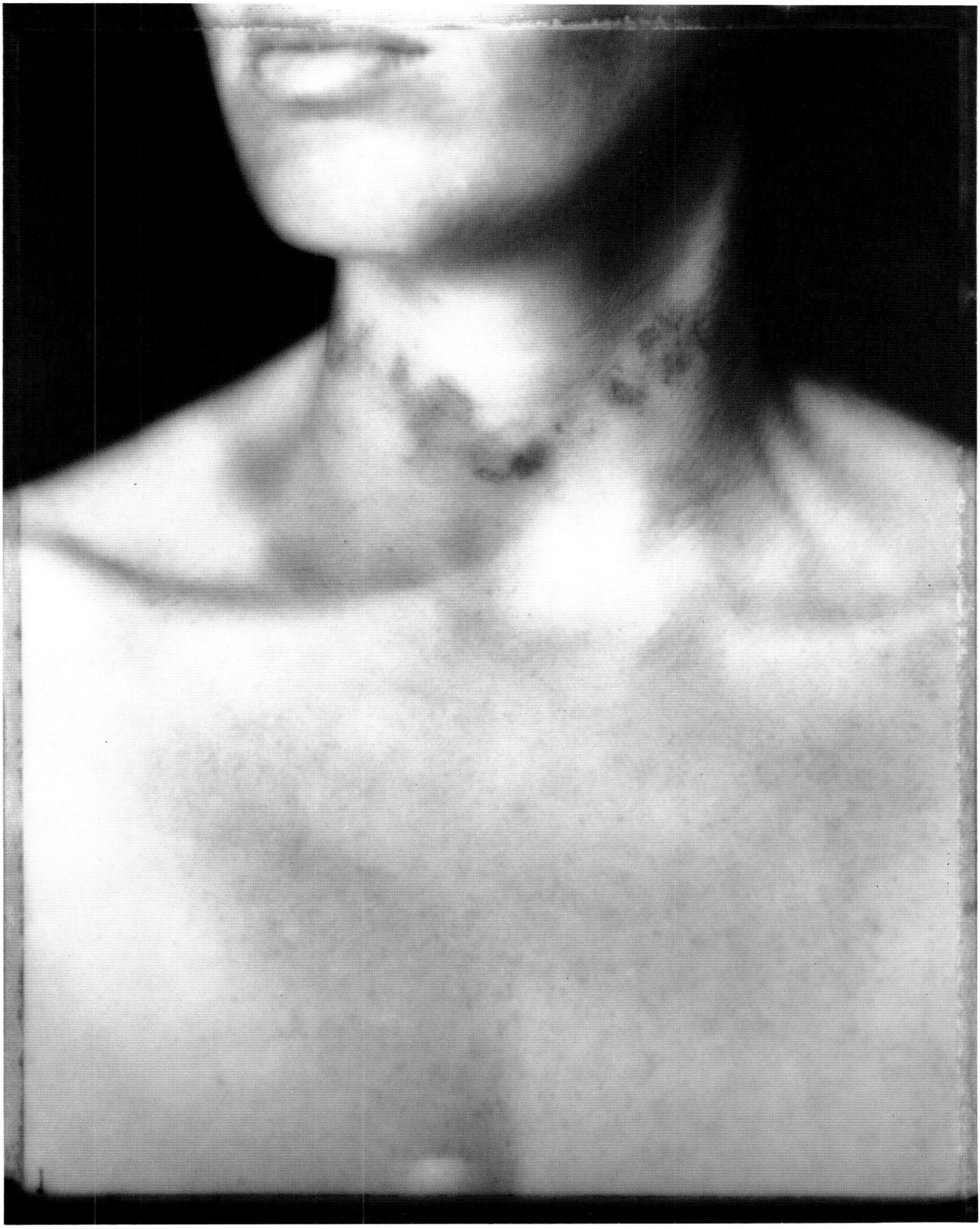

68

MICHAEL PAREKOWHAI

Born Wellington 1968.
BFA, UA 1990; DT, Auckland College of Education 1991.
Lives in Auckland.

Parekowhai is a Maori sculptor who is examining firstly the relationships between the colonists and the tangata whenua with intelligence and irony (cf. Cotton, 100NZP, 16; Robinson 100NZP, 78) and secondly aspects of modern art from his own perspective. He works mainly in the traditional Maori carving medium of wood, but meticulously fashions and paints so that it looks like plastic. In 1990 he was concerned with rendering words in three dimensions, using the extra dimension (size, colour, finish, positioning) to set up ironies and multiple readings. In one work the words 'I AM HE', taken from a McCahon painting in which they were rendered in distorted 3-D perspective, were made hugely real as he turned them into a showdown between young sculptor and old master. More recently Parekowhai's sculptures have imitated the plastic kitsets from which realistic models are made. One noticeable difference is the scale (Parekowhai's simulations are about 10 times larger than the models), and another is subject matter. Model sets come in sheets, like a trampoline frame with all the components suspended within and held in place by tiny points of contact. To get a piece out of the frame, one twists it a little and breaks the join. Parekowhai still owns a model set of a truck given to him by his elder brother in 1981. He never made it up because he so enjoyed the look of the unbroken matrices. Within Parekowhai's frames, or sometimes free of them, we find sets of objects that speak of the physical colonisation of New Zealand: spades, axes and guns refer to the pioneers, while gas-welding apparatus refers to the evolution of a settled, westernised society. Other sets refer to an artistic colonisation, such as huge kitset versions of Walters' koru paintings (100NZP, 93) made from laser-cut steel. The 'frames', when they are shown with their contents popped out and only the sprues remaining, make wistful statements about absence, loss and waste. Like Walters' paintings they are that rare commodity: minimal art with a message.

A more international, postmodern statement is made when Parekowhai clones copies of Marcel Duchamp's readymades, such as his *Urinal*. Art that was never made by an artist originally now appears as if mass-produced. We see large-scale versions of small-scale models of originals of yet another scale, and we are left with a range of possible meanings. One is that the artist is playing games with us, as indicated by his works incorporating game pieces, such as pick-up-sticks and chessmen — but then again, the enlarged sticks look like pa palisades, and chess was an abiding passion of Duchamp. Parekowhai has also made a number of other imitation artworks, such as a big Henry Moore figure. In shiny, lumpy fibreglass, it makes nonsense of the original, which was intended to resemble water-smoothed stone. This continues an interest Parekowhai demonstrated at art school, when he laboriously made an impeccable wooden copy of Duchamp's readymade bicycle wheel.

Parekowhai puts things into his own frames of reference and twists them out again. Viewers are left to assemble their own meanings (cf. O'Connor, 65).

Acts, 1993
Enamel on wood
Variable dimensions
Courtesy Gregory Flint Gallery, Auckland

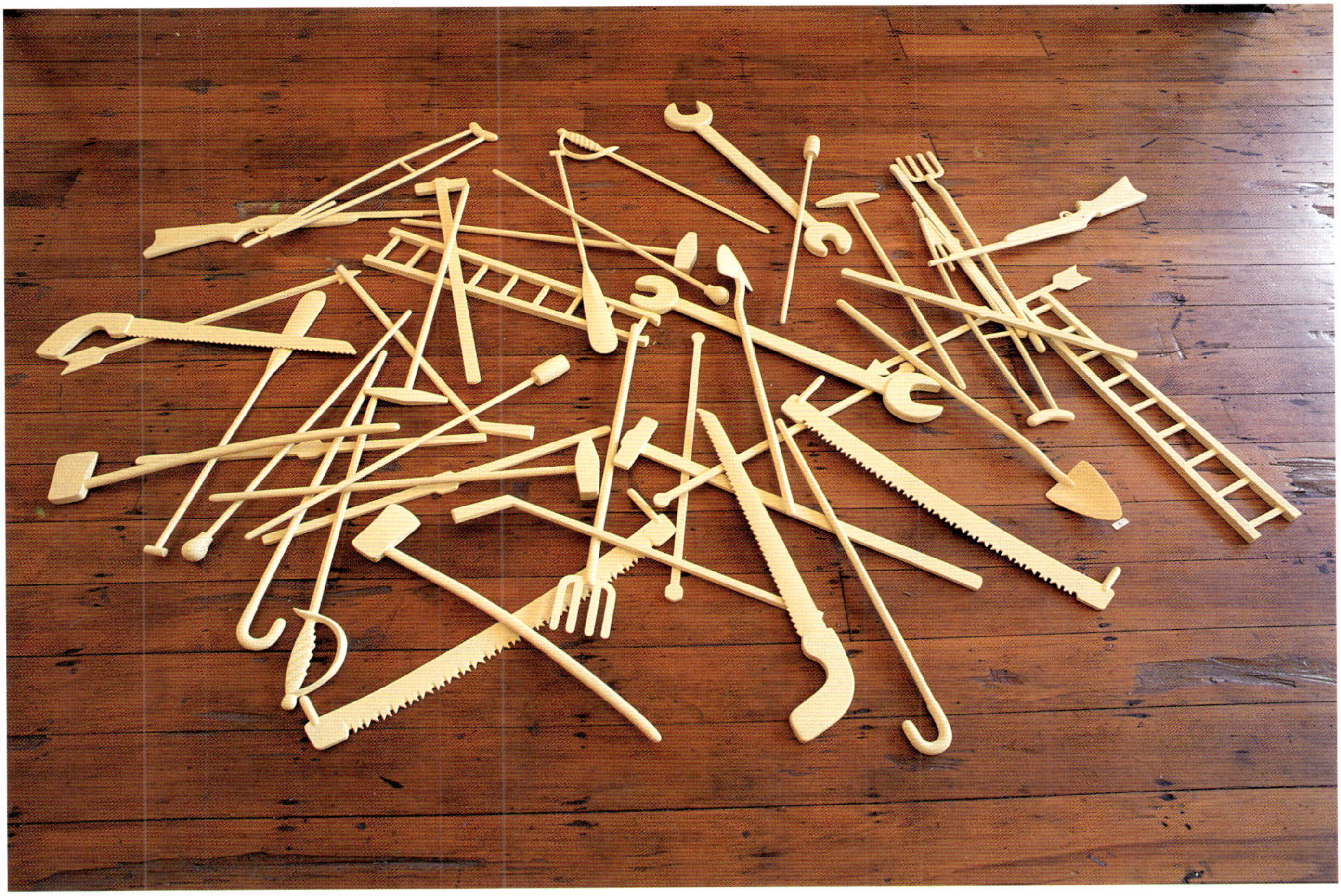

69

ANTON PARSONS

Born Palmerston North 1968.
BFA, UC 1991.
Lives in Auckland.

From his first exhibition as a student sculptor in 1989, Parsons has shown consistent inventiveness, professional workmanship and an ability to invest a comparatively simple object with elegance, humour and intellectual depth.

His early works were ribbed and flanged forms, based on oval and cone shapes, displaying potential for movement and traction. His 1990 work had a pop feel to it. A scaled-up pen was held off a wall by its own drawn line; a model zeppelin was held down by a simulated 12-ton weight; and on one curve of blue-green wood an airship was convincingly portrayed above the sea and a submarine below it. In 1991, in common with other artists (see Haffern, 100NZP, 30; Budd, 7; Pardington, 67), Parsons began making works involving text. One was a Möbius strip, seemingly made of box-section riveted steel, covered on all sides with random lettering — an endlessly unrolling, meaningless stream of text. Another version of this work, in the form of a knot, found an ideal home in a jurors' waiting room. *Yin and Yang* was a book 1 metre thick, with a curved spine which reversed itself halfway, at which point a third cover was inserted. *Pencil Holder* was a 1.7-metre-long hollow steel pencil. Random letters were cut out of each of its six faces, revealing an inside full of pencil sharpeners made in the shape of little planet Earths. Here were worlds of meaning in one pencil . . . or maybe a fatal conceptual error multiplying. In his 1992 show, *About the Size of It*, Parsons presented immaculately made gigantic pencils and a wooden ruler. This cheeky piece offered viewers writing utensils and the means of measuring the dimensions of their unusability. The pencils, seen as gender symbols, are open to many further interpretations.

Guide, 1994–5
Wood, paint, steel, plastic
2000 x 1200 x 250mm
Courtesy 23a Gallery, Auckland

Time spent overseas in 1993 directed Parsons' art into more serious mode. During 1994–95 he exhibited works on the theme of seeing/not seeing . On the related theme of not communicating, *He Had Nothing to Say*, a tall, wardrobe-shaped piece, black on one side and white on the other, looked like an oversized version of the back of a switchboard. On going around to the other side, one discovered that the 'wires' just looped back the other way. A piece of the same shape consisted of a black plywood chest edged with aluminium and perforated by holes in a Braille pattern, like the switchboard with the wires ripped out — a negative version of *Guide*. Glimpses of light (but not enlightenment) came through from holes on the opposite side. Lying on its side, this work was elegantly matched with a set of pure black and pure white photo prints showing the full film — frame bars, sprocket holes and all.

The idea of seeing and not doing is also of interest to Parsons. *Dumb Box* of 1994 is a black box with a stiff white carrying cover and a set of bolts. With the cover taken off and set down beside the box, the piece looks minimal and puzzling. A gallery-goer bold enough to disrupt its symmetry and pick it up finds that it can be assembled in seven different combinations (all, it must be said, equally minimal). In February 1996 Parsons made a window-work for Auckland's new New Gallery, which consisted of an opticians' test chart so large that one had to back across the road for it to work properly, thus getting the Big Picture (or maybe killed by traffic).

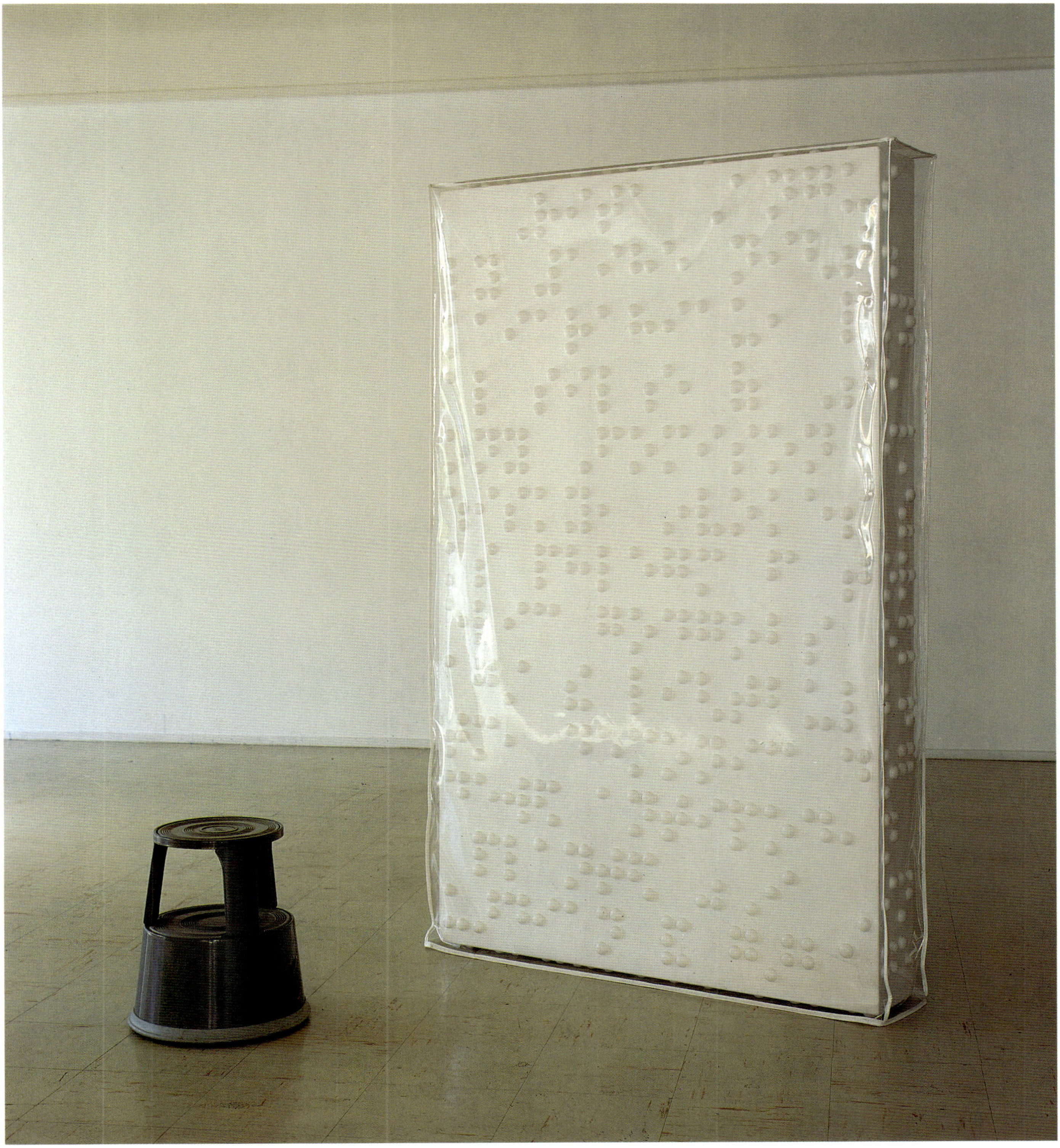

70

PETER PERYER

Born Auckland 1941.
MA (Education), UA 1972.
Lives in Auckland.

Peryer's photographs are often deceptively simple. He works in black and white, and his subjects can appear so ordinary one wonders why he bothered photographing them. He is self-taught, uses basic equipment and makes no attempt at image manipulation or glitzy effects. He does not take many pictures and often spends a great deal of time preparing for the ones he does take. He also is always awake to the possibilities of serendipitous happenings. Peryer uses a camera to put before us images that have engaged his mind as an artist. Just as we can miss many interesting things in life by not paying attention, so the content of a Peryer photograph can elude us if we do not give it adequate consideration. He does not make it easy for us: he changes the *raison d'être* of his photographs all the time. Texture, design, mood, identity, multiple readings, oddity, even banality can be the point, and sometimes it will be a mixture of these.

Peryer's work has moved from experimentation through portraiture to aspects of formal design of the picture, to an interest in the natural world. In 1975, in common with other photographers at the time who were seeking a new look, Peryer used a Diana camera for six months. This cheap camera has a fixed aperture, distorting wide-angle lens, poor focus and slow shutter speed. In his *Mars Hotel* series Peryer created images with a furtive look, as if they had been taken through a periscope or with a spy camera. Peryer first came to wide notice in 1978 with a series of posed portraits of himself and friends. These were grainy and melodramatic, the subjects seemingly captured off-guard at a time when they were under some stress. One of the best known of this series is a self-portrait holding a rooster with tied legs. With these works Peryer was in the forefront of a movement in photography popularised by Cindy Sherman from 1978 on. This type of work seeks to break down the impersonal, finger-on-the-button factor by ironically putting the photographer in front of the lens, so that he or she is seen in a narrative situation which, by definition, is most unlikely to be factual, but may be symbolic. The idea of the set-up shot has been used occasionally by Peryer since — for example, in his pictures of a Meccano bus climbing a steep clay road.

In *Frozen Flame*, 1982, everything within the frame is grainy by nature — a path, kerbing, garden soil and tree trunk. As the dominant part of the image is a severely geometric V where a garden comes to a point, the result is a study in line and tone. In a photograph of Braille, *Seeing*, 1989, the sense of scale is ambiguous — we could be looking at rivets on a sheet of steel or at orderly grass huts seen from a plane. The same applies to *New Zealand*, 1991, which looks like a remarkably clear satellite view of the country, but is actually a playground inlay. Peryer's attitude to the infinite replicability of a photograph is illuminating. He is reluctant to 'print back' (reprint copies of images from the past). As an artist who uses a camera, he prefers to be printing, showing and selling what he is currently doing.

Chicken, 1996
Black and white photograph
132 x 208 mm
Collection of the artist

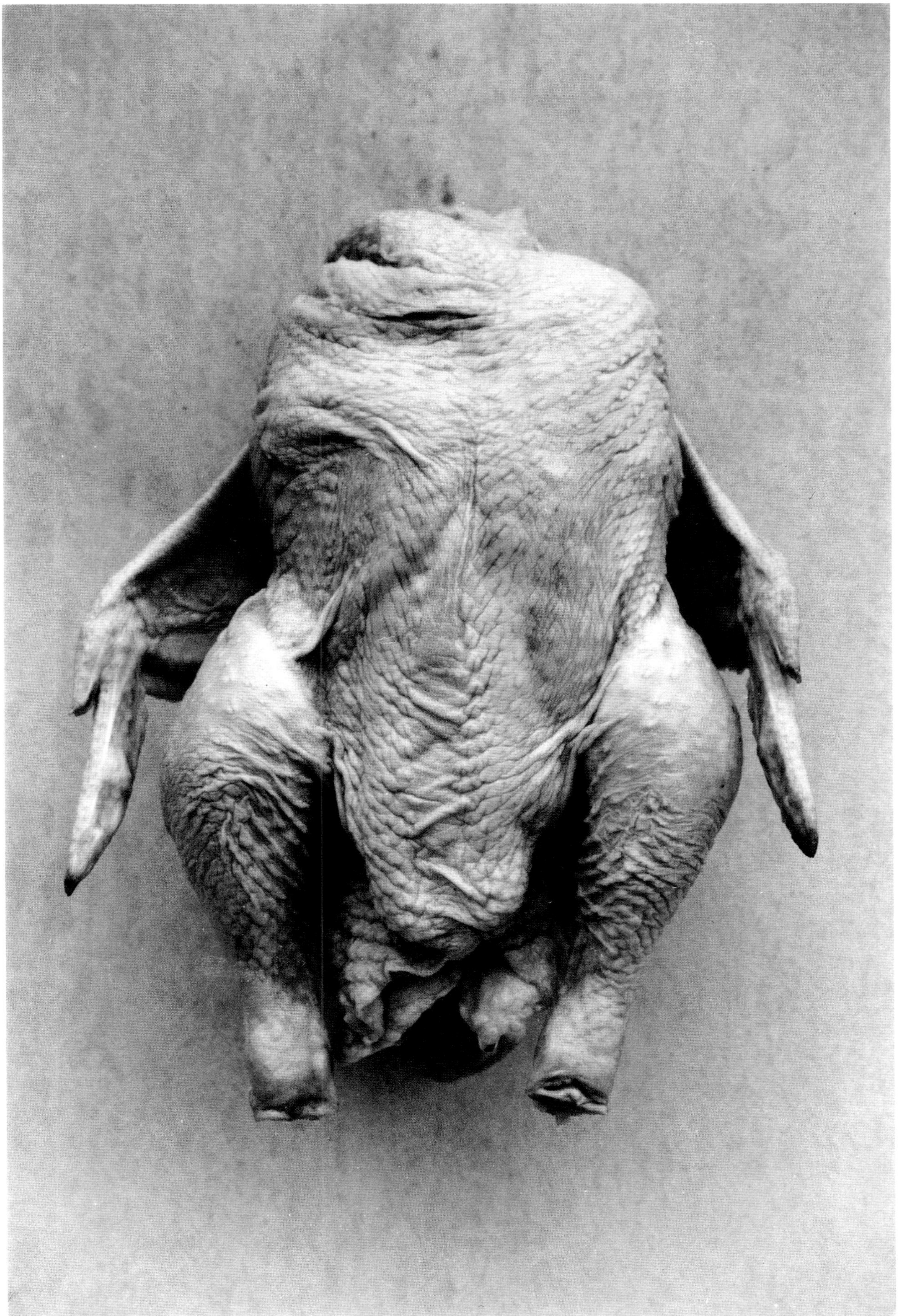

71

MATT PINE

Born Wanganui 1941.
DFA, UA 1962; Hornsey College of Art, London 1962–64.
Lives in Taihape.

Pine is perhaps the most classically modern New Zealand sculptor, and he is certainly one of the most prolific. He lived for 10 years in London and absorbed the 1960s sculptural styles of Judd, Andre, Smith, Le Witt, Smithson and Morris. Those styles can broadly be described as constructivist and minimalist — a reaction to the rounded surrealist forms of Picasso, Moore and Hepworth. Pine has continued working in this manner ever since, with remarkable diversity and originality. His range of forms is extremely wide and he has served younger sculptors as a one-man demonstration of the possibilities for working with such basic materials as sawn timber, rough stone, concrete blocks, wire, rope, sheet iron and perspex. Throughout his career he has made innumerable drawings, both as studies for sculpture and as finished works; he paints, makes prints and has done some conceptual photography.

While in London Pine produced his *Open Series*, open forms in wood, metal and plastics, and some very elegant work in perspex, the *Colour Works*, abstract studies in primary colour relationships. On his return to New Zealand in 1974, Pine set about applying what he had learned to making sculpture based on local structural designs. He found in his Maori heritage and New Zealand's colonial past a wealth of inspiration. The year 1977 was a particularly creative one for Pine. The *Structure Series* looked at meeting house construction details, transformed into chrome-plated steel. The forms of the houses themselves were abstracted into the rough-sawn plank *Constructions*. He also began his important *Fortifications* series based on the shapes of Maori defensive earthworks, and the *Lineworks* series, large outdoor works using rope and wire which traced the outlines of tent forms and sail rigging. The balancing of opposites is a feature of much of Pine's work. The *Equivalent* series was about differences in materials, setting one type against another, while the *Untitled* series in galvanised steel was about differences in shapes. The *Ground Level* series of 1979 analysed Maori food store structures, and the *F* series of that year re-created the complex, angular outlines of Maori trenches in PVC pipe, making sinuous, minimal, absolutely contemporary sculptures. The solid *Blockworks* of 1980 and the open *Outrigger Series* of 1981 showed Pine working in diametrically opposed materials and forms. The *High Water* series of 1982 were small cast-aluminium works based on partly submerged structures in the Wanganui River, while the *Traps*, based on traditional Maori bird and fish traps, made elegant suspended forms out of aluminium strips and wire. In the *Placement/Displacement* series of 1982–85, rough stones were placed within carefully constructed wooden slat cages. The *Circles*, begun in 1985, were concrete block mazes that called to mind igloos and archaeological excavations. The elegant, inventive *Above Ground* series of 1987 re-presented the essential outlines of historic Maori architecture, and the *Pacific Pieces* of 1989 re-created the outlines of Polynesian canoes, huts and temples in modern materials. In the 1990s Pine has made a number of stone pieces derived from forms from ancient cultures, and installations made up of separate sculptures in diverse media, some in memory of relatives who died in battle and others dealing with extinct birds and the threatened environment.

These descriptive references are but a sampling of Pine's diverse output, which ranges in scale from tiny to huge and is presented both inside and outside.

Ground Level no. 1, 1977
Rough-sawn pine using interlocking joints
2135 x 1525 x 1220 mm
Courtesy Sarjeant Gallery, Wanganui

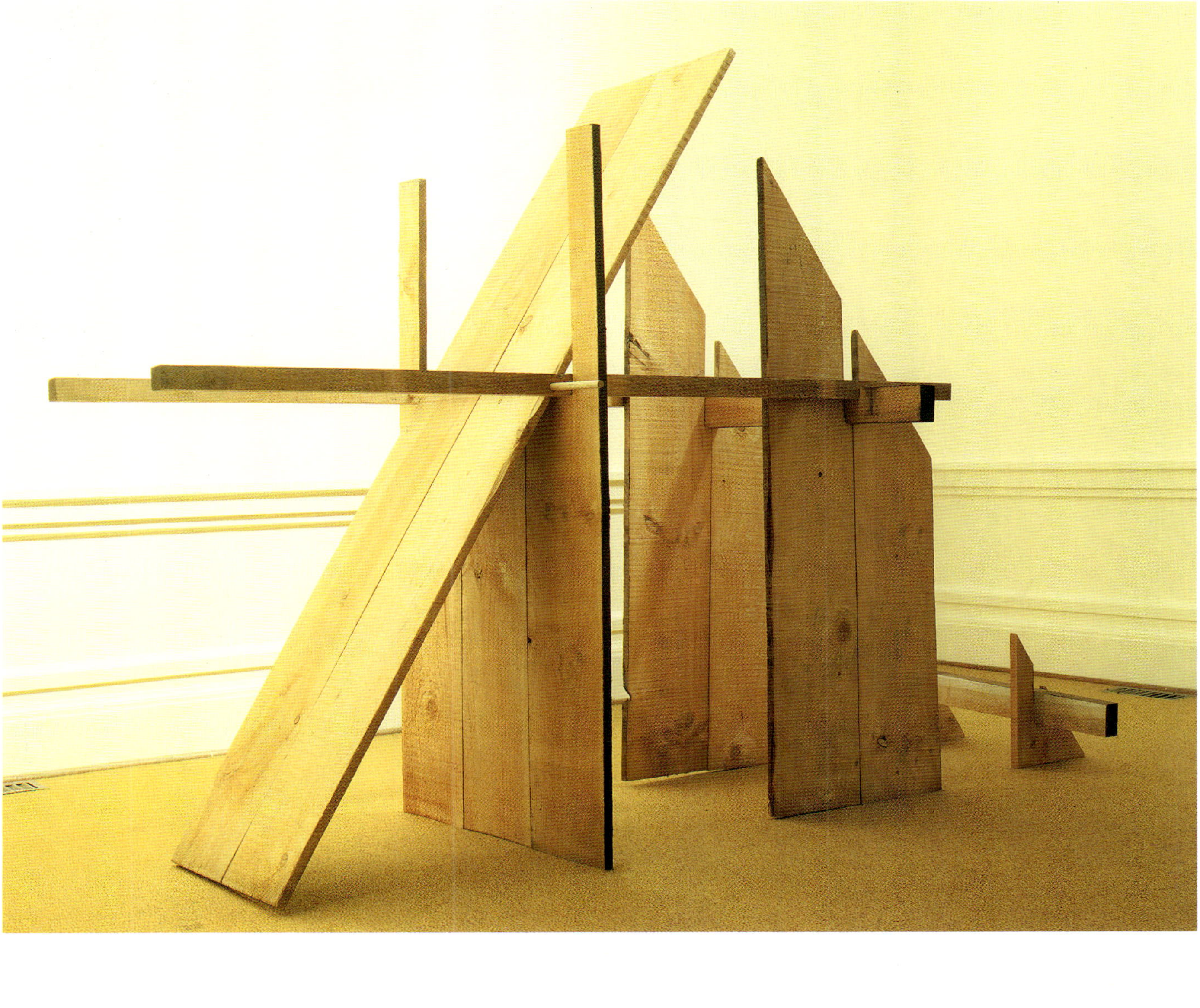

72

RICHARD REDDAWAY

Born Lower Hutt 1962.
DFA, UC 1985.
Lives in Wellington.

Reddaway is a photographer and sculptor, and his subject is the human body. His themes relate to architecture as a symbol, first of human achievements and secondly of human subordination to systems necessary to make 'progress'. Reddaway's photographs and drawings can be seen as two-dimensional explorations of ideas which he has also pursued in three, but there is a difference in the presentation of the two media. The photographs are of real bodies, usually the artist's, and by definition they are perfect replications. The sculptures are simplified and generic, either roughly expressive or mutely cubic. The photographs are montages of multiple copies of black and white prints combined in various inventive ways that call to mind architectural elements, such as the rose windows of medieval cathedrals and the decorative reliefs found in their arched doorways. They are seemingly simple works which on reflection are seen to be full of references — to the New Zealand artist viewing the gothic tradition, to the self-supporting artist boldly revealing himself and yet appearing vulnerable and entrapped in an unbreakable system, and to the biological phenomenon of mimesis (one creature masquerading as another). Beyond these insights are further complexities — the salacious male gaze at female nudity is reversed; the artist's gender is always hidden from view and he seems capable of self-replication; his role-playing as the perfect physical specimen of Greek art is patently flawed; and there is obvious fragility where a support structure of bodies is dependent upon the man at the bottom.

Shining Star, 1993–4
Mirror tiles, silver leaf on cardson & wood
ca. 1.6 m dia.
Courtesy of the artist

Reddaway's sculptures are variations on a blocky, stylised figure of the type drawn by students trying to master the dynamics and positions of body movements before getting on to any expressive detail (cf. Cherrie, 12). The figures are usually in passive postures and often hang on the wall in the slumped attitude of a crucifixion, but with the arms tied at the back. This bent-knee position is similar to that of praying, or, again, of a trussed captive. An air of vulnerability and pathos is created. Other figures made out of square concrete blocks are lonely sentinels prepared, like buildings, to stand impassively for ever. To this basic approach in presenting the human figure Reddaway adds a range of expressive finishes, or skins, which affect the viewer's perception of and reaction to each figure. His early mannikins were made of sticks wrapped in sack-cloth strips, giving a mummy-like dimension to the forms and at the same time binding them together in groups. They hung together like chains of ants, individually helpless but mutually supportive.

Beginning in 1990 the artist has fleshed out his forms by covering them in mirrorglass fragments, broken vinyl records, small ceramic bathroom tiles, shells and other materials found in our everyday environment. Strangely, the accretions of flat, angular shards give the figures an expressive life lacking in the boxy understructure. Light is reflected and shadows created, artificially modelling the forms. There is illusion, and also allusion — to expressionism, cubism and minimalism, art styles literally embodied in the works. In 1992 Reddaway echoed his figures in text pinned on the adjacent wall, the sheets of paper themselves making up a blocky silhouette. These works presented a view of modern men as part of a featureless mass, and any textural legacy they may leave to the future as fragmentary and ephemeral.

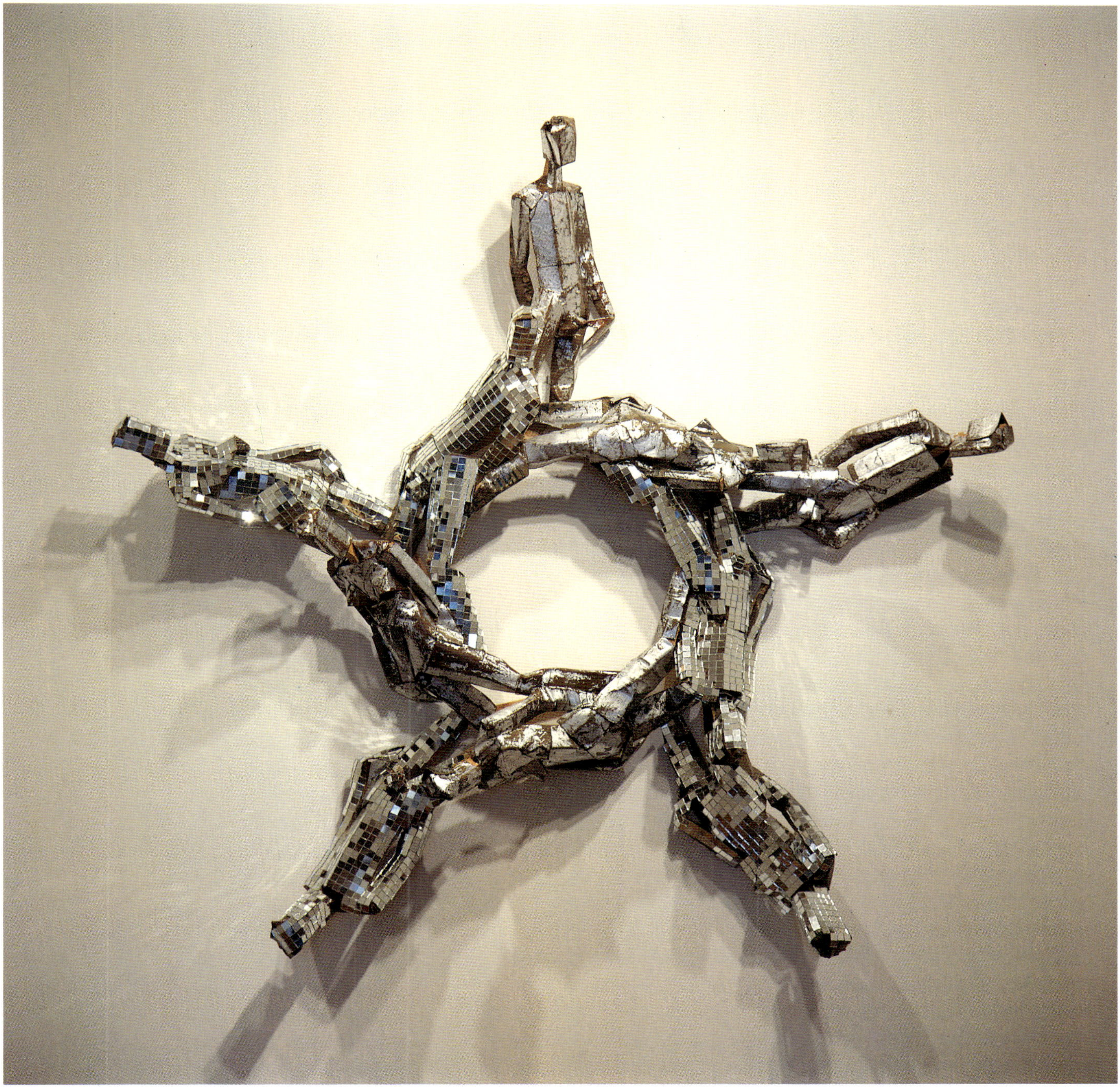

73

MICHAEL REED

Born Christchurch 1950.
DFA (Engraving), UC 1969.
Lives in Christchurch.

Reed works mainly on and with paper, but he has designed rugs, and made medallions, works in etched brass and wall sculpture. He has been a printmaker since 1970 and he has used pastel, pencil and paint on both flat and folded paper in a wide variety of ways. A love for rich, saturated colour is another feature of his art, and this can be traced back to his love of Bonnard's work.

Reed studied etching with Barry Cleavin (14) and his work from 1972 to 1975 had some similarities to Cleavin's in that it was figurative, detailed and sometimes mordantly humorous. Some works expressed Reed's social conscience, a side that was to underlie his work of the 1990s, at which time some elements of realism also returned after a long absence. In retrospect, Reed's love of decoration and the expressively drawn line which supported his later abstraction is also evident in these works.

By 1977 Reed was moving away from realism and traditional perspective, with works in which card-like shapes appeared to float against a patterned background. He introduced paper-sculpting techniques to create real, shallow spaces. By the early 1980s he was working in a style with affinities to that of Bennett (4), exploring the representation in two dimensions of geometric planes and shapes which, because of the sharp shadows they threw out, appeared to be in three dimensions. This blending of surrealism and analytical cubism created perceptual conundrums. Scribbled gestural marks and the use of unusual colour prevented the drawings from becoming academic exercises. *Bright Lights, Dark Corners* of 1981 looked at the abstract forms made by light falling into Reed's newly acquired cottage. As these works developed he began adding more interest to the reliefs by tearing and overlaying papers. The *Concertina Impositions* of 1984 sunk repeated triangles and trapezoids into the paper, like erratic louvres. The pastels of the mid-1980s featured velvet-rich textures in powerful colours, setting up intense contrasts heightened by real and drawn shadows. Reed's screenprints and lithographs of the 1980s appear to depict a surrealist stage upon which variously coloured pyramids, walls and poles are set up, casting shadows and making a strong composition with spatial illusion. Prints of the latter part of the 1980s also have floating elements such as moons, and the spotlight on the 'stage' becomes a palette-shaped island in a sea of expressive marks. It is here that we see the beginnings of an overt Pacific reference which has occupied Reed in the 1990s.

A trip to Mexico in 1987 imbued Reed with a clear sense of his origins and place as a Pacific dweller. Constructed drawings of 1988 depicted a ridged sea and, on the island, forms representing habitation and natural growth. By 1990 specific images drawn from around the Pacific were worked into colourful prints, painted collages and wall-based constructions which, at first glance, seemed to be celebrations of the Pacific Paradise. A closer look showed them to be subtle comments about the pollution of lagoons by run-off from tree clearance and land development, and of the sea by nuclear tests, lost fishnets and waste plastic. Wrinkled surfaces coloured the deep, dark blue of the ocean were cracked and fissured, and some works contained relevant but barely readable texts and finely drawn geometric shapes. Cowrie shell eyes, evocative of the Pacific, were a reminder that we should look at what is happening there. Reed's works of 1995 were direct representations of eyes, using wood, seagrass, paua and mirrors.

Postcard from the South Seas/ Fromage Moruroa, 1995
Mixed media on paper
960 x 600 mm
Collection of Cashmere High School, Christchurch

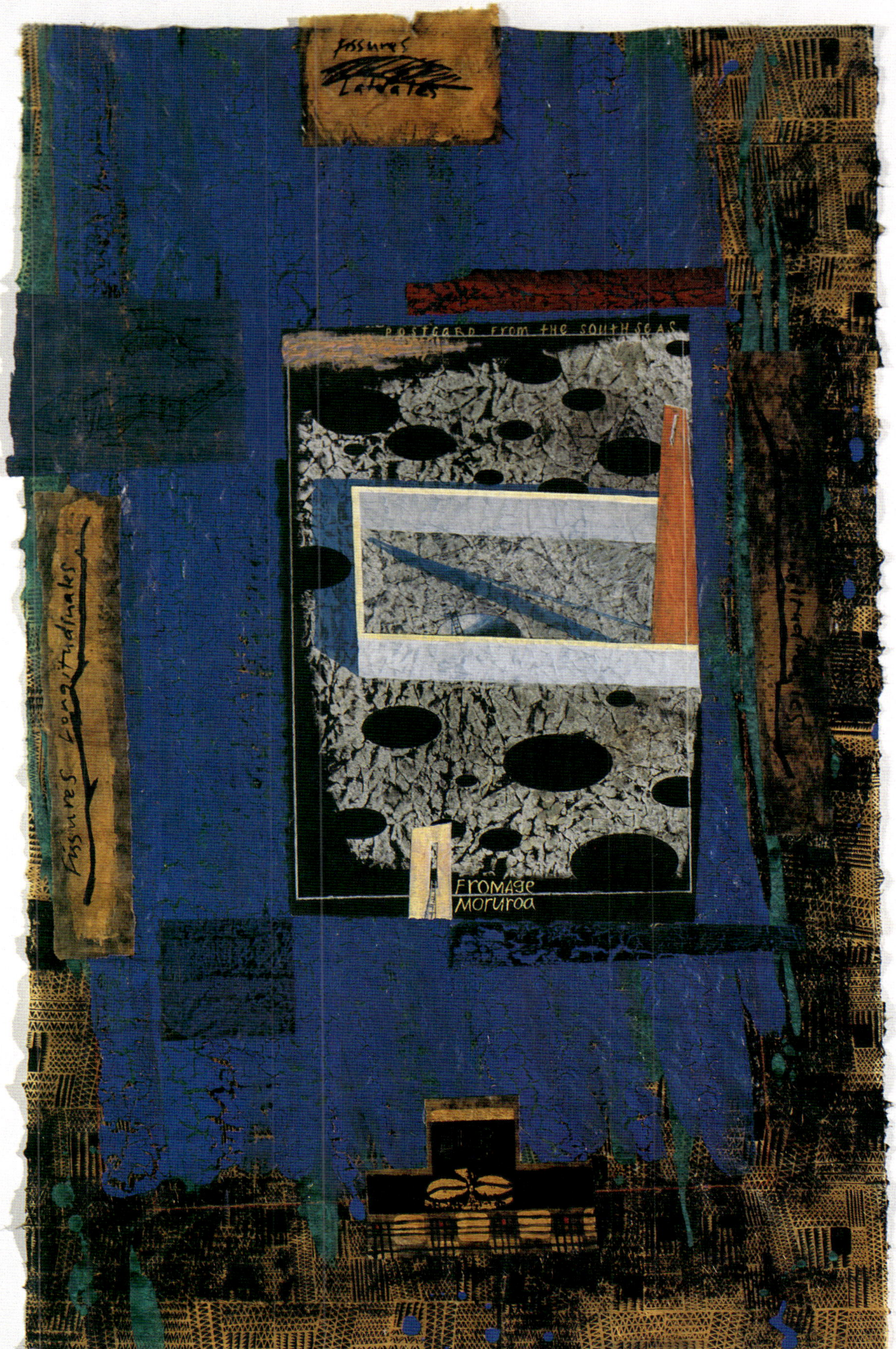

Fissures
Laterales
POSTCARD FROM THE SOUTH SEAS
Fissures Longitudinales
Fromage
Moruroa

PATRICK REYNOLDS

Born Auckland 1962.
BA (History), UA 1984; studied photography, UA 1982–83.
Lives in Auckland.

Reynolds loves the photographic medium and his work is an exploration of its possibilities, but without recourse to such extreme actions as cutting or manipulation. He prefers to use natural light rather than studio set-ups, although he does make extensive use of flash. Between 1985 and 1987 Reynolds lived in England and Italy. While there he took many photographs on colour positive film, and these formed the basis of his first exhibition on his return, the *Candela* of 1987. These were multi-part cibachrome works in which the cypress trees of Tuscany were equated with candles. The device used in this series, of bracketing a number of photographs together in sets, was a link back to Reynolds' early work of 1984. He began using colour negative film in 1988 and has used this for his colour work since then.

Reynolds' black and white *Landscape* series of 1988 remains one of his most important bodies of work. He found in Auckland's Waitakere Ranges a hilly, coastal landscape very different from Tuscany. He noted the forms of flax bushes, toitoi and cabbage trees which previously he had taken for granted. At night, lit from below and standing out against the blackness, this growth seemed strange and Dr Seuss-like. Wandering in the scrub in sight of the sea at dusk, Reynolds took a series of photographs of solitary toitoi stalks. These were lit first by a flash and then, by leaving the shutter open, by available light. The results made the toitoi appear as a flame or a wraith, with the rest of the landscape moody and indistinct. Applied to cabbage tree leaves, this technique resulted in some extraordinary pictures in which the leaf fans seemed to vibrate, caught sharply by the flash and less distinctly by the hand-held time exposure. In the related series, *Night is my Fire* and *Nature is a Language*, 1989, Reynolds continued his investigation of the use of multiple light sources in dark conditions, using starlight, moonlight and firelight in conjunction with flash to create images that the eye (including the photographer's eye) does not see. A fine example of this is a diptych which shows a punga frond seemingly in positive and negative. The black on white version was the result of the flash failing to work.

The Structure of the Universe III, 1988
Selenium-toned silver gelatin print
480 x 480 mm
Courtesy of the artist

A desire to get away from the picturesque and not to fulfil viewers' expectations of what a photograph should be about is a continuing motivator for Reynolds. He has applied this approach to portrait photography, where his definitive and arresting images are often the result of an unposed snap (e.g. *Some Painters*, 1991). His most extreme application of the principle of letting the camera do the seeing was the seven large (1 x 1.5 metre) prints in the *Headlands* series of 1991. Over one summer Reynolds ran the same films through several cameras more than once, shooting pictures of whatever interested him inside, outside, at night and by day. The resulting negatives were multiple exposures, a surreal mix of real people, places, times and objects. Works such as these done as paintings would become silly and psychedelic. As photographs they became evocative journeys for the mind.

Reynolds' work since 1991 has been more documentary in nature. One three-year project which culminated in 1995 was *Owners*. A panoramic camera was used to photograph the owners of pieces made by the artist/jeweller Warwick Freeman: all were wearing their pieces, and these plus the photographs were all exhibited together.

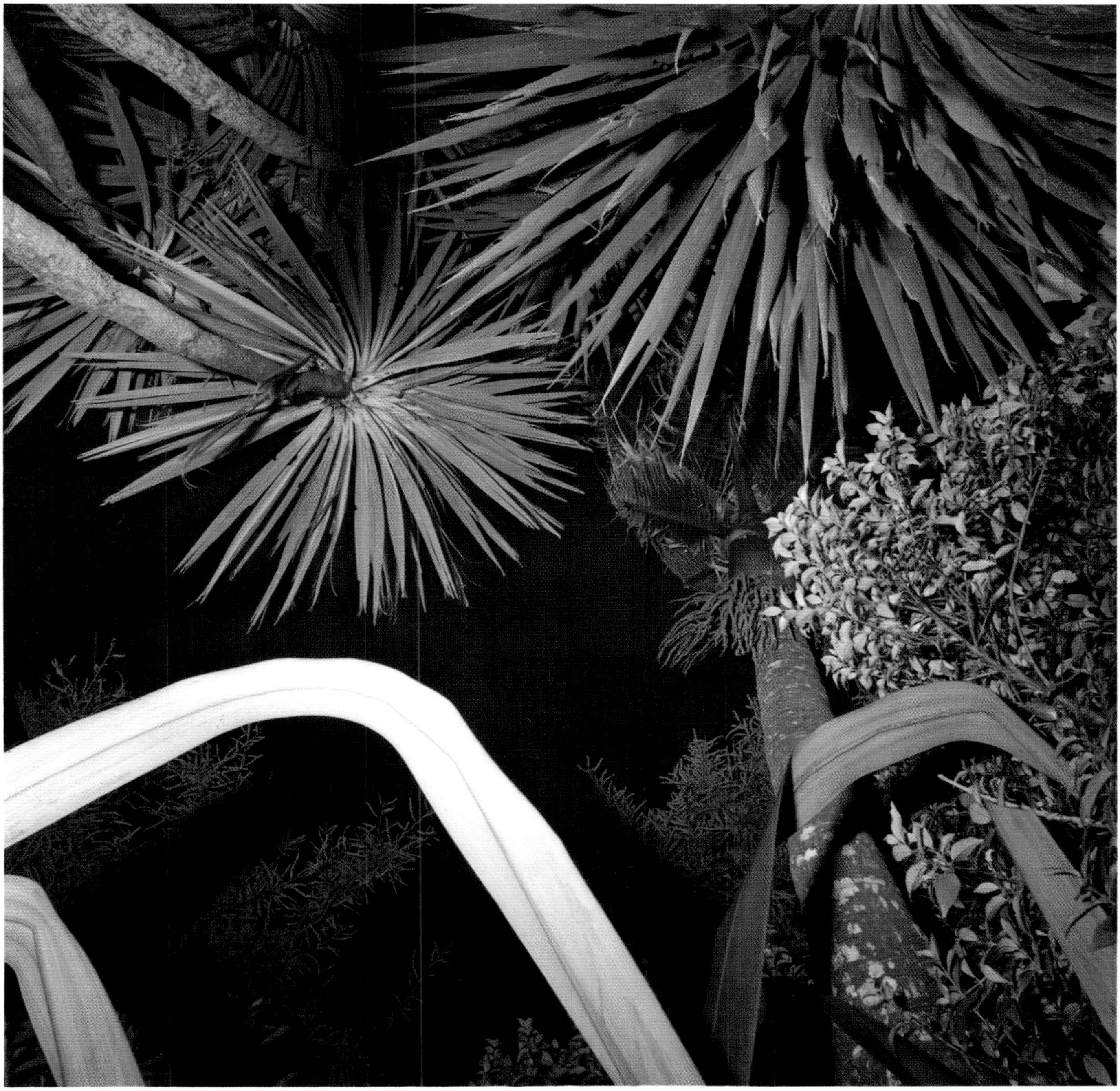

75

PAULINE RHODES

Born Christchurch 1937.
Studied art, WP 1960 and UC 1972–74.
Lives in Christchurch.

Between 1961 and 1971 Rhodes made sculpture in terracotta, wood and bronze in New Zealand, Nigeria and England. She began working outdoors in 1973, establishing herself as one of New Zealand's few environmental sculptors, working with and in nature. This form of art is based on pioneering work done in America in the 1960s by artists such as Smithson and Heizer. Much of their work involved alteration of the landscape by marking or digging it, as well as carting bits of it into galleries. Rhodes's alterations are much more colourful, gentle and temporary, and in this she anticipated artists such as Goldsworthy. Rhodes's studios are the Southern Alps and the coastline and hills of Banks Peninsula, which she modifies by placing contrasting coloured elements and forms within them. Green sticks may be planted in yellow summer grass or on black sand; driftwood or stones may be assembled on a beach, or red leaf shapes floated on a blue tidal pool. Materials are functional and economical and anything brought to a site is removed after the scene has been recorded on colour transparencies.

Another activity has been to use natural outdoor processes to achieve modification of material, such as the rusting of steel plates and mesh to stain cardboard, wood and cloth. Some of this, as well as other material, is shaped by the artist into jagged or round-topped screens or other shapes found in nature. Materials are then used in gallery installations, which can be compact or very large and dispersed. Elements can be assembled quite formally or appear to have been just dumped in a pile. The components may show marks of having been wetly pressed together, such as the grid of the mesh on the cardboard and the random stains of rust on the cloth. So, although an assemblage may be flimsy, it is cohesive and balanced. Some of the elements are kept and reused in related installations elsewhere and at other times.

from 'Land Extensum Projects', Banks Peninsula, 1994
Dyed cloth
Variable dimensions
Courtesy of the artist

Rhodes entitles her outdoor works *Extensums*, things being created over a wide area on an ongoing basis as extensions of the artist's thinking and experience. The indoor works are *Intensums*, the collecting together of elements which then relate to each other in accordance with their temporary placement. The spanning of space and time is important to Rhodes. With the *Intensums* there is the feeling of past time conveyed by objects which have obviously been subjected elsewhere to weathering processes. For followers of Rhodes's work there will also be the recognition of some elements seen in earlier installations. The *Intensums* can only be fully experienced by being there and taking some time to look at them. Strangely, in photographs they lose the intensity imparted to them by their confinement and the lighting within the white cube of the gallery. Photography has the opposite effect on the *Extensums*. It concentrates the viewer's vision on the work and enables the artist to pick the best angle of view and conditions of light. Through photography, these ephemeral events can last for ever, or at least much longer than the installations, and viewers can mentally re-create them in other settings.

Rhodes's art is perceptual, experimental and vital rather than something to be acquired. The artist says: 'The projects are ephemeral, just as life is. The materials are related in size to the human body and its movement through space. I like to be doing work which is self-generating, has its own continuum of energy and evokes universal life forces.'

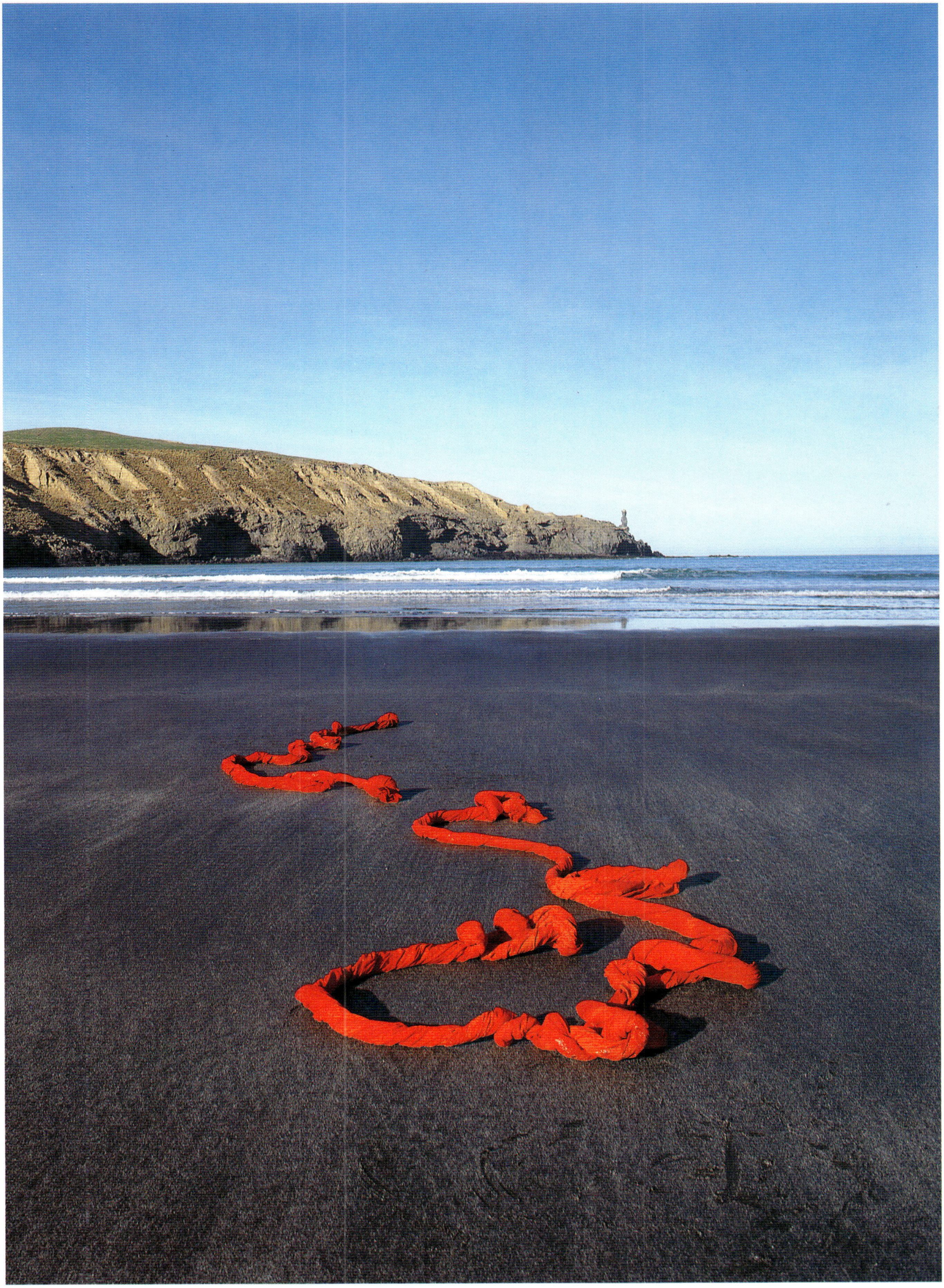

76

PETER ROCHE

Born Auckland 1957.
BFA, UA 1979.
Lives in Auckland.

Roche is a worthy successor to Len Lye (53) in the field of kinetic sculpture. Unlike Lye, who made simple forms from pure stainless steel, Roche has used galvanised sheet metal, plastic and wood. Where Lye relied on the reflectivity of his metal for light effects and on its natural timbre for sound, Roche has built lighting and sound into his works. He shares with Lye a sense of the dramatic: a sculpture that appears immobile or quiet can suddenly light up and become mobile or noisy.

Roche began his career in 1979 as a performance artist, conducting various activities designed to puzzle and shock, or to investigate the nature of human relationships, including that of the artist with the audience. He regards this sort of art, to which he has recently returned, as 'sculpture in real time'. In 1984 he began working on large, coloured drawings with mechanical attachments and on other rather dangerous, loosely constructed, electrically driven sculptural constructions. These somewhat ephemeral pieces employed sound, light and movement, and could work on viewers in the artificial time of a gallery exhibition. Loose, gestural charcoal drawings were associated with these works. In 1988 Roche exhibited a group of carefully constructed wall and floor-based sculptures. Made of sheet metal and brightly coloured in shiny enamels, they resembled equipment in the laboratory of a sci-fi scientist. They were precursors of the major series *Trophies and Emblems* of 1990. Large, sharp-edged devices, circular, triangular, star-shaped or winged like a large bird on a perch, they had a certain elegance of form. Wall-mounted and free-standing, the pieces were made of raw, tarnished sheet metal covered in mysterious stencilled insignia. Some displayed an erratic light sequence; others emitted aggressive noise when approached. One even included a whirling circular-saw blade at face height. We live in a world where whizz-bang technology, both real and of the TV/movie/computer-game fantasy kind, is becoming ever more pervasive. Roche's art ironically reflects this, just as the pop artists reflected the arrival of the image overload of the 1960s. Part of the irony is that an artist, like a fighter pilot, is always supposed to be in absolute control. Roche's objects before 1994 were often surly, ill-mannered creations, asserting their independence and refusing to be commodified. They worked against traditional expectations of sculpture: that it be a pleasing adjunct to gracious living, polished to perfection by the artist.

Roche's less threatening sculptures have connections to pop, evoking the decorative elements in jukeboxes and pinball games. In 1994 Roche exhibited small, circular, wall-mounted works, each lit internally in various ways. Wiring and electronic circuit-boards were visible elements, and the effect was cool and slickly elegant. These were followed in 1995 by the *Tribal Fictions* series, stylised robot figures made from junked circuit-boards collaged onto big, black-lacquered circular disks. Iridescent and jewel-like, these pieces seemed like kitsch decor for a starship, twenty-second-century versions of mokoed Maori painted on velvet. This was futurised nostalgia for a technology long since replaced . . . but by what? Roche's sculptural work reminds us that the effects of technology are unpredictable. Totalitarian terror and lotus-eating torpor are only two possible outcomes.

Landcrab, 1992
Enamel on board with electri-mechanical components
1.9 x 2.2 m
Collection of the artist

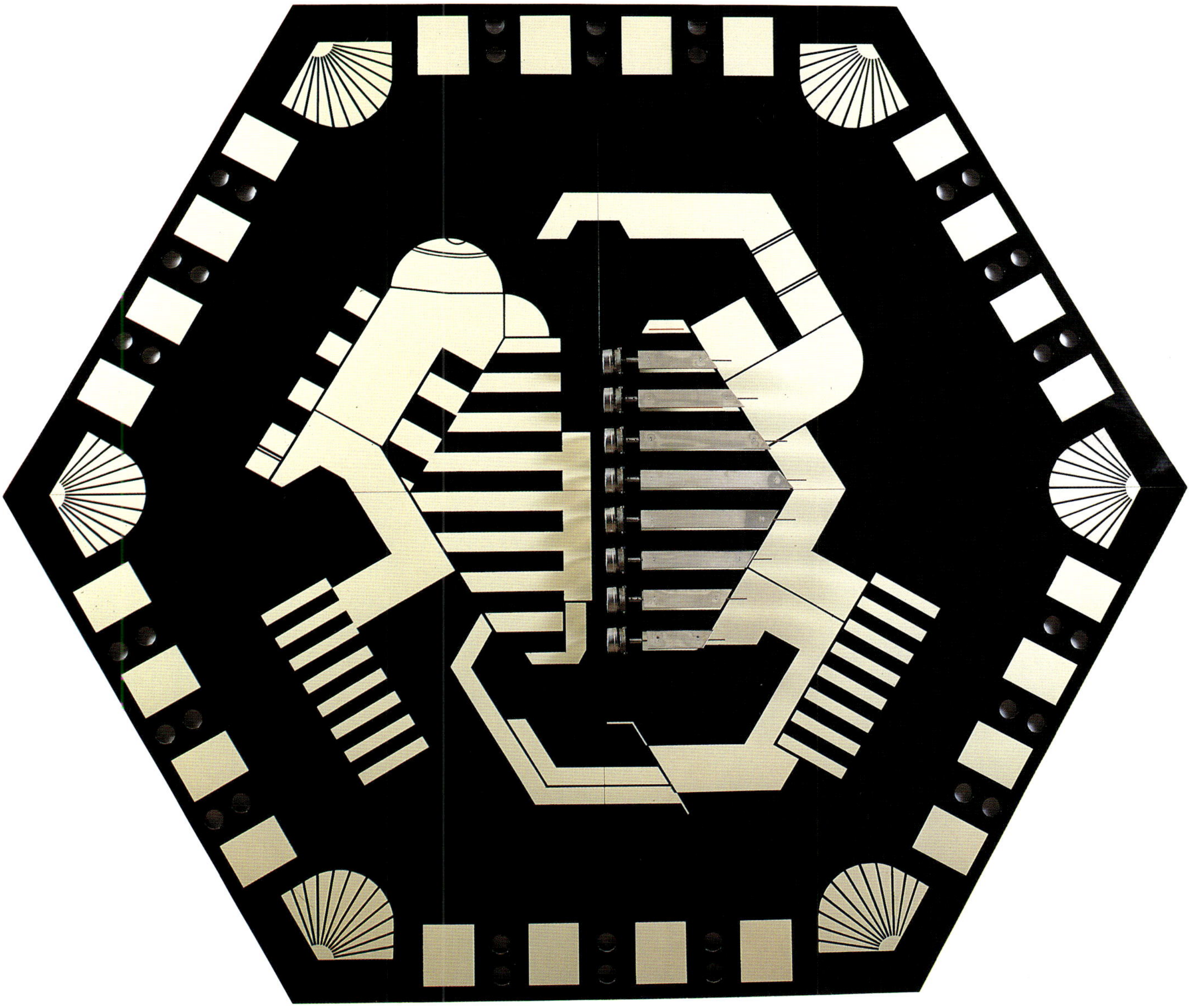

77

NICHOLA SHANLEY

Born Waimana, Bay of Plenty 1969.
Bachelor of Visual Arts, Auckland Society of Arts, 1994.
Lives mainly in the South Island.

Shanley has had the urge to make art from an early age. She studied art history at school and felt a strong affinity with pre-Renaissance religious painting, with its semi-naive figures and lack of perspectival depth. In her recent drawings this interest has led to some interesting stylistic similarities with the work of Paladino and with Hanly's drawings of the 1980s (100NZP, 32), although both bodies of work are unknown to her. She loves poetry, and is a visionary who believes that only a part of herself inhabits the physical world. Consequently, she feels the need to relate to something outside herself in a focused, religious sense. Setting down her visions is a necessity for her, and she draws and writes continuously as a 'survival tool'. She understands the need of people in the past to worship icons, and has taken an interest in the early days of Christianity before it became institutionalised and corrupted. One of her parents was a devout Catholic and the other an atheist. She did not receive a religious upbringing, but as she grew older she began to see visions of Mary in various forms, and this has become a sustaining source of inspiration. This is not to say that Shanley is a beatific artist; much of her imagery can be seen as pagan rather than Christian. She dislikes cities, feeling more comfortable in a natural environment which can provide a framework for the realisations of her visions in art. Landscape has always been an important part of her work, dealt with imaginatively and expressively in prints and drawings.

Shanley's accessible body of work is not large. She is unique among the artists profiled in this book in that her reputation at present rests almost entirely upon the series of intaglio prints that she made while still at art school. These remarkable works, mainly quite small fall into two groups. One consists of spidery, black and white etchings of thin, elongated fiends and female figures, such as *I am Vanity, the Beast Itself,* and *I Saw a Hovering Pearshaped Dream*, 1990. The other group is a series of coloured etchings which depict strange happenings. They are best described by their titles, inscribed on the prints in the artist's personalised text: *and he then alighted upon his wife and ate her; The dragon fly flew up from the swomp to taste the wife's skeletall waste.* They are like illustrations for most unusual fairy tales. Figures are recognisable but dreamlike, as are the settings and backgrounds. Prints in Shanley's final ASA year, 1993, were from multiple shaped, cut-out plates, with drypoint imagery superimposed on monochromatic, cloudy grounds.

Shanley has only recently resumed working on zinc plates after a period of two years travelling in the South Island. Most of the considerable number of charcoal drawings on newsprint made during that period were sold or given away. Those that are accessible show a figure of Mary in a landscape, surrounded in a glow of light and accompanied by floating heads within cartouches. Lines vibrate, and the handling of the landscapes is very graphic and expressive. Small animalistic altars or temples and what may be a burning bush can be discerned. The time spent on the road could prove to be an important period in Shanley's development. Her new prints, a mixture of drypoint imagery set in aquatint grounds, distil the essence of the drawings.

Untitled, 1996
Drypoint and aquatint
208 x 195 mm
Courtesy of the artist

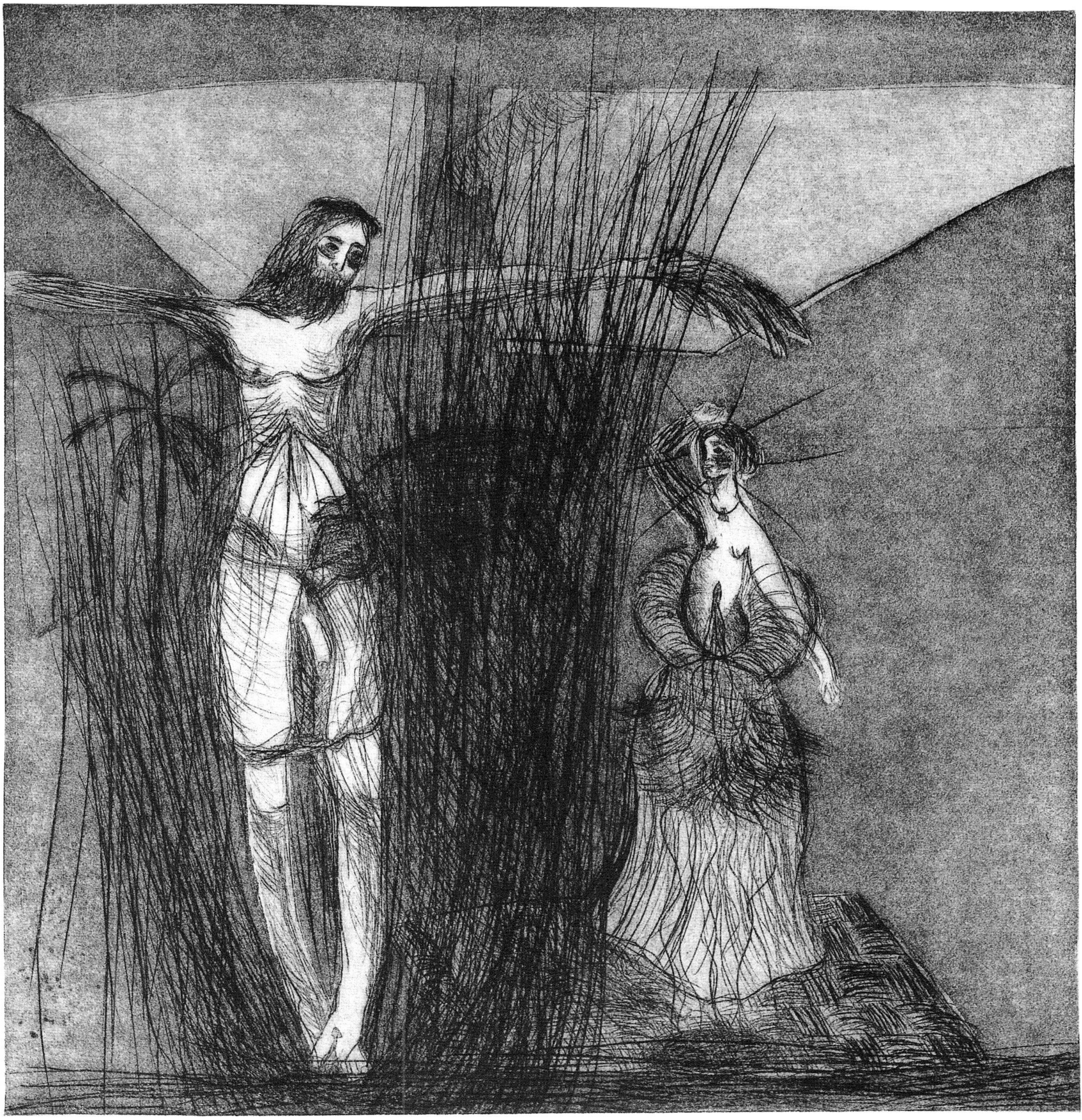

78

CAROLE SHEPHEARD

Born Taumarunui 1945.
DFA (Hons), UA 1967; DT, Auckland Teachers College 1968.
Lives in Auckland.

Shepheard has worked in many media over the last 20 years — painting, sculpture, photography, assemblage, printmaking and these combined, creating a very considerable body of work. This, and her indefatigable activity as a teacher, organiser of symposia and promoter of women's issues through art, has made her an influential force. Much of Shepheard's work has been based on dreams, myths, rituals, spiritual journeys and pacifist/feminist thinking. Her multi-media skills have proved invaluable in realising these ideas, resulting in works in which narrative plays a greater or lesser part, and which shift in focus, scale, detail and intensity. Her approach has been one of pulling disparate images and materials together to make a new reality. Her choice of medium is dictated by her ideas and how they can best be expressed. Interestingly, Shepheard's training was in stage and costume design, and her earliest work was illustrative. She soon moved to an intuitive, assemblagist approach, using stitching, handmade paper and found objects in boxed presentations. Her first major series of prints, the *Body Coverings* of 1982, were photo-etchings of sections of the female body conjoined with fabrics. Because this early work coincided and clashed with current feminist thought and fashion, she found herself being adopted or rejected by various groups, and this led to her deciding to read widely to understand the issues. This thoughtful approach has typified all her work since. She has never made work to a political agenda; rather she sees her work as investigating universal issues of life and location.

In 1984, after a period spent making small works, and an American trip, Shepheard increased the scale of her work dramatically in paintings overlaid with wood and bamboo matrices. Unstretched canvas segments were assembled in forms of kites, mats, shields and scrolls, and painted expressively to resemble whirling leaves or windblown grass. The overlays operated to trap and contain this movement, symbolising not only humanity's impositions on nature but also the invisible order inherent in the structures of life and matter. This imagery has reappeared in her prints. The *Dreams and Realities* of 1985–86 were etchings and painted assemblages based on notes the artist took of her own dreams, at the urging of a friend. The wide, painted frames became an integral part of each piece. The public success of these colourful, evocative works put pressure on Shepheard, and a sojourn in Australia in 1988 gave her the space needed to move on. She discovered Bruce Chatwin's writings, and the sharp contrast of land and sky in the Australian interior. This led to her *Songlines* series of etchings and many semi-abstract paintings, large and small, in which humanity's historical presence was reduced to mere scratchings on the earth.

In contrast, the *Home Hearth and Garden* paintings of 1990 were romantic celebrations of domesticity — a reminder that Shepheard, a wife and mother, had never rejected those roles. In 1991–92 the artist moved on to multi-method prints. Shepheard's work over the last three years has been built around installation and commissioned work, using the multi-part concept to build large-scale works of great authority, elegance and expressiveness. Two examples are *Enraptured Love*, which challenged the viewer to use and then examine all his or her senses, and *Abjection/Absolution,* which forced a similar focus on the fluids emanating from the body.

Essence, Shadow & Signs Part II, 1996
Xerox transfer and oil on plywood, bronze-coated thorns
1960 x 1490 mm
Collection of the artist

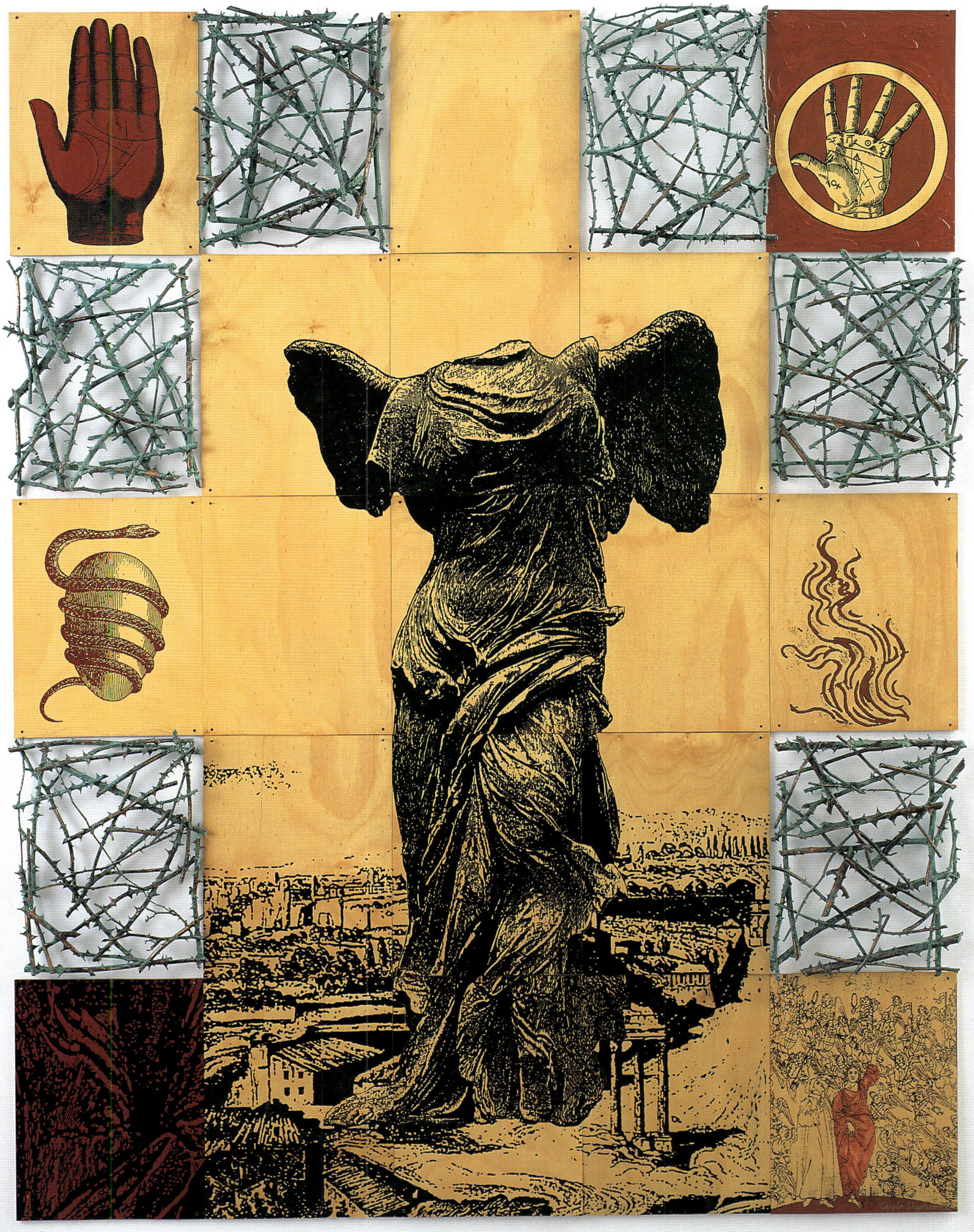

79

SIMON SHEPHEARD

Born Whangarei 1961.
BFA, UA 1983.
Lives in Paekakariki.

Shepheard is something of a magician. He works with unmeritorious waste material, touches it and brings out hidden beauty. His method differs from that of an assemblagist such as Copeland (16) who associates evocative items to set up resonance and spark memory, or Driver (30) who works with colour, texture and shape to make large-scale collages. Like Paul Johnson (45), Shepheard has an affection for weathered plywood, but his style is baroque whereas Johnson's is austere. He enjoys going against the grain of severe intellectualism demanded by some critics and just being himself.

He studied painting at art school and in his final year experimented unsuccessfully with junk materials. He then went travelling in China and Tibet, making innumerable figurative sketches and small paintings on matchboxes, card or anything he could find. He saw this activity as a more honest way of recording what he saw than using a tourist's camera. When he returned to New Zealand he decided to frame the best of these small works for exhibition and, to increase their impact and isolate them from the background, he made very wide frames from cheap wood. This got him thinking about assemblage and he soon began making 'scenes' to go inside the frames and treating the frames themselves as sculptural/figurative elements. His early work continued to include paintings, and from time to time he will still do this.

Beaten, 1993
Enamel paint on aluminium
800 x 700 mm
Private collection, Wellington

Since 1989 he has made some 200 works. Shepheard treats driftwood as a joiner would treat perfectly squared timber, cutting and splicing it so that slabs and branches can be made into frames, spirals, signboards, brackets and figures. Paint is added sparingly where needed and other found fragments are incorporated. A knothole may be inlaid with paua shell, decorative studs may be made of sliced bone, or a spoon may simulate a moon He has also used rubber, metal, and formed and foam plastic. The final results are delightful without being trivial. Whittled, sanded, cobbled together, they look like the folk art of an eccentric retired sailor. Every piece is different and Shepheard has no fixed agenda, allowing the materials to suggest ideas: few broad generalisations can be made about his work. He likes spirals and moonscapes, and his work has become increasingly confident and refined over the years. *Far From Le Metro*, 1995, is an oval wooden form covered entirely with aqua-coloured Metro tickets, their red magnetic stripes making a tranquil, tropic seascape into a diagram of shockwaves and radiation. Description of a few more pieces may give an indication of the artist's quirky vision, skill and sense of humour. *Miti Miti*, 1992, is a little masterpiece and yet there is nothing to it. The rectangular frame, made of once-planed wood now worn and cracked, has rusty spots around it where nails once were. It encloses a scene of bare, dry hills or dunes with a pinkish sky streaked with high, flat clouds partly covering the sun. This convincing scene is full of detail, but faded and nostalgic. After looking at it for a while we realise that it is just a piece of bark overlaid on worn plywood. The fact that so-called 'bark paintings' are a standard kitsch item makes the success of this piece more remarkable. *Voyage to Uluru*, 1993, is similar but is an uncannily real view of Ayer's Rock. *Estuary*, 1993, and *Offshore*, 1995, both use the grain and faults in plywood to recreate rippling sand, sea and sky. We know we are being fooled, but that somehow makes the works even more enjoyable.

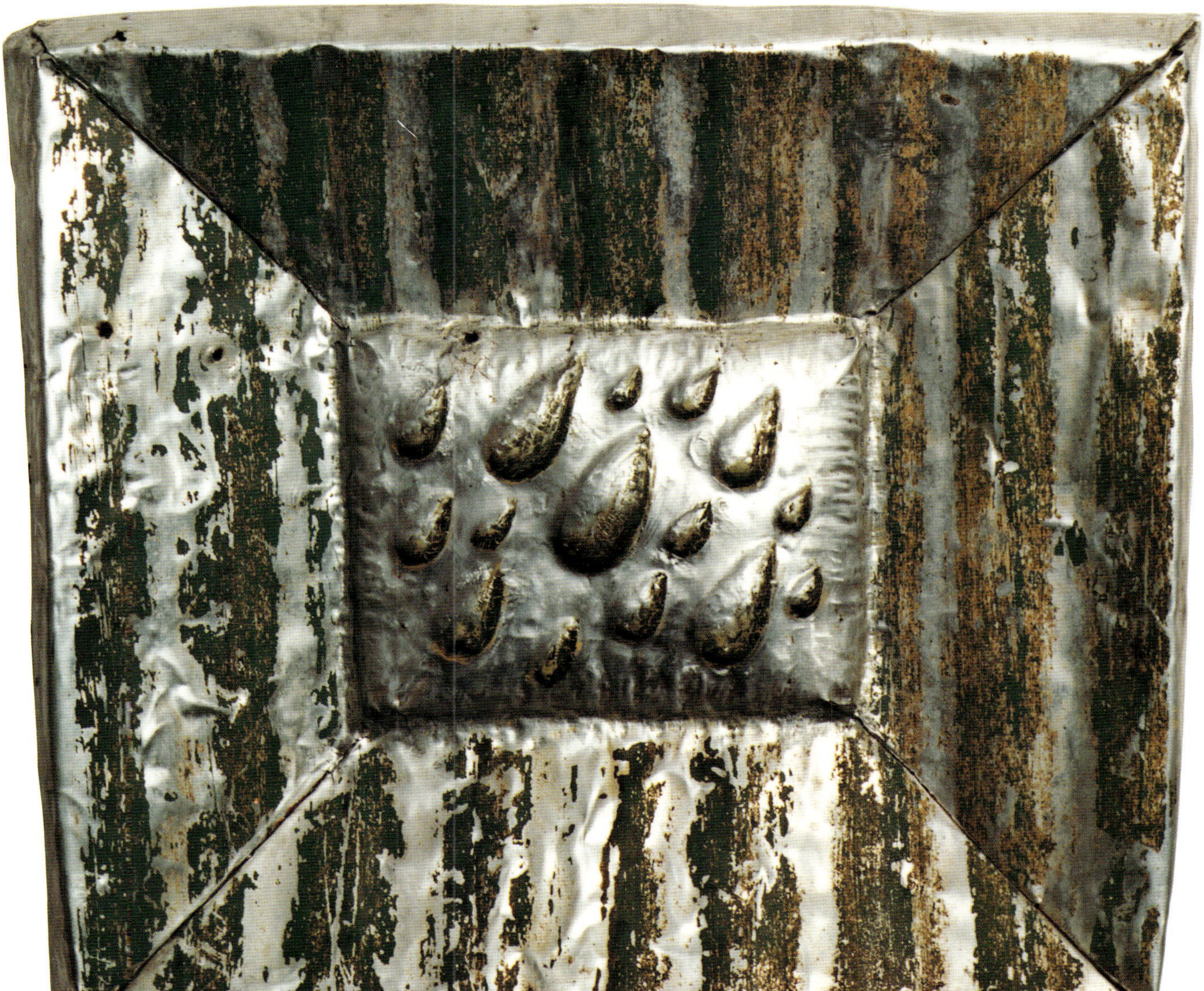

80

SYLVIA SIDDELL

Born Auckland 1941.
Auckland Teachers College 1964–65.
Lives in Auckland.

Siddell's drawings are a good example of style in art (cf. Chilcott, 100NZP, 13; Tricker, 88). She has developed a unique style of drawing that is immediately recognisable, linked to a very personal, restricted range of subjects. 'Frazzled' is an appropriate description for a typical Siddell drawing. Although everything is familiar, shapes are a little wobbly and there is an atmosphere of anxiety and confusion. Siddell, who for many years was both a working wife and mother, draws scenes of domestic chaos. They are everyday happenings, but changed into surreal nightmares by the artist's wicked sense of humour. Daily chores and clutter take on a gleeful animation as they gang up on the hapless housewife. Beneath wildly prancing taps a sinkful of dishes writhes about. A teapot spout becomes a snake, a dishmop a frenzied dancer. In the laundry the washing billows around a machine with controls reading 'Smoke', 'Hellfire' and 'Brimstone'. In the hall the vacuum cleaner has become a rampant dragon. In the bedroom, amid the tangled sheets, the woman's handbag, her lifesaving carry-all, has erupted, spewing out a fantastic array of contents, including a dead fish. The latter has almost become a Siddell trademark, appearing often in the midst of other out-of-control household accoutrements. It stands for hopelessness, the last straw. A plucked and dressed fowl is a similar symbol for a wife and mother trussed up by the demands of her family and ready to be made a meal of. Siddell sometimes includes herself in the drama, always assailed, usually hiding under the bedsheets hoping it will all go away. In some drawings the artist concentrates on just one object, such as a cut-in-half cabbage or a can-opener attacking a can. When she does so, she imbues the subject with such surprising life that we are taken aback.

Objects in a Siddell drawing seem to be made of buffed brass. Areas of light and shade are delineated in fine zig-zag lines which build up energy in the objects, adding to the feeling that they are about to leap, nip, cut or jab.

Making serious humorous art is very hard to do successfully. Siddell's work has a note of desperately poignant relevance that lifts it well above cartooning. She makes a feminist statement more effectively than many other artists who take a polemic or symbolic approach. Referring to her drawings in the context of the paintings of her husband (see Peter Siddell, 100NZP, 82), the artist says, 'The calm exteriors of the houses in Peter's paintings belie the inner turmoil.'

Although Siddell uses colour occasionally, her best work is monochromatic. The artist's style adapts readily to lithography and she has made many fine prints in that medium, as well as some screenprints. In recent years she has branched out into painting, retaining the graphic look by duplicating her oscillating shading lines with the brush.

Banquet, 1993
Conté on arches
920 x 690 mm
Collection of the Robert McDougall Art Gallery, Christchurch

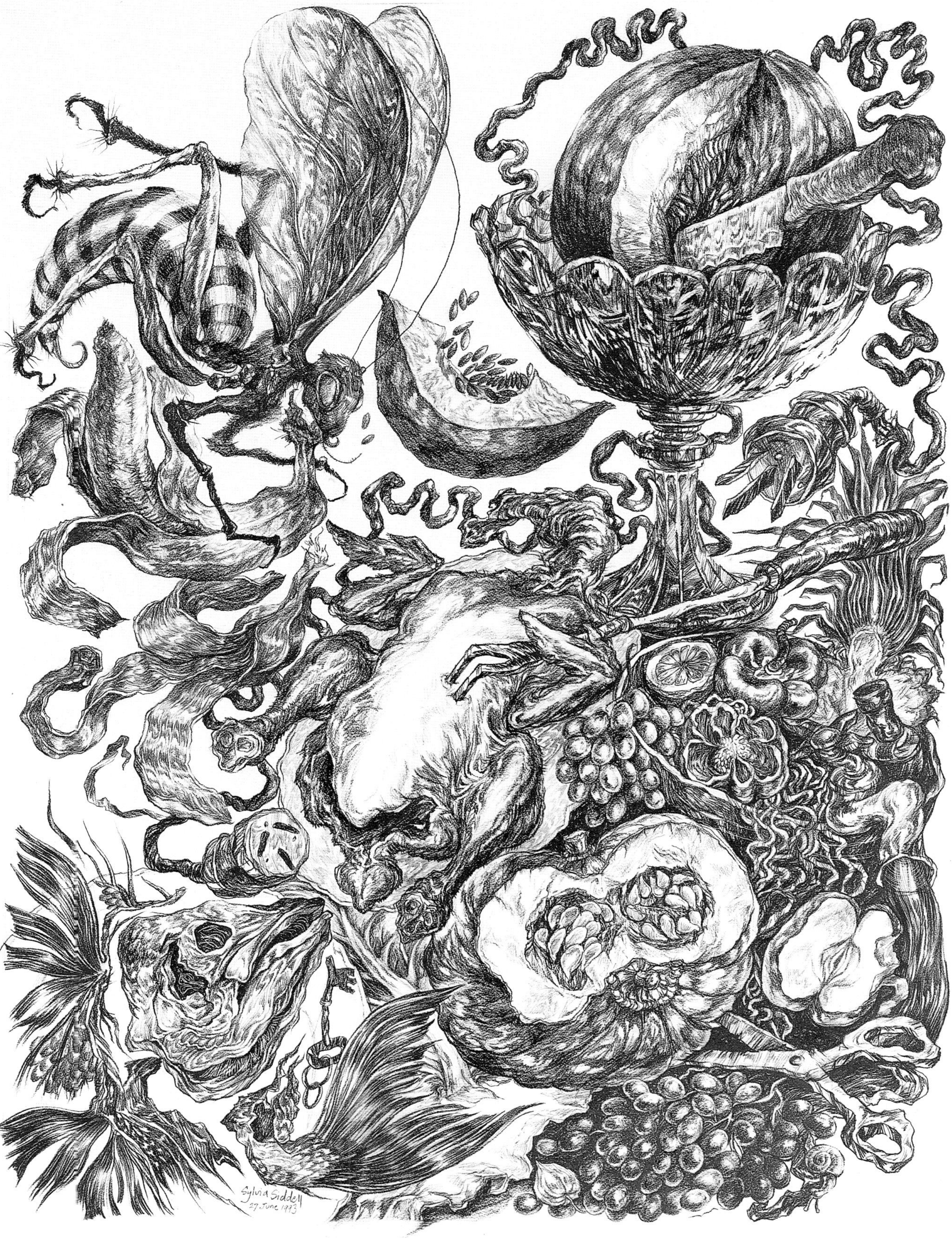
Sylvia Siddell
27 June 1993

81

GRAHAM SNOWDEN

Born Wellington 1955.
DFA (Hons in Sculpture), UC 1978.
Lives in Auckland.

Snowden's earliest sculptures, made when he was a student, were collections of *art povera* materials such as old buckets and bricks. By graduation he had arrived at a minimalist, geometric position which set the direction for all of his subsequent sculptural work. In 1978 he exhibited small white architectural elements, mainly flange forms, which sat on the floor. In 1979 and 1980 he experimented with screenprinting and a gallery performance piece involving projected slides and music. Between 1979 and 1985 he worked on a series of pastel drawings based on his own photography. The first works were of leaf forms lying on a plane surface. Then followed drawings of details of industrial yards, where containers and all manner of leftovers pile up. These successful works achieved separation from the photographic sources, becoming real-life geometric abstractions. They led on to a series of oil paintings done in 1985 which took the distancing process further towards complete abstraction. Some of these paintings were the direct 2-D precursors of Snowden's acclaimed plywood wall sculptures, begun in 1986 and continued up to the present time. These come in two types — square reliefs, and multi-part works in which the elements relate to, but do not touch, each other. The latter are usually rectangular in cross-section and resemble oversized extrusions or joinery offcuts, some curved, some straight. They are painted in flat white, black or bright primary colours, and the arrangement is random. They protrude from the wall seamlessly, as if a collection of geometric shapes has been flung into quick-drying cement. This work is an extension of the reductive art developed by the Russian suprematists and Dutch neo-plasticists after the First World War. The work of one of the masters of that period, Mondrian, took the form of sections of grids enclosing coloured rectangles, both of which ran off the edge of the paintings and needed to be completed in the mind. Snowden's sculpture also takes us beyond what we see. His curves and columns, blocks and planks seem to extend into the substance of the wall — to have a life in another dimension. The forms could be entering our time and space, or leaving it. This effect would be quickly shattered if there was the slightest imperfection on the sculptures' surfaces or any gap where they touch the wall. Snowden's joinery is so perfect that each angled element appears to be embedded in and moving through the wall. Like Dawson (26), Snowden uses the wall as an integral part of his work, not just a backdrop. Although Snowden's elements are not very long, their lines and curves have a dynamism that seems to extend them in space. The tangled, clashing orbits of subatomic particles may come to mind, or the spatially enigmatic paintings of Al Held.

The artist's other works are square wooden painted reliefs, again geometric, seemingly random and painted in primary colours. Some of these also include smaller pieces of the flying, embedded elements. These are not dependent upon, and so lose the sense of engagement with, the wall, but use light and shadow most effectively.

Since 1994 Snowden has been working on paintings in black and white and in pastel colours which seem to show us the invisible lines suggested by the sculptures, or perhaps their shadows. They resemble Held's paintings, but without the outlines he uses, so they appear flatter. There are also similarities with Ian Scott's late lattice paintings (100NZP, 80).

Yellow II, 1992
Enamel on wood
1380 x 1300 x 350 mm
Collection of the artist

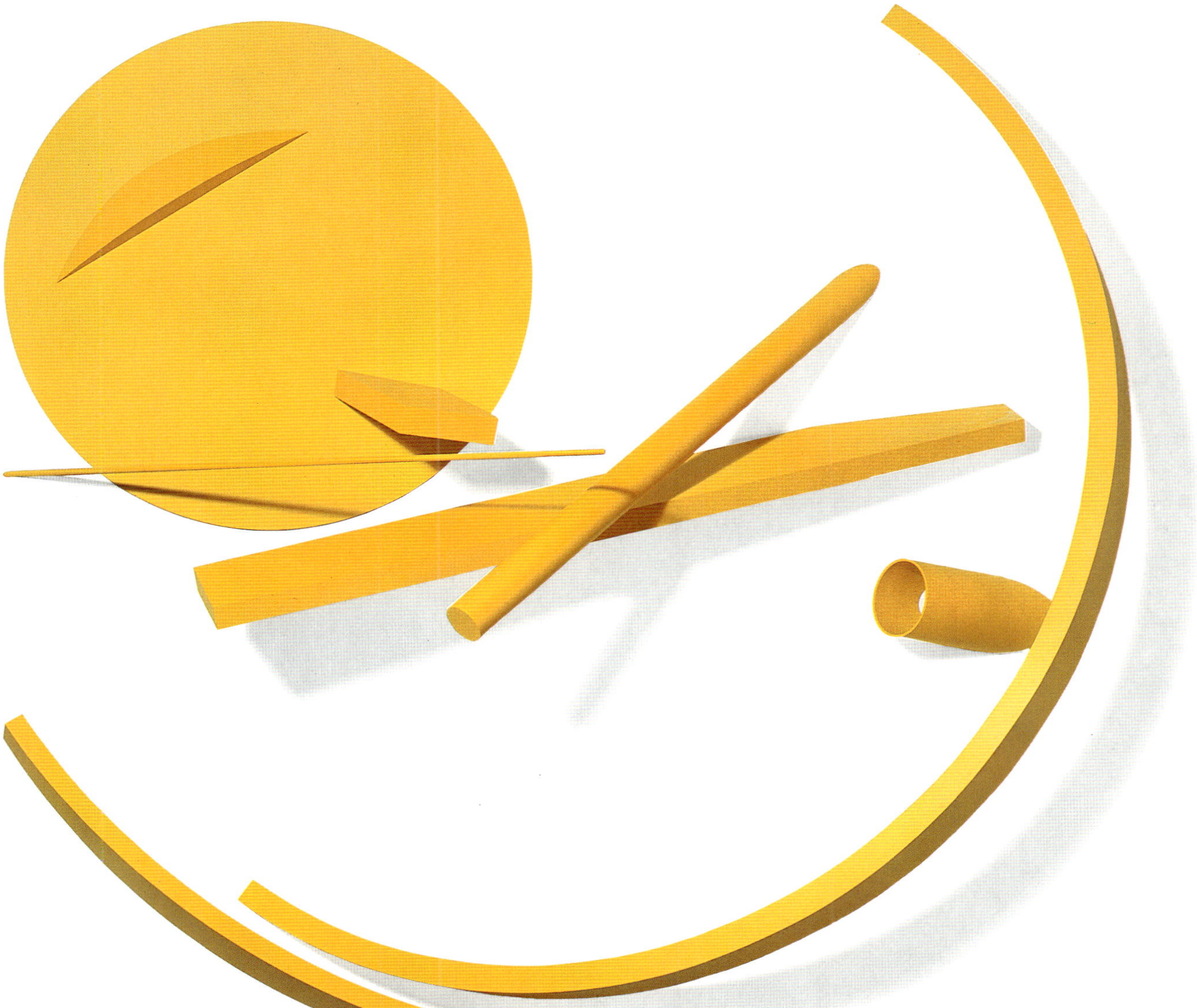

TERRY STRINGER

Born England 1946.
Came to New Zealand 1952. DFA, UA 1967.
Lives in Auckland.

Stringer is best known as a sculptor, although he has done many fine watercolours of figures, accurately capturing the forms with light, fluid brushstrokes. Two of his major public sculptures are the fountain in Auckland's Aotea Square, erupting through the paving slabs like a bronze iceberg, and a white lightning bolt performing similarly in Rotorua. However, most of Stringer's work is domestic scale, and figures and domestic objects make up much of his subject matter. Rather than making sculptures to occupy space, Stringer uses sculpture to manipulate space in various ways. In some works he adopts one of the devices invented by the cubists. To break away from the classical illusionistic perspective of earlier art, around 1912 the analytical cubists flattened out the space in their pictures, creating an effect similar to that produced by a telephoto lens. To aid this process they tilted up horizontal surfaces towards the viewer, so that tabletops and floors seemed more like screens. Stringer's bronzes do this, and, as if denying their three-dimensionality, they seem slightly squashed and creased at the corners. A table with objects on it may be only 15 centimetres deep; a sleeping cat or a portrait head may be no thicker than a book. The origin of these works was in a series of realistically painted wooden sculptures made between 1972 and 1976 which used flat boards joined so that the planes twisted and tilted. In other works, instead of suppressing volume, Stringer enhances depth. In wall-mounted reliefs made of painted sheet aluminium, skilful shading and a sure sense of perspective create the illusion of depth where there is actually very little. What looks like a vase on a shelf across a room corner proves to be an almost flat construction. A wooden table, partly covered with a cloth and bearing a plate and glass, seems to recede into the wall it hangs on. These works are part of the tradition of *trompe l'oeil* and also relate to the work of such contemporary American artists as Ron Davis and John Okulik. By bringing the two-dimensional conventions of drawing and painting into the viewer's space, Stringer makes art out of artifice

Colour is used sparingly and very subtly in all Stringer's work. His watercolours are washy and muted; his bronzes are patinated in satiny dark greens and browns; and his drawing and painting is kept within a narrow range of faded colours. This lends an air of nostalgia to many pieces. Stringer does not seek to make any social, environmental or political statements. He creates sophisticated objects for pleasurable contemplation, without sentiment but with a touch of gentle humour. For example, one piece includes a flower stem in a glass of water. Just as refraction cuts and repositions the stem in the real world, so it appears in the bronze image. Again, Stringer's flat cat, intended to lie on the floor, sums up the sculptural style of such early modernists as Lipchitz, but it also looks like it might have been stepped on. Some of his recent works incorporate hidden lighting, which spills out onto the wall from behind the forms in an ironic link with art deco ornamentation.

Mask of Fortune, 1996
130 x 55 x 40 cm
Bronze, edition of 3
Courtesy of the artist

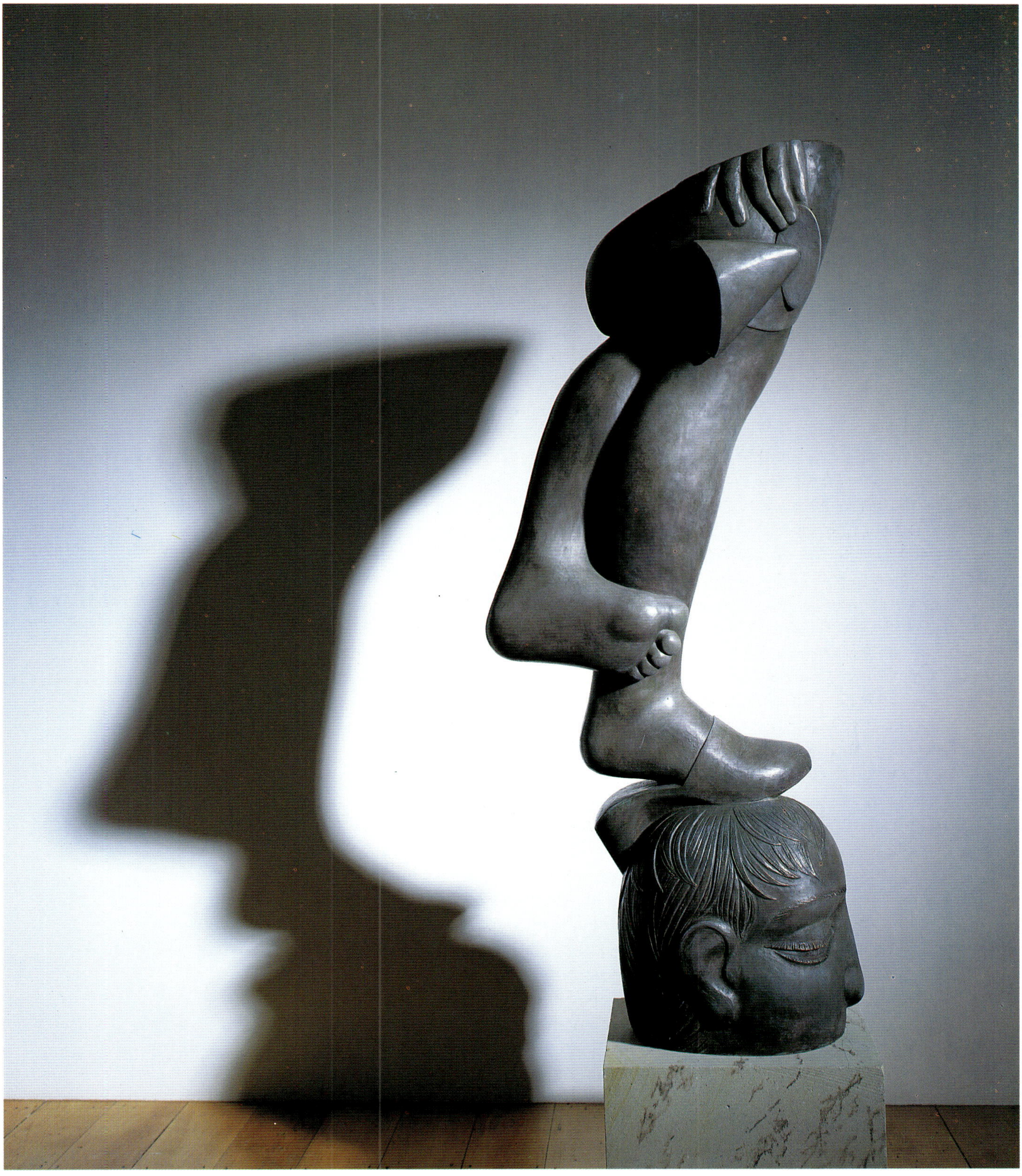

CARL SYDOW

Born Takapau 1940.
DFA, UC 1961; DFA (Hons), UA 1963.
Died Christchurch 1975.

Although he died more than 20 years ago and many of his works are lost, the influence and example of Sydow's sculpture live on. Echoes of his remarkably original work can be found in the subsequent production of at least six living New Zealand sculptors. He pioneered constructivist sculpture here, and was succeeded by Pine (71), Jones (47) and Cullen (22). Between 1962 and 1963, Sydow worked in a figurative mode in the style of the British sculptors Chadwick, Armitage and Moore. Forms were welded, or modelled in clay and cast. He then spent some time in London working with fellow Christchurch students John Panting and Stephen Furlonger. They were both constructivists, and Panting's work done in England, before he too died tragically young, was of a minimal, linear type using square-section steel rods (cf. Twiss, 90). Like Pine, also in London at that time, Sydow observed and absorbed the directions sculpture was taking in the use of modern, industrial materials. He said, 'It all constituted a great upheaval in sculpture and left me in a great state of confusion.' On his return to Christchurch in 1967 Sydow worked briefly in bronze, casting figures which seemed to demonstrate a move towards abstraction. The bottom half of each figure was realistically modelled, but the top was squashed flat into a rectangular flange. Pursuing a typical working method, Sydow did many drawings between 1967 and 1969, and then abandoned the traditional approach in favour of large-scale assemblages incorporating PVC piping, plastic hose, roofing iron and other commercial material. This was revolutionary, and critical response was largely negative. The works reflected Sydow's careful planning, being simple yet fully resolved and satisfying. *Flow*, 1970, was just eight PVC pipes lying together, with transparent hose curving between each segment.

In 1971 Sydow made his *Meander* series, using coloured plastic hose winding in and out of clear perspex support frames. These works alluded to the natural and fabricated environments: water carried through pipes, waterfalls and the braided rivers of the Canterbury Plains. Although static, these pieces seem to be moving — an effect enhanced by the use of magnifying mirrors which come into play as the viewer moves. In 1974, after working with suspended netting and trellis and doing lots more drawings, Sydow began working on a series of zinc mesh screens, stretched like vertical trampolines on aluminium rod frames. By mounting one sheet in front of another, an interference pattern, like watered silk, was set up in the eye as one moved past. Sydow used no colour, and achieved an impressive balance between the ethereal shimmering and the severe, tight, metallic constructivism of his materials. In his last two years Sydow continued with drawings using Letratone film. This dotted film comes in various densities and colours, and if one sheet is laid over another, density increases and interference patterns are set up. Sydow 'drew' three-dimensional geometric shapes in two dimensions, as seen from various angles: origami folds which came together to make patterns and then resolved back into shapes. At the time of his death Sydow was pondering the sculptural possibilities inherent in these beautiful drawings. Neil Dawson (25) achieved spectacular success with similar ideas in 1978 and 1985. All the work of Sydow's final five years still looks as fresh and original. As with other artists cut off in their prime (Marc Macke, Boccioni, Schiele, Morris, Smith), we can only guess what Sydow might have done had he lived.

Meander II, 1971
Perspex, mirror, PVC tubing
1900 x 867 x 1495 mm
Museum of New Zealand, Te Papa Tongarewa

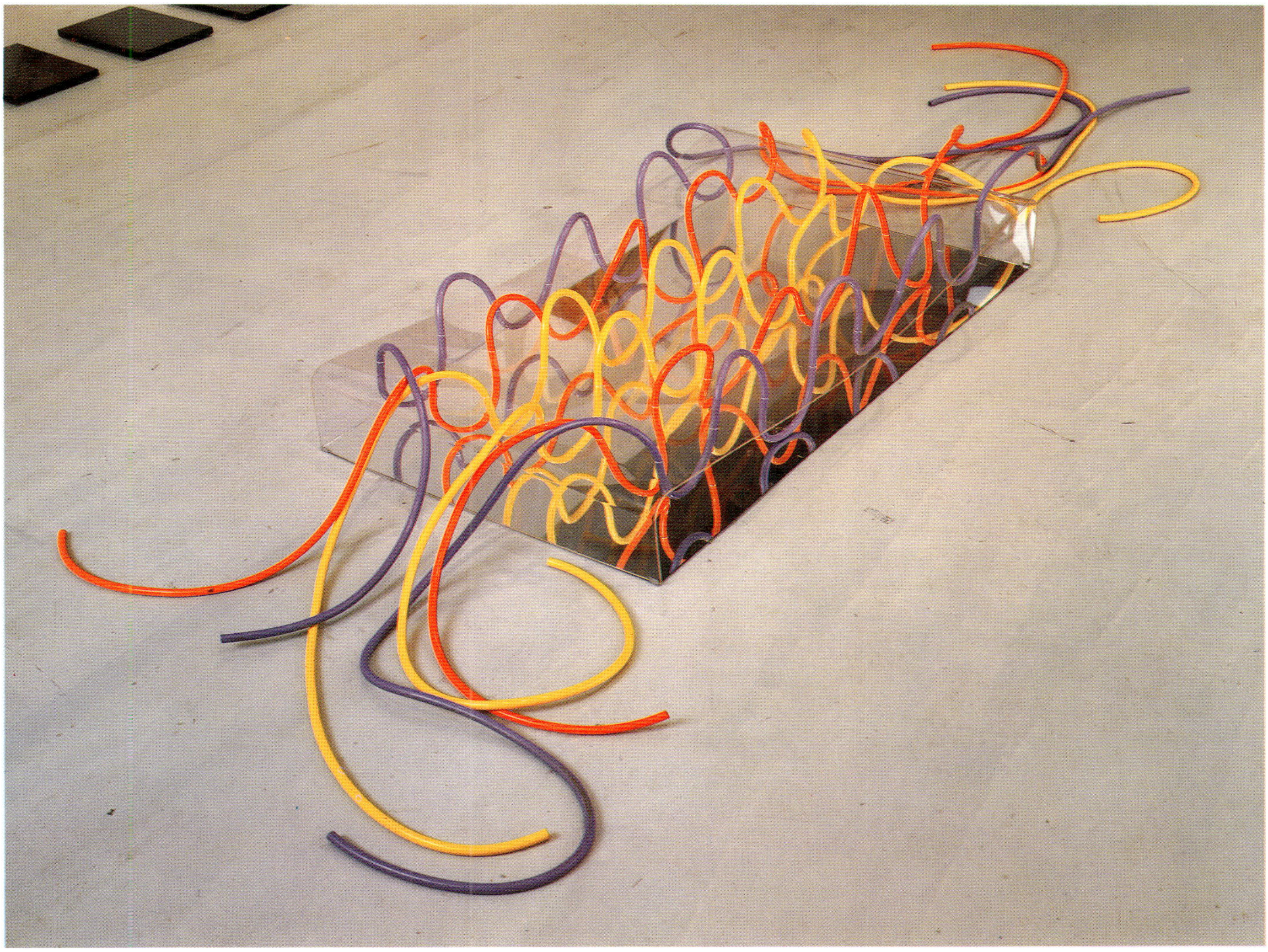

MARTÉ SZIRMAY

Born Budapest, Hungary 1946.
Came to New Zealand 1957.
DFA (Hons), UA 1968; DT, Auckland Teachers College 1969.
Lives in Auckland.

Among contemporary New Zealand sculptors Szirmay is the closest to the European modernist tradition. Hers is sculpture in the round: solid, three-dimensional, aspiring to the monumental even when tabletop-sized. She stands at the other end of the spectrum from such artists as Twiss (90), Dawson (26) and Dawe (24) with their interest in open forms which articulate empty space. On the other hand, the New Zealand environment has shaped Szirmay's work — she shares with other local artists a desire to celebrate the natural world (cf. Hellyar, 41). Spiral and hemispherical motifs, used repetitively in many different ways, allude to the Pacific Basin, its currents, winds, atolls, shells and cycles of life. However, Szirmay also has a keen interest in ancient European civilisations and she is not wedded to the use of natural materials. She has always relished the opportunity to use new technologies to make new forms. Her first show 25 years ago used plastic spheres, mirrors and anodised metal, and since then she has made artificial marble, used resin and fibreglass in various ways, and employed metal-spraying and laser-cutting technology.

Szirmay's early work of the 1970s included chromed gunmetal pieces which seemed like sweeps of movement made solid, shell-like forms in painted aluminium, and flanged forms which suggested unfolding growth and the internal structures of fruits and seeds. By 1978 Szirmay was using cast marble to make smooth, tactile objects, some of which were exhibited in tanks of water. They called to mind the rounded forms of Arp, Brancusi, Hepworth and Moore, but whereas their sculptures moved in the dreamworld of surrealism, Szirmay's might have been beautifully presented fossils or exotic shells. Later pieces resembled wave forms, water-shaped stone and melting icebergs. In 1981 cracks and textures were introduced to prevent the pieces becoming too ornamental.

Work of 1983 was formed out of fibreglass, like a boat hull, and Szirmay used this method throughout the 1980s, predominantly in spiral shell forms. The effect was raw: surfaces were often bumpy and edges rough. Occasionally Szirmay abandoned beauty, with glutinous objects which spoke of pollution and decay.

Szirmay's first commission in 1969 was in stainless steel, a big mechanistic form which still impresses viewers today in the Auckland suburb of Newmarket. Since then Szirmay has executed many large sculptures in cut metal sheet, and these constitute a separate body of work, only some of which has been publicly exhibited. Most are elegant leaf, petal and spiral forms, while one or two are more like flags or folded ribbons.

In 1991 Szirmay used metal-plated fibreglass, changing the look of her work completely. The forms were like rich theatre curtains or, in ironic contrast, golden rags blowing in the wind. Her most recent work, the *Emerging Orders* in resin and fibreglass, retains some forms from the past but makes them more geometric and austere, like fonts or altars. There is a balancing of opposites — concave/convex, opaque/translucent, curve/angle, container and contents.

Over the years Szirmay has made many small bronze pieces and medallions, some cast paper forms and innumerable drawings. The artist sums up her work to date as a search for a unifying logic in nature and for a universal visual language in which to represent it.

Marine Stainless Steel, 1990
Stainless steel
1.5 x 2.4 m
Private collection, Auckland

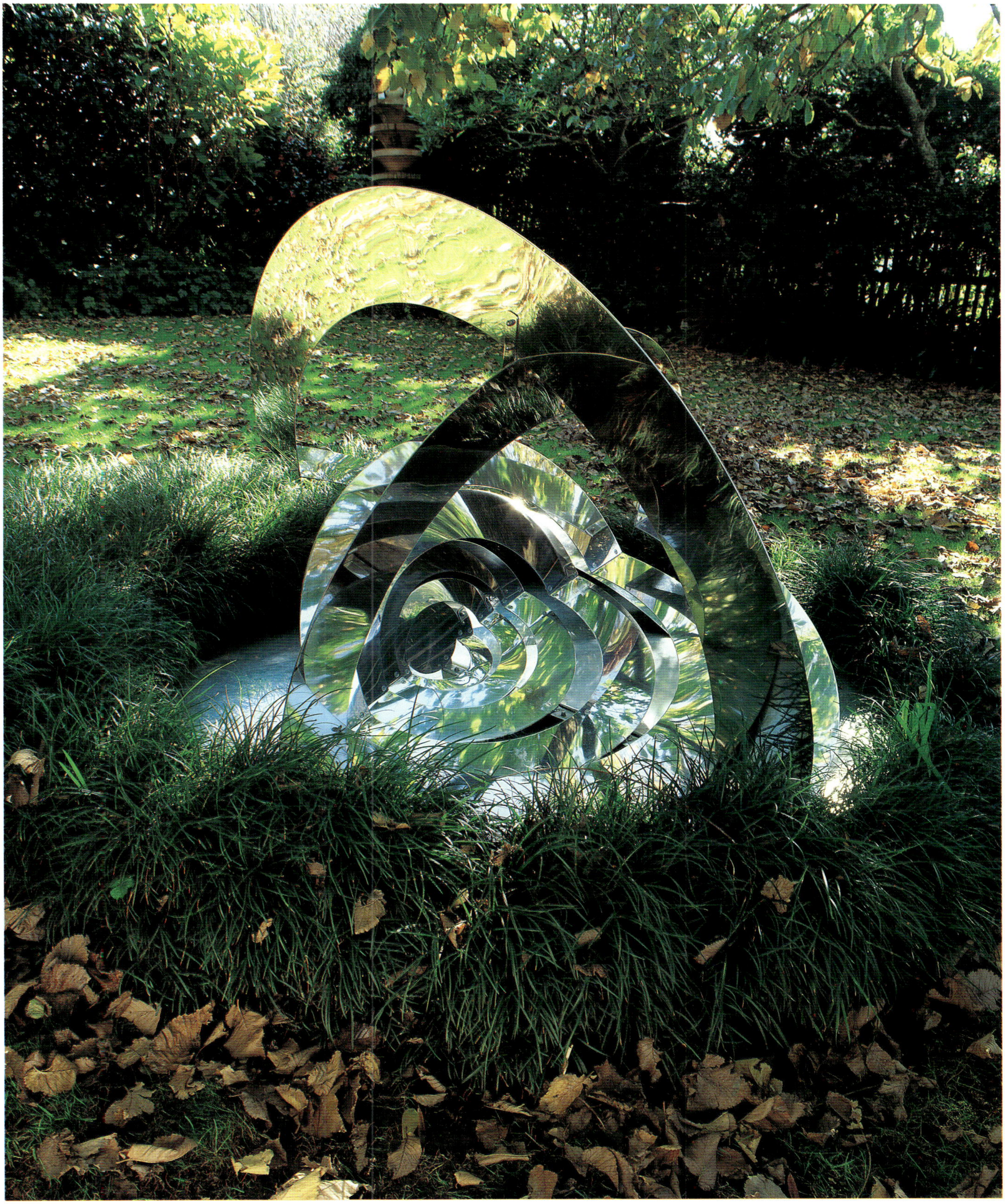

85

JOHN TARLTON

Born 1950 Long Beach, California. Came to New Zealand 1972.
Certificate of Proficiency in Painting, UC 1972;
MA (Fine Arts), State University of New York 1974.
Lives on Waiheke Island.

Tarlton is a figurative artist who has worked in the media of drawing, printmaking, painting and collage. His drawing skills are of the highest standard and enable him to generate whatever image he requires for the work currently in hand. He describes himself, paradoxically, as a classicist whose sensibilities have been time-warped by exposure to American pop art, and that is just what his graphic work looks like. He has done many charcoal drawings of everyday objects, isolated on an otherwise blank sheet of paper but loaded with innuendo and easily grasped symbolism. As with all other art of this type, the viewer's subjective response is an important part of the 'meaning' of the work. All Tarlton's work is marked by a gentle wit, usually displayed through the juxtaposition of images and, sometimes, text. Textural description of these works makes them sound corny, but this is because corniness is part of their delightful levity. A good example is Tarlton's 1988 drawing *The Horn of Plenty*, in which some bread, cheap wine and a spinach are shown with a trumpet and the inscription 'Flugel Repast'. In a 1989 series of seven drawings on the theme of fish, Tarlton drew things relating either to fishing or a fishy quote. Thus massage parlour paraphernalia accompanied the words 'Whipper Snapper', while *Cod Defend New Zealand* showed a cod and a slingshot.

In 1988 Tarlton embarked on a collage project, *Adventures in Paradise*, which consumed a year and about 800 copies of the *Listener* magazine. At that time it had a large format and contained many full-page, coloured advertisements and illustrations. Tarlton cut all of these out and indexed them by subject, then used them to create witty collages about the state of the nation and its people. The same image, used more than once, could be expanded to make expanses of grass, sky, sea and buildings, and groups of people could be made into crowds. By carefully selecting the size of image to fit the perspective of the collage, Tarlton achieved an oddly surreal reality, belied by the outrageous happenings in each work. Each collage was photographed to create a seamless image and released as an archival cibachrome print (cf. Crook, 20).

The mild conceptualism of the *Listener* collages was accentuated in Tarlton's 1993 exhibition, *Endangered Species*. He covered the entire wall of a large gallery with one complete edition of a screenprint depicting a tuatara and a copy of the artist's small bank balance. The prints were so designed as to create a wallpaper effect, and were very reasonably priced. As each copy sold it was taken down, eventually creating a random chequerboard and then a sparse, minimalist display. Sadly, the artist's aim of complete extinction of the edition was not achieved.

Tarlton has a sure command of watercolour, as befits a classicist, and in this medium his collections of objects appear in colour and on backgrounds of wash. Often the effect is like a family noticeboard. These paintings offer a greater sense of depth and a wider range of expression than the drawings and prints, but are otherwise consistent with them.

One for the Road, 1989
Cibachrome print from collage
590 x 410 mm
Courtesy of the artist

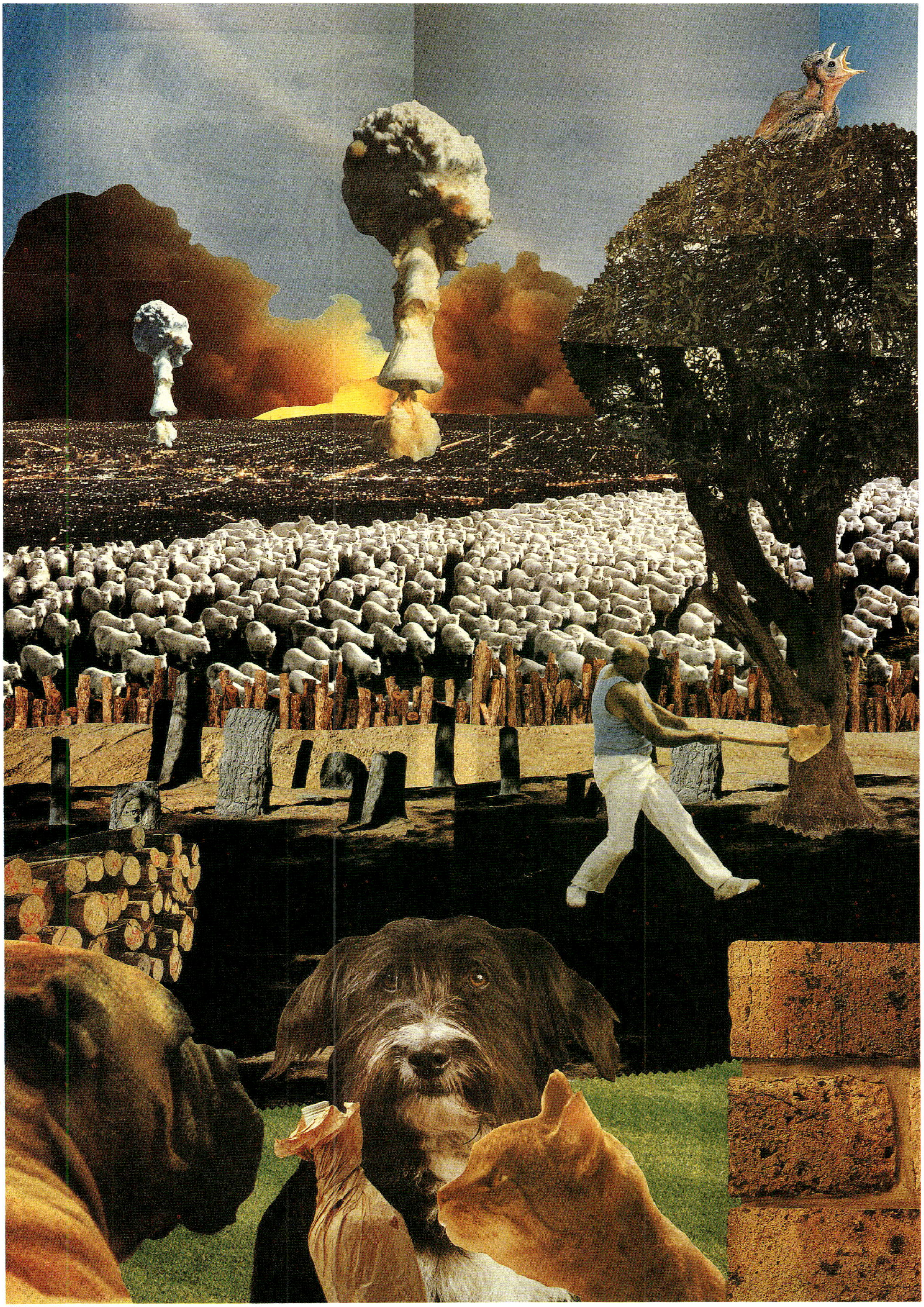

86

ELIZABETH THOMSON

Born Auckland 1955.
MFA, UA 1988.
Lives in Wellington.

Thomson made her reputation initially as a printmaker. Her etchings were taken into the collections of our National Gallery and the Victoria and Albert Museum in London while she was still a student. Using techniques that she developed herself, Thomson's prints involved aquatint and photo-etching. The photographs were of sculptural heads and collages made especially for the job, as well as other photographic source material. The resulting etchings had a strange monumentality and 3-D quality, playing tricks with scale. Tiny figures of mountaineers could be found scaling a 'face' that revealed itself to have eyes and ears. A vast, crumbling human head sat in the sea like a natural headland. Photo-etching can with care produce a reasonable facsimile of a grainy photograph, but Thomson's prints had the look of provisional proofs, retaining lots of white paper. These monochrome works were tough, ironic and surreal, usually relieved by the humour of the obvious artifice.

In 1987 Thomson had her first exhibition of sculpture, and she was immediately recognised as an original and dedicated artist in the medium of cast bronze. Her first works were of schools of fish, creating the impression in viewers that they were under the surface of the sea. The most sensational of these was *The Fearless Five Hundred*, 1989. A graphic reference was retained, in that the gallery wall could also be read as a sheet of paper with images printed on it. Later pieces took the form of over-size insects, moths and beetles, including stick insects over 2 metres long. Given that real bugs often have a metallic look, and moths' wings can resemble patinated bronze, Thomson's pieces can be a bit scary, but their immobility and size give them away. The enduring impression is one of vulnerability — we are confronted with fragile life forms which normally hide in dark places and disguise themselves. The camouflage of moths' wings provides a further link between the prints and the sculptures. The real eyes found staring from the fake cliffs in the etchings remind us of the fake, predator-scaring eyes on moths' wings. The chemistry of the etching process is repeated in Thomson's masterful use of patination.

Thomson grew up in Auckland's Waitakere Ranges, an area of dramatic, surf-girt headlands backed by extensive native bush. The rocky cliffs of the prints and the insect sculptures reflect that environment, as do her more recent bronze leaves. Over the last two years Thomson has been developing in new directions. For a long time she has been interested in the world of the very small, and she has begun making sculptures based on micro-photographs of leaf hairs, insect feelers and mould spores. These works combine sculpted customwood, blown glass and moulded bronze, and are elegant, delicate, surreal and, still, a little scary. Thomson's interest in different-sized scales comes to the fore again. A separate group of works is collections of leaves cast in bronze, once again using the wall as a page. Thomson has also returned to printmaking, with photo-litho works depicting elderly people inhabiting strange micro-worlds.

Trichomes and Leaf Hairs II (not so soft) from the 'Natural Abstraction' series, 1994
Patinated bronze, glass, gesso, shellac, casein, shaped MDF
1600 x 1700 x 220 mm (spikes)
Collection of the artist

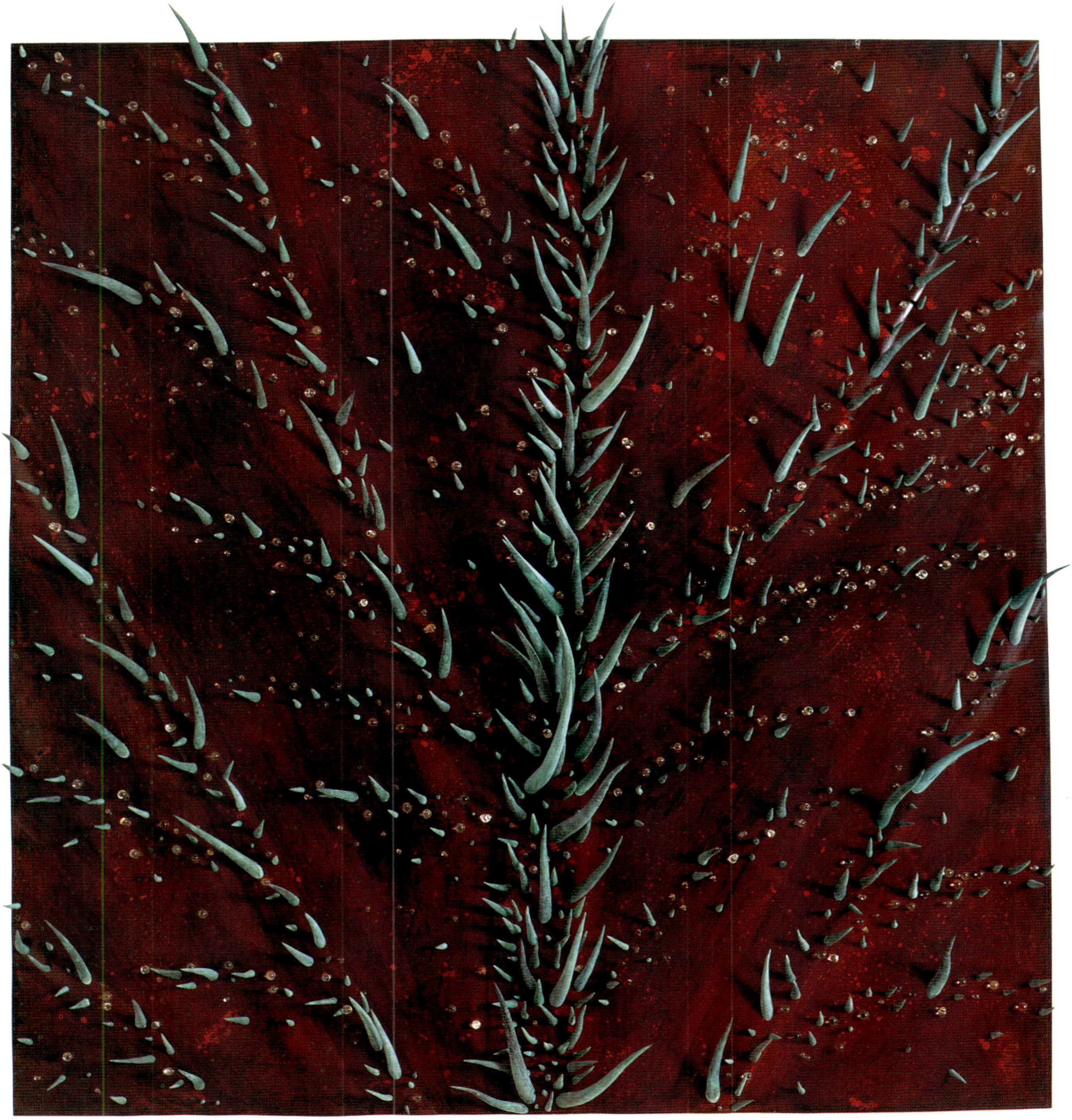

87

JEFF THOMSON

Born Auckland 1957.
BFA, UA 1981; DT, Auckland Teachers College 1982.
Lives in Helensville.

Corrugated iron, that ubiquitous material which is literally part of the fabric of New Zealand society, has undulated its way into the country's art. Ralph Hotere (100NZP, 37) has given it grandeur in his rich, black Aramoana panels, and Neil Dawson (26) has used ragged-edged bits in his sculptures. However, Jeff Thomson is the undisputed master of the medium. Who else would attempt to make a typewriter, a camera and tripod, or a lawnmower out of it? In a 1986 exhibition in Auckland, Thomson offered a country storeful of zany objects. Some were done in multiple versions and lined up in rows: letter boxes, mowers, cows and motorbikes. There was a field gun (a visual pastoral pun), a sheep's skull and a crayfish. Around the walls a herd of elephants looked on, most advancing, one retreating. Thomson has followed the lead of Claes Oldenburg by making familiar objects out of wildly inappropriate material. The American made drum sets and giant fans out of stuffed vinyl. Their floppy uselessness was part of their charm. In contrast, Thomson's artefacts look like the creations of a manic do-it-yourselfer isolated from technical aids and working up some remote back road, with only an old water tank and some tin snips at hand. One wonders whether they might not work just once before flying to pieces, like Richard Pearse's plane. Notwithstanding the fun and fantasy, Thomson is a serious artist. Just as Oldenburg's use of vinyl reflected the tacky modernism of the sixties, so Thomson's use of iron is ironic. It speaks of deliberate regionalism, anti-elitism and low tech in an international art scene. It is a blatant (and successful) attempt to bring art to the people.

Thomson's art evolved from a project that he started in 1981. On long country walks, undertaken for enjoyment, he was able to take in the landscape slowly and in detail. The normally insignificant, and mailboxes in particular, became important. The latter seemed to Thomson like roadside sculptures, every one different, bearing the marks of age and fate. He had the idea of dropping off letters which offered property owners free painted tin sculptures to attach to their mailboxes, each one reflecting the identity or activity of the owner. Conceptually, Thomson saw this as a means of enlivening the roadside, a communication between owners and travellers, with art as the medium. In 1982 Thomson exhibited a number of these mailboxes, plus maps of his walks and correspondence with owners. In his easy-going way the artist had carried art from town to country and back again. People started asking him to make bigger objects out of tin, and from these early commissions his work increased in both scale and complexity, and from two into three dimensions.

Thomson's pieces now stand about in gardens and houses throughout New Zealand. Farm animals have been popular, but the artist has even clad his stationwagon in corrugated iron. His most recent work has become abstract and includes lacy filigrees, curled like wood shavings, and screenprinted pieces. With an inexhaustible supply of raw material available, Thomson's horizons are limited only by his imagination.

Dahlia Suite, 1994
Screenprinted corrugated steel, downpipes, guttering, barge rolls, ridging, ridge caps and gas cowls
2.4 x 2.4 x 1.6 m
Courtesy Bowen Galleries, Wellington

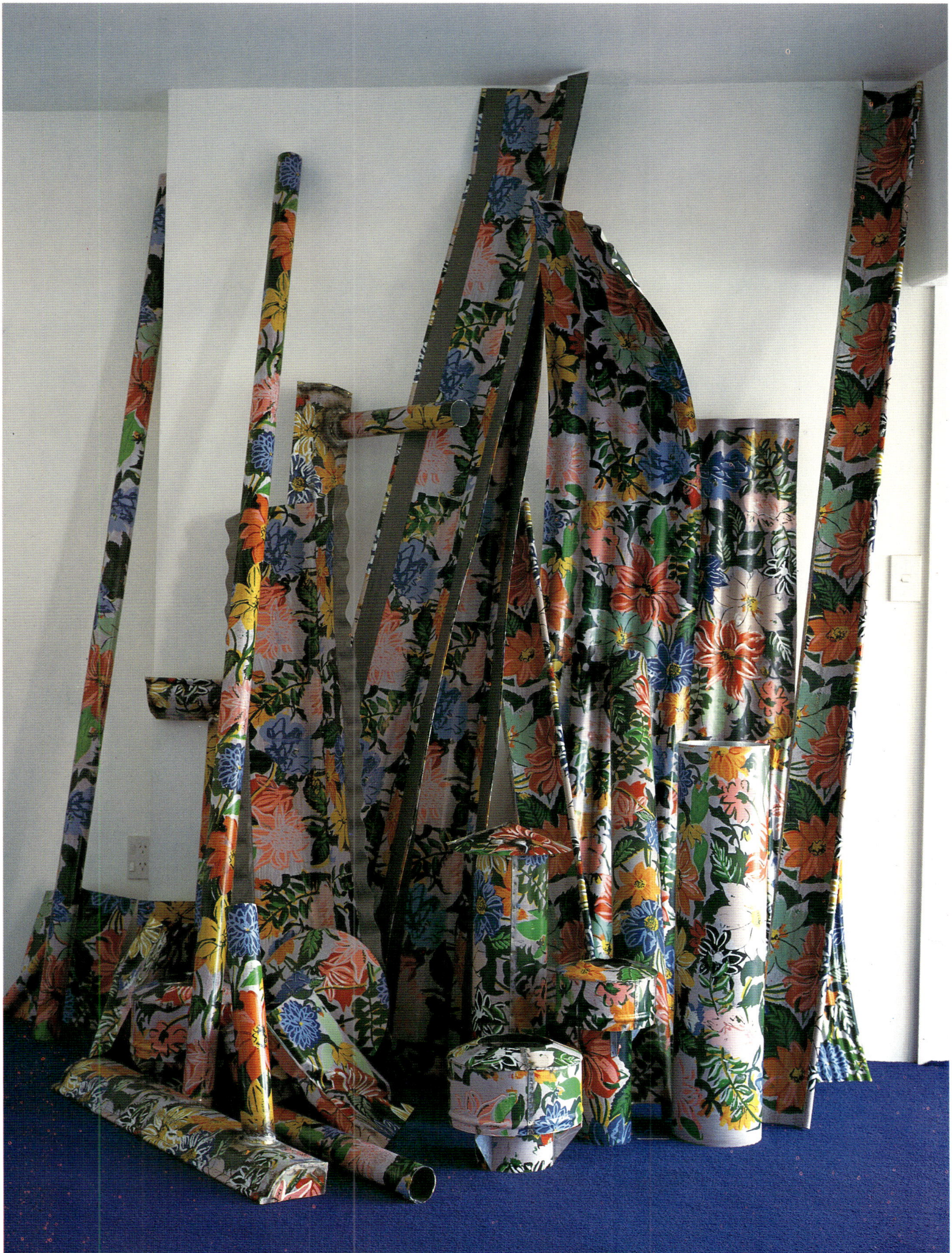

88

GARY TRICKER

Born Wellington 1939.
Lives in Greytown, Wairarapa.

Tricker is self-taught as an etcher, but the uniqueness of his vision and style has won him a following around the world. Much of his childhood was spent in the country, and that relatively unsophisticated environment, plus a severe hearing disability, set the scene for the development of a gentle, introspective, literary artist. Tricker found talk, and sometimes listening, too difficult to be bothered with. Art provided a way to say what he wanted to say.

Tricker's father was a railway maintenance inspector, and he took his son, from the age of five, on trips up and down the North Island main trunk line. Many journeys were made by hand jigger, and the scenery, characters and equipment encountered on these trips so impressed young Gary that the memories have sustained him over 20 years as a full-time artist. Among those memories were the endless cups of tea, that life-sustaining ritual of the working man. To this we must add a love of cats — Tricker's ears as he describes them — and of books: quiet companions for a quiet man. Some combination of railways, tea, cats and self-portraits is found in most of Tricker's etchings. His world is one of delightful whimsy. All is not obvious in a Tricker print, and time needs to be taken to appreciate its niceties.

Like Morandi and his jars and bottles, Tricker seems constantly to be able to derive fresh inspiration from his chosen subjects. They are usually portrayed in surreal conjunctions as visual puns (*Untrained Cat, Purrfection*). As well as staking claim to comfortable parts of the house, the imperturbable cats are found in all sorts of unlikely situations — perched above tunnels waiting for trains, flying, riding engines and freight cars, or muscling in on a tea party. Teapots and cups can appear anywhere at any time. Trains, seen square-on, are often found on only enough track to hold one carriage. Fine detail is another Tricker speciality: exquisite little vistas seen through windows, pictures on walls, rows of titled books, the wheels and other moving parts of trains. Tricker often incorporates proverbs and literary quotes into his images in well-schooled script — quite a demanding undertaking, as words have to be inscribed backwards on the plate. A further Tricker trademark is his 'snowstorm' effect, a random spread of small white blotches covering each image. This is produced by a stopping-out procedure during the etching process. There are also various small marks, like hairs or twigs, found at random on the image, the sort of little defect that other printers go to great lengths to get rid of. Unlike some etchers, who print in one dark colour and then hand-colour the image with watercolour, Tricker colours the printing plate *à la poupée*, dabbing on different inks with a rag. This results in clouds of soft-focus colour which are not always restricted to discrete objects. All of these effects, applied consistently over the years, impart a distinctive, dreamy quality to the prints.

Invention is the Mother of Necessity, 1987
Etching
210 x 210 mm
Collection of the artist

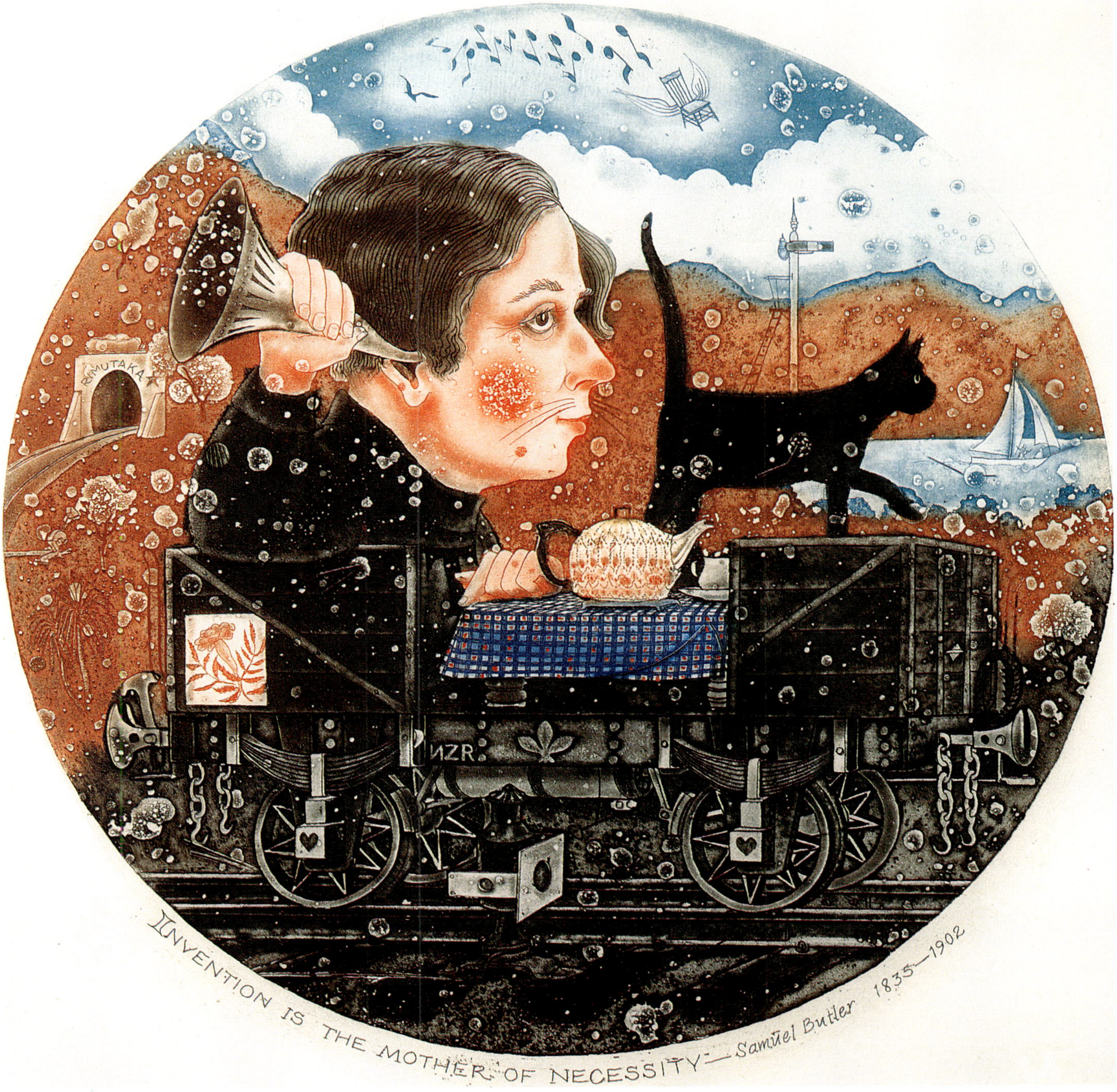
RIMUTAKA
NZR
INVENTION IS THE MOTHER OF NECESSITY — Samuel Butler 1835—1902

89

MICHEL TUFFERY

Born Wellington, 1968.
DFA (Hons), Dunedin Polytechnic 1988.
Lives in Wellington.

Tuffery can now be seen as the advance guard of a special group of young Polynesian artists who have emerged in the last five years (see Cotton, 100NZP,16; Pule, 100NZP, 69; Robinson, 100NZP, 78). Each of these artists has developed a sophisticated personal style which draws on his Polynesian heritage in a confident new way. Unlike some of their predecessors, they have not sought to 'modernise' traditional forms or to accentuate the primitive by using expressionism. Tuffery's approach has been to use his exceptional graphic skills to communicate visions of the fauna and human activity of the Pacific region, specifically his ancestral homeland of Samoa. Success in this endeavour has been continuous since he left art school. His works have immediate appeal to young and old alike; they can be enjoyed at a decorative level, and thereafter studied and appreciated for their inventiveness, fine drawing and sense of spirituality. Tuffery's work is totally lacking in sentiment, but it conveys the interdependent harmony of life on a Pacific island — fishes, birds, animals, people, plants, land, sea, sun and stars, all in balance. There is a sense of homage being paid to this harmony, be it God or Gaia. There is a sense of organic growth to a point of stasis, as if the components of the work had somehow come together on their own. There is harmony too in Tuffery's use of colour. While he may use the high-keyed blue of the deep Pacific, the yellow of the sun or the red of blood, these colours are moderated by gentle browns and greys. Tuffery's use of black and white is equally skilful, whether it be the sharp contrasts of woodcuts or the shadings of the lithographic crayon.

Tuffery suffered from dyslexia in his youth, and drawing became a way of communicating beyond writing. He was fortunate in having at all stages supportive teachers who recognised his talent and persuaded him, when a sporting career beckoned, to take his art right through to tertiary level. Along the way, like Pule, he abandoned an involvement with expressionism and found a clear source of subject matter in the motifs of Polynesian culture. In addition to being surrounded by stories and images of Samoa in his youth, Tuffery made a visit there when he was 10 or 11 and has returned since; he has also travelled to other Polynesian cultural centres. One of his tutors at the polytechnic was Marilynn Webb (87), and she and others taught him printmaking skills ideally suited to his graphic style. His work now ranges across many media: printmaking, painting, carving, assembled and painted sculpture, and drawing, including colour pencil work. He uses tapa and handmade paper as well as conventional paper. Several forms appear regularly: the zig-zag shape used in much Polynesian pattern-making, the lattice of woven mats, small human heads and figures, and the vaka (canoe), fish, leaves and shells (all of which share the same general shape). In lesser hands these archetypical forms could remain merely decorative; Tuffery welds them into compelling, compassionate icons.

Over the last three years Tuffery has diversified into theatrical work, designing sets, costumes and lighting. He has also spent a great deal of his time in the Solomon Islands, assisting unemployed young people there to develop paper and printmaking skills with a view to producing saleable art.

Lua Pili Siva, 1992
Lithograph with chine collé
530 x 380 mm
Courtesy of the artist

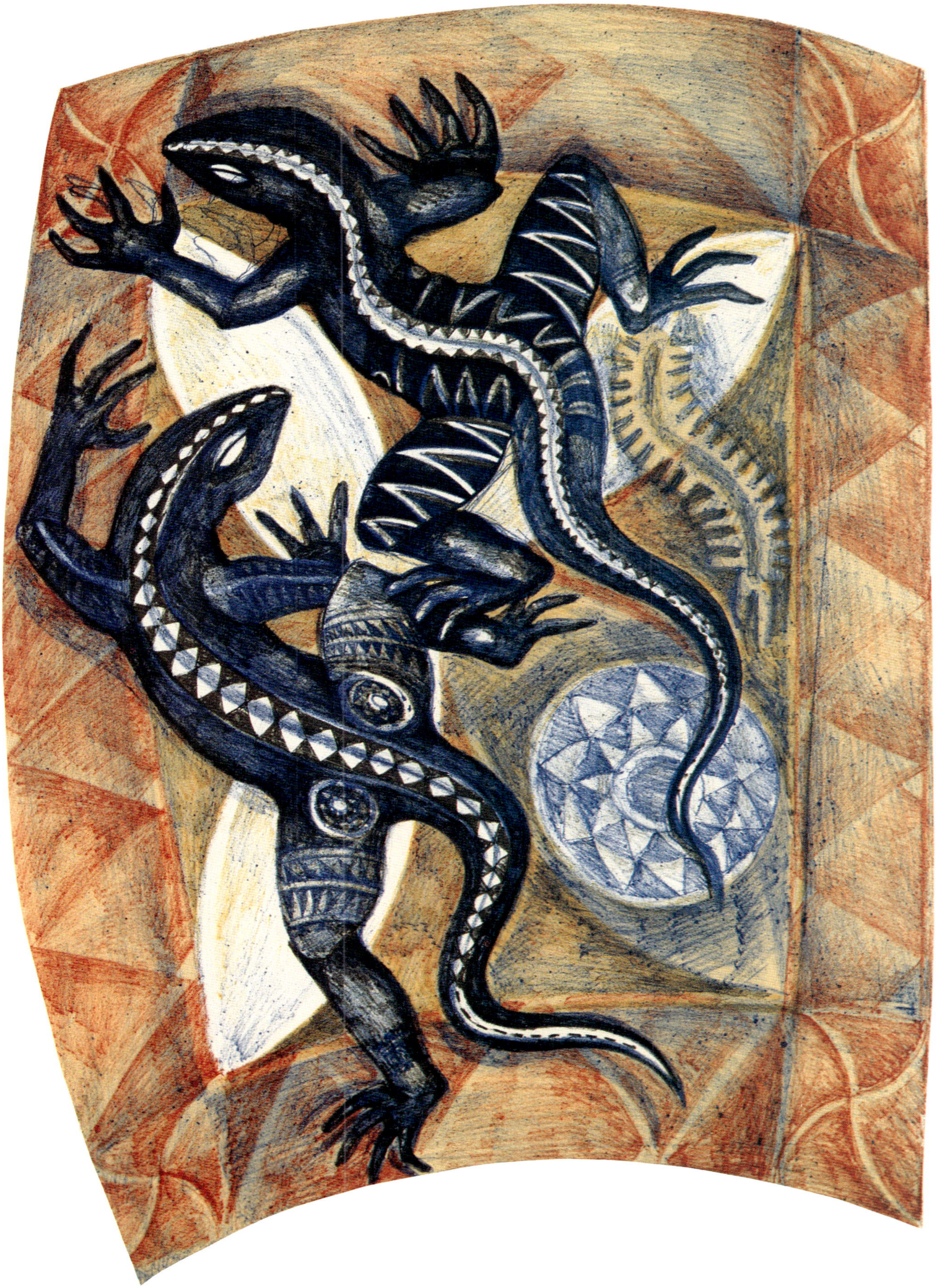

90

GREER TWISS

Born Auckland 1937.
DFA (Hons), UA 1957.
Lives in Auckland.

Twiss was one of the first contemporary New Zealand sculptors to realise new ideas in a public forum. His Karangahape Road fountain of 1969 sparked controversy because its misshapen figures and spaceship backdrop departed from public conventions. The work was based on ideas that Twiss had been developing since 1964, the year he showed his well-known *Athletes* series of floor and table sculptures. These images, modelled in wax and cast in bronze, showed influences from Moore, Armitage and Giacometti. Taking a popular (and, in the past, idealised) image as a starting point, Twiss distorted and generalised it to create poignant figures that seemed to be struggling with the burden of competition. Often coalesced in groups, these lumpen forms were not heroic; indeed, they looked more like Hiroshima victims than Olympians. Twiss was able to take these forms and readily redefine them into his *Protest Marchers* series of 1965. In later works the figures were sliced off at the waist, or only a limb was portrayed. Shadows became the plate upon which the figure was displayed. Some pieces were lacquered in bright primary colours.

From 1970 onwards the figures edged out of Twiss's work as he changed his style to one that was both more realistic and constructivist. He began casting hands, ropes and tools in bronze, and juxtaposing them with thin elements such as rods and bars. Works of 1974 were concerned with formal qualities, such as the hang of a lead rope from bronze rings on a vertical steel plate. Around 1976 and again in 1980 Twiss was concerned with the formal delineation of site areas using linear elements. Works of 1979 were about support systems, both soft (cushions and straps) and hard (plates and struts). During this period Twiss explored the forces of compression, gravity and movement frozen in time. He also exploited the natural colours of metal, contrasting yellow bronze with grey steel. In his austere *Tripods* of 1980, Twiss belied the apparent utility of the forms by attaching small, useless, bronze-cast appendages such as clamps and scraps of material.

Venus in the Park, 1996
Zinc-coated steel
2.5 x 2.5 x 1.5 m
Collection of the artist

In 1985 Twiss began working with cast lead and beaten lead sheets, ironically sculpting balloons, boats, cloth and other lightweight forms out of it, sometimes associated with model buildings. Lead has, obviously, a leaden quality: uniformly sombre, depressing and dense. Twiss exploited these characteristics in tableaux that could be whimsical, sad, surreal and puzzling all at the same time. Twiss has made tools, hats, spectacles, animals, birds and fish out of lead, and sometimes combined lead 'canvas' with real wooden chairs or screens.

Since a major installation at the Fisher Gallery, Auckland, in 1993, Twiss has been working with soldered galvanised-iron sheeting. The properties of that material have given a more provisional, constructivist look to his work, but retains the uniform grey tonality. Using a range of pre-cut and folded elements, the artist follows intuition in creating each sculpture. He retains a sense of the handmade, making no attempt to disguise folded flanges and braised joints. However, the finish is much finer and more detailed than in Jeff Thomson's work of the 1980s (87). The complexity of the objects Twiss is making in this medium increases. His most recent show on the subject of colonialism included opossums, .303 rifles, chainsaws and folded fabric. As in the past, the new work calls for an intuitive viewer response.

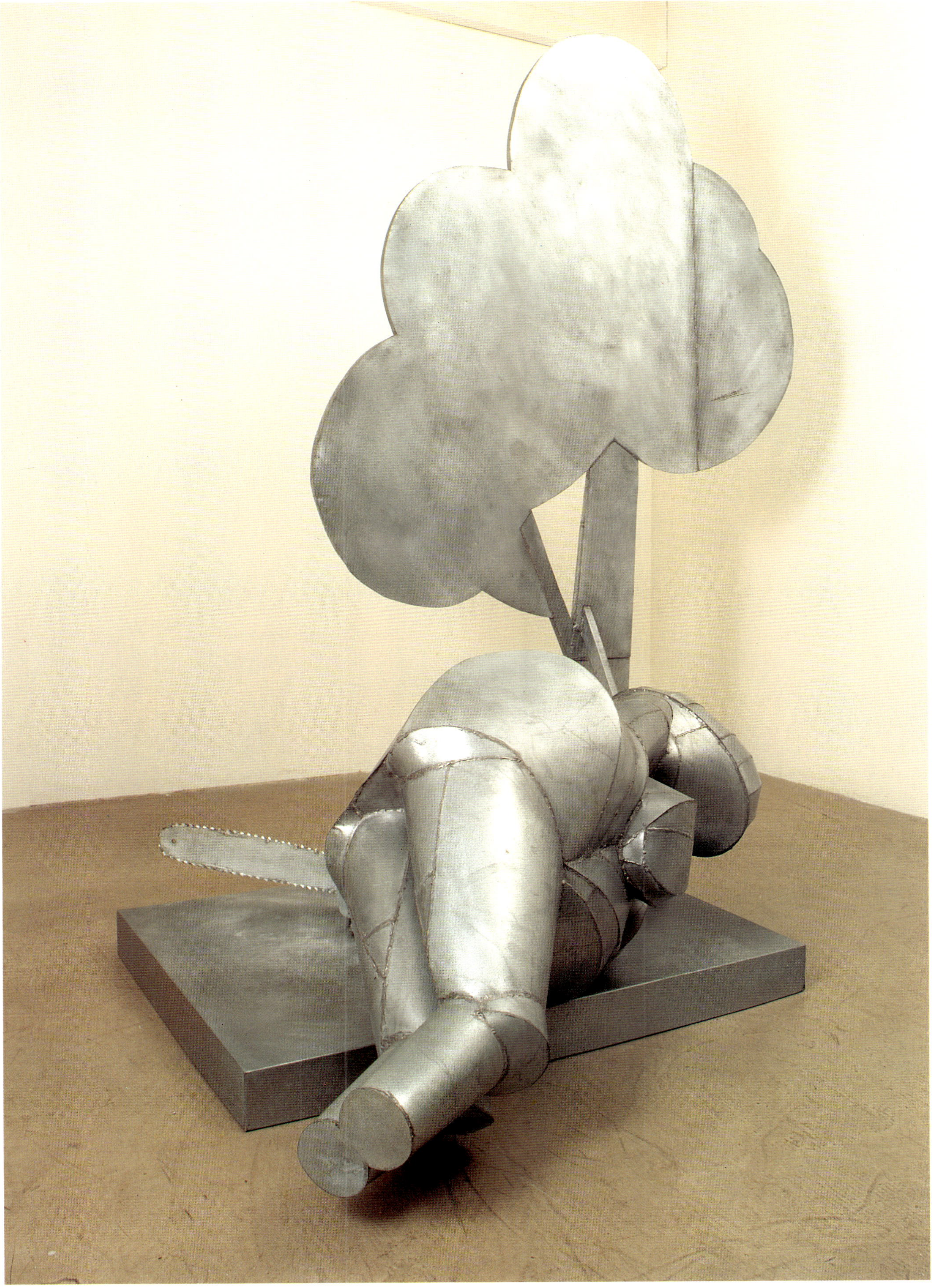

91

TERRY URBAHN

Born New Plymouth 1961.
BFA, UC 1985.
Lives in Wellington.

Urbahn is a painter, sculptor, photographer and graphic artist, and does mixed media installations. His early paintings were semi-abstract, expressive, colourful and painterly, although executed on boards cut to geometrical shapes. His ensuing work of 1988–89 changed completely, pursuing the interest in geometry into emblematic drawings and assembled sculpture. The drawings were based on a blocky cross shape in the centre, placed upon other shapes which resembled daises, altars or coffins. Collaged elements emphasised the straight lines, and colour was sombre, applied in drippy washes which suggested tears or rain. The sculptures were made of formicas, stainless steel and other commercial materials, combined with painted and textured areas. Very much sculptural objects, these pieces had authority, some almost to the point of becoming totalitarian emblems (cf. Roche, 76).

The architectural feel of those works foreshadowed Urbahn's next project. After the business crash in New Zealand in 1987, the central retailing area of New Plymouth was devastated by business failures and competition from a new centre nearby. Many large shops were vacant and Urbahn noticed that the interiors had a special articulation of space caused by their fitting-out for retail display. When everything was removed, arches, niches, stages, ramps, daises, plinths, recessed lighting and stairwells remained. The stores were like deserted stages set for some existential play. They called to mind Kurt Schwitters' famous *Merzbau*, built in Hanover before the Second World War. Urbahn did a suite of drawings of these spaces, shown in 1992, more or less faithful to the subject but in some works introducing imaginary sculptures to grace the emptiness. These works were again notable for their subdued, washy colour, their 1930s look and convincing sense of depth. Some were very large.

Vocal PA, 1992
Window sign, empty shop, scaffolding, planks, painted home appliance cartons, rope
ca. 3 x 3 x 6 m
Courtesy of the artist

In 1994 Urbahn took his art and his audience into an actual derelict space, an empty Wellington hotel. Using abandoned material found there, he made a large site-specific sculpture like a plughole or cosmic vortex. In an adjoining space, videos shot in the empty rooms were screened while closed-circuit cameras showed live surveillance of empty rooms upstairs. Letters and other personal ephemera left behind by the last occupants of the hotel were then used in *Hangover*, a group exhibition of grunge (trash) art. Urbahn's art thus moved in 1992–94 from abstract absences to actual absences, from suprematist high art to low art, from the spiritual to the mundane.

Moving on in this direction, Urbahn's installation *Alien Space* at the Govett Brewster Art Gallery in 1995 looked at the subcultures of surfing, rugby and heavy-metal rock in Taranaki. Local heroes in those pursuits were featured on videos in a setting of surfboards and guitars. Urbahn's most recent work retains architectural spaces in fuzzy, enlarged photographs, but populates them with collaged cartoons, tattoo designs and crudely lettered text. Another group of works is based on an abandoned set of travelling museum display boxes which Urbahn has altered so that they become ironic altarpieces for a banality cult. Using a computer, Urbahn has also produced posters of himself made over as famous rock stars (he is a performing rock musician). The texts on both these sets of works run counter to the imagery, being sober and portentous statements about life and aesthetics. In company with a number of younger New Zealand artists, Urbahn is at present in a neo-Fluxus mode, using anti-art ideas to probe the way forward.

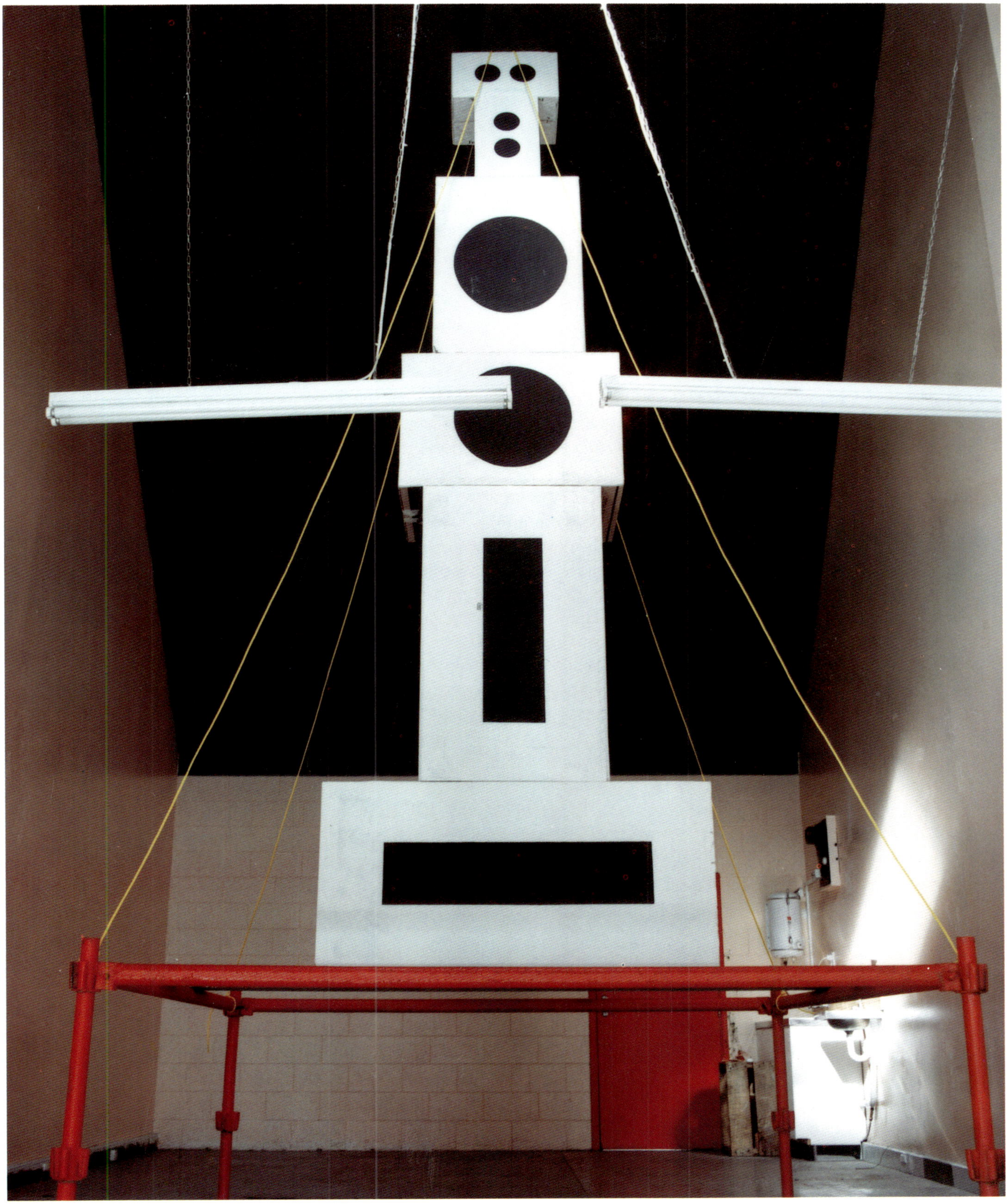

RONNIE VAN HOUT

Born Christchurch 1962.
Lives in Christchurch.

Van Hout is one of a new breed of artists who are not wedded to any particular style or medium. Such artists regard art as an activity, and are prepared to use any means to make art as they define it from time to time. Van Hout's art of the last decade inclines toward the experimental, often in the form of installations, and cannot be easily categorised or described. He is more interested in memory and how the mind works than in creating new things, so he sets up environments in which the viewer's mind can wander. His installations have themes, but more than one thing may be going on at once and items can be included to make meaning deliberately 'a little cloudy'.

The artist studied film-making in 1980–82, sings in a rock band, and thinks that both rock and art encompass ideas of rebellion, sexuality and fame. He has worked with film, painting, photography, computer graphics, print, ceramics and embroidery. Embroidery? Why not? Van Hout is of Dutch extraction, and many Dutch homes have embroidered decorations on their walls. In 1993 he decided to reproduce in stitching some of the notices he saw posted around town by groups advertising for musicians. He also did some works in this medium involving speech balloons and hellfire flames.

Van Hout's first show of paintings was in 1985. The works were texts (one-liner jokes) superimposed on images with obscure related meanings. His 1986 paintings, done at the height of an economic boom, superimposed corporate names on composite images which included quotes from past art, figures, a lacework like cracks in dried mud, and variations of tone as in a double-exposed photo. In his 1987 paintings *Believing is Seeing*, Van Hout used a pointillist technique to duplicate the appearance of a reproduced photograph, but the source photos (supposed shots of UFOs) were so fuzzy that the paintings became nearly abstract, glowing with a strange light. Other paintings of 1987 experimented with advertising imagery and slogans. In 1988 Van Hout exhibited multi-panelled photographic works which contrived to show a relationship between fiction and reality, the reality being snapshots of a Wellington street. Between 1989 and 1991 he was making dioramas in which he placed scale models, creating his own fictitious reality. The first works superimposed text on the images, exploring the cultural and personal effects of narrative on perception. Later the theme was colonisation of New Zealand, and Van Hout included cut-out lettering in the backgrounds, evoking both Colin McCahon and the famous Los Angeles HOLLYWOOD sign.

Installations of 1992–95 dealt with diverse topics: unfinished art projects, how art is contextualised by a museum in its stick-on wall notes, drawings done by a serial killer, parallels between wartime battles and digestive systems, totalitarianism and personal memories. In 1995 Van Hout made a suite of soft-focus photographs, again using scale models, in which the figure of a schoolboy walked from a landscape into a simulated art gallery setting, where other figures gathered, indifferent to the art. These 'art' photographs, exhibited in a gallery, had art, artifice and the relevance of both as their subject, leaving the viewer stranded somewhere in the middle. In 1996 Van Hout has extended the personal reference into casts of his own body, in association with increasingly haphazard and anti-aesthetic assemblies of objects, 'as if put together by a disturbed mind'. The meaning of each object in such an assembly becomes subjectively affected by its proximity to another object.

Art School, 1980
Black and white photograph
247 x 192 mm
Courtesy of the artist

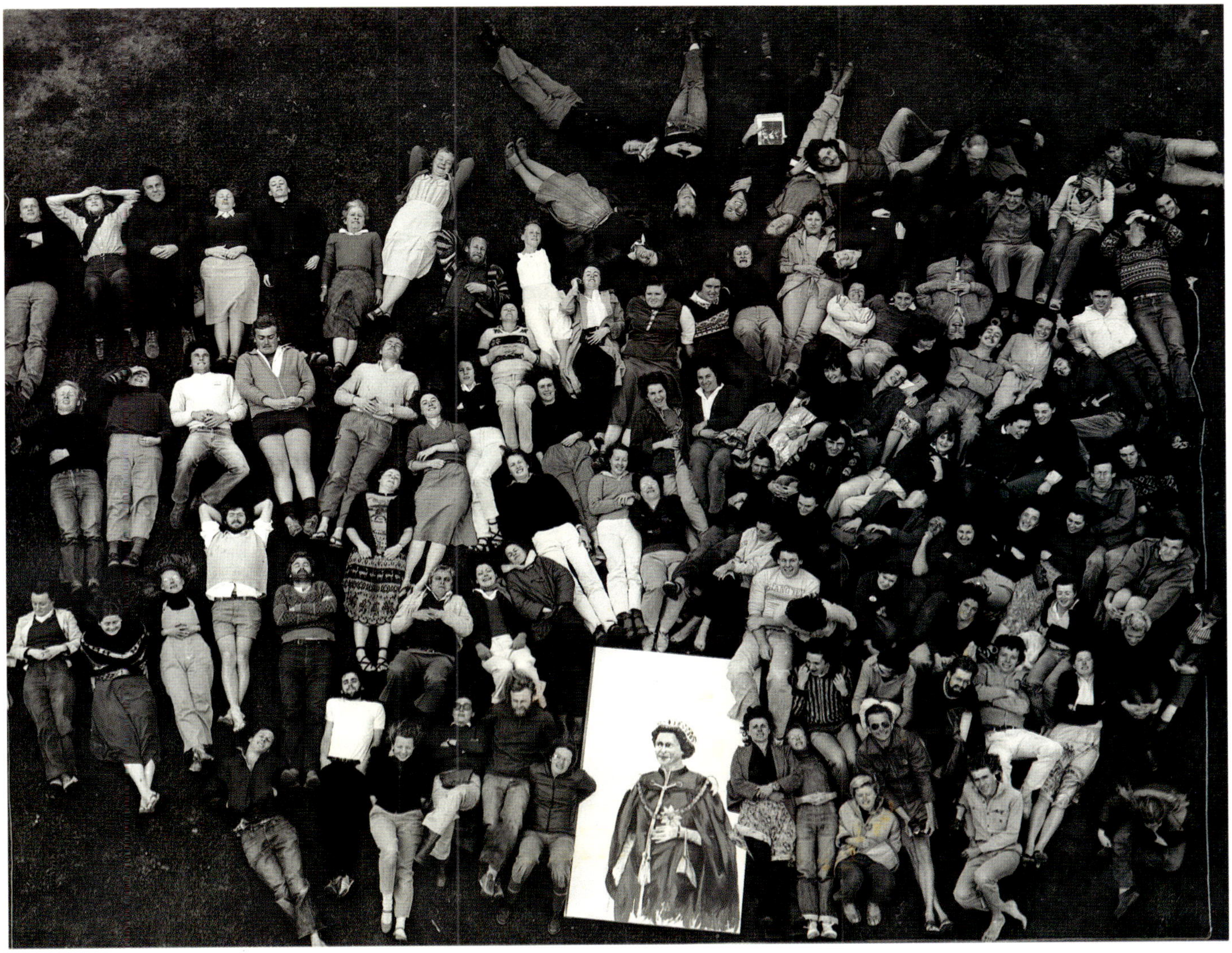

93

WARREN VISCOE

Born Auckland 1935.
Trade Certificate in Building Construction 1957;
studied painting, Chelsea Polytechnic, London 1958; DFA, UA 1965.
Lives in Auckland.

Over 30 years Viscoe's work has moved from avant-garde and conceptual to accessible and witty. Throughout he has made many drawings, indirectly related to his sculpture. Before 1969, Viscoe's sculpture was volumetric and smoothly modelled. Then, until 1981, it was ephemeral, in the form of installations using pine planks, wire, buckets, scoria, shells, earth and rocks. These constructions dealt with the effects of gravity and with systems by which natural materials were levitated, graded or confined. Some pieces were informal; others, using perspex, were angular and carefully put together.

In the early 1980s Viscoe began combining natural, found timber with the milled boards he had been using. Gradually his work became more figurative and, at the same time, underwent a style change. He began a cheerful involvement with raw radiata pine. He sawed, adzed, drilled and chiselled it, usually leaving the surface rough and making no attempt to disguise the way parts were added to make up the whole. Occasionally pieces were glossily painted. The effect was like funky/folk art, renouncing sentiment and blending organic and humorous human forms. Society and the environment have been continuing themes, but the effects gained from particular tools, or the demands of an installation space, could also spark off a sculptural idea. Many of Viscoe's pieces of the 1980s involved males engaged in activities, singly or in groups and accompanied by zany props. The sturdy, stylised figures (quarrymen, woodsmen) were bullet-headed and muscly, but they were witty caricatures. In many cases heads were flat cut-outs, hands and feet were oversized, and poses were stiff.

Hydra's Rack, 1986
Partly painted wood
2820 x 625 x 220 mm
Private Collection, Wanganui

In 1985 Viscoe made some important figures. *DSIR Man* was a pin-headed figure striding on enormous, muscled legs. Articulations of wood suggested mechanical elements and the man seemed like the uncertain driver of a robot. *Egg Preserver Man* was a stick-like form that also read as a tree which struggled with a row of drawings of eggs placed precariously above his head. In *Guided Tours*, a nine-piece work of 1986, a well-built man relaxed on a sunbed while all around him alligators and other snappy creatures gathered, baring their teeth in anticipation. In 1987 Viscoe, who has worked as a builder, made some small sculptural buildings. His fish smokehouse was a framework resembling a Greek temple with big wooden forms hanging inside — metaphors for the flesh and the spirit. A similar piece was a big playhouse, full of large painted wooden forms suggesting organs and a ribcage. These works introduced a note of surrealism, which has recurred since in Viscoe's less playful work.

The work of 1988 was abstract, but the forms were bony and contained sunken, elongated recesses which had a visceral look. In 1989 Viscoe built very large exterior installations of do-it-yourself Greek columns and gateways topped with sculpted figures. In 1990 his *Pink and White Bathers,* a group of figures shown at the old Rotorua bath-house, played games with art history. Two smooth, life-size figures of 1991 were each painted in one colour. *Sower* resembled a giant twisty-toy figure, striding across the furrows, while *Sleeper* lay on a bench swathed in a blanket, becoming an almost abstract form. The trend towards abstraction continued in 1993 with white-painted wooden columns and tubes with evenly gouged surfaces which resembled stanchions, leis, coral branches and/or exploding A-bombs. Symbolic forms rather than figures make up Viscoe's most recent work.

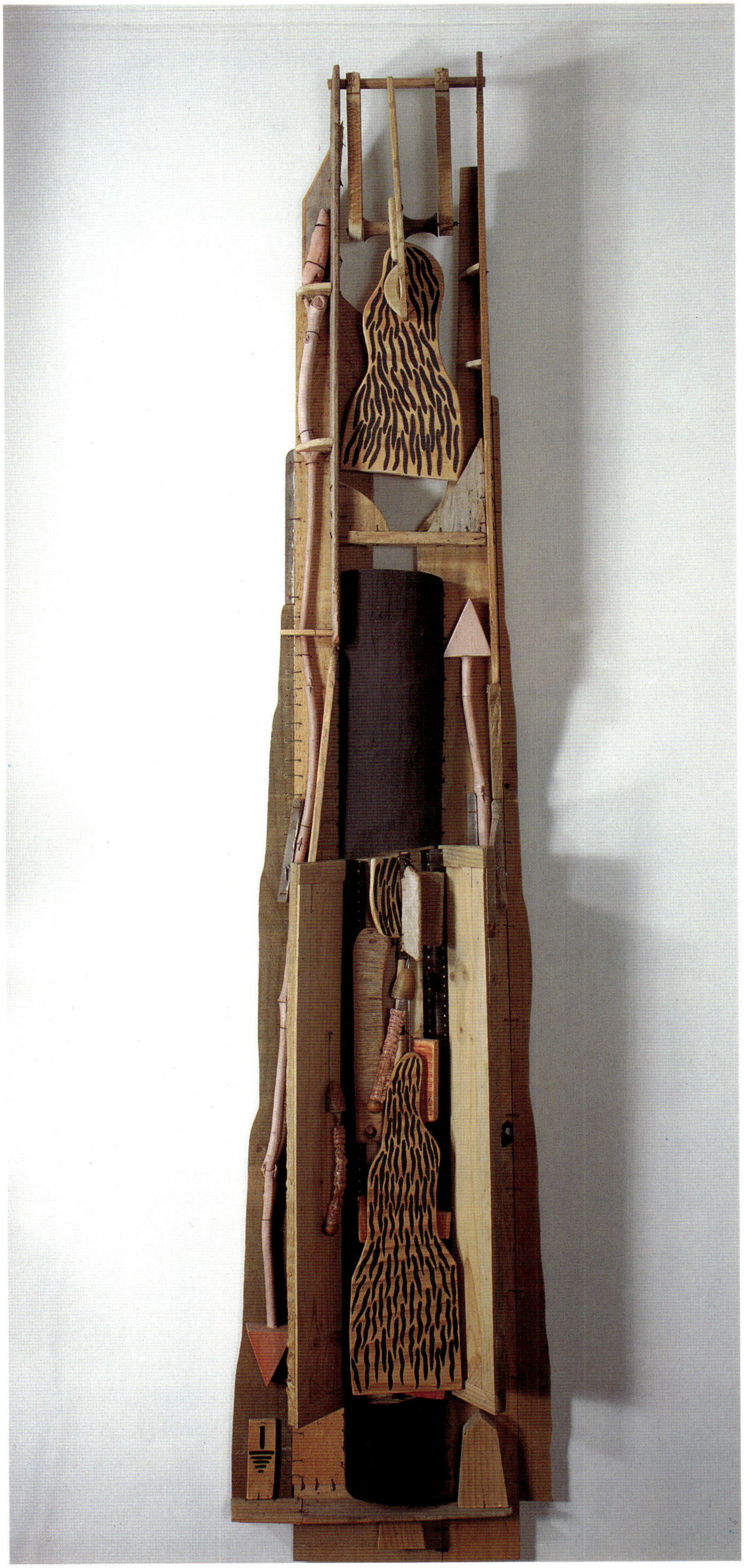

94

BARBARA WARD

Born Christchurch 1955.
Lives in Auckland.

The activity of stone carving goes back into prehistory. This heavy historic baggage has made stone unpopular with many contemporary artists, who prefer trendier materials. Ward got into carving gradually, and without tuition, not knowing or thinking at all about art history or politics. She arrived independently at conventions of carving that link through Khmer, Aztec, Mayan and modernist sculpture in a fresh, unselfconscious way. Although Ward's sculpture is chunky, compact and sometimes leaves part of the original block 'in the rough', it is always imaginative, well composed and convincingly modelled. Ward makes no preliminary sketches, selects her stone blocks carefully and studies them for some time before starting to chisel. Until recently she has not even made maquettes. She does not use power tools because she enjoys the handworking process and believes that it gives a more sympathetic feel for the stone. She uses Mt Somers limestone as well as the softer Hinuera stone, formed from compacted volcanic ash.

In 1981 Ward began carving blocks of plaster, then Chinese soapstone, making small works that were fragments of bodies or bird skulls or other forms that interested her. She moved on to Hinuera stone in 1985 and since then she has learned by doing, improving her range of tools and knowledge of how to use them, a process which she sees as ongoing. She was an organiser of and participant in the first stone symposium in Auckland in 1986, and her first large-scale piece done there, the image of a human foetus carved from a 2-tonne block, remains one of her best works. It was the first of many pieces, handled in a direct but sensitive way, which deal with the birth process and women's bodies.

Untitled, 1995
Mt Somers limestone
940 x 410 x 400 mm
Courtesy of the artist

Ward sees her work as falling into two groups: imaginative, intuitive pieces made for fun; and those dealing with the human body, which reflect indirectly the artist's thoughts and experiences. She makes works of both types at the same time. The human forms are often in groups, demonstrating Ward's interest in the relationships of bodies. Even when only one figure appears, she eschews the aloofness typical of a statue, and seeks to create a dynamic situation involving the viewer.

In her work of 1989, Ward was concerned with society's downtrodden, or trodden-in. Some pieces referred to drug addiction, some to death (in the form of excavated bones) and some to dying (the *Ground Under* series). The latter were floor pieces depicting huddled forms gaping and gesturing feebly like famine victims. In 1990–91 Ward was working in relief on limestone slabs. Her *Celebration of Death* series depicted the desiccated bodies of animals, while the *Helping Hands* showed truncated hands holding ropes or umbilical cords. These works were about the ties that bind and hands that heal in social and family situations.

In 1992 Ward carved a series of Amazonian female figures in seated or crouching poses. In style they resembled the paintings of women Picasso did around 1921, with enlarged hands and feet, and were saved from stolidity by delicately carved details. In 1993 she made a series of lithe, heraldic beasts, subjects beloved of medieval gargoyle-carvers. Cats that looked like lizards and dogs resembling dragons crouched prepared to spring, their bone structure showing through their smooth skins. Her small female figures of 1994 celebrated pregnancy. Ward's most recent female figures in limestone demonstrate mastery of the medium and are more classical than before.

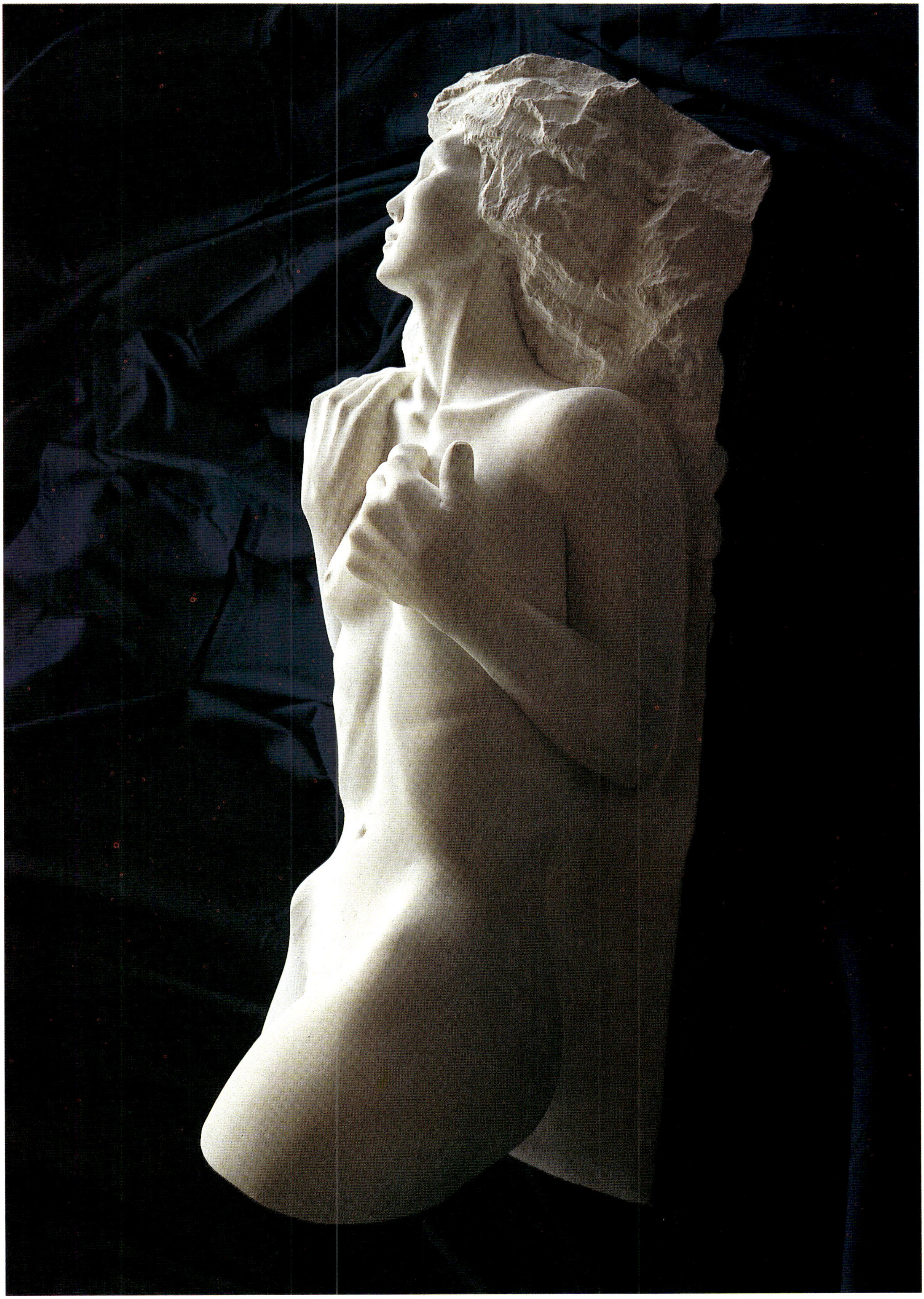

95

VIVIAN WARD

Born Greymouth 1950.
MFA, UA 1992.
Lives in Auckland.

Ward is one of the few New Zealand printmakers making mezzotints. The process is laborious and leaves little room for error. Such a long time is taken preparing the plate with a serrated tool that mezzotints are usually small. Most of Ward's works are smaller than the print reproduced opposite, but their size does not diminish their impact. Indeed, one series of nude male figures seem imprisoned and compressed within a plate 45 mm square. Ward uses the contrast between white and velvety black — the distinguishing feature of mezzotints — to give her images iconic power. Her concerns and themes are with the human presence in the landscape and urbanscape, demonstrating 'transition, silence and ambiguities'.

Ward's work divides roughly into three categories. The first are realistic studies of flowers, figures or parts of the figure (heads, hands, feet). In choosing these difficult subjects the artist seems to be challenging herself to succeed and then to repeat that success. Using tiny highlights on tendons and bone structure, on curling leaf edges and stalks, Ward models the forms as if spotlit. This sort of fine highlighting is a feature of her work.

The second category is studies of small groups of people and animals. These are little vignettes or slices of life. A woman sits in a doorway with a dog at her feet; another strokes a cat; a bird sits on the finger of another. Two women pull aside the curtain of their flat to view passers-by. A woman adjusts her hair in a shop window reflection.

The third group of works incorporates fantasy and surrealism. Here can be found some of Ward's earliest, as well as some of her most compelling, images. Early works included pierrots and staring eyes in the manner of classic surrealism. In the more recent *Counterweight*, a huge black cube balances on a corner at one end of an inclined plane. At the other end, a greyhound leaps toward the cube while a man throws his weight against the right-hand edge of the plate. In *Man with Birds* the man has his feet on the top of the image but the birds are orientated to the bottom edge.

Ward adopts unusually elongated formats with great success. She has done rows of heads, feet and running figures. In *Woman and Washing Line*, a tall, thin work, a woman hangs out or takes in washing while above her looms a stack of roiling clouds. *Great Great Grandmothers* is a tall column of figures standing on each other's shoulders. In *Sleeper II*, a work in a thin, horizontal format, a woman sleeps in a house on the left while on the right a barking dog leaps at a flock of gulls, with a night seascape beyond. Marvellous is not too strong a word (albeit a hackneyed one) to describe these works. One is drawn into the tiny spaces, which then open out like a Cinerama screen, totally absorbing one's attention. It is the velvety blackness of the mezzotint, unobtainable by any other method, which aids this process.

People and Pigeons, 1996
Mezzotint
235 x 135 mm
Courtesy Portfolio Gallery, Auckland

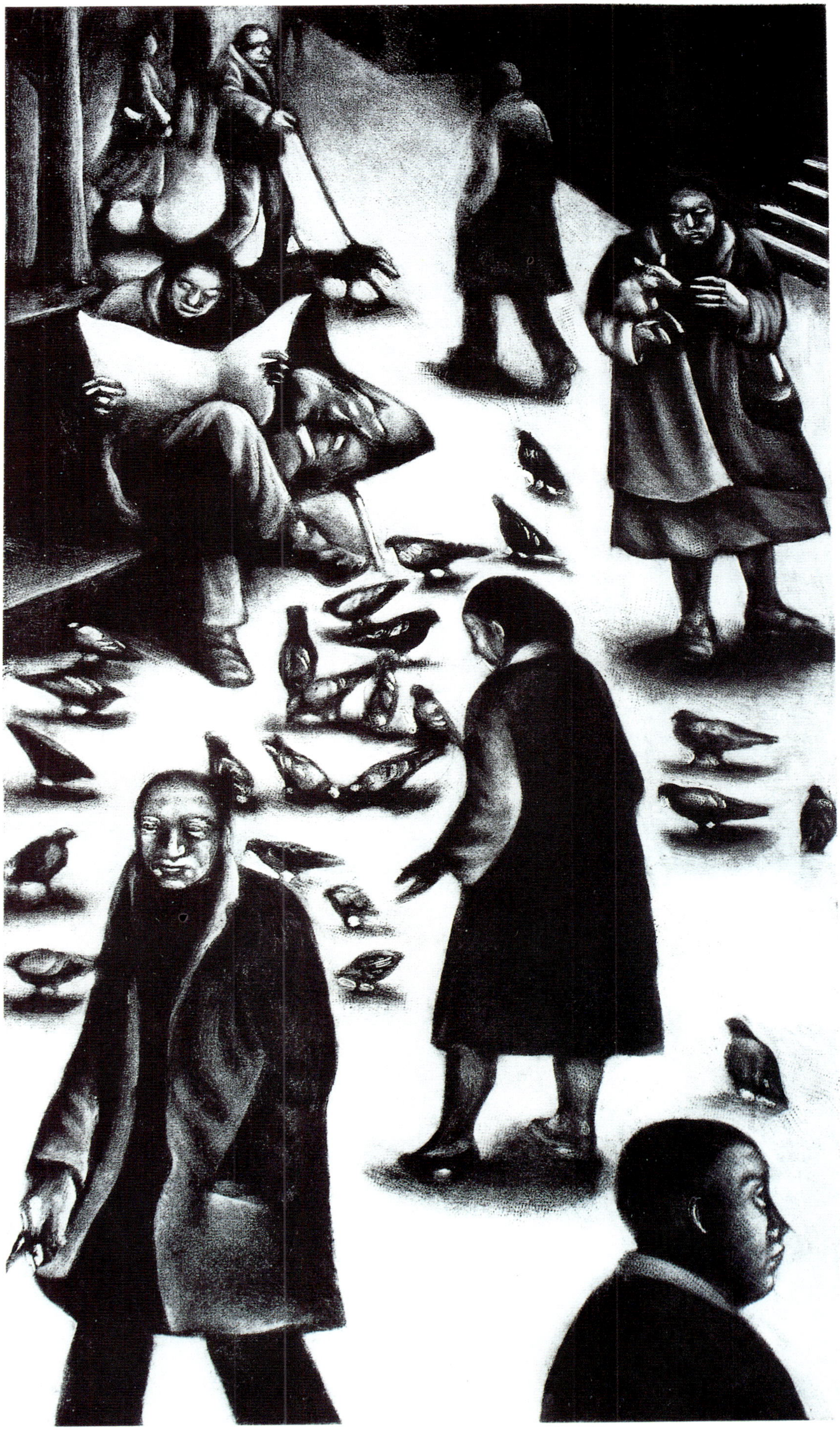

96

RUTH WATSON

Born West Melton, Canterbury 1962.
BFA, UC 1984.
Lives in Sydney.

Watson's inventive *oeuvre* between 1986 and 1993 is an important contribution to the body of deconstructivist work which absorbed the attention of many New Zealand artists over that period (cf. Budd, 7; Haffern, 100NZP, 30). These works illustrated the doctrine that we cannot have 'pure' experiences or memories — they will always be affected, even directed, by past experiences and learned codes of behaviour and interpretation.

Capitalising on this theory while illustrating it, Watson has used easily assimilable images to capture viewers' attention. In 1990 she even used a billboard. Her 1986 works resembled vellum pages from an illuminated manuscript, but with most of the text blacked out so that only the odd word and some small circular illustrations were left visible. In 1987 Watson further developed her long-standing interest in maps. Maps purport to meet a need for direction and meaning, but they have always been biased guides and part of the process of colonisation. Watson's large, mixed-media works looked like surreal versions of medieval maps, some using the Gores projection (which displays the globe as a row of leaf-shaped segments). She achieved the effect of wrinkled, yellowed vellum by skilful use of wax, tissue paper and paint. Mixed in with ill-defined land masses and fine background lines were body parts, staring eyes, brain and embryo shapes, and atomic and planetary structures, making dream maps of the past and future. A Gores map segment resembles a shield, canoe, leaf or lips, and Watson made a series of personally significant sculptural reliefs using this form in 1987. In 1988 she extended the astronomy metaphor by constructing her own planetarium in which projected colour slides made ironic commentaries on male domination of science. In 1989 Watson continued with map-like works, introducing as a unifying background element a faint swirl of lines derived from greatly enlarged fingerprints. She also exhibited *Tour of New Zealand,* an enlarged board game based on a 1960s original. Her game subverted a comforting trip around scenic spots with fragmentary texts from postmodern and feminist theorists, suggesting that hidden subtexts control our bland society. A number of other board games were made at this time. Also in 1989 Watson moved on to sculpture with an exhibition of 12 chairs identical in shape but covered with differing skins of material. The chair design and some of the surfaces were appropriated from other artists' work. In 1990, in her *Second Nature* series, Watson began using photography and found images. Taking a kitsch poster of breaking waves at sunset as a background, she foregrounded a number of other flat, image-bearing objects, such as jigsaw puzzles and books, as well as three-dimensional ones, such as a china-doll trinket container. In 1992 Watson turned her attention to another metaphor for meaning being created by systems (rather than vice versa) — the game of Scrabble. She made a series of enlarged Scrabble tiles which, seen in the clinical space of an art gallery, seemed very cool and minimal. Another work reproduced the whole Scrabble board, but with faded colour and multiple overprinting of letters as a metaphor for a grubby, played-out game (life?). Much of Watson's work from 1990 on has been concerned with taste in the context of memory. She has placed and photographed china ornaments, postcards and other knick-knacks in front of various nostalgic backgrounds. This overlay device was used in a series of lithographs in 1986 and in the 1990 photos, and is consistent with Watson's extensive use of collage.

Small Book, 1990
Edition of 10, photographic cibachrome print
360 x 280 mm
Private and public collections throughout New Zealand

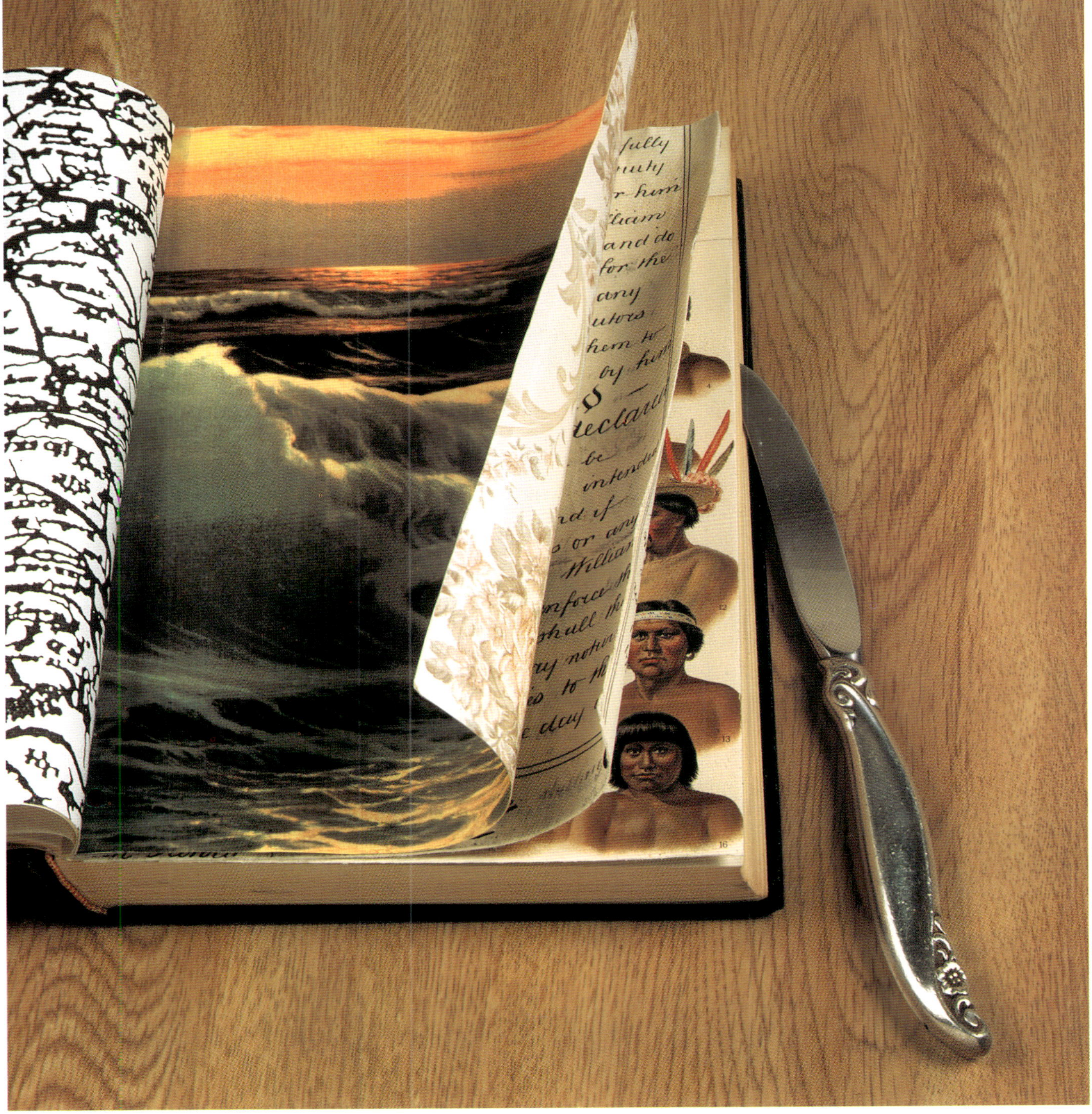
fully
and do
for the
any
be

97

MARILYNN WEBB

Born Auckland 1937.
Ardmore and Dunedin Teachers Colleges 1955–57.
Lives in Dunedin

Webb is one of New Zealand's senior printmakers and an artist who is well known outside the country; she has participated in many international print exhibitions since 1970. Her long involvement with teaching has added to the considerable influence of her prints in encouraging younger printmakers. Webb's prints exemplify the effects that can be found only in the print medium — paper embossing, sensitive wiping of inked plates, and subtle linear and tonal qualities.

Although much of her work is landscape-based, Webb is no scenic-view maker. Her works are products of lengthy contemplation of one particular area in Central Otago, and often record nothing more than clouds, water and a line of low hills. Lake Mahinerangi (Maori for 'daughter of the sky') is situated 60 kilometres inland from Dunedin. The water is coloured brown in summer and leaden-grey in winter. It is a strong, harsh, treeless landscape which exhibits constant changes of light and weather effects. In summer it shimmers with heat and the sunsets flush the sky red. In winter the lake freezes over and icy winds sweep across it. Over years of observation Webb has captured the essence of these fleeting events. In a process which duplicates what happens at the lake, she makes a linocut plate of the topography, prints multiple copies and then hand-colours the skies and water areas to produce unique images of particular times of day and weather conditions. Webb's watercolour washes convincingly evoke the original atmospherics, yet maintain a contemporary, expressive approach. She has used the same techniques in her ongoing suite of prints and drawings *Being in the Maniototo*. The weather dominates on this bleak plain between Ranfurly and Omakau.

Another of Webb's concerns is for the environment, internationally and locally. In works of 1970, 1985 and 1995 she addressed nuclear testing. Her observations of a burnoff of native tussock country to convert it for grazing inspired one 1983 series of prints. Proposals to dam the Clutha River prompted studies of its blue waters while they still flowed freely.

Celtic art, medieval illuminated manuscripts and runic inscriptions have also been an influence. Embossed or inscribed originally, those sources were readily incorporated into Webb's printmaking. Her *Protection* and *Garden* series, begun in 1985, emphasise geometric and symbolic elements. In some works mystical lettering could be magic, protective spells; in some, hands reach out to guard delicate leaves; others seem to take a microscopic view in which protozoa or DNA strands swim in a liquid medium contained within a rectangle. These latter, abstract works remind us of the source of life and that water in nature is intensely vulnerable to pollution.

Webb's early prints were notable for their sparse inking, restrained colour and embossed lines outlining billowing clouds. More recent works utilise rich reds, purples, blues, pinks and oranges, as well as embossed silver and gold lines, numbers and letters. A series of pastels, ongoing since 1987, use dramatic colour and boldly drawn landforms to make almost apocalyptic statements, with ambiguity of space and distance. Circular woodcuts, ongoing since 1993, move towards a balanced abstraction.

Cloud Pools, Ida Valley, from 'Being in the Maniototo Suite', 1988
Hand-coloured monotype on 300 gsm arches rives paper, hand-coloured with watercolours
846 x 605 mm
Collection of the artist, Dunedin

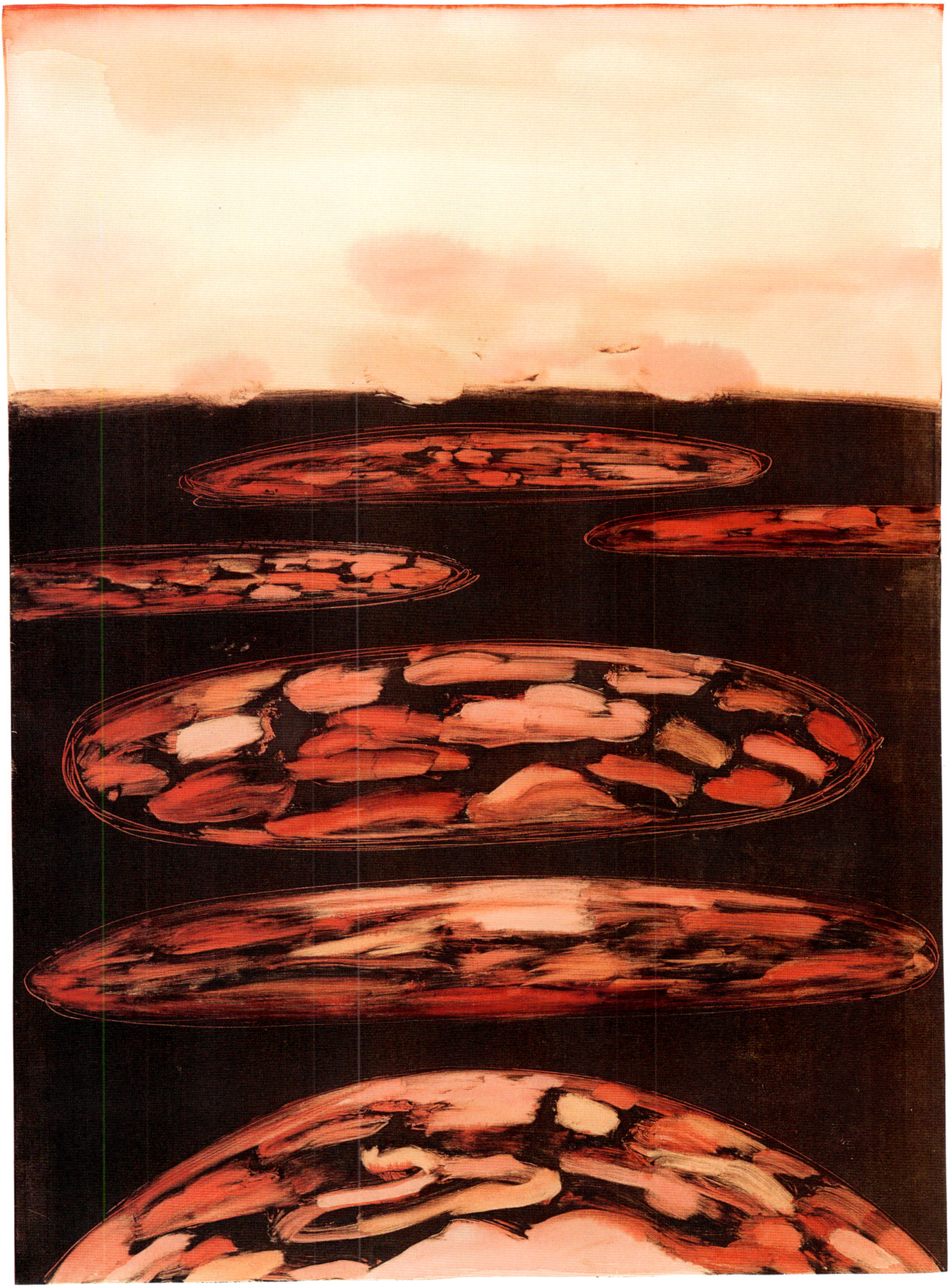

98

CHRISTINE WEBSTER

Born Pukekohe 1958.
Studied at Massey and Victoria Universities 1976–78;
Diploma in Photography, WP 1979;
DT Wellington College of Education 1979.
Lives in Auckland.

From her first exhibition in 1981, Webster has made her intentions clear — to use photography purely as a medium to make her art. Her photographs have been carefully considered and set up in advance. Her theme has been the strangeness of life: its fears, rituals, dreams and paranoias; its loneliness and anguish; its mortality. Exploration of the part played by self-awareness and sexuality in all these complexities of life has been a primary concern.

In a 1982 series Webster used the blurring effect which occurs when a subject moves too fast for the shutter speed to freeze it. Figures were turned into wraiths, seemingly trying to assert themselves in desolate but otherwise sharply defined environments. This concentration on the figure and the occasional use of blurred images runs through all Webster's subsequent work. In 1984–85 she began working with props and the artificial light and blackness of night photography. Memorable images from this period were washed with tones of yellow, green and red.

Precursors to the works from 1987 were a number of wide-angle, close-up polachrome portraits of a woman in which Webster had treated the film before printing it, causing the exposed emulsion to mottle, crack and slump. The resulting large prints were rent by black, curving voids with glowing edges. The effect was to create an intensely vulnerable, introspective and indefinably tragic figure.

Over the last nine years Webster has developed a distinctive style which has gained her an international reputation. She has presented her large, unframed cibachrome prints in a thin, vertical format surrounded by black, and (until 1991) with a plaque of text at head or foot. These uncluttered but complex works make much use of masks, costumes, allegory and symbolism, with nude or semi-clad models in soft focus as the 'subjects'. Webster trained in drama and has always sought theatrical effects. Light falls on the figures, but the surrounding space is dark, so the effect is very much like a spotlit performer in front of a stage curtain. The dark, shiny surfaces of the prints reflect the viewer as well as random light effects. This forges a direct link to our subconscious, tapping in to our own particular set of Freudian predispositions.

New Myths, 1988, was a series exploring gender and sexuality. In *The Players* of 1991, one model played various roles, such as Provider, Rescuer or Seducer. *Possession and Mirth,* 1992, was a series looking back to Caravaggio and the classic nude in a provocative, disquieting mix of the sacred and the profane. The major series *Black Carnival,* 1993–95, consists of 49 photographs of different models in a frieze covering 50 metres of wall. The over-lifesize figures are either self-absorbed or stare frankly at the viewer. Many are wholly or partly unclad; some wear masks, cross-dress or sport fetishistic adornments. They are designed to surround the viewer, who is drawn into this parade of strange creatures of the night.

The *Can-Can* series of 1994 presented details from *Black Carnival* isolated by ripped black gaffer tape. Here the viewer became voyeur, and the images spoke of the way people suppress some aspects of themselves and flaunt others. And 1996 has seen the presentation of two new series: *The Hunt, The Seduction and The Kill,* shown in Melbourne, and *Circus of Angels,* with the dancer Douglas Wright as model.

Rags, 1992
Cibachrome on five sheets of plastic
2137 x 1788 mm
Hocken Library, University of Otago, Dunedin

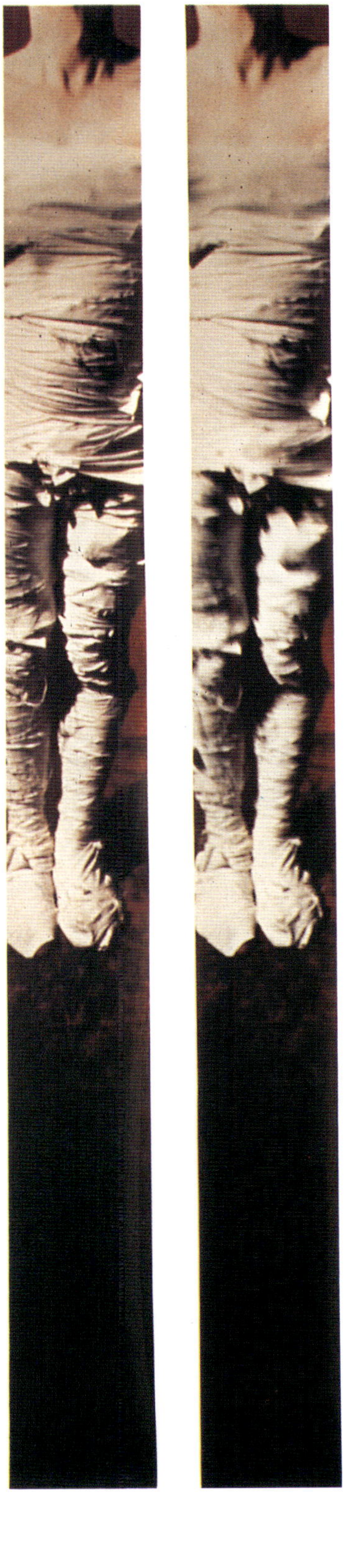

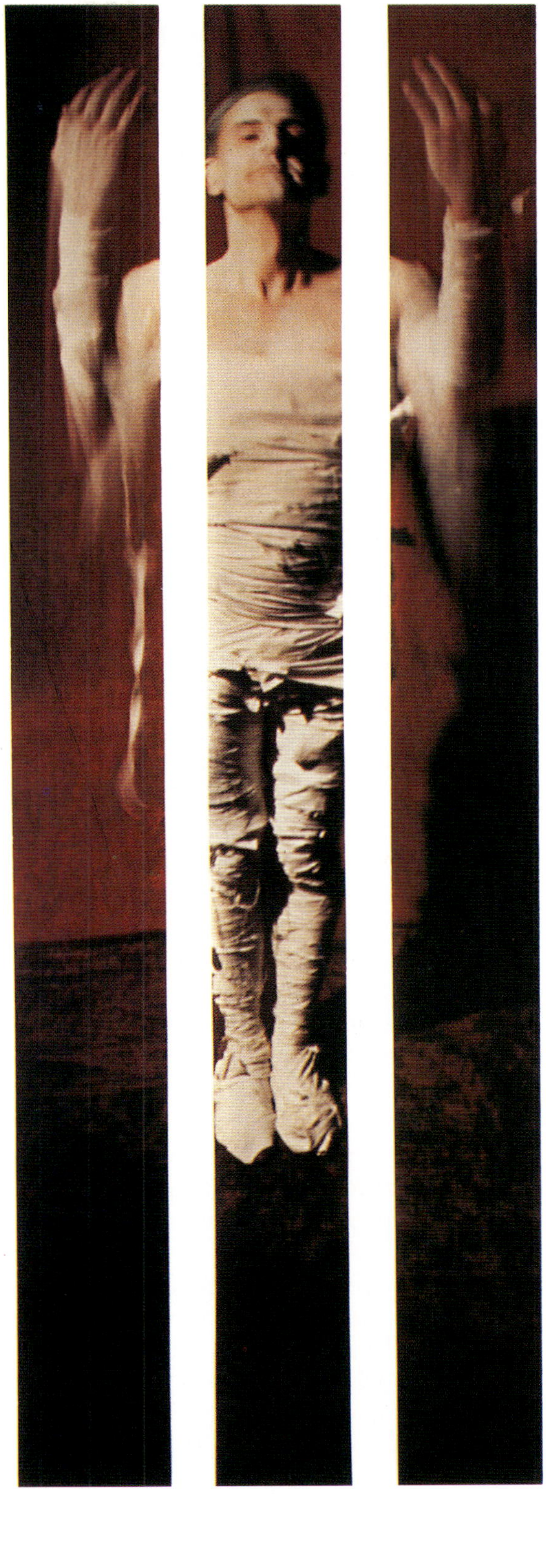

99

FELICITY WEST

Born Auckland 1945.
Attended Elam Art School 1962–64.
Lives in Helensville.

Although she has worked with the media of photography and drawing, West's reputation is based on the intaglio prints she has made since 1982. Printmaking by definition involves the production of multiple images, and there can be a temptation to popularise an image so that it will have wide appeal. West, though committed to landscape-based imagery in her work, has never compromised her tough, analytic style. For her the landscape is, as it was for McCahon (100NZP, 50), a reservoir of spiritual values. McCahon tutored West in painting and supported her in 'staying with her own truth'. That truth has involved living in and contemplating the New Zealand landscape while struggling to bring up a family in difficult financial circumstances and coping with a visual impairment.

West lived on the coast north of Blenheim for five years and has lived on a hill overlooking the Kaipara Harbour for 27 years. From there she has made frequent visits to the expansive vistas of Muriwai, one of McCahon's sources of inspiration. No specific 'scenes' emerge from West's response to these environments; rather her prints have distilled out essential elements, small details and snatches of memory that we all share. These include the blurred sweep of beach, sandhill, sea and sky; lone trees sculpted by the wind; isolated rocks and stumps; and the changing weather. In 1983–84 West was endeavouring to express the different qualities of the west and east coasts — one softly feminine and the other ruggedly masculine. Blue predominated, the colour of sea and sky. In 1985 she began introducing autobiographic figures inked in brown to symbolise their links to the earth. In1986 she devoted herself to large and small studies of the Kaipara environment, seen as a stage upon which humans played out their acts of exploitation while small, unnoticed and vulnerable beauty lay all around.

Before 1991, West's prints were coloured in a limited range of blues, browns and orange-red with touches of gold. In 1991, with the *Unacknowledged Sacrifices* series, she began restricting her colours to black and gold, and used engraving techniques in preference to acid etching. At the same time her work took on a much more dreamlike, spiritual quality. She describes these changes as a search for a greater sense of depth in the images, a move away from the seduction of colour and a desire to open her work to a broader range of expressive responses. After a series in which gold shapes of shells and chalices lay nestled within black backgrounds, she began using a gothic arch shape in a variety of evocative ways. It appeared as the space between bending grasses and trees; as a sea-cave floored with wet, rippled sand reflecting light; and as an abstract symbol of peace and protection. As an opening or entry, the arch shape also stands for the steps into the dark one must make in life in order to progress.

Survival Strategies, 1986
Etching
260 x 160 mm
Courtesy Portfolio Gallery, Auckland

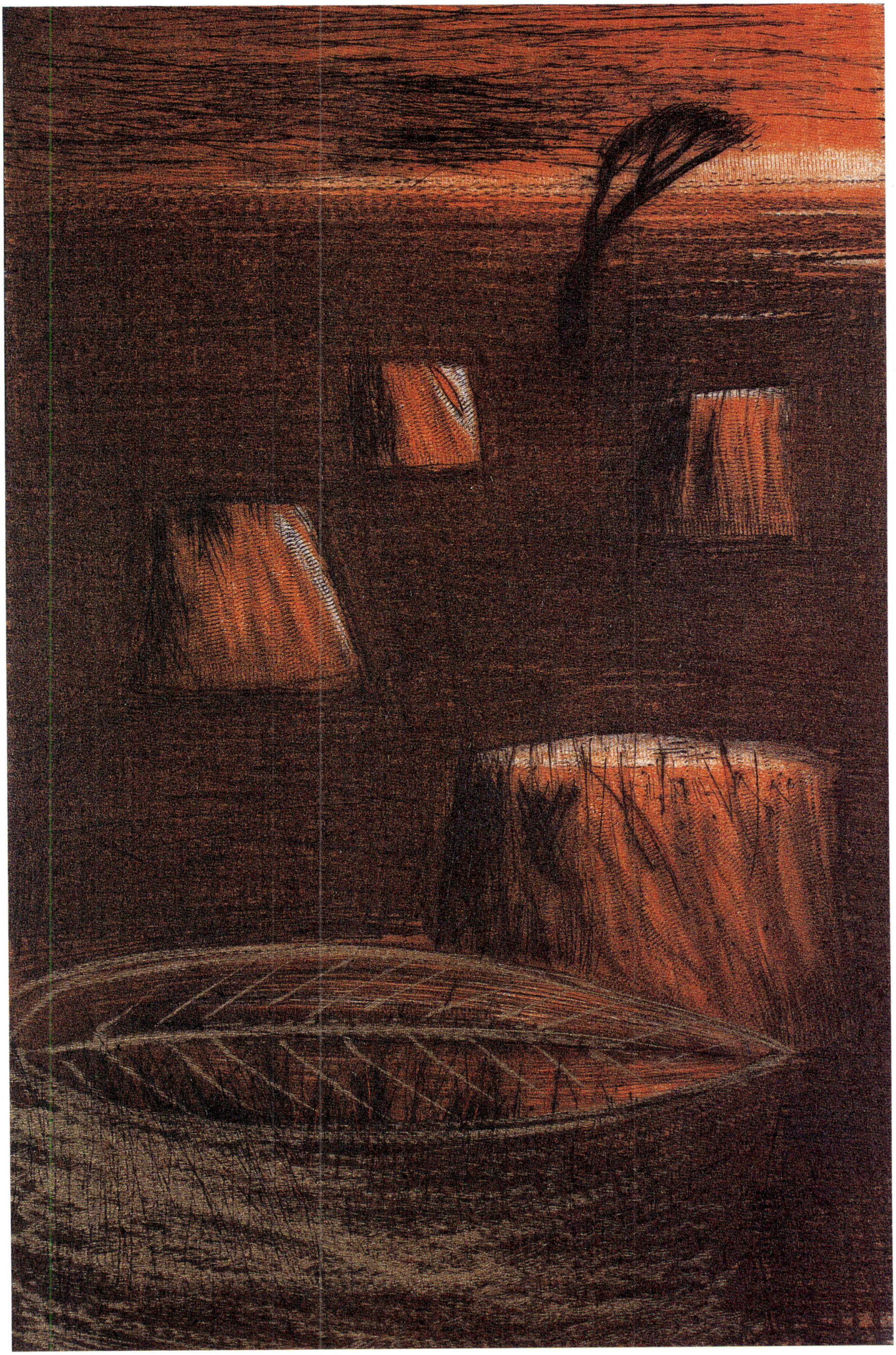

100

FRANK WOMBLE

Born San Francisco 1945.
Came to New Zealand 1972, departed 1988 and returned 1993.
Lives in Auckland.

Womble was an irrepressible, high-profile artist in Auckland in the late 1970s and early 1980s. He often dressed as a clown, but he took his art and his philosophy of life most seriously, and would debate it forcefully with anyone at any time. To discuss such issues as nuclear Armageddon, totalitarian government, the insidiousness of big-money marketing or the cliqueishness of the art scene with someone in whiteface and wearing a Mickey Mouse hat was an unnerving experience. However, there was method in Womble's madness. He was more committed than most of his contemporaries to his lifestyle as a serious artist and pacifist. Like the Dadaists before him, Womble suggested that in a world gone mad only the clown is sane. Images of clowns, Disney characters and Charlie Chaplin appeared in much of his work at that time. He used them to point out the absurdity, as he saw it, of spending megamillions on armaments and the space race when much of humanity (including artists) languished in poverty, both physical and spiritual. Womble included plastic model war toys in his anti-war assemblages with telling effect.

A professional clown must also have unexpected skills, such as juggling or acrobatics. Contemporary critics generally agreed that Womble's ability to juggle commonplace images was without parallel. He attracted media attention with his large outdoor junk sculptures, such as *Oblivion Express* of 1983, a truck which came from oblivion (selected scrap metal parts) and rapidly returned there. His collages, paintings and small wall sculptures made from found objects were thought-provoking and endlessly inventive. Devices or images used repetitively by Womble included masks, flags and targets, Mickey Mouse and Donald Duck, the cover of *Time* magazine, advertising logos, and cruciform and totemic shapes. These were exploited for their visual, symbolic and emotive content, and often combined together. The artist could lull viewers with a series of delightful visual witticisms and then hit them with irony, pathos or tragedy. A feature of Womble's paintings was his use of drips, creating a sense of multiple surfaces (depth) and alluding to things being in flux, under attack and metamorphosing. His collages ranged from a few deft alterations to an image to more complex surreal rearrangements.

In 1978 Womble mounted his unforgettable *Zpace Zhow* at the Auckland City Gallery, one of the first installation-type shows seen there. A very large space was filled with a wide selection of his work in collage, sculpture and painting, which delighted crowds of adults and children alike. In addition to regular gallery shows he also put on exhibitions in cafés, vacant shops and other non-gallery spaces around Auckland.

Womble's first show on his return to New Zealand, *New Money*, was a series of collages based on the design of the American dollar bill. Mixing humour with seriousness as usual, this was a quest to bring into focus the figureheads and institutions responsible for the industrial-materialist takeover of much of the world.

Zaza (Mickey Meta), 1985
Enamel on wood and aluminium
650 x 350 x 230 mm
Collection of the artist

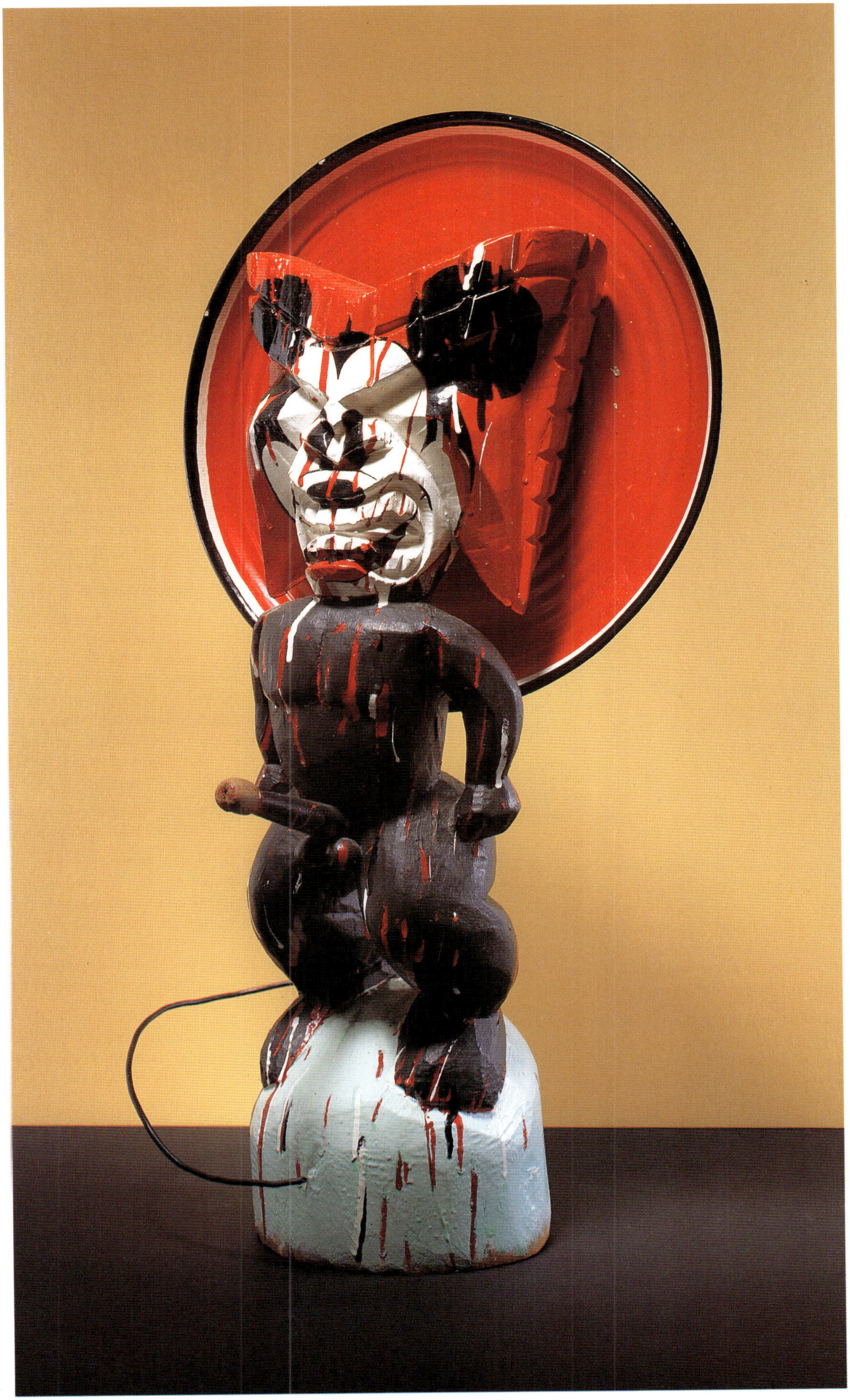

NOTES ON THE ILLUSTRATIONS

1. This drawing has links back to Ball's earliest work, in that the handling of the background plays an important part. It has depth and can be seen as a receding, misty landscape. The work is a development of the 1994 paper-scrap drawings. Both Ball and McCahon have examined the contrasts between darkness and light, and it is interesting to see how contemplation of such different things as paper scraps and rocky, vertical cliffs can produce consistent results. Here we see Ball arriving, via Mondrian, at a similar position to that reached by McCahon in his *Necessary Protection, Jump* and *Angels and Bed* series, and taking the opportunity to pay homage to both artists.

2. This 1986 photograph prefigures Barrar's *Shifting Nature* series made in the Wanganui area and elsewhere in 1990–92. The theme of the series was erosion and attempts at controlling it. The picture shows an embankment made of steel piles, backfilled and topped with a protective railing, but this is not immediately apparent. Take 1 is of an abstract composition with surreal overtones. The rusted pile tops resemble an alien city from a sci-fi movie. Take 2 is a view across water to gently rising land with cloudy sky above. Take 3 shows that it is not distant land we see but a close-up section of wooden railing. Take 4 reveals an amazing correlation between the clouds and the lichen growing on the railing. We are left in a spatial limbo, with near and far, water, sky and land all rendered uncertain.

3. Beadle made a number of these open rotunda towers, buildings stripped of their outer walls revealing the human activity within. This one shows vignettes of life indoors and outdoors in a big city.

4. One of a number of small sculptures made between 1990 and 1995 in which angular forms sink into rounded stones. It makes reference in miniature to Bennett's large exterior project on Nelson's Boulder Bank. The rectangular panel is similar to the glass panels in that assembly, and also relates to the artist's graphic work in which diagonals are a standard feature. Here we see a perfect balance between natural and artificial forms.

5. This sculpture was originally displayed in Wanganui, a city at the mouth of a river which reaches into the central plateau and carries down quantities of pumice. This material has a foamy, organic texture, adding to the feeling that the forms may be big fungi or tubers. Works such as this relate directly to Booth's linear stone compositions, because they are a spiral of stone on flexible, rather than stiff, steel. The form is built up in the same way as a coil-clay pot. The light weight of this material goes some way towards ameliorating the problem of transporting piles of rock over long distances.

6. One of a number of large works on metal with similar coloration in which structures and the tools that build them form the backbone of the composition.

7. The illustration shows part of an installation which also included a TV set playing a continuous tape, a record player with no needle playing its turntable, a projector throwing out a beam of light which silhouetted a vase filled with milk, a pile of books (all these objects roughly painted white) and a number of plastercasts of the inside of cardboard containers. The theme of the show was a critique of mass media — amid the accoutrements of a comfy home (chair, heaters, ornaments) these media were communicating nothing — and the overall effect was of hopeless sterility. This installation was made by the artist in her Merit Gröting persona.

8. This work was made in London at the apogee of the British pop movement. Its sexual overtones link it with other work of the period, such as that of Peter Phillips and Allen Jones, which was concerned with the 'packaging' of people as sex symbols. There is also some affinity with the work of Richard Lindner. However, Bullmore's work is more symbolic and, of course, more sculptural. It is a synthesis of pop, synthetic cubism and surrealism; a modern coat-of-arms or tribal shield.

9. This recent woodcut demonstrates Campbell's variety of line, and includes many of his repeated images — the fountain, monuments, rowboat, tree and car. The car here is on a roller-belt, whereas in other less optimistic works it sits propped up, wheel-less, on sticks. The heart shape in the centre relates to a series of paintings of hearts impaled on trees done in 1994. Overall, the scene calls to mind Bosch's famous *Garden of Earthly Delights* (*ca.*1500), and the cautionary message is the same.

10. Although the brown paper backing and smudged text are typical of Cane's work, the use of relief collage is unusual.

11. One example of a body of work which draws upon issues of masking and layers of reality. Chaplin's cloth theme is apparent here, serving as a symbol for both the theatre and for veiling. The mask also veils, and its face — Pierrot's — is a theatrical one. It is an adult face, but its wearer is a young boy. Pierrot appears as a supplicant before a votive figure, once richly clad but now just an empty frame. The lighting and soft focus turn the cloth to stone.

12. The blanket and careful joinery all indicate that this is a piece of equipment designed for a very specific recreational use, but just how it works evades our understanding.

13. The influence of Maori convention is seen in the three-fingered hands and elongated form, but the carving on the hands is more like a bicycle chain, while the head reminds us of Picasso and Epstein. This remarkable figure switches from being goofy to imposing, from being a supplicant to an adjudicator. The head made from engine parts is a fine example of Christensen's ability to integrate found objects into his wooden sculpture.

14. Everything about this bird suggests a museum specimen, except for the perch which is designed for a live bird. The aquatint background has been developed in two degrees of density to produce the shadow.

15. In 1974 Coolahan began the *Immigrants* series of images

based on the problems of transition, a subject that has held its interest for her over the years (cf. O'Connor, 65). This particular print, with its cut and interleaved paper, shows Coolahan's inventive approach to the medium.

16. The basic structure is a stand made especially for the display of 'limited edition' collectors' items. Copeland's display is full of surrealist symbols: eyes, clock, playing card, old photographs and corpse. This is a *vanitas*, a reminder that we can't take our accumulated baubles with us when we die.

17. This is a good example of Copland's etchings of twisted trees. Somehow this low-angle view involves us with the tree as a living organism much more than a distant view would do.

18. The pieces of this work do not have to be displayed in set positions but can be moved around from time to time to set up fresh relationships or to take advantage of changing light directions. The artist prefers placement on a mirror surface to create a floating effect.

19. Cornish has made many small temples, both as individual pieces and as components of her multi-part floor installations. Their crusty surfaces are like bread, and they are symbols of physical and spiritual nourishment as well as shrines to the art of ceramics.

20. These two small tapestries are part of an 18-piece work woven in Melbourne. The patterning shows Crook in expressive mood — in other tapestries, the imagery is more geometric and realistic.

21. This huge floor piece is an example of Culbert using plastic bottles and neon tubes in an informal way to create an overall environment. The power leads become part of the abstract composition. The artist has done a number of similar installations.

22. One of a set of four works which involve the pumping of water around an unlikely circuit between reconstructed chairs and cardboard boxes. Sucking and gurgling sounds, and the movement of air bubbles along pipes are part of the overall concept. A better sculptural example of kinetic *arte povera* would be hard to find.

23. This work shows Darragh moving away from works crammed full of plastic knick-knacks towards a more restrained, if no less kitsch, image. Darragh likes using roses, and here they act sumptuously with the gold torso to make a piece of classic surrealism. The foetus is not immediately apparent — an example of the little shocks which Darragh often sneaks in to her assemblages.

24. A skeleton pinned against a grid is an image which Dawe has used several times. The grid calls to mind the site layout of an archaeological dig, a reading initially denied by the absurdity of the umbrella. However, umbrellas are used at such digs — to protect the site from sun and rain. As usual with Dawe's work, a close inspection of the skeleton reveals beautifully crafted joints, polished wood and small metal components.

25. The source of the disposition of figures in this manipulated photograph is *Madonna del Parto*, a painting by Piera della Francesca. The artist is the stand-in for the madonna.

26. The theme of levitation runs through much of Dawson's outdoor sculpture. Here the sky and trees play the same role as does the wall in his indoor pieces.

27. This piece shows how De Boer is moving away from strictly natural forms toward more abstract compositions. The vertical leg at the right evokes both gothic architecture and the form of the punga tree. The leg on the left functions as a water channel for overflow from the bowl, which calls to mind a kidney and a boat, which in their separate ways both deal with water. The piece is sand cast from wooden patterns developed from natural tree forms.

28. The work delightfully depicts the modern woman on the run in several different directions, balancing her roles as shopper and office worker and still making time for tea with her friends. The device of delineating a breast by a cut-out crescent is a Dibble trademark and is possible only because of the thinness of his seemingly monumental forms.

29. This typical work from the 1980s shows how Drawbridge can create a fascinating composition of lines and tones from a very simple subject. There is a clear difference in appearance from a pencil or ink drawing — marks on a metal plate have much greater complexity.

30. This very large collage demonstrates Driver's use of cubism and his sure grasp of colour. The conjunction of sack, material, strap or rope tensors and vinyl backing has been used by him in a number of similar hangings over the years.

31. One of a number of small 'devices' in bell jars which incorporate sphagnum moss and what seems to be scientific apparatus for weighing or measuring within these trapped atmospheres.

32. An example of a recent installation by Endres in the interior of a Wellington city carpark building. Drivers of cars spiralling up and down the ramps were treated to a stroboscopic display of pink bars relieved by the occasional glimpse of what could be a TV ad — a metaphor for a controlled, candy culture in which we all spin meaninglessly.

33. Over recent years Ffrench has been doing a lot of drawing and painting, and incorporating this material into her photographs along with other photographs and objects as before. This innovation has taken her work one step further into the mysterious area where truth and fiction mix. She has also sought to increase the sense of perspectival depth and realism in the backgrounds, which formerly were quite intangible. The illustration comes from the artist's 1996 show which explored the romantic vision, something done at the end of the last century by the symbolists and late Victorian novelists. At the mouth of the Wanganui River we see the city in the background. A man works on a laptop computer watched by a female figure from Poussin's painting *Et in Arcadia Ego.* The plumb-bob pendulum indicates time.

34. This horned form is one of several variations made by Fisher. It is simple yet powerful, graceful yet authoritative. It pays homage to past art as far apart in time as the work of Arp and the Norsemen.

35. This print combines three subjects used extensively by Fumpston – the clear sky seen at dusk when it takes on unusual hues, the angular form of a building in shadow, and bright flowers rendered simply and boldly. The sky shows the artist's skill at inking the etching plate with blended colours.

36. Monochrome reproductions of 12 other works from this series can be found in the 1982 catalogue *Rudolf Gopas*, published by the Govett Brewster Art Gallery, New Plymouth.

37. This disturbing image of an aged, scarred, distorted woman's torso is derived from a photograph of a detail of a tree root. Other works in this series depict equally disturbing male and hermaphroditic forms, and gargoyles. The step away from the original photos using the solarplate printing method (a new way of photo-etching) gives these images a graphic look that

makes them all the more compelling.

38. The back side of this form is hollow and smooth. The parallel grooves are based on traditional Maori heihei carving. The form evokes an exotic flower, a pouring vessel and a benign god-figure. It is a feminine form, balanced in the original exhibition by a symbolically male one.

39. The hammer used in chiselling the wood in this piece has been incorporated into it. The spines at the top are old rock-drilling bits and the metal rose was handmade by the artist. On the tile is an image of ancient Greeks digging clay for pottery.

40. One of the more light and open of Handscomb's scrolls; others have substantial areas of dark pigment obscuring the writings.

41. As much of Hellyar's work over the years has been contained in one form or another, it was a logical extension for her to set her works out in old china cabinets or cupboards. Roots, nests, feathered head-dresses, stone tools and items made of clay are displayed in these, as if in a rather primitive, run-down museum. Hellyar extended this concept in a very fine show in 1992 called *Food for Thought,* in which smooth domes made of wood, wax and other materials were placed in old post office pigeon-holes, interspersed with folded and crumpled cloth and paper, slate, clay and wood sheets to make a repository.

42. One of a number of haunting portraits done over the last two years. Close examination will reveal that the lines are full of random bits of colour from the underlying maps. These works are examples of the laws of chance at work — or chaos theory, as some would have it. At a large enough scale the seemingly random lines take on a strange overall cohesion. Viewers familiar with the earlier Christchurch map works may see this as a portrait of the artist in the New Zealand landscape, but it is neither. The self-portrait is based on one by Josef Albers, and the maps are British road maps.

43. One of a series of works using photographs of different types of chairs as metaphors for a range of cultural misalignments. One is asked to consider chairs and photographs as images, as products of culture, as constitutions of materials or substance and as imported symbols of western values. Photography was used to document the Maori people, supposedly dying out. Late-19th-century Maori artists perceived the chair as a symbol of authority and power, and this one clearly is intended for a professor, magistrate or head of a wealthy family. The sawdust in the bowls signifies both substance and temporality. One can imagine the sawdust coming from the chair which we see only in reproduction; we see a patinated copper structure which is in fact made of wood. Jahnke's sculptures are full of such subtleties.

44. The starting point for this multi-part work is the photograph in the centre of a chandelier in the Villa D'Este in Tivoli, Italy. What the artist describes as 'objects of fragile adornment and delicate consumption' are arrayed around it -- a moulded jelly, jewels, beads, etc. All of these are collaged from differently coloured prints of one blurred photograph of the chandelier. The strip below the beads shows the spectrum of colour obtainable from the processing machine.

45. Part of a series using jetsam, of which there is always a plentiful supply in Wanganui. All of this material had seen hard service and much weathering, being stained, torn, partly painted, and with rusty nail holes along edges. A sensibility shared with Tapies, Burri, Styll, Rothko and Diebenkorn comes to mind when viewing these pieces. Johnson does not strain for effect and lets the subtle colours and found linear elements speak for themselves. This work is one of the least abstract in the series. The sea, sky and rocks at the harbour entrance emerge clearly, seen past a wharf or marker structure in the foreground. There is an interesting correlation between this work and Wayne Barrar's photograph (2), as in each case Wanganui wood simulates landforms.

46. This work was commissioned for this publication and combines elements from earlier series of prints, all of them fragments of the natural and the fabricated. The work speaks of the passage of time and its relentless breaking down of all forms of organised matter.

47. These three pieces come from Jones's *Flight* exhibition at the CSA Gallery in 1990. The unfolding concertina forms on top of these stylised 1930s petrol bowsers call to mind the Shell symbol. Here, they symbolise the journey through life. On the opposite side of the set the stencilled words are GAS, GASSING, GASSED, and the gas pumps become monuments to the Holocaust.

48. This perforated leaf sculpture is one of a number of similar forms, some cast in bronze. The pieces cut out of the holes have been used to make separate works. King is now using her sculptures for the purpose of creating photographic works (cf. Rhodes, 75)

49. An overall view and a close-up of the artist's 1988 lawn and roof installation at Wellington's old library building. Vandalisation of the lawn layout was a frequent occurrence, a matter which the artist accepted philosophically as a measure of the public's tolerance of art and artist.

50. Kum's materials are usually placed in or on minimalist, rectangular containers, a joke at both Donald Judd's and Joseph Beuys' expense. The stacked shelves in this work call to mind Judd's wall-mounted columns of metal trays. The trolley wheels suggest that this icky collection may be part of some unpleasant procedure, perhaps in a hospital, where it may be necessary to move it (or collect it?) quickly. The forms were created by heating EVA and dropping it into water so that it set rapidly.

51. This detail from a huge installation in Christchurch's Robert McDougall Gallery shows the scale at which Lander can work with his handmade papers.

52. Modelled on the artist's daughter, there is a male companion-piece to this work, modelled on his son. The blocky, square-on figure is a carry-over of the style used by Lett in his stone figures. A figure presenting a precious vessel is found in much tribal art, and calls to mind some of Illingworth's (100NZP, 39) small sculptures. The roughness of the wood surface is used to advantage to enliven the colour.

53. This beautifully poised work is one of Lye's most popular. It has been much copied commercially in a smaller scale as an ornament, using optic fibres to carry light out to the tips. An electric motor in the base makes it swirl slightly, producing a tinkling noise as the wands touch.

54. This work can be seen as a celebration of femininity, aligned with the decorative women's art of 1978–82 in America. It represents an easing up by the artist of the more issues-based agenda she set herself decades ago.

55. This frame/sculpture can be adjusted to grip any flat, round object of the owner's choice. It is part of the series of works which utilise piano parts.

56. This drawing includes several images used elsewhere by the artist: the cat-person, the angel, the curtain, the receding

hills, the light on the horizon and the strange UFO-like clouds. The black sky relates to earlier black and white mezzotints and lithographs while acting to key up the colours. The frightened figure is being comforted by the angel, whose wings echo the shapes of the curtain and hills in a very satisfying way.

57. This piece demonstrates Matchitt's precisionist, constructivist, machine-tool approach to carving, with an extreme simplification of traditional Maori motifs.

58. The manufacturer's trade markings remain visible on one of the raw customwood sheets making up this piece. It does not comfortably stand upright and square; it is more stable tipped over. It looks like a half-finished shop fitting.

59. One of a group, some of similar size and some table-sized, which incorporate discs and cones. It can be read as the artist (on the left) making a drawing (below), and its realisation in steel (above). The two halves are interdependent, as neither could stand safely without the other; this imparts balance to the work.

60. The title reminds us of two of the virtues which are worth preserving down through successive generations. Though the flesh of the virtuous may decay, the memory of their virtue remains.

61. Sadly, this fine, asymetrical and expressive work was not sited at the top of the steps at the front door of Auckland's characterless Aotea Centre as originally intended. If it had been, it would have worked to alleviate the cold, slab-like horizontals of the building and would have formed a sculptural pair with Matchitt's mural. It stands as an entry onto Aotea Square, where it seems somewhat disconnected, lacking a palisade on either side to give it purpose. The forms at the top represent the sun, the moon and gods of the wind, sea and forest.

62. This sculpture consists of 100 wooden balls, each one held up by a tripod. Each ball required 4000 individual bandsaw cuts to make, and the spherical shape was achieved by eye alone. Each tripod stick was spokeshaved into cylindrical form from a square-section length. The finished work can be viewed as a model of planetary orbiting, a monument to patience or as a pure construct.

63. In 1985 Nicholls began developing an idea which stemmed from *100 Degree Twist* of 1982, a stack of short hardwood blocks mitred together and spiralling as it rose. Over the next four years he made about 12 dramatic, stacked works using baulks a metre or more long, loosely dovetailed together. These highly successful sculptures take on a unified, dynamic personality, and can be seen as symbolic books, feathered head-dresses, spreading fingers, sails or wings. Although rough-cut and blocky, they are elegant and, being taller than a tall man, they have presence, flaunting their fans of wood like strutting peacocks. Depending on the viewpoint, *Luff* can be seen as a slack sail, a cloaked warrior or falling water. It is one of the many private commissions executed by Nicholls throughout New Zealand.

64. Noble's recurring interest in women as subjects for her photography here takes the form of a classical nude study, but by using montage and an unusual camera angle the artist approaches surrealism. This links the work with Noble's *Song for Debbie,* 1988 — separately framed black and white pictures of five male necks, with bird and insect overlays, plus a woman's eye.

65. Part of the collection *Theatre of Dust*, this sculpture shows the artist's use of found material in the heavy-grade sandpaper. It makes a rich, grainy, refractive background, like one of Di Ffrench's cibachrome prints (33). The theme is emigration — the oars touch stone cairns representing past and present, the old land and the new. On the left (past) side the candles are extinguished, a reference to fading memory and to the title of the work, the last three days of Holy Week during which church candles are successively extinguished. The arm reaches out through the bell of night from the lock/spade to the fishtail/key on the right (future) side. The engraved text is a stanza from Geoffrey Hill's poem *Tenebrae*, the Latin word for darkness.

66. The work is about seeing and thinking, and perhaps about the influence of European and Japanese products on life in New Zealand (or perhaps not).

67. This photo is deliberately out of focus so that we cannot tell whether the marks on the neck (ostensibly love bites) may not be a skin ailment or marks of violence. As John Daly-Peoples said about *Tainted Love,* the show in which this work appeared, 'Pardington's work sits in a strangely real environment between the debasing images of pornography and the elusive images of romantic love.'

68. This work refers to the children's game 'pick up sticks', in which the object is to remove sticks of a certain colour without disturbing the others. Here the sticks, all white, are implements of colonial settlement. The only action which seems to have any point is to remove them all. The pieces resemble the model-making components popped out of plastic frames of the type depicted elsewhere by the artist.

69. The Braille text on *Retainer* was written by a blind friend of the artist, recounting his visit to an artist's studio. Without the plastic cover, it was exhibited in Christchurch together with a set of completely black and pure white photographs entitled *Six Days and Nights in Canterbury* and also two white bags, zipped up to conceal kidney-shaped, Arp-like formica sculptures. In 1994–95 Parsons showed works wherein the raised hemispheres of Braille, greatly enlarged, were affixed directly to the wall, effectively turning it into a huge sheet of paper spelling out the names of blind musicians. Like his pencils, Parsons' wall Braille is dysfunctional, being too big for a blind person to get a grip on. The addition of the cover on *Retainer* makes that unreadable also, while relating it to his other bagged sculpture pieces and to Christo's wrapped sculptures. The moveable stool is an ironic aid, given the obstructing cover.

70. Because it is not something one normally contemplates for any length of time before putting it in the oven, the plucked chicken at first seems strangely alien in its drastically altered state, then becomes accusatory. After a while this image takes on some aspects of an old, wrinkled human face and assumes great poignancy. It is an eloquent symbol of vulnerability, temporality and exploitation.

71. The *Above Ground* works are semi-abstract excerpts from Maori food store structures, an elegant way of making constructivism relevant to a New Zealand audience.

72. The generic mannikins in this work are typical of those used in a number of other sculptures, while the rosette form (a feature of gothic architecture) has been used in some of Reddaway's photomontages.

73. Crinkled cobalt-blue paper and a skull head symbolise turbulent times in Pacific waters. In the upper centre we see a series of craters and a walled compound, references to the French test site at Moruroa. The underlying tapa design can be read as the vibrations of a nuclear blast.

74. This image is one of a number shot amid flax and cabbage trees. Spatial relationships become confused, and the work

becomes a study in shapes and contrasts. The curving flax leaf is an uncanny evocation of McCahon's 1960s waterfall paintings.

75. Recording one's country in painting is no longer regarded as valid contemporary art activity. Rhodes's use of the outdoors as the setting for her modifications celebrates the New Zealand landscape in a new way. She has often used the mirror-like inter-tidal zone. Twisted lengths of red silk, painted wooden laths, sinuous meanders of rope or thin tripods are placed in this ethereal space between earth and sky (cf. Cross, 100NZP, 17). The placement of thin, curved shapes against rugged coastline rocks is another continuing activity.

76. This work falls between two quite different series of sculptures, one metallic, mechanical and warlike and the other glossy, electronic and domesticated. It combines elements of art deco with futuristic spaceship design as seen in countless TV and film imaginings. Its purpose, as well as its place in time, is uncertain — is it functional or decorative? If it is functional, is the function benign or malign?

77. The use of drypoint, scratched into the metal, is a direct, expressive equivalent of drawing in this first series of prints made by the artist after a period of intense drawing activity.

78. Since 1990 Shepheard has been exploring the possibilities of printing from fragments of borrowed images, or from computer-generated ones. Using xerography, solvents and a printing press, she has selected and enlarged images, then transferred the copy to archival paper, wood or mylar. In the latter case, the image can then be made into a screenprint. All these graphic pieces can then be further combined into larger assembled works. This is one example of decontextualisation, a postmodern device akin to pop art's borrowing of images, but ranging much more widely over historical sources. As in pop art, surrealism and Dada, the artist presents carefully selected, resonant images. The artistic experience is a product of their interaction with the viewer's personal knowledge and experience. This particular presentation has been made especially for this book. It centres around the Nike of Samothrace, goddess of victory. Shepheard attempts 'to reclassify her power, her strength, her spirit and the respect she commanded'. The rose thorn panels, symbolising beauty/pain/protection, are made using a special process which deposits a thin film of bronze on real objects.

79. The beating of rain against a window is here equated with the method of making the work — by beating the forms out of sheet metal.

80. Siddell often includes insects in her drawings, capitalising on most women's horror of creepy-crawlies, especially when encountered in a domestic situation. They add the final touch to what is already a housekeeper's nightmare. There is also a topical reference, as Auckland has been invaded by wasps in recent years.

81. The elements of Snowden's sculptures contain only curves or straight lines. In this work, the large segment of a circle operates as a frame for the rest of the piece. The delicately poised, very thin rod is like an antenna reaching out and inviting the viewer to make contact.

82. In this piece Stringer takes his fondness for optical illusion, usually expressed as false depth, into the fanciful area of surreal 'invisible visages' pioneered by Dali.

83. There is a vertical version of this sculpture in the collection of the Robert MacDougall Gallery, Christchurch.

84. Szirmay has made a number of outdoor pieces using sheet stainless steel. Some, like this one, take on the form of a flower or plant, while others are more formal, set within parallel rectangular frames and setting up changing optical overlaps as one moves past.

85. Tarlton's vision of the apocalypse. The final collage was photographed and printed in cibachrome, thus overcoming the problems of the visibility of the collage cuts and the non-archival material used. By restricting his source material to the *Listener*, a New Zealand media institution, Tarlton ensured consistency, vague familiarity and a convincing sense of the local scene.

86. An example of Thomson's new interest in the amazing world of the very small. As there are no clues to the correct scale of the subject, this could be vegetable, animal or insect life — or a landscape on an alien planet.

87. An example of Thomson's recent work that has been screenprinted with text and illustrations from the *Lysaght Manual,* the bible for those using galvanised sheet metal. After printing, the sheets are commercially fabricated into pipes, gutters and flanges, as well as being corrugated. Thomson applied paint to iron in the past, but often used iron as found with its old, faded paint. Thomson is now moving into an abstract mode, but he still avoids a minimalist, formal look.

88. A good representative print by Tricker, showing most of his themes and techniques. He has used the tondo format periodically, but most of his works are rectangular.

89. Tuffery has used the lizard in several other works, capitalising on its sinuous form as a compositional device and a means of energising the drawing. For a review of Tuffery's development as an artist, refer to Tim Walker's article in *Art New Zealand* 70 (p.64) which includes further illustrations.

90. Irony abounds in this huddled form based on the Milenburg Venus, a prehistoric statuette of a footless fertility goddess. She has been turned into a version of the tin woodsman from *The Wizard of Oz,* but the tree has turned to tin as well. The tinman's axe has become the ancient tinwoman's modern chainsaw, and supplies the answer to the mystery of the missing feet.

91. This installation in an empty shop was a realisation by the artist of an idea previously expressed in two dimensions in the 1991–92 drawings, which showed imaginary abstract sculptures in retail spaces. He limited himself to six painted cardboard cartons and some scaffolding. The work was visible through the shop window for one week. The light fittings which make up the arms of the anthropomorphic figure were already in place, and the narrow, dark-ceilinged shop with the red rear door makes a perfect setting. The figure, in more ways than one, is a simulated speaker, dominating the space and silently announcing its tenuous presence.

92. The artist offers this picture as an artwork existing only in this book. It shows the artist with his contemporaries at the point of graduation from art school, and therefore returns his 16-year career to its beginnings, inviting readers to assess its worth at this point of time. As much of Van Hout's work is ephemeral, it is his reputation as an artist which carries him along and which is at stake here. The pagework represents his career in both its inception and maturity.

93. This work neatly sums up a number of aspects of Viscoe's sculptural practice: folksy woodwork, painted elements contrasted with unpainted ones, wire stitching joining elements, flanges and boxes contrasted with more organic shapes and a stylised head at the top. The work refers to human interference with the flow of rivers.

94. Moving on from her blocky crouched figures modelled in Hinuera stone (which will not carry fine detail), Ward has started to use limestone and as a result her work has taken on a more classical look.

95. A good example of the contrast, detail and depth of perspective typical of Ward's mezzotints. One's eye is led into the far background by the turning pathway. All the figures are going somewhere except the central, seated man. Although the scene is an everyday one, there is a sense of individual isolation reminiscent of the works of Edward Hopper and George Tooker.

96. One of a series of images featuring a book altered by the artist for use as a prop. The kitschy seascape has been used as a background in several other photographs.

97. One of Webb's more abstract compositions, although it is still based on landscape (cloud shadows moving across burned grassland). It is an apocalyptic vision which contrasts with her more quiet water- and sky-scapes.

98. This work contrasts with much of Webster's other current photography in which the subjects are more bold and confident. It is interesting to compare these slumped, bandaged figures with the sculptures of Reddaway (72) done in the late 1980s. The pathos and sense of helplessness are the same.

99. This small work, reproduced actual size, encompasses a great vista of land and sky. It was a response to commercial manuka-cutting for firewood in the Kaipara area. The red colour signifies fire, sunset and the day of judgement — devastation and beauty combined; the gold leaf is an ironic comment on both preciousness and greed.

100. The starting point for this work was a found Hawaiian war god figure, no doubt carved for the tourist market. Womble has transformed it by overpainting a Mickey Mouse image and adding a tin-lid halo. The result is a synthesis of three idols — a pagan, Pacific one; a Christian one; and a popular, highly marketed Western one, the latter emanating from California, Womble's home state. The work alludes to the artist's own blending into the Pacific culture, but it has more to say. Viewed frontally, the Mickey image dominates; viewed obliquely the cheery face morphs into a skull — a powerful metaphor for the insidious influence of Californian culture on life in the Pacific.

FOREIGN ARTISTS MENTIONED IN THE TEXT

The notes very briefly mention some relevant facts to contextualise the reference in the main text. Artists are painters unless otherwise stated.

Agam, Yaacov (1928– , Israeli). Visual kinetics created by flanges on constructed paintings which reveal changing forms and colours as the angle of view changes.

Albers, Josef (1888–1976, German). Painter and designer who went to America in 1939 and influenced the development of abstraction there.

Andre, Carl (1935– , American). Minimalist, floor-based sculpture using assemblies of equal-sized square metal plates, bricks and other repetitive forms.

Annigoni, Pietro (1910– , Italian). Fine draftsman noted for his somewhat sentimental portraits and drawings of handsome young men and women.

Armitage, Kenneth (1916– , British). Sculptures of groups of figures merged into a matrix; vestigial limbs and heads, swollen torsos.

Arp, Jean (1887–1966, French). Wooden relief constructions and sculptures evoking human anatomy, water-worn stones and fruit. Influenced Henry Moore and countless other sculptors of 'modern' rounded forms.

Artschwager, Richard (1923– , American). Took the concept of utilitarian, formica furniture into the realm of art by making finely finished shapes which resembled oversized tables, chairs and counters.

Benton, Thomas Hart (1889–1975, American). Founder of the realist style now known as regionalism, noted for its rhythmic simplification of land and body forms.

Beuys, Joseph (1921–86, German). Merger of life and art; revival of alchemy and shamanism; consistent use of limited range of humble materials to create a style in sculpture and drawing.

Blackwell, Tom (1938– , American). Photorealist paintings of details of highly polished and chromed motorbikes, exploiting the reflections and convolutions of pipes, petrol tanks and mudguards.

Blake, Peter (1932– , British). Pop art pioneer. Use of media imagery combined with figures, handled with a gentle sense of humour.

Blake, William (1757–1827, British). Visionary painter, engraver and poet with a highly individual style. Integrated words and images in dramatic, figurative works on the theme of heaven and hell.

Bonnard, Pierre (1867–1947, French). Impressionist who stressed pattern and design at the expense of definition. Luminous use of colour verging at times upon fauvism.

Bosch, Hieronymus (*ca.*1450–1516, Netherlandish). Painter of allegorical scenes of heaven and hell, full of extraordinary imagery which anticipated surrealism.

Brancusi, Constantin (1876–1957, Romanian). Rugged, fetishistic wood sculpture and smooth, flame-like forms in marble and bronze.

Brueghel, Pieter (1525–69, Netherlandish). Wide-angle paintings of rustic life, filled with a wealth of narrative detail.

Burri, Alberto (1915– , Italian). Abstract collage paintings involving burned sacking and found objects.

Caravaggio, Michelangelo (1571–1610, Italian). Bold, strongly lit figures emerging dramatically from dark shadows; a sense of the theatrical and the hedonistic in life.
Caro, Anthony (1924– , British). Very wide range of innovative sculptural forms, small and large scale, using cut pieces of preformed metal, usually painted in one colour.
Chadwick, Lynn (1914– , British). Sculpture in welded iron to make spiky, ribbed, bird-like forms.
Christo (Christo Javacheff, 1935– , Bulgarian/American). Huge, temporary exterior projects involving wrapping up landscapes and buildings in plastic, erecting fences or installing umbrellas across large areas.
Close, Chuck (1940– , American). Photorealist painter specialising in close-ups of heads, examining the changes of focus which result from use of a narrow depth of field in the camera setting.
Cornell, Joseph (1903–72, American). Found object assemblage using boxes. Strong sense of nostalgia for times past and yearning for foreign places.
Cragg, Tony (1949– , British). Wall-mounted fragments of coloured plastic debris filling in a recognisable outline.
Dali, Salvadore (1904–89, Spanish). Surrealist painting using meticulous, old-master technique to create dream-like images of unlikely or impossible occurrences.
Daumier, Honore (1808–79, French). Precursor of expressionism in his use of black and white, distortion of figures and concern with the plight of the poor.
Da Vinci, Leonardo (1452–1519, Italian). Encouraged artists to study the random forms and patterns of nature. Made many expressive drawings incorporating text and images which speculated about the future.
Davis, Ron (1935– , American). Sculptor and painter whose works resemble coloured diagrams or architectural drawings. Flat wall pieces have a strongly illusionistic 3-D look.
Diebenkorn, Richard (1922–93, American). Abstract painting based in landscape, straight lines dividing the picture into areas of soft colour.
Dubuffet, Jean (1901–85, French). Inventor of *art brut.* Looked to the art of children and the insane for inspiration. Painted and sculpted comic figures and wobbly shapes; used earth in his paint and later used primary colours, outlining and cross-hatching to make art that looked like doodling.
Duchamp, Marcel (1887–1968, French). Invention of conceptual art, merger of life and art, the idea of the found object.
Dürer, Albrecht (1471–1528, German). Consummate draftsman and master of engraving and woodcut, notable for his ability to convey detail and suggest space and movement in two dimensions.
El Greco (1541–1614, Greek). Painted in a loose, highly original style which anticipated expressionism, particularly his handling of landscapes.
Epstein, Jacob (1880-1959, British). Sculpted in Vorticist style, a dynamic variant of cubism.
Friedrich, Caspar David (1774–1840, German). Silent figures confronting vast spaces; a sense of the sublime in skies flooded with light.
Giacometti, Alberto (1901–66, Swiss). Haunted, expressionistic figures delineated by swirling, wire-like lines of paint or charcoal; skeletal sculptures in which figures are stripped down to bare essentials like burnt matches.
Goldsworthy, Andy (1956– , British). Sculptor who works outdoors making ephemeral and environmentally friendly modifications to the environment which are then photographed. Also works with piles of stone and slate, forming arches, columns and cairns.
Gonzalez, Julio (1876–1942, Spanish). Pioneer of welding and riveting techniques in the making of metal sculpture which was open, thin and resembled drawing in space.
Goya y Lucientes, Francisco de (1746–1828, Spanish). Precursor of expressionism in his imaginative, dark, freely brushed, distorted paintings of pagan rites and the horrors of war.
Heizer, Michael (1944– , American). Earth artist noted for large-scale manipulation of the desert environment with structures and excavations.
Held, Al (1928– , American). Paintings crowded with linear, geometric forms which overlap and interlock in puzzling ways, with a strongly 3-D look.
Hepworth, Barbara (1903–75, British). Abstract sculpture. Curved, hollowed-out forms strung with wires like harps; organic rather than angular shapes.
Hoch, Hanna (1889–1978, German). Anarchic, Dada photocollages in which found photos were sliced up and reassembled, sometimes making strong social comments. Precursor of pop art.
Hockney, David (1937– , British). Pop art pioneer with a light, loose, gestural style that contrasted with the sharp delineation of other contemporary work.
Hogarth, William (1697–1764, British). Caricaturist who ridiculed the hypocrisy, greed and corruption of his time, and used engraving to publish his works.
Hopper, Edward (1882–1967, American). Realist painter who conveyed a sense of lonely isolation in the midst of 20th century urban life.
Jones, Allen (1937– , British). Pioneer pop artist with an erotic bent. Based his work on 'pin-up' art.
Judd, Donald (1928–95, American). Minimalist sculptor, identical boxes and trays made of metal or wood presented in sets.
Klee, Paul (1879–1940, Swiss). Worked small in scale but with a huge diversity of style, ranging from child-like to abstract. Paintings were often like coloured-in line drawings. Generated many ideas taken up by others in larger paintings.
Leger, Fernand (1881–1955, French). Developed own version of cubism, emphasising the cylinder, with figures looking like they were made of pipes. Later work influenced the art deco style.
Le Witt, Sol (1928– , American). Minimalist sculptor and graphic artist. Works with geometric, linear, constructivist forms.
Lindner, Richard (1901–78, German/American). Anticipated pop art with erotic, hard-edged figurative works derived in part from Leger.
Lipchitz, Jacques (1891–73, Lithuanian). Sculptor, first a cubist, later a surrealist, defining many forms in those styles.
Malevich, Kasimir (1878–1935, Russian). Pioneer of geometric abstraction using rectangles, lines and primary, all-over colours.
Mapplethorpe, Robert (1946–89, American). Finely-grained black and white photography of flowers and bodies, homo-erotic photography and self-portraits.
Martin, Agnes (1912– , American). Minimalist noted for her paintings with extremely refined use of pale colour and almost imperceptible pencil lines, and her folded, origami-like drawings.
Matisse, Pierre (1869–1954, French). His figurative style has been one of the most influential of the century. Confident, sweeping, simplified drawing; bold, clean colour; assured, unusual composition; use of decorative elements; dynamism of figures and objects creating a rhythm.
Mondrian, Piet (1872–1944, Dutch). Developed an abstract geometric style which involved a black grid, seemingly extending beyond the canvas, with some rectangles within the grid in primary colours.

Moore, Henry (1898–1987, British). Influenced by surrealist ideas, he made many sculptures based on the human form, but greatly abstracted into forms resembling water-worn stones.
Morandi, Giorgio (1890–1964, Italian). Showed in his still lifes that it is possible to interpret and re-interpret limited subject matter, using a limited palette, without becoming formulaic.
Morris, Robert (1931– , American). In the mid-1960s he was making minimalist geometric sculpture: elongated box shapes which articulated the space around them.
Motherwell, Robert (1915–91, American). Maintained a consistent style over many years — big black blob shapes in his *Elegy to the Spanish Republic* series and a direct, clean-cut look in his collages, which utilised brown paper and other packaging with coloured rectangular elements, often in pale blue.
Nadelman, Elie (1882–1946, Polish/American). Smooth, simplified figures with a flowing line imparting a sense of movement. Moved *art nouveau* into art deco.
Nevelson, Louise (1899–1988, American). Painted her large assemblages (of found wooden bits and pieces placed within stacked boxes) in one overall colour (black, white or gold) to create remarkably intricate and cohesive reliefs dominated by the play of light and shadow.
Okulick, John (1947– , American). Realist sculptor whose flat wooden reliefs are so dimensionally illusionistic that they appear to be receding into the wall.
Oldenburg, Claes (1929– , American). Pioneer pop artist, inventor of soft sculpture, recently noted for huge enlargements of everyday objects.
Paladino, Mimmo (1948– , Italian). Neo-expressionist who merged expressive brushwork with slightly abstracted figurative imagery based on Italian religious art of the past. Instead of angst his work conveys a feeling of spiritual transcendence.
Paolozzi, Eduado (1924– , British). Pop sculptor who made colourful totemic objects which resembled robots, and photo-screenprints based on found text and images.
Phillips, Peter (1939– , British). Pioneer pop artist with a decorative style based on popular designs for customising cars and bikes.
Picasso, Pablo (1881–1973, Spanish). Co-invented cubism and went on to explore a wide range of modernist distortions of objects and the figure in his paintings and sculpture. Some figures were thick-set and adopted classic poses; others were wobbly surreal forms; still others like angular cardboard cut-outs or stick figures.
Rembrandt (1606–69, Dutch). A master of chiaroscuro and of the portrait. Regarded as one of the greatest painters of all time.
Rothko, Mark (1903–70, American). Abstract expressionist who developed works in cloudy fields of colour rather than gestural brushmarks.
Ryman, Robert (1930– , American). Large, ongoing series of white paintings, all differing in tone, coverage or type of brushwork.
Sant' Elia, Antonio (1888–1915, Italian). Futurist architect who envisioned remarkably modern city buildings with sculptural qualities in the balance between solid and glazed elements.
Seurat, Georges (1859–91, French). Neo-impressionist who used the pointillist technique, whereby a scene was built up out of a myriad of colour dots which blended in the eye to create subtle tones and shading.
Sherman, Cindy (1945– , American). Cast herself in various stereotyped B movie roles and photographed herself, then made large prints.
Smith, David (1906–65, American). Follower of Gonzalez who took his methods further into welded, boxy, anthropomorphic sculpture, sometimes painted and sometimes in stainless steel with a buffed surface.
Smithson, Robert (1938–73, American). Pioneer earthworks artist (indoor and outdoor), used industrial and construction materials in minimalist, conceptual, floor-based sculpture.
Snelson, Kenneth (1927– , American). Towers of aluminium pipes connected by wires, which seem to hold themselves up.
Steinberg, Saul (1914– , American). Cartoonist for the *New Yorker* magazine with a finely penned, flourishing, distinctively whimsical style.
Still, Clyfford (1904–80, American). Abstract expressionist whose large paintings feature jagged areas of unusual colour.
Suvero, Mark Di (1933– , American). Large, heavy baulks of timber and steel swung into space and held there at various angles by counterbalances, hawsers and chains.
Taeuber-Arp, Sophie (1889–1943, Swiss). Abstraction in rhythmic, colourful, geometric shapes, similar in style to Delaunay. Worked in the medium of tapestry as well as painting.
Tapies, Antonio (1923– , Spanish). Abstract painter. Uses impasto to create scratched, cracked surfaces which resemble wet sand or old walls, and often incorporates flat found objects.
Tooker, George (1920– , American). Realist images of haunted-looking people in soulless urban environments such as subways, all ignoring each others' presence.
Turner, J.M.W. (1775–1851, British). His light-filled, turbulent sea- and storm-scapes can be seen as forerunners of both impressionism and abstract expressionism.
Twombly, Cy (1929– , American). Developed a recognisable style out of the consistent use of arbitrary scribbles and smudges drawn on a plain background.
Vermeer, Jan (1632–75, Dutch). Carefully composed interiors into which light slanted, striking objects obliquely. His use of geometric shapes was a step towards abstraction.
Wesselmann, Tom (1931– , American). Pioneer pop painter whose work has concentrated on the female nude. In the last decade he has been making metal wall pieces in which everything but the image is cut away and the wall becomes the background to the work.